International Debt Statistics 2014

International Debt Statistics 2014

THE WORLD BANK
Washington, D.C.

1 2 3 4 17 16 15 14

ISBN (paper): 978-1-4648-0051-1
ISBN (electronic): 978-1-4648-0052-8
DOI: 10.1596/978-1-4648-0051-1
ISSN (paper): 2310-2667
ISSN (electronic): 2310-2675

Cover design: Jomo Tariku, World Bank
Cover image: original artwork by Jomo Tariku, World Bank

Table of Contents

Preface

This year's edition of *International Debt Statistics*, successor to *Global Development Finance* and *World Debt Tables*, and the second in the series, is designed to respond to user demand for timely, comprehensive data on trends in external debt in developing countries. It also provides summary information on the external debt of high-income countries and public (domestic and external) debt for a select group of countries.

The World Bank's Debtor Reporting System (DRS), from which the aggregates and country tables presented in this report are drawn, was established in 1951. *World Debt Tables*, the first publication that included DRS external debt data, appeared in 1973 and gained increased attention during the debt crisis of the 1980s. Since then, the publication and data have undergone numerous revisions and iterations to address the challenges and demands posed by the global economic conditions.

Presentation and access to data have been refined to improve the user experience. The printed edition of *International Debt Statistics 2014* now provides a summary overview and a select set of indicators, while an expanded dataset is available online (datatopics.worldbank.org/debt/ids).

By providing comprehensive and timely data that reflects the latest additions and revisions, and by expanding the scope of the data available online, we aim to serve the needs of our users and to reach a wider audience. Improvements in data dissemination are matched with ongoing efforts to improve the quality and timeliness of data collection. In partnership with the major providers of debt data management systems to developing countries, the Commonwealth Secretariat (COMSEC) and the United Nations Conference on Trade and Development (UNCTAD), we are working toward an established standard code and system links that will enable countries to provide their DRS reports electronically, in a seamless and automated data exchange process.

As these changes take place, we welcome your feedback and suggestions for further improvements at data@worldbank.org.

Haishan Fu
Director, Development Data Group

Acknowledgments

This volume was prepared by the Financial Data Team of the Development Data Group (DECDG), led by Ibrahim Levent under the management of Neil Fantom, and comprising Wendy Huang, Hiroko Maeda, Patricia Olmedo, Iulian Pogor, Malvina Pollock, Evis Rucaj, Rubena Sukaj, Sun Hwa Song, Maryna Taran, Rasiel Vellos, and Alagiriswamy Venkatesan, who worked closely with other teams in DECDG. The team was assisted by Elysee Kiti. The overview of current developments was prepared by Malvina Pollock, Evis Rucaj, and Rasiel Vellos in consultation with the staff of DECDG; country economists reviewed the data tables. The work was carried out under the direction of Grant Cameron and Haishan Fu. Valuable advice was provided by the Operations and Strategy unit of the Vice Presidency.

The production of this volume was managed by Azita Amjadi. The online database was prepared by Shelley Fu and William Prince. International Debt Statistics electronic products were prepared by a team led by Malarvizhi Veerappan under the supervision of Soong Sup Lee and comprising Ying Chi, Rajesh Danda, Jean-Pierre Djomalieu, Ramgopal Erabelly, Shelley Fu, Omar Hadi, Gytis Kanchas, Siddhesh Kaushik, Ugendran Machakkalai, Nacer Megherbi, Shanmugam Natarajan, Parastoo Oloumi, Manish Rathore, Ganeshkumar Sathiyamoorthy, Ashish Shah, and Atsushi Shimo. The cover was designed by Jomo Tariku. Denise Bergeron, Susan Graham, and Stephen McGroarty from the Publishing and Knowledge Division of the World Bank coordinated the publication and dissemination of the book.

User Guide to Tables

International Debt Statistics 2014 focuses on financial flows, trends in external debt, and other major financial indicators for developing and advanced economies. The report includes more than 200 time series indicators from 1970 to 2012 for most reporting countries. This edition of *International Debt Statistics* (IDS) has been reconfigured to offer a more condensed presentation of the principal indicators, along with additional tables showcasing Quarterly External Debt Statistics and Public Sector Debt.

Tables

Summary and Aggregate Tables

The summary tables are labeled by the type of data presented for 2012: present value of debt and public and publicly guaranteed debt by multilateral creditors. The aggregate tables are labeled by region name. Data are shown for all developing countries and six regional groups (East Asia and Pacific, Europe and Central Asia, Latin America and the Caribbean, Middle East and North Africa, South Asia, and Sub-Saharan Africa).

Country Tables

Country tables are labeled by country name and ordered alphabetically. Data are shown for 124 developing countries that report public and publicly guaranteed external debt to the World Bank's Debtor Reporting System (DRS). The tables also include key debt ratios and the composition of external debt stocks and flows for each country.

Each table shows a time series with the most recent six years, as well as 2000 and 2005 as companion years. Full time series data is available for all countries in the World Bank's Open Data website (http://data.worldbank.org/data-catalog/international-debt-statistics).

Statistics

The general cutoff date for countries to report data for this publication is end-September 2013. The economic aggregates presented in the tables are prepared for the convenience of users. Although debt ratios can give useful information about developments in a debt-servicing capacity, conclusions drawn from them will not be valid unless accompanied by careful economic evaluation.

The macroeconomic data provided are collected from national statistical organizations, but in some cases may be subject to a considerable margin of error. The usual care must be taken in interpreting the ratios, particularly for the most recent years, because figures may be preliminary and subject to revision.

Notes at the bottom of each country table summarize major events that have taken place in the country in recent years; describe the sources of information for short-term and private nonguaranteed external debt if the reports were not provided by the country; and highlight main issues in the data collection process. Unless otherwise specified, data on long-term public and publicly guaranteed external debt for 2012 are based on reports provided by the country.

More detailed information on data sources, methodology, and compilation is provided in the About the Data section at the back of this book.

Aggregate Measures for Income Groups and Regions

Aggregate measures for income groups and regions include the 124 developing countries that report public and publicly guaranteed external debt to the World Bank's DRS, whenever data are available. The aggregate "All developing countries" is the sum of data for 124 countries.

Classification of Economies

For operational and analytical purposes, the World Bank's main criterion for classifying economies is gross national income (GNI) per capita (calculated by the *World Bank Atlas* method). Every economy is classified as low income, middle income, or high income. Low- and middle-income countries are sometimes referred to as developing countries. The term is used for convenience; it is not intended to imply that all countries in the group are experiencing similar development or that other economies have reached a preferred or final stage of development. Because GNI per capita changes over time, the country composition of income groups may change from one edition of *International Debt Statistics* to the next. Once the classification is fixed for an edition, based on GNI per capita in the most recent year for which data are available, all historical data presented are based on the same country grouping.

Symbols

0 or 0.0 means zero or small enough that the number would round to zero at the displayed number of decimal places.

.. means that data are not available or that aggregates cannot be calculated because of missing data in the years shown.

$ indicates current U.S. dollars unless otherwise specified.

User Guide to IDS Online Tables

The extended version of country tables that were previously available in the *International Debt Statistics* print edition is now available online. Using an automated query process, these reference tables will be updated based on the revisions to the International Debt Statistics database.

Users can access all the online tables, download the PDF version of the publication, view the report as an eBook on ISSUU, as well as access the database and download the archived editions of the publication by going to http://data.worldbank.org/products/ids.

How to Access IDS Online Country Tables

To access the IDS online tables, visit http://datatopics.worldbank.org/debt/ids and select from "Country," "Region," or "Topic" options.

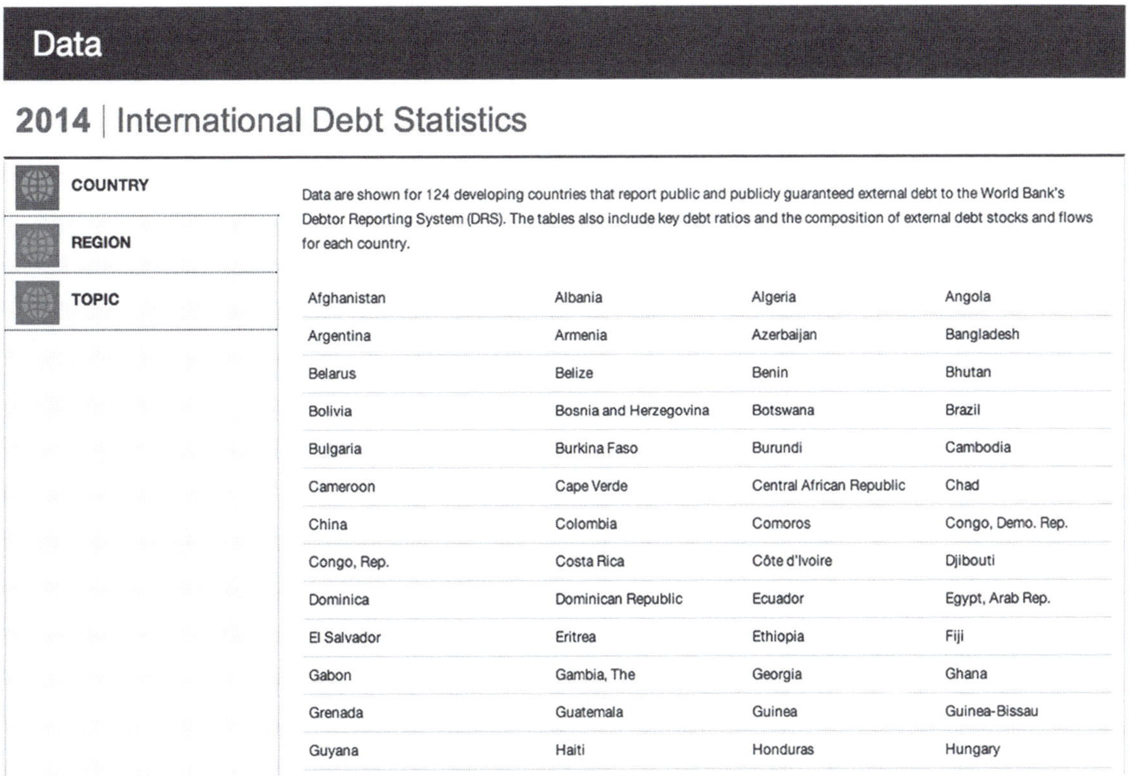

To access a specific country table directly without going through the above landing page, use the URL http://datatopics.worldbank.org/debt/ids/ and the country name (for example, http://datatopics.worldbank.org/debt/ids/country/argentina to view the table for Argentina). Similarly, to view the regional table, click on the "Region" tab and select one of the listed regions (for example http://datatopics.worldbank.org/debt/ids/region/south-asia to view the table for South Asia).

2014 | International Debt Statistics

Data > Data Topics > Debt Data > Country Tables > Algeria

$ millions	2008	2009	2010	2011	2012
External debt stocks	3,232.4	3,332.4	2,333.4	3,433.4	3,333.3
Long-term external debt	**6,246**	**7,405**	**7,246**	**6,045**	**5,643**
Public and publicly guaranteed	4,745	4,035	3,623	3,064	2,597
Private nonguaranteed	1,304	1,492	1,778	1,142	1,205
Use of IMF Credit	0	0	0	0	0
Short-term external debt	4,745	4,035	3,623	3,064	2,597
of which interest arrears on long-term	**4,745**	**4,035**	**3,623**	**3,064**	**2,597**
Official Creditors	4,745	4,035	3,623	3,064	2,597
Private Creditors	4,745	4,035	3,623	3,064	2,597
Memo: principal arrears on LDOD	4,745	4,035	3,623	3,064	2,597
Official Creditors	**675**	**211**	**43**	**30**	**29**
Private Creditors	4,745	4,035	3,623	3,064	2,597
External Debt Flows					
Disbursements	4,745	4,035	3,623	3,064	2,597
Long-term external debt	4,745	4,035	3,623	3,064	2,597
IMF purchases	**675**	**211**	**43**	**30**	**29**
Net flows	4,745	4,035	3,623	3,064	2,597
of which short-term debt	4,745	4,035	3,623	3,064	2,597
Interest payments	4,745	4,035	3,623	3,064	2,597
long-term debt	4,745	4,035	3,623	3,064	2,597
IMF charges	**675**	**211**	**43**	**30**	**29**
Short-term debt	**675**	**211**	**43**	**30**	**29**
Short-term debt	**675**	**211**	**43**	**30**	**29**

Indicators

The indicator codes for each indicator that appears online and in the publication are listed below. To view a specific indicator online, go to http://data.worldbank.org/indicator/ and add the indicator code at the end of the url; for example, to view a page for total debt stocks, this line should be in your browser:

http://data.worldbank.org/indicator/DT.DOD.DECT.CD

1. SUMMARY EXTERNAL DEBT DATA

External debt stocks	DT.DOD.DECT.CD
Long-term external debt	DT.DOD.DLXF.CD
Public and publicly guaranteed	DT.DOD.DPPG.CD
Private nonguaranteed	DT.DOD.DPNG.CD
Use of IMF credit	DT.DOD.DIMF.CD
Short-term debt	DT.DOD.DSTC.CD
interest arrears on long-term	DT.IXA.DPPG.CD
Memorandum items	
Principal arrears on long-term	DT.AXA.DPPG.CD
Long-term public sector debt	DT.DOD.DPPG.CD
Long-term private sector debt	DT.DOD.PRVS.CD
Public & publicly guaranteed commitments	DT.COM.DPPG.CD
External debt flows	
Disbursements	DT.DIS.DLTF.CD
Long-term external debt	DT.DIS.DLXF.CD
IMF purchases	DT.DIS.DIMF.CD
Principal repayments	DT.AMT.DLTF.CD
Long-term external debt	DT.AMT.DLXF.CD
IMF repurchases	DT.AMT.DIMF.CD
Net flows	DT.NFL.DECT.CD
Long-term external debt	DT.NFL.DLXF.CD
Short-term external debt	DT.NFL.DSTC.CD
Interest payments (INT)	DT.INT.DECT.CD
Long-term external debt	DT.INT.DLXF.CD
IMF charges	DT.INT.DIMF.CD
Short-term external debt	DT.INT.DSTC.CD

2. OTHER NON-DEBT RESOURCE FLOWS

Foreign direct investment (net)	BX.KLT.DINV.CD.WD
Portfolio equity flows	BX.PEF.TOTL.CD.WD

3. CURRENCY COMPOSITION OF PUBLIC AND PUBLICLY GUARANTEED DEBT (%)

Euro	DT.CUR.EURO.ZS
Japanese yen	DT.CUR.JYEN.ZS
Pound sterling	DT.CUR.UKPS.ZS
Swiss franc	DT.CUR.SWFR.ZS
U.S. dollars	DT.CUR.USDL.ZS

4. AVERAGE TERMS OF NEW COMMITMENTS

Official creditors	
Interest (%)	DT.INR.OFFT
Maturity (years)	DT.MAT.OFFT
Grace period (years)	DT.GPA.OFFT
Private creditors	
Interest (%)	DT.INR.PRVT
Maturity (years)	DT.MAT.PRVT
Grace period (years)	DT.GPA.PRVT

5. MAJOR ECONOMIC AGGREGATES

Gross national income (GNI)	NY.GNP.MKTP.CD
Exports of goods, services, and primary income	BX.GSR.TOTL.CD
Personal transfers and compensation of employees	BX.TRF.PWKR.CD.DT
Imports of goods, services and primary income	BM.GSR.TOTL.CD
Primary income on FDI	BX.KLT.DREM.CD.DT
International reserves	FI.RES.TOTL.CD

6. RATIOS

External debt stocks to exports (%)	DT.DOD.DECT.EX.ZS
External debt stocks to GNI (%)	DT.DOD.DECT.GN.ZS
Debt service to exports (%)	DT.TDS.DECT.EX.ZS
Short-term to external debt stocks (%)	DT.DOD.DSTC.ZS
Multilateral to external debt stocks (%)	DT.DOD.MLAT.ZS
Reserves to external debt stocks (%)	FI.RES.TOTL.DT.ZS
Current account balance	BN.CAB.XOKA.CD
Reserves to imports (months)	FI.RES.TOTL.MO

7. LONG-TERM EXTERNAL DEBT			
Debt outstanding and disbursed	DT.DOD.DLXF.CD	**Interest payments**	DT.INT.DLXF.CD
Public and publicly guaranteed	DT.DOD.DPPG.CD	**Public and publicly guaranteed**	DT.INT.DPPG.CD
Official creditors	DT.DOD.OFFT.CD	Official creditors	DT.INT.OFFT.CD
Multilateral	DT.DOD.MLAT.CD	Multilateral	DT.INT.MLAT.CD
of which: IBRD	DT.DOD.MIBR.CD	of which: IBRD	DT.INT.MIBR.CD
IDA	DT.DOD.MIDA.CD	IDA	DT.INT.MIDA.CD
Bilateral	DT.DOD.BLAT.CD	Bilateral	DT.INT.BLAT.CD
Private creditors	DT.DOD.PRVT.CD	Private creditors	DT.INT.PRVT.CD
of which: Bonds	DT.DOD.PBND.CD	of which: Bonds	DT.INT.PBND.CD
Commercial banks	DT.DOD.PCBK.CD	Commercial banks	DT.INT.PCBK.CD
Private nonguaranteed	DT.DOD.DPNG.CD	Private nonguaranteed	DT.INT.DPNG.CD
of which: Bonds	DT.DOD.PNGB.CD	of which: Bonds	DT.INT.PNGB.CD
Disbursements	DT.DIS.DLXF.CD	**Principal repayments**	DT.AMT.DLXF.CD
Public and publicly guaranteed	DT.DIS.DPPG.CD	Public and publicly guaranteed	DT.AMT.DPPG.CD
Official creditors	DT.DIS.OFFT.CD	Official creditors	DT.AMT.OFFT.CD
Multilateral	DT.DIS.MLAT.CD	Multilateral	DT.AMT.MLAT.CD
of which: IBRD	DT.DIS.MIBR.CD	of which: IBRD	DT.AMT.MIBR.CD
IDA	DT.DIS.MIDA.CD	IDA	DT.AMT.MIDA.CD
Bilateral	DT.DIS.BLAT.CD	Bilateral	DT.AMT.BLAT.CD
Private creditors	DT.DIS.PRVT.CD	Private creditors	DT.AMT.PRVT.CD
of which: Bonds	DT.DIS.PBND.CD	of which: Bonds	DT.AMT.PBND.CD
Commercial banks	DT.DIS.PCBK.CD	Commercial banks	DT.AMT.PCBK.CD
Private nonguaranteed	DT.DIS.DPNG.CD	**Private nonguaranteed**	DT.AMT.DPNG.CD
of which: Bonds	DT.DIS.PNGB.CD	of which: Bonds	DT.AMT.PNGB.CD

8. DEBT STOCK-FLOW RECONCILATION	
Total change in external debt stocks	DT.DOD.DECT.CD.CG
Net flows on external debt	DT.NFL.DECT.CD

9. DEBT STOCK-FLOW RECONCILATION	
Total amount rescheduled	DT.DXR.DPPG.CD
Total amount forgiven	DT.DFR.DPPG.CD
Debt buyback	DT.DSB.DPPG.CD

10. CONTRACTUAL OBLIGATIONS ON OUTSTANDING LONG-TERM EXTERNAL DEBT	
Official creditors	
Principal	DT.AMT.OFFT.CD
Interest	DT.INT.OFFT.CD
Private creditors	
Principal	DT.AMT.PRVT.CD
Interest	DT.INT.PRVT.CD

How to Use the Databank

DataBank (http://databank.worldbank.org) is an online web resource that provides simple and quick access to collections of time series data. It has advanced functions for selecting and displaying data, performing customized queries, downloading data, and creating charts and maps. Users can create dynamic, custom reports based on their selection of countries, indicators, and years. All these reports can be easily edited, shared, and embedded as widgets on websites or blogs. For more information, see http://databank.worldbank.org/help.

Actions

Click to share the table using either the embed code or the URL

Click to edit and revise the table in DataBank

Click to export all metadata to Excel

Click to export the table to Excel

Click to export the table and corresponding indicator metadata to PDF

Click to print the table and corresponding indicator metadata

Click to access the IDS Online Tables Help file

Overview

International Debt Statistics 2014 presents data and analytical information on the external debt of developing countries for 2012, based on actual flows and debt-related transactions reported to the World Bank Debtor Reporting System (DRS) by 124 developing countries. It provides users with comprehensive stock and flow data on the external debt of individual developing countries and for regional and analytical groupings. In addition, *International Debt Statistics* (IDS) showcases the broader spectrum of debt data collected and compiled by the World Bank. These include the high frequency, quarterly data for high-income and select developing countries reporting to the joint World Bank–International Monetary Fund (IMF) Quarterly External Debt Statistics (QEDS) and the Public Sector Debt (PSD) database launched in 2010. In common with the DRS, these databases promote consistency and comparability across countries through standard definitions and valuation methods. IDS also includes a summary analysis of aggregate net capital flows (debt and equity) in 2012. The main messages from the 2012 data are:

(a) Net debt flows to developing countries were $412 billion in 2012, 9 percent lower than the comparable figure for 2011. However, the aggregates mask the impact of the sharp contraction in net debt flows to China, which fell to less than 30 percent of their 2011 level. When China is excluded, net debt flows to developing countries increased in 2012; they rose by 20 percent in 2012 with long-term debt flows 14 percent higher and short-term debt flows 55 percent higher than in 2011.

(b) Debt flows in 2012 were characterized by important shifts in both borrowing patterns and sources of financing. Inflows to public and publicly guaranteed borrowers rose 83 percent and accounted for one-half of long-term debt inflows, compared with one-third in 2011. In contrast, net flows to private nonguaranteed borrowers fell 17 percent, and short-term debt flows contracted sharply (41 percent). Private creditors accounted for more than 90 percent of net debt flows in 2012 and were dominated by the surge in bond issuance by developing-country borrowers, which rose by 30 percent over the 2011 level.

(c) Aggregate net capital flows, debt, and equity combined totaled just over $1.1 trillion in 2012, little changed from 2011. Foreign direct investment proved resilient despite being 6 percent lower than in 2011, and this decline was more than offset by the surge in portfolio equity flows. Measured relative to developing-country gross national income (GNI), aggregate capital flows have fallen sharply: to 4.7 percent in 2012, well short of the 7.7 percent recorded in 2007.

(d) Countries reporting to the QEDS and PSD databases confirm that external debt and public debt levels in high-income countries are, on average, much higher than in developing countries. The ratio of external debt to GDP in high-income countries averaged 143 percent in 2012, and in some cases surpassed 200 percent. This was the antithesis in developing countries, where the ratio of external debt to GNI averaged 22 percent in 2012. Similarly, general government debt relative to GDP in high-income countries is, on average, twice the comparable ratio for the largest borrowers among developing countries.

Table I.1. External Debt Stock of Developing Countries and Selected Ratios, 2005–12
$ billion

	2005	2006	2007	2008	2009	2010	2011	2012
Total external debt outstanding	2,338.0	2,534.4	2,993.5	3,262.1	3,542.1	3,987.5	4,437.8	4,829.6
Long-term external debt (including IMF)	1,856.8	1,975.1	2,293.4	2,559.4	2,792.7	2,987.1	3,265.3	3,552.0
Public and publicly guaranteed (including IMF)	1,292.2	1,223.4	1,304.7	1,369.3	1,559.7	1,688.0	1,768.5	1,911.3
Private nonguaranteed	564.6	751.7	988.7	1,190.0	1,233.0	1,299.1	1,496.8	1,640.7
Short-term external debt	481.2	559.3	700.1	702.8	749.4	1,000.3	1,172.5	1,277.6
Ratios								
External debt stocks to GNI (%)	27.2	25.0	23.9	21.9	23.7	22.3	21.4	22.1
External debt stocks to exports (%)	80.5	71.8	69.4	63.0	83.4	75.4	69.3	71.9
Reserves to external debt stocks (%)	74.3	88.4	104.8	111.7	120.8	124.2	122.3	117.6

Sources: World Bank Debtor Reporting System and International Monetary Fund.

I. Trends in External Debt Stocks and Flows

The pace of debt accumulation slowed to 9 percent in 2012, from 11 percent in 2011 with both long-term and short-term debt increasing at the same pace. This was in marked contrast to 2011, when the rise in short-term debt, 17 percent, grew almost twice as fast as that in long-term debt. The combined stock of developing countries' external debt rose from $4.4 trillion in 2011 to $4.8 trillion at the end of 2012, reflecting net debt inflows of $412 billion and debt forgiveness in the context of the Heavily Indebted Poor Country (HIPC) Initiative. It also includes the effect of the year-on-year exchange adjustments of foreign currencies relative to the U.S. dollar, in which approximately one-third of developing countries' external debt is denominated. The stock of long-term debt at the end of 2012 was fairly evenly divided between publicly guaranteed debt, 54 percent, and debt owed to private, nonguaranteed borrowers, 46 percent. The stock of short-term debt, as a share of total outstanding debt, was 26 percent at the end of 2012, unchanged from the previous year (table I.1).

Net debt flows to developing countries fell 9 percent in 2012, to $412 billion, and were characterized by some important shifts in borrowing patterns and sources of financing. Viewed from the borrower perspective, net flows of public and publicly guaranteed debt drove the overall increase in long-term debt flows in 2012. They jumped 67 percent, to $155 billion, in contrast to a 17 percent fall in net flows to private, nonguaranteed borrowers, accompanied by a sharp 41 percent contraction in short-term debt flows. As a result, public and publicly guaranteed borrowers accounted for one-half of long-term debt inflows, as compared with one-third in 2011. Regarding the source of financing, private creditors remained dominant and accounted for more than 90 percent of net debt flows in 2012. Long-term debt flows from private creditors continued their upward trajectory, rising by an additional 15 percent in 2012 on the back of the surge in bond issuance by developing-country borrowers. These rose to $179 billion (from $121 billion in 2011), offsetting both the fall in long-term lending by commercial banks and a large part of the decline in short-term debt flows (table I.2).

The rapid contraction in net debt flows to China dominated the global trend. They plummeted to $38 billion in 2012, less than 30 percent of their 2011 level. If China (the single largest borrower among developing countries) is excluded, then net debt flows to developing countries rose 20 percent in 2012 with long-term debt flows 14 percent higher and short-term debt flows 55 percent higher than the 2011 level (figure I.1).

Just ten of the 124 countries reporting to the World Bank DRS received more than 70 percent of net debt flows in 2012 and owed 65 percent of

Table I.2 Net Debt Flows to Developing Countries, 2005–12
$ billion

	2005	2006	2007	2008	2009	2010	2011	2012
Net inflows								
Total net debt flows	120.7	204.6	382.1	248.4	206.7	481.2	451.9	411.8
Long-term net debt flows	35.5	126.5	243.6	245.5	159.3	225.6	276.7	308.4
Public and publicly guaranteed (including IMF)	–23.2	–42.1	35.7	50.3	117.3	157.6	92.6	154.8
Private nonguaranteed	58.7	168.6	207.9	195.1	42.0	67.9	184.1	153.6
Short-term debt flows	85.2	78.1	138.5	2.9	47.4	255.6	175.1	103.4
By creditor								
Official creditors (including IMF)	–41.5	–40.1	3.2	42.7	93.8	80.1	32.0	27.9
Private creditors	162.2	244.7	378.9	205.6	112.9	401.0	419.9	383.9
of which:								
Long-term debt flows	77.0	166.6	240.4	202.7	65.5	145.4	244.8	280.5
Bonds	41.8	29.5	75.6	7.8	49.9	115.5	120.6	178.7
Banks and other private	35.2	137.1	164.8	195.0	15.6	29.9	124.2	101.8
Net short-term debt flows	85.2	78.1	138.5	2.9	47.4	255.6	175.1	103.4

Source: World Bank Debtor Reporting System.

developing countries' outstanding external debt.[1] This group is comprised of developing countries with the largest economies wherein the volume and trends in financing may differ from, and mask the size and direction of, flows to other developing countries. As a group, the top 10 borrowers saw net debt inflows fall 15 percent in 2012, driven by the 73 percent decline in net debt inflows to China. Excluding China, the other top 10 borrowers saw net debt inflows jump by 26 percent on average in 2012. At the individual country level, there was wide disparity in the direction of flows, which ranged from massive net debt outflow (in the case of Hungary and Ukraine) to the more than doubling of net debt inflows in South Africa and Turkey. Mexico was the largest

Figure I.1 Net Debt Flows to All Developing Countries 2000–12, Including and Excluding China

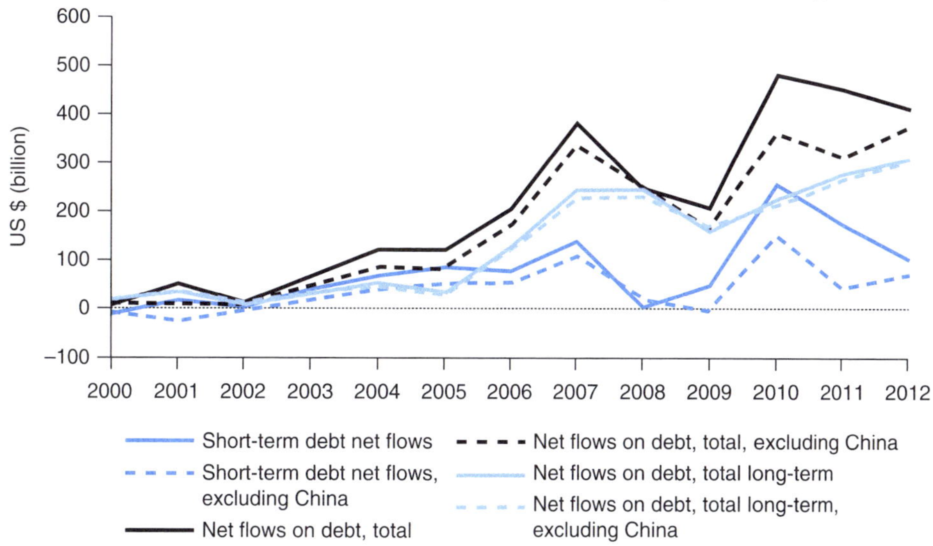

Source: World Bank Debtor Reporting System.

1. Defined as countries with the largest stock of outstanding external debt at end 2012.

Table I.3. Top Ten Borrowers, External Debt Stocks 2012, and Net Inflows 2011–12
$ billion

	External debt stock end 2012		Net inflow 2011	Net inflow 2012		
Country	Amount	% of total	Amount	Amount	% change in net inflow 2012	% of total net flow 2012
China	754.0	15.6	140.1	37.8	–73.0	9.2
Brazil	440.5	9.1	46.3	39.5	–14.8	9.6
India	379.1	7.8	43.4	44.3	1.9	10.8
Mexico	354.9	7.3	42.9	84.4	96.7	20.5
Turkey	337.5	7.0	17.5	40.1	129.0	9.7
Indonesia	254.9	5.3	22.9	30.2	31.8	7.3
Hungary	203.8	4.2	1.8	–10.7	–685.6	–2.6
South Africa	137.5	2.8	4.4	11.7	168.7	2.8
Kazakhstan	137.0	2.8	6.4	12.4	93.3	3.0
Ukraine	135.1	2.8	11.5	–3.5	–130.5	–0.9
Total top 10 borrowers	3,134.2	64.9	337.2	286.1	–15.2	69.5
Other developing countries	1,695.4	35.1	114.6	125.7	9.7	30.5
All developing countries	4,829.6	100.0	451.9	411.8	–8.9	100.0

Source: World Bank Debtor Reporting System.

net borrower in 2012, accounting for 20 percent of net debt inflows to all developing countries (table I.3).

Developing countries' external debt burdens are moderate. Despite uncertainty surrounding the global economic and financial crisis, the majority of developing countries have seen their economies rebound strongly since 2010 with a concomitant improvement in the ratio of outstanding external debt to GNI and to export earnings; this improvement translates to an average of 22.1 percent of GNI and 71.9 percent of export earnings at the end of 2012. Risks associated with the fact that short-term debt constituted 26 percent of external debt stock at the end of 2012 were mitigated by international reserves equivalent to 118 percent of the external debt stock at the end of 2012. Most short-term debt was trade related; measured against developing countries' imports, it was 18 percent—virtually unchanged from 2011. Developing countries have also seen a significant improvement in their external debt payment servicing capacity over the past decade, primarily as a consequence of increased export earnings, but also as a direct outcome of debt restructuring and outright debt relief from official and private creditors. Most HIPC- and MDRI-eligible countries have now fully benefited from HIPC, MDRI, and additional bilateral relief. The average debt service to export ratio fell to 9.8 percent in 2012, a marginal decline from the 10 percent recorded in 2011, but well below half the 21.1 percent at the start of the decade (figure I.2).

Bond issuance by developing countries' public and private borrowers rose nearly 30 percent in 2012, to an all-time high of $226 billion. The principal driver was a surge in new bond issuance by sovereigns and public sector entities in international capital markets and the purchase of domestically issued sovereign bonds by nonresidents, particularly in Mexico and Thailand. Issuance by public borrowers rose 43 percent in 2012, to $137.8 billion, and their share of total bond issuance rose to 61 percent, from 55 percent in 2011. Public borrowers in Latin America and the Caribbean claimed the largest share (39 percent)

Figure I.2. **Key Debt Indicator Trends, 2000–12**

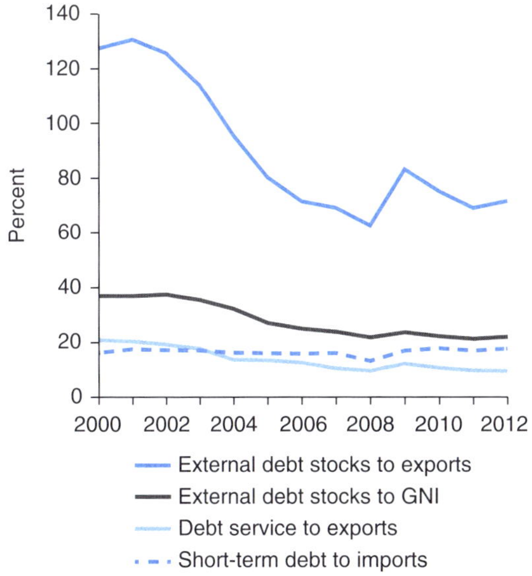

Sources: World Bank Debtor Reporting System and International Monetary Fund.

followed by those in Europe and Central Asia (25 percent). Issuance by corporate borrowers rose at a more moderate pace, to $88 billion, up 12 percent from 2011. The dominant players were private-sector borrowers in Latin America and the Caribbean, particularly in Brazil and Mexico, who commanded well over half of all corporate bonds issued in 2012. However, the sharpest increase was in Europe and Central Asia, where corporate bond issuance rose more than threefold to $14.7 billion led by Turkey (table I.4).

Aggregate Net Flows to Developing Countries

International capital flows, debt and equity combined, totaled just over $1.1 trillion in 2012, only marginally higher than 2011, but 7 percent above their 2007 precrisis level. Measured relative to developing country GNI, net capital flows declined sharply to 5.1 percent in 2012, well short of the 8.4 percent recorded in 2007. Net equity flows rose 8 percent in 2012 driven by a sharp rebound in portfolio equity flows. The increase to almost $100 billion in portfolio equity flows offset both the 7 percent fall in foreign direct investment inflows and the 9 percent decline in net debt inflows. However, this global trend is dominated by development in China, which accounted for more than one-third of net capital flows to developing countries in 2011 and 2012, and in which the net inflow of debt and equity combined fell to $321 billion in 2012, 25 percent below their 2011 level. In contrast, other developing countries saw net capital flows rise 17 percent in 2012 (table I.5).

Foreign direct investment is the single largest component of capital flows to developing countries and the most resilient, accounting for almost 55 percent since 2008. UNCTAD's *World Investment Report 2013* confirms that a record 52 percent of global foreign direct investment in 2012 was directed at developing countries with investors attracted by improvements in the business and regulatory environment, growth prospects, and buoyant domestic markets. Although an

Table I.4. **Bond Issuance by Developing Country Borrowers, 2011–12**
$ billion

	Public borrowers		Corporate borrowers	
	2011	2012	2011	2012
East Asia and Pacific	23.5	28.7	16.4	20.3
Europe and Central Asia	18.6	35.1	4.5	14.7
Latin America and the Caribbean	42.5	53.9	55.1	48.7
Middle East and North Africa	4.0	8.3	0.0	0.5
South Asia	3.0	8.5	0.7	0.8
Sub-Saharan Africa	4.5	3.4	1.7	3.1
All developing countries	96.1	137.8	78.5	88.1
Of which:				
Top ten borrowers	62.3	97.3	68.5	69.3

Source: World Bank Debtor Reporting System.

Table I.5. Net Capital Flows to Developing Countries, Debt and Equity, 2007–12
$ billion

	2007	2008	2009	2010	2011	2012
Net private and official inflows	1,049.8	831.2	698.0	1,116.1	1,109.3	1,121.6
Percent of GNI (%)	8.4	5.6	4.7	6.2	5.3	5.1
Net equity inflows	667.7	582.8	491.3	634.9	657.4	709.7
Net FDI inflows	558.6	623.4	380.3	511.6	654.7	612.2
Net portfolio equity inflows	109.0	-40.6	110.9	123.4	2.7	97.6
Net debt flows	382.1	248.4	206.7	481.2	451.9	411.8
Official creditors	3.2	42.7	93.8	80.1	32.0	27.9
World Bank	5.7	7.8	18.3	23.0	7.0	12.1
IMF	-5.2	16.6	31.8	13.4	0.5	-13.4
Private creditors	378.9	205.6	112.9	401.0	419.9	383.9
Net medium- and long-term debt flows	240.4	202.7	65.5	145.4	244.8	280.5
Bonds	75.6	7.8	49.9	115.5	120.6	178.7
Banks and other private	164.8	195.0	15.6	29.9	124.2	101.8
Net short-term debt flows	138.5	2.9	47.4	255.6	175.1	103.4
Change in reserves (– = increase)	-898.5	-506.9	-632.8	-673.4	-475.8	-252.8
Memorandum items						
Workers remittances	255.2	294.5	280.4	310.1	342.9	348.1

Sources: World Bank Debtor Reporting System, International Monetary Fund, and Bank for International Settlement.

increasing number of developing countries are beneficiaries of foreign direct investment, these flows remain highly concentrated among the ten largest recipients who absorbed more than 75 percent of inflows in 2012. This concentration is also reflected at the regional level with 81 percent of foreign direct investment in the East Asia and Pacific region going to China, while India absorbs almost 90 percent of foreign direct investment into the South Asia region, and Brazil accounts for half of the foreign direct investment going to Latin America and the Caribbean region (figure I.3).

Portfolio equity flows remained by far the most volatile of all capital flows. Following a near total collapse in 2011, portfolio equity flows shot up to close to $100 billion in 2012 as investors piled into select emerging markets, where growth prospects remained good and returns were anticipated to be high. Only a handful of developing countries benefited in any significant way from portfolio equity flows. In 2012, more than half of such flows went to China ($29.9 billion) and India ($22.8 billion), and the top six recipients combined accounted for 86 percent of inflows

Figure I.3. Net Foreign Direct Investment Inflows to Major Recipients, 2010–12

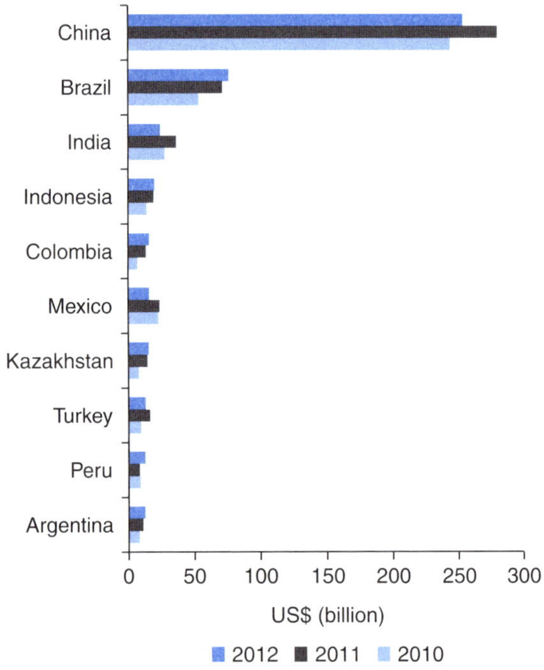

Source: International Monetary Fund.

to all developing countries—almost identical to their share in 2010. Over the past three years, most recipients experienced extreme volatility in portfolio equity flows. Nigeria stands out as the only country in which the portfolio equity flows have remained positive, and in 2012, on a sharp upward trajectory, portfolio equity flows rose more than fourfold in Nigeria, to $10 billion (table I.6).

Table I.6. Net Inflow of Portfolio Equity to Major Recipients, 2010–12
$ billion

	2010	2011	2012
Primary recipients	105.5	3.5	84.6
China	31.4	5.3	29.9
India	30.4	-4.0	22.8
Mexico	0.4	-6.6	10.0
Nigeria	2.2	2.6	10.0
Turkey	3.5	-1.0	6.3
Brazil	37.7	7.2	5.6
Other developing countries	17.9	-0.8	13.0
Total all developing countries	**123.4**	**2.7**	**97.6**
Primary recipients as a share of total (%)	85.5	128.5	86.7

Source: International Monetary Fund.

Regional Trends

East Asia and Pacific

External Debt Stock and Net Capital Flows to East Asia and Pacific, 2007–12
$ billion

	2007	2008	2009	2010	2011	2012
External Debt Stocks	746.7	775.3	883.3	1,080.6	1,286.6	1,412.4
Net private and official inflows	298.4	208.2	259.0	529.6	546.4	485.8
Percent of GNI (%)	6.5	3.6	4.1	7.1	6.0	4.8
Net equity inflows	231.4	203.6	184.7	331.5	346.6	351.6
Net FDI inflows	196.4	211.2	154.5	291.1	339.9	313.7
Net portfolio equity inflows	35.1	-7.6	30.2	40.3	6.7	37.9
Net debt flows	67.0	4.6	74.3	198.1	199.8	134.2
Official creditors	–3.2	–0.4	3.9	4.0	–0.4	3.3
World Bank	–0.3	1.2	2.2	2.7	0.9	1.0
IMF	0.0	0.0	0.1	0.0	0.0	_0.1
Private creditors	70.2	5.0	70.4	194.1	200.2	130.9
Net medium- and long-term debt flows	17.2	18.3	5.4	45.2	55.0	74.2
Bonds	2.6	2.7	9.5	28.1	30.6	45.7
Banks and other private	14.6	15.6	-4.2	17.1	24.4	28.6
Net short-term debt flows	52.9	-13.3	65.0	148.9	145.1	56.7
Memorandum items						
Change in reserves (– = increase)	-538.6	-431.2	-513.9	-536.2	-393.2	-162.1

Sources: World Bank Debtor Reporting System, International Monetary Fund, and Bank for International Settlement.

In 2012, net capital flows to the region fell 11 percent to $486 billion, equivalent to 4.8 percent of the region's gross national income (GNI), on account of a precipitous, 33 percent drop in net debt flows from the previous year. The downturn was driven primarily by the sharp contraction in short-term debt flows to China, which fell to $33 billion, less than a quarter of their 2011 level. Equity flows at $351 billion were largely unchanged from 2011, as an increase in portfolio equity flows (from $7 billion in 2011 to $38 billion in 2012) offset a 26 percent fall in foreign direct investment.

Since 2007, China has absorbed 74 percent of net capital flows into the region, and at the end of 2012, it accounted for 54 percent of the combined external debt stock of the East Asia and Pacific countries. China is by far the largest recipient of non-debt flows to all developing countries: it accounted for about 40 percent of all such flows over the past five years. In 2012, the slowdown in GDP growth in China had a knock-on effect on capital inflows, in particular short-term debt flows. They contracted to $33 billion (down from $129 billion the previous year), dictating both the global and regional trend, and bringing net debt flows to China down to just a little over one-quarter of their 2011 equivalent. Foreign direct investment flows also fell 10 percent from their 2011 peak, but the decline was more than offset by the $30 billion surge in portfolio equity flows, which resulted in an overall net equity flow that remained unchanged from their 2011 level.

Other East Asia and Pacific countries saw net capital flows rise 36 percent in 2012 with net debt flows jumping 62 percent and equity flows up 11 percent over their 2011 level. Consistent with the trend in previous years, Indonesia received around one-third of net capital flows to countries in the region, excluding China. It recorded $ 51.5 billion in debt and non-debt flows in 2012, a 23 percent increase over the 2011 level. But Thailand was the main driver of the 2012 increase with net debt flows up fivefold, to $32 billion, and non-debt flows, primarily foreign direct investment, 55 percent higher than 2011. Although small in the regional context, Mongolia saw net debt flows skyrocket, to $2.6 billion, and external debt stock double as a result of bond issuance by public- and private-sector entities. Similarly, in Papua and New Guinea, net debt flows were up 157 percent because of long-term commercial bank financing to private-sector borrowers.

Both public- and private-sector Asian borrowers profited from advantageous market conditions and investor appetite to issue almost $50 billion in bonds, an increase of 23 percent over 2011. The percentage share of issues by public- and private-sector borrowers, about 60 percent and 40 percent, respectively, was almost identical to 2011 with important shifts happening at the individual country level. Indonesia accounted for 45 percent of issuance by public sector borrowers in 2012. Public sector borrowers in China were absent from the markets, but in contrast, issuance by public sector borrowers in Thailand almost doubled to $9 billion, including domestically issued Thai bhat bonds purchased by nonresidents in search of attractive yields. Mongolia came to the market for the first time in November 2012 with a $1.5 billion 5- and 10-year note that was heavily oversubscribed. Chinese corporations accounted for the majority share of bond issuance by private-sector borrowers, at 54 percent, and those in Malaysia accounted for an additional 20 percent.

Countries in the region have, on average, the lowest external debt burden in relation to GNI compared with all developing countries. The stock of external debt rose 10 percent in 2012, but the ratio of debt outstanding to GNI, 13.9 percent, was below half the comparable ratio of 29 percent for other developing countries. The ratio of debt to exports, 42.3 percent, was also among the lowest of any other region. East Asia and Pacific countries accumulated an additional $160 billion in international reserves in 2012. The reserves now stand at 36.5 percent, the level of outstanding external debt—a stark contrast to the much higher ratio of external debt stock to reserves of 189 percent in other developing countries.

Net Capital Flows to East Asian Countries, 2007–12

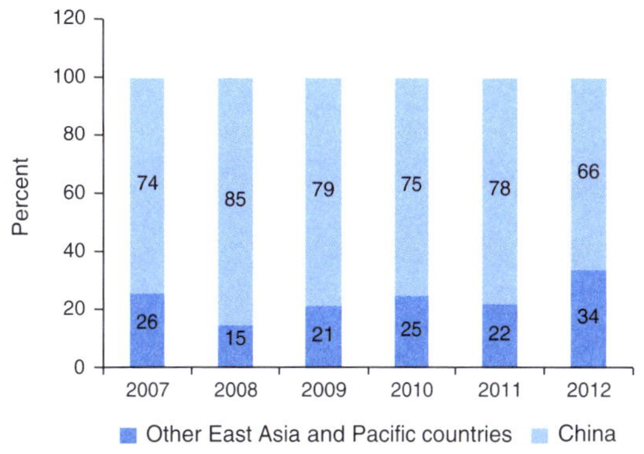

Sources: World Bank Debtor Reporting System and the International Monetary Fund.

Ratio of external debt stocks to GNI, exports and reserves, 2012

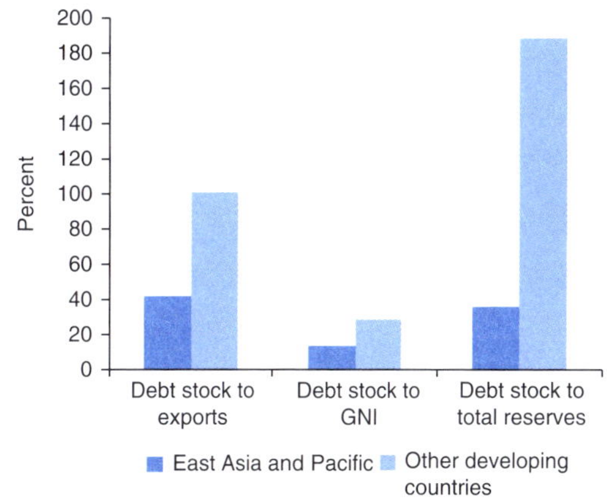

Sources: World Bank Debtor Reporting System and the International Monetary Fund.

Trends in Net Capital Flows to East Asia and Pacific countries, 2007–12

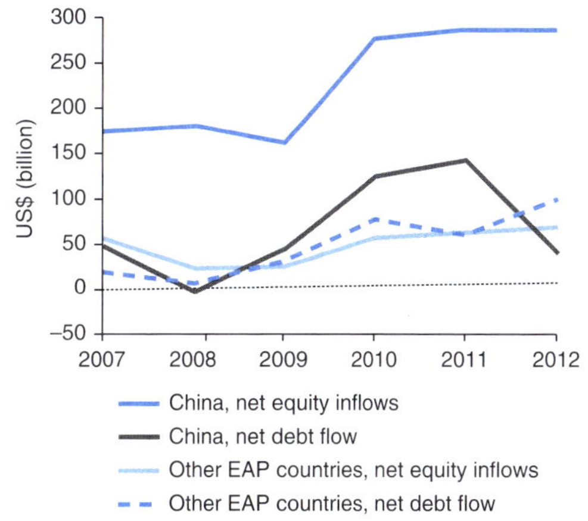

Sources: World Bank Debtor Reporting System and the International Monetary Fund.

Europe and Central Asia

External Debt Stock and Net Capital Flows to Europe and Central Asia, 2007–12
$ billion

	2007	2008	2009	2010	2011	2012
External Debt Stocks	806.1	966.6	1,023.2	1,060.5	1,095.3	1,149.5
Net private and official inflows	263.6	249.9	104.3	105.9	126.1	112.7
Percent of GNI (%)	18.5	14.7	7.4	6.6	7.0	6.3
Net equity inflows	91.7	90.5	57.8	48.2	63.8	63.8
Net FDI inflows	88.2	91.0	54.1	44.5	64.5	55.8
Net portfolio equity inflows	3.5	-0.4	3.7	3.7	-0.7	8.0
Net debt flows	171.9	159.3	46.5	57.7	62.2	48.8
Official creditors	-0.9	24.6	49.0	28.0	6.9	-6.9
World Bank	0.7	1.2	3.4	3.9	2.9	2.0
IMF	-5.0	12.8	25.5	9.0	-1.0	-13.0
Private creditors	172.8	134.8	-2.5	29.7	55.3	55.7
Net medium- and long-term debt flows	131.1	129.1	7.4	-11.8	41.3	46.8
Bonds	31.5	-3.2	-6.8	7.1	8.2	38.7
Banks and other private	99.6	132.3	14.2	-18.9	33.0	8.0
Net short-term debt flows	41.7	5.7	-9.9	41.6	14.1	9.0
Memorandum items						
Change in reserves (– = increase)	-49.5	-5.6	-18.9	-21.8	-7.2	-9.1

Sources: World Bank Debtor Reporting System, International Monetary Fund, and Bank for International Settlement.

Net capital flows to the region fell 11 percent in 2012 as a consequence of a downturn in net debt flows. These dropped to $49 billion in 2012, largely as a consequence of a $13 billion net outflow to the IMF as the rescue packages extended in the wake of the global economic and financial crisis were repaid. Net equity flows were broadly unchanged with a fall in foreign direct investment compensated by increased portfolio equity flows.

Important changes to the composition of the Europe and Central Asia region in *International Debt Statistics 2014* should be noted. The Russian Federation is excluded from the regional analysis because it is now classified as a high-income country. Conversely, Hungary has been reclassified from a high- to a middle-income country and is included in the regional aggregates.

Net inflows to the region fell sharply in 2012 as new inflows declined while payments on emergency loans extended in response to the 2008 global economic and financial crisis rose appreciably. Countries in the region were among some of the hardest hit by the global economic and financial crisis. Thus, external support from official creditors, notably institutions like the IMF and the World Bank, was essential for the creation of financial buffers and acted as a catalyst in addressing macro-economic imbalances. However, 2012 saw a sharp fall in net inflows from official creditors to –$7 billion in 2012, a sharp contrast to the $50 billion net inflow of 2009. Gross disbursements continued on a downward trajectory, falling by 20 percent in 2012, while those from the World Bank Group (IBRD and IDA) fell 16 percent, to $3.9 billion. In parallel, there was a sharp rise in repayments, especially with regard to the IMF, with an outflow of $13 billion in 2012; largely the result of repurchases (payments) by Hungary, Romania, Turkey, and Ukraine.

Regional net debt inflows from private creditors were almost identical to their 2011 level, with a major change in composition of borrowers and loan instruments. Public- and private-sector entities across the region took advantage of lower borrowing costs and investor interest to issue international bonds totaling $50 billion in 2012, well more than double their 2011 level and equivalent to 22 percent of the 2012 international bond issuance by all developing countries.

Issuance by sovereign and public-sector borrowers rose to $35 billion, of which close to two-thirds was accounted for by Hungary, Romania, and Ukraine. Bulgaria came back to the market for the first time since 2002 with a $1.2 billion 5-year sovereign issue, and Serbia raised $1.8 billion in two offerings. In parallel, international bond issuance by private entities surged to $14.7 billion whereas long-term lending by commercial banks, particularly private-sector borrowers, fell sharply in 2012, in large part due to deleveraging by banks in the Euro Area.

Sixty percent of net capital flows into the region in 2012 were in the form of foreign direct investment. While almost all countries in the region benefited from some investment flows, they were fairly heavily concentrated in five countries: Azerbaijan, Hungary, Kazakhstan, Turkey, and Ukraine, who together accounted for more than 75 percent of net foreign direct investment to the region in 2012. As in previous years, much of the investment in Kazakhstan, the largest recipient in 2012, and inflows into Hungary, slowed in response to economic uncertainties. Those to Turkey fell 20 percent but were offset by the surge in portfolio equity flows, which shot up to $6.3 billion, an all-time high and a marked turnaround from the –$1 billion outflow in 2011.

Countries in Europe and Central Asia are the most indebted of those in any other region, but debt indicators have improved. The average ratio of external debt stock to GNI for the Europe and Central Asia countries at the end of 2012, 63.8 percent, was three times the comparable ratio for all developing countries combined. Similarly, external debt stock measured in relation to exports at the end of 2012 was double the developing country average at 144.7 percent. However, there has been a 12 percentage point reduction in the external debt stock to GNI ratio since 2009, and an even more pronounced improvement in the external debt stock to exports ratio over the same period, 23 percentage points. The principal drivers of growth and improved export earnings are the oil exporters, notably Kazakhstan and Turkey, followed by Hungary and Ukraine.

Bond Issuance, Public- and Private-Sector Borrowers, 2011–12

$ billion

	Public borrowers		Corporate borrowers	
	2011	2012	2011	2012
Albania	0.1	0.0	0.0	0.0
Azerbaijan	0.0	0.5	0.0	0.0
Bulgaria	0.0	1.2	0.0	0.2
Belarus	0.8	0.0	0.0	0.0
Georgia	0.5	0.3	0.0	1.0
Hungary	6.3	11.2	0.0	4.7
Kazakhstan	0.0	2.3	0.8	1.8
Montenegro	0.2	0.0	0.0	0.0
Romania	2.1	5.1	0.1	0.0
Serbia	1.0	1.8	0.0	0.0
Turkey	4.8	7.9	2.1	7.0
Ukraine	2.8	4.9	1.6	0.0
Total	18.6	35.1	4.5	14.7

Source: World Bank Debtor Reporting System.

Net Inflow of Foreign Direct Investment, 2011–12

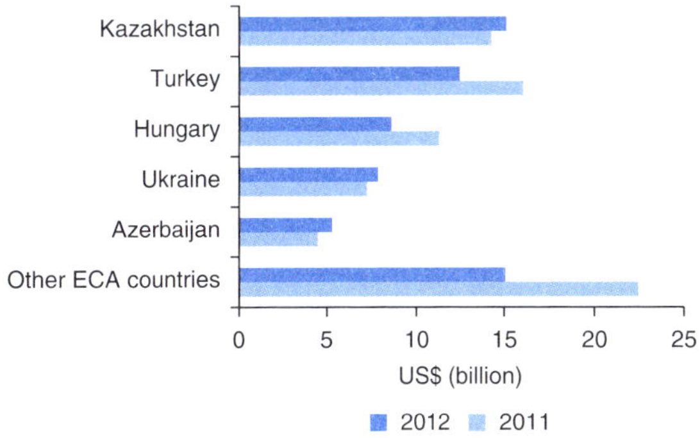

Source: International Monetary Fund.

Select Debt Ratios for Europe and Central Asia, 2007–12

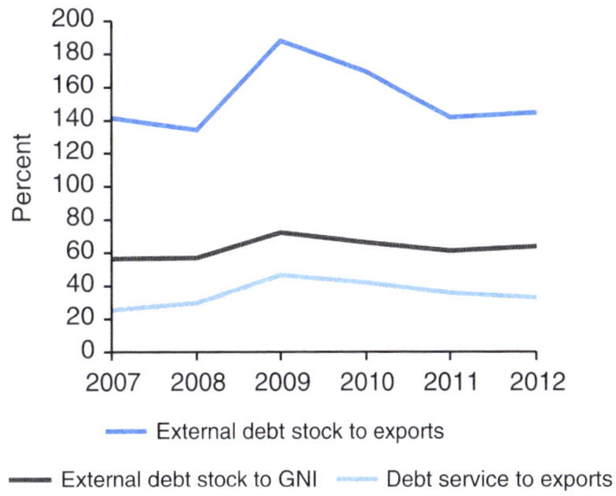

Sources: World Bank Debtor Reporting System and the International Monetary Fund.

Latin America and the Caribbean

External Debt Stock and Net Capital Flows to Latin America and the Caribbean, 2007–12
$ billion

	2007	2008	2009	2010	2011	2012
External Debt Stock	782.3	831.1	866.3	1,000.9	1,133.5	1,257.9
Net private and official inflows	213.1	163.1	160.4	303.4	267.7	312.2
Percent of GNI (%)	6.3	4.1	4.3	6.6	5.2	6.1
Net equity inflows	140.9	109.9	112.5	150.1	147.5	170.5
Net FDI inflows	112.5	121.5	71.2	110.9	145.0	150.3
Net portfolio equity inflows	28.4	-11.6	41.2	39.3	2.6	20.2
Net debt flows	72.2	53.2	47.9	153.3	120.2	141.6
Official creditors	-1.0	6.4	17.2	22.6	4.9	11.8
World Bank	-0.2	2.5	6.2	8.3	-2.9	3.6
IMF	0.0	0.0	0.4	1.3	0.2	-0.1
Private creditors	73.2	46.8	30.7	130.7	115.3	129.8
Net medium- and long-term debt flows	51.7	44.2	38.6	84.8	121.2	117.5
Bonds	22.5	9.1	43.3	65.6	75.6	79.8
Banks and other private	29.2	35.1	-4.7	19.1	45.6	37.7
Net short-term debt flows	21.6	2.6	-7.9	45.9	-5.9	12.3
Memorandum items						
Change in reserves (– = increase)	-136.1	-40.8	-46.3	-81.4	-87.9	-55.8

Sources: World Bank Debtor Reporting System, International Monetary Fund, and Bank for International Settlement.

Net capital flows to the region rose 17 percent in 2012, to $312 billion, equivalent to 6.1 percent of GNI (5.2 percent in 2011), and 28 percent of comparable flows to all developing countries. Debt and non-debt flows rose by broadly the same percentage, with changes in composition. The principal drivers were, for debt flows, the doubling of net inflow from official creditors and a sharp rise in short-term debt, and with regard to non-debt flows, the surge in portfolio flows.

Equity flows accounted for 55 percent of net capital flows to the region in 2012, and for many countries in the region were the most important source of external financing. They rose by 16 percent in 2012, to $171 billion, of which almost 50 percent was directed to Brazil. Concomitant with the slowdown in growth, equity flows to Brazil rose only a moderate 4 percent in 2012. Despite the slowdown, Brazil remained the second most important developing country destination, after China, for foreign direct investment. However, foreign direct investment inflows rose sharply across the region, spurred by the presence of natural resources, a fast expanding middle-class, and inter-regional investments. They were up 13 percent in Argentina, 17 percent in Colombia, 49 percent in Peru, and 76 percent in the Dominican Republic (to $3.9 billion), boosted by the acquisition of the country's main brewery by the Belgian company Ambev for $1 billion. Among the major economies in the region, Mexico was the only one to see foreign direct investment decline in 2012. The foreign direct investment fell 34 percent in large part due to disinvestment by Banco Santander of Spain, where 25 percent of its share is its Mexican affiliate. But this decline was more than offset by the surge in portfolio equity and overall equity inflow to Mexico, which rose 50 percent in 2012.

Net debt flows to Latin America and the Caribbean remained robust in 2012, despite slower growth in much of the region, rising by 18 percent, to $171 billion. This reflected a record pace of bond issuance and a rebound in short-term debt flows. The region also had the sharpest increase among all regions in net debt flows from official creditors, up nearly 143 percent to $12 billion. This was in large part due to the turnaround in net inflows from the World Bank Group (IBRD and IDA), which increased to $3.6

billion from an outflow of $2.9 billion in 2011. The principal driver was Mexico where net debt flows came close to doubling in 2012, to $84 billion, more than offsetting the 15 percent decline in net debt flows to Brazil and 43 percent fall in those to other countries in the region. Short-term debt flows returned to positive territory in 2012, rising to $12.3 billion, from an outflow of –$5.9 billion in 2011, but remained well below the $45.9 billion recorded in 2010. Here again the aggregate masks disparate trends at the individual country level, in particular, the direction of flows to the two largest economies. In the case of Brazil, short-term flows continued to contract by an additional –$9.6 billion in 2012; in marked contrast, short-term inflows to Mexico almost doubled from their 2011 level, to $21.3 billon.

Public and private entities in Latin America and the Caribbean took advantage of low funding costs and strong investor demand and raised $103 billion through bond issuance in 2012, equivalent to 45 percent of bonds issued by all developing countries. The overall level of bond issuance in 2012 was only marginally higher than in 2011, but the aggregate figure masks important changes at the individual country level and with regard to the type of issuer. Mexico remained by far the largest borrower with total issuance of $73 billion, a little more than 70 percent of the regional bond issuance in 2012 (up from 62 percent in 2011). Public sector borrowers accounted for close to 60 percent of this, much the same as in 2011, including a large component of domestically issued government bonds purchased by nonresidents in search of attractive yields. Issuance by Mexican corporations also jumped over 70 percent in 2012 across all sectors, but led by Mobil Corporation. In sharp contrast, bond issuance by Brazil was down 71 percent, primarily on account of Brazil's private sector, which after considerable activity in 2011, was largely absent from the market, reflecting both their prior borrowing and the country's economic downturn.

Net Debt and Equity Flows, Percentage Share, 2012

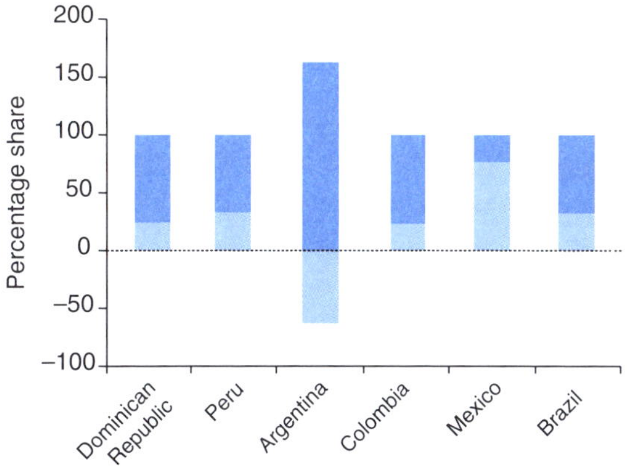

Sources: World Bank Debtor Reporting System and the International Monetary Fund.

Net Short-term Debt Inflows to Select Countries in Latin America and the Caribbean, 2011–12

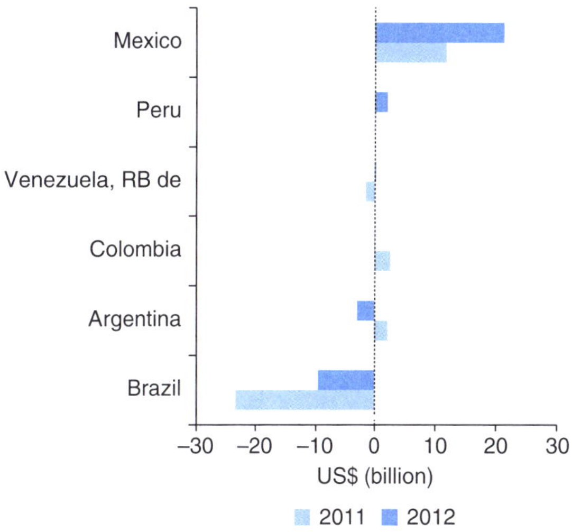

Sources: Bank for International Settlements and national authorities.

Bond Issuance, Public- and Private-Sector Borrowers, Latin America and the Caribbean 2011–12
$ billion

	Public-sector borrowers		Private-sector borrowers	
	2011	2012	2011	2012
Brazil	3.6	6.6	30.8	8.8
Colombia	2.6	2.3	2.7	2.6
Mexico	26.8	41.7	18.1	31.0
Peru	0.0	0.9	1.7	3.0
Other	9.4	2.5	1.8	3.3
Total LAC countries	42.5	53.9	55.1	48.7

Source: World Bank Debtor Reporting System.

Middle East and North Africa

External Debt Stock and Net Capital Flows to the Middle East and North Africa, 2007–12
$ billion

	2007	2008	2009	2010	2011	2012
External Debt Stocks	156.3	148.7	160.6	166.6	162.9	177.1
Net private and official inflows	30.1	23.8	30.9	31.4	10.2	32.7
Percent of GNI (%)	3.9	2.6	3.3	..	..	..
Net equity inflows	26.0	30.0	27.5	24.2	13.0	18.0
Net FDI inflows	28.1	29.6	26.3	22.3	13.7	19.3
Net portfolio equity inflows	-2.1	0.4	1.2	2.0	-0.6	-1.3
Net debt flows	4.1	-6.2	3.4	7.1	-2.8	14.7
Official creditors	1.2	-1.7	2.5	1.3	1.2	4.8
World Bank	1.0	-0.3	0.9	0.8	0.9	0.8
IMF	-0.1	-0.1	-0.1	0.0	-0.1	0.5
Private creditors	2.9	-4.4	0.9	5.9	-4.0	9.9
Net medium- and long-term debt flows	-0.5	-2.5	-2.1	1.4	-1.5	6.0
Bonds	0.7	-0.8	0.1	3.2	-0.6	5.8
Banks and other private	-1.2	-1.7	-2.2	-1.8	-0.8	0.1
Net short-term debt flows	3.3	-1.9	3.0	4.5	-2.6	4.0
Memorandum items						
Change in reserves (– = increase)	-44.1	-42.8	-19.9	-17.9	23.8	-4.6

Sources: World Bank Debtor Reporting System, International Monetary Fund, and Bank for International Settlement.
Note: .. = not available.

Net capital inflows rose by 220 percent in 2012, far faster than any other region, to an all time high of $32.7 billion. Driving this was the spectacular turnaround in net debt flows that climbed to $14.7 billion, more than double their previous 2008 peak and a marked contrast to the –$2.8 billion outflow in 2011. The key elements were sovereign bond issuance by several countries in the region, a fourfold increase in net flows from official creditors, and an expansion in short-term debt. Non-debt flows, notably foreign direct investment, regained momentum and were up close to 40 percent from their 2011 level.

The combined net debt flows to the four largest borrowers in the region, the Arab Republic of Egypt, Lebanon, Morocco, and Tunisia, of $16.5 billion, were more than five times their 2011 level. Egypt saw the most spectacular rise, a $6.9 billion turnaround from the net debt outflow that was recorded in 2011, but net debt flows to Lebanon and Tunisia also surged. There was, however, wide divergence in the pattern of financial instruments used across countries. In Egypt, net debt inflow in 2012 was composed entirely of short-term debt inflows, about 72 percent, and the rest from official creditors, primarily bilateral inflows from Saudi Arabia. In contrast, almost 90 percent of net debt flows in Lebanon came from bonds issued in international capital markets, partly to refinance upcoming maturities. Morocco returned to the international bond market in 2012 with a $1.5 billion sovereign bond that combined a 10-year and a 30-year note, and was heavily oversubscribed. Tunisia successfully issued its first bond since the Arab uprising in July, 2012—$485 million guaranteed by the U.S. Agency for International Development.

Net equity flows, primarily foreign direct investment, rose over 40 percent in 2012 with the majority of countries in the region recording higher inflows. The Islamic Republic of Iran was the single largest recipient, receiving on average 28 percent of foreign direct investment into the region in 2011–12, primarily into the hydrocarbon sector. However, but the most pronounced rises were in Egypt and, to a lesser extent, Tunisia. The net inflow of net foreign direct investment to Egypt jumped to $2.8 billion in 2012, from 2011, but remained far short of its precrisis peak of $11.6 billion in 2007. Tunisia also saw foreign direct investment rebound in 2012 to a net inflow of \$1.6 billion, close to four times its 2011 level.

External debt stocks, in relation to export earnings, were the lowest of any region in 2012. They averaged 42.1 percent at the end of 2012, compared with 74 percent in other developing countries. This outcome is the result of a very high share of non-debt capital flows to the region and relatively robust export earnings. Debt service payments absorbed only a moderate 5.1 percent of export earnings, almost half the average of 9.9 percent in other developing countries. International reserves stood at 158 percent of external debt stocks at the end of 2012, but the regional aggregate was heavily weighted by Algeria's high level of international reserves and low external debt level. In contrast, Egypt, which accounted for nearly one-quarter of the external debt stock of the region at the end of 2012, has international reserves equivalent to 29 percent of outstanding external debt.

Net Foreign Direct Investment Inflows to Major Recipients, 2011–12

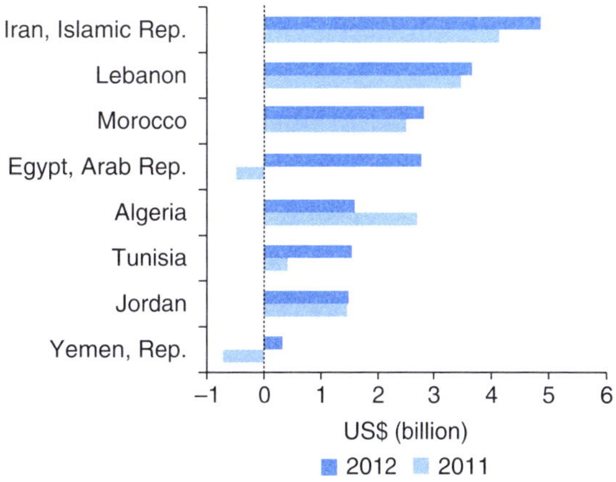

Source: International Monetary Fund.

Ratio of External Debt and Debt Service to Exports, 2007–12

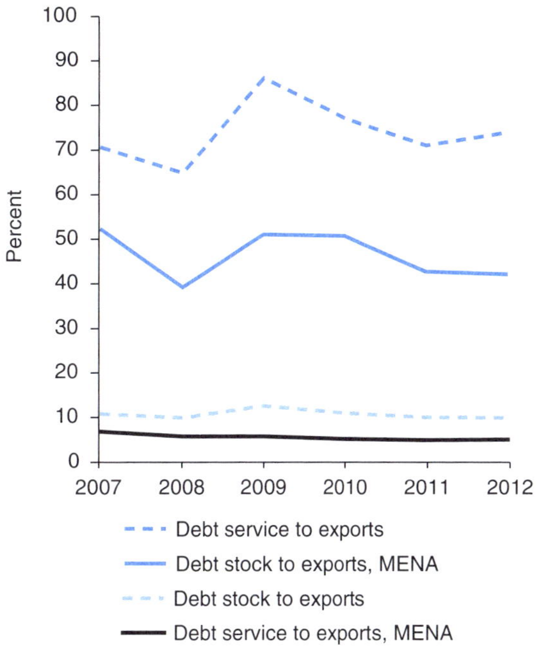

Sources: World Bank Debtor Reporting System and the International Monetary Fund.

Net Debt Flows to Select Countries, 2011–12

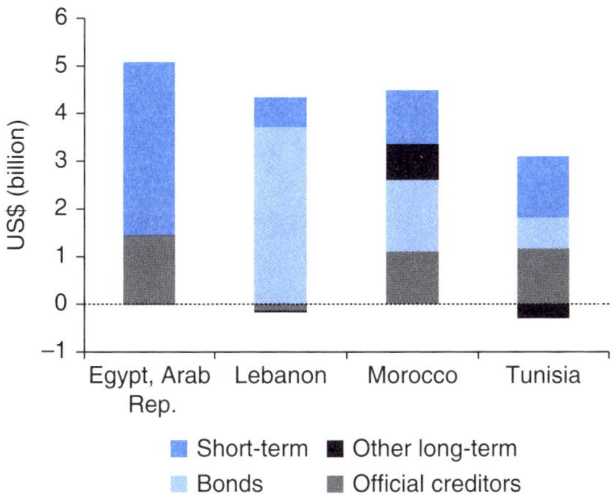

Source: World Bank Debtor Reporting System.

South Asia

External Debt Stock and Net Capital Flows to South Asia, 2007–12
$ billion

	2007	2008	2009	2010	2011	2012
External Debt Stock	289.2	322.7	363.1	409.8	461.8	501.5
Net private and official inflows	115.8	64.6	89.9	107.0	84.7	96.1
Percent of GNI (%)	7.7	4.2	5.3	5.2	3.7	4.2
Net equity inflows	66.4	35.1	63.6	61.1	36.1	50.8
Net FDI inflows	32.5	50.9	39.5	31.2	40.4	27.4
Net portfolio equity inflows	34.0	-15.8	24.1	29.9	-4.3	23.4
Net debt flows	49.4	29.6	26.3	45.9	48.6	45.3
Official creditors	4.4	8.8	11.0	10.8	6.6	4.0
World Bank	2.0	1.4	2.4	3.3	2.0	0.9
IMF	-0.1	3.1	3.6	2.0	0.0	-1.6
Private creditors	44.9	20.7	15.4	35.0	42.0	41.3
Net medium- and long-term debt flows	32.0	12.9	12.7	23.3	19.3	27.9
Bonds	10.7	1.7	1.9	10.1	0.7	5.1
Banks and other private	21.3	11.2	10.9	13.2	18.5	22.8
Net short-term debt flows	12.9	7.9	2.6	11.7	22.7	13.4
Memorandum items						
Change in reserves (– = increase)	-101.1	24.0	-30.1	-16.6	4.8	-0.2

Sources: World Bank Debtor Reporting System, International Monetary Fund, and Bank for International Settlement.

The region saw net capital inflows rise by 13 percent in 2012, equivalent to 4.2 percent of GNI (versus 3.7 percent in 2011) because of an increase in portfolio equity flows of $28 billion. These offset the slowdown in foreign direct investment and pushed non-debt flows up by 41 percent over their 2011 level. In contrast, a sharp contraction in short-term debt flows overshadowed the rise in long–term debt flows from private creditors and pulled total net debt flows down by 7 percent in 2012.

India has absorbed 95 percent of net capital flows into the region since 2007. In 2012 India's share was $91 billion, fairly evenly divided between debt and non-debt flows. The level of net debt flows was broadly unchanged from 2011, but the composition of debt by maturities changed. A 29 percent fall in short-term debt flows was offset by new long-term financing, primarily from bond issuance by public sector entities (up fourfold from 2011) and a 30 percent increase in net long-term flows from commercial banks to private-sector borrowers, often supported by an export credit guarantee. Even though foreign direct investment flows fell by a third in 2012 to $24 billion, their lowest level since 2005, India remained the third most important developing country destination for investment flows, after Brazil and China. The downturn was additionally offset by a significant turnaround in portfolio equity flows of $28 billion, which pushed 2012's total non-debt flows up by 44 percent from their 2011 level.

Countries in the region are relatively poor: with the exception of Sri Lanka, all are IDA-eligible countries, but official creditors account for a small share of net debt flows. In the wake of the global economic and financial crisis, debt related flows from official creditors, including from the IMF, averaged $11 billion in 2009–10. This accounted for about 60 percent of net debt flows to the public sector and close to one-third of total net debt flows. Thereafter they have been on a declining trajectory and by 2012 had fallen to $4 billion, their lowest level since 2005, less than 9 percent of net debt flows. An important element was the $2.3 billion IMF repurchase (payment) by Pakistan in the context of the Standby Agreement concluded in 2008. Net outflows from Pakistan to IBRD ($82 million) and from India to IDA ($250 million) lowered net inflows to the region from the World Bank Group (IBRD and IDA) by 56 percent, compared with 2011. Regional aggregates mask an increase in bilateral flows in 2012, principally to Bangladesh and Sri Lanka.

External debt stocks at the end of 2012, measured in relation to exports and to GNI, remained moderate, 93.7 percent and 21.9 percent, respectively. However, the regional averages mask important differences between countries. The external debt to export ratio ranged from 83.5 percent in India to 194.3 percent in Pakistan; and the external debt to GNI ratio ranged from 20.8 percent in India to 43.6 percent in Sri Lanka. Similarly for India, international reserves stood at 71.4 percent of external debt stocks at the end of 2012, compared with 16.6 percent in Pakistan.

Net Debt Flows from Official Creditors, 2007–12

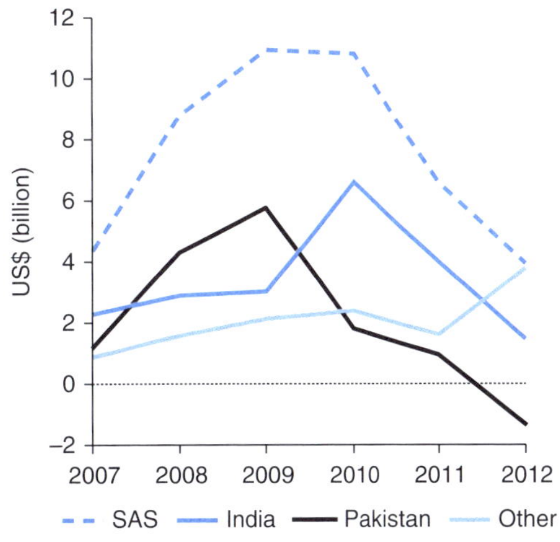

Source: World Bank Debtor Reporting System.

India, Composition of Net Capital Flows, 2011–12

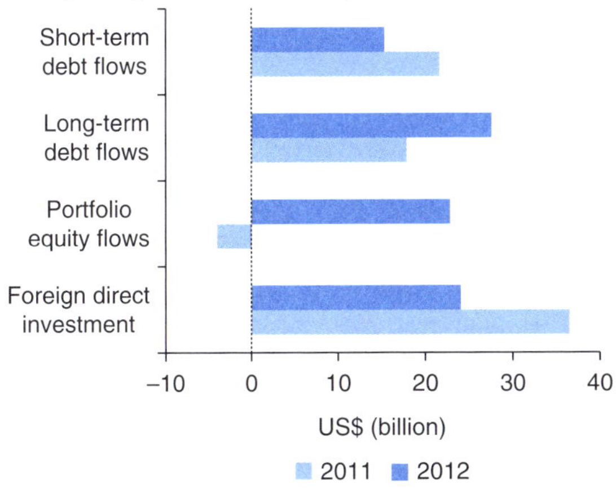

Sources: World Bank Debtor Reporting System and the International Monetary Fund.

Ratio of External Debt Stocks to GNI and Exports, 2012

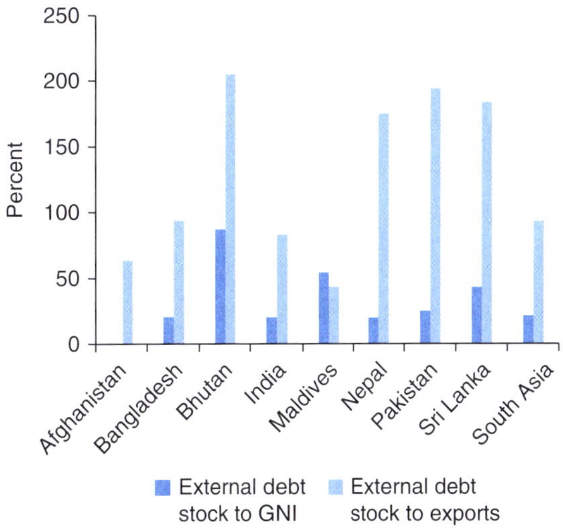

Sources: World Bank Debtor Reporting System and the International Monetary Fund.

Sub-Saharan Africa

External Debt Stock and Net Capital Flows to Sub-Saharan Africa, 2007–12
$ billion

	2007	2008	2009	2010	2011	2012
External Debt Stock	213.0	217.7	245.7	269.1	297.6	331.2
Net private and official inflows	58.1	46.6	56.5	59.5	62.9	73.6
Percent of GNI (%)	7.2	5.1	6.4	5.6	5.3	6.1
Net equity inflows	40.6	38.7	48.2	40.4	39.0	46.4
Net FDI inflows	30.4	44.3	37.7	32.2	40.0	37.0
Net portfolio equity inflows	10.2	-5.6	10.5	8.2	-1.0	9.4
Net debt flows	17.6	7.9	8.3	19.1	23.9	27.2
Official creditors	2.7	5.0	10.2	13.5	12.8	11.0
World Bank	2.4	1.9	3.1	4.0	3.2	3.9
IMF	0.1	0.7	2.2	1.2	1.4	0.9
Private creditors	14.8	2.8	-1.9	5.6	11.1	16.2
Net medium- and long-term debt flows	8.8	0.9	3.6	2.6	9.5	8.2
Bonds	7.5	-1.6	2.0	1.4	6.0	3.6
Banks and other private	1.3	2.5	1.6	1.2	3.4	4.6
Net short-term debt flows	6.0	1.9	-5.5	3.0	1.6	8.0
Memorandum items						
Change in reserves (– = increase)	-29.1	-10.4	-3.7	0.5	-16.1	-21.0

Sources: World Bank Debtor Reporting System, International Monetary Fund, and Bank for International Settlement.

Net capital flows to Sub-Saharan Africa rose 17 percent in 2012, primarily as a consequence of a sharp rise in portfolio equity flows to Nigeria and a surge in short-term debt inflows to South Africa. Almost two-thirds of the $74 billion 2012 inflows constituted non-debt flows. Net capital flows as a share of GNI increased to 6.1 percent (5.3 percent in 2011), and to almost 7 percent, excluding South Africa.

In 2012, just two countries, Nigeria and South Africa, absorbed 45 percent of net capital flows to Sub-Saharan Africa. Even though it saw the net inflow of foreign direct investment fall by 20 percent compared with its 2011 level, Nigeria received the highest share, over one-third, of net equity flows into the region in 2012, mostly to the hydrocarbon sector. This was more than offset by the surge in portfolio equity flows, which totaled $10 billion in 2012, due to investors increasingly attracted by the country's economic prospects. Nigeria is the only developing country in Sub-Saharan Africa where portfolio equity flows have been on a continuous upward trajectory since the global financial and economic crisis. In contrast, the 142 percent jump in net capital flows to South Africa in 2012 was largely debt-related. Net debt flows jumped to $11.7 billion, from $4.4 billion in 2011—mostly due to an increase in short-term debt flows, which surged to $7.3 billion from an outflow of $1.2 billion in 2011.

Net debt flows to countries in Sub-Saharan Africa, other than South Africa, declined by 21 percent in 2012. The reason for the downturn lay in the sharp 75 percent contraction in short-term debt flows and a 23 percent fall in net inflows from official creditors, on which many countries in the region depend. In addition, inflows from private creditors fell by 18 percent over their 2011 level. Net inflows from multilateral creditors constituted over two-thirds of official flows, with IDA being by far the most important creditor. It provided $3.3 billion to the region in 2012 in net concessional loans, equivalent to half of all net multilateral debt inflows, and an additional $1.4 billion in grants. Inflows from IDA were heavily concentrated with 50 percent going to three countries, Ethiopia, Nigeria, and Tanzania. Most bilateral debt inflows came from nontraditional developing country creditors, notably China and, to a lesser extent, Brazil and India. The bulk of these inflows were directed at large-scale infrastructure projects and half of net inflows in 2012 was concentrated in four countries: Ethiopia, Ghana, Mozambique, and Senegal. Long-term inflows from private creditors rose 19 percent, to $5.2 billion, of which the largest share went to private-sector borrowers. Inflows to public-sector borrowers were largely confined to East Africa: Zambia joined the ranks of countries in the region to tap international bond markets with a $750 million debut issue that was 15 times oversubscribed, and Kenya raised $600 million for infrastructure financing through a syndicated bank loan.

Foreign direct investment has become the most important element of net capital flows for countries across the region, accounting for 55 percent of net capital inflows in 2012, excluding South Africa. In 2012 they were again boosted by high commodity prices, the wealth of natural resources across the continent, and relatively high levels of return on investment. A large share of foreign direct investment inflows went to the hydrocarbon and other extractive sectors in Nigeria, the single largest recipient. The region also experienced a jump in investment in large-scale infrastructure projects. In some of the large economies like Ghana and Nigeria, demographic changes, such as a growing middle class, resulted in an increasing share of investment flows directed to consumer-oriented manufacturing and rapidly expanding consumer service sectors.

Debt indicators have improved significantly since 2000 due to economic reforms, a favorable external environment, increased aid, and debt restructuring and debt relief. External debt stocks at the end of 2012 were 71.5 percent of exports and 27.2 percent of GNI, a marginal deterioration from 63.3 percent and 25.2 percent, respectively in 2011. Two more countries in the region, Côte d'Ivoire and Guinea reached the HIPC Completion Point in 2012 and received around $6.3 billion in debt relief under the HIPC and Multilateral Debt Relief Initiative and additional debt relief from bilateral, Paris Club creditors.

Net Capital Flows to Sub-Saharan Africa, 2007–12

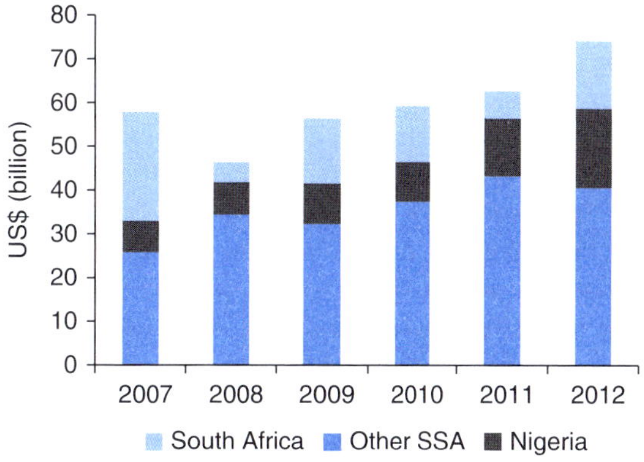

Sources: World Bank Debtor Reporting System and the International Monetary Fund.

Net Debt Flows to Sub-Saharan Africa, excluding South Africa, 2007–12

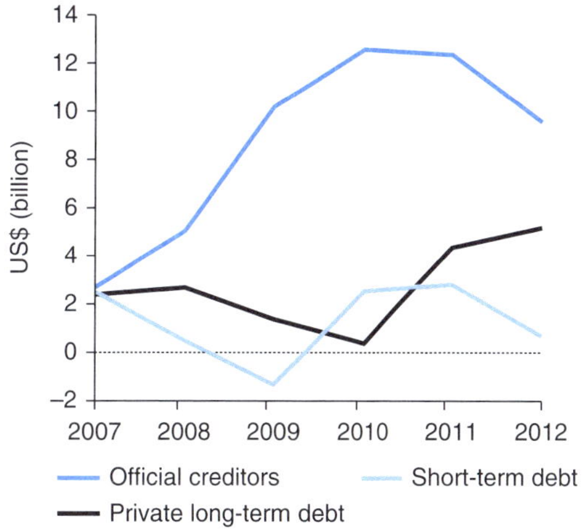

Source: World Bank Debtor Reporting System.

Net Inflow of Foreign Direct Investment to Select Countries, 2011–12

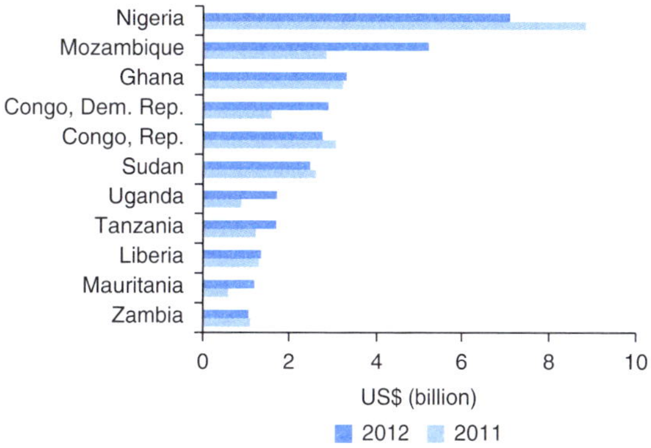

Source: International Monetary Fund.

II. Quarterly External Debt Statistics

About the data

The Quarterly External Debt database (QEDS) was developed jointly by the International Monetary Fund and the World Bank in the wake of the 1997 Asian crisis, in response to the widespread demand for comprehensive and readily available high frequency data to facilitate macroeconomic analysis and cross-country data comparisons at the global level. The data are compiled and classified in accordance with the International Monetary Fund Special Data Dissemination Standard (SDDS) or General Data Dissemination Standard (GDDS). They provide quarterly information on the stock of outstanding external liabilities, categorized by maturity as well as by borrowing entity and instrument. Reporting is voluntary, but to date 70 countries have agreed to participate in the SDDS/QEDS database, of which 69 countries currently provide data. An additional 48 countries have agreed to participate in the GDDS/QEDS database, of which 43 countries have thus far reported. Unlike the World Bank Debtor Reporting System, to which countries borrowing from IBRD and IDA are obligated to report, QEDS is open to any country, developing or high-income, that accepts the reporting standards and agrees to participate: 41 of the countries currently providing data to the QEDS are high-income countries.

Trends in 2012 External Debt of High-Income Countries

The external debt stock of high-income countries rose moderately in 2012, and the maturity structure improved, although short-term debt, as a share of total external debt, 42 percent, remained high. The total external debt stock (measured on a gross basis) for high-income countries[2] reporting to the Quarterly External Debt Statistics (QEDS) database rose 3 percent in 2012, to $66.7 trillion, much slower than the 5 percent increase recorded in 2011, and considerably less than the 9 percent rise in the external debt stock of developing countries in the same period. Most of the increase in high-income countries' external debt stock was driven by the rise in the debt of the general government, particularly in France, Germany, Greece, Italy, Spain, and the United States. Together these six countries accounted for just over three-quarters of the $1.4 trillion rise in external debt owed by governments of high-income countries. In 2012, there was a perceptible shift toward long-term debt, which increased to 58 percent of total external debt, up from 55 percent the previous year.

External debt, measured relative to GDP, is on average very high, and the situation worsened in 2012. Additional borrowing in 2012, coupled with the slow growth in output, led to an increase in the level of external debt relative to GDP in most of the high income countries; on average, the level was 143 percent in 2012 compared with 138 percent in 2011. There was, however, a wide disparity between countries that ranged from upward of 230 percent of GDP in the case of Finland, Greece, and Portugal, to below 40 percent for the least indebted countries like Israel, the Republic of Korea, and Russia. (figure II.1).

The Group of Seven (G7) countries together owed almost two-thirds of the external debt of high-income countries: $43 trillion at the end of 2012 (see table II.1). As a group, they saw debt rise much more slowly than the average for other high-income countries in 2012, 1.1 percent as compared to 7.6 percent, and at a much slower pace than the 5 percent rise recorded in 2011. There was, however, wide disparity at the individual country level. Canada had the sharpest increase in external debt in 2012, 11.7 percent, followed by Germany and Italy, 7 percent. A more moderate increase was recorded by France and the United States, 3.8 percent and 1.1 percent, respectively, while in Japan and the United Kingdom, the stock of external debt contracted: 3.2 percent and 5.1 percent, respectively. The combined stock of external debt of G7 countries was 127 percent of GDP at the end of 2012, virtually unchanged from the previous year, with improvements in some countries offsetting the deterioration in others (see figure II.2).

2. High-income countries reporting to the SDDS QEDS database include: Australia; Austria; Belgium; Canada; Chile; Croatia; Czech Republic; Denmark; Estonia; Finland; France; Germany; Greece; Hong Kong SAR, China; Iceland; Ireland; Israel; Italy; Japan; Republic of Korea; Latvia; Lithuania; Luxembourg; Malta; Netherlands; New Zealand; Norway; Poland; Portugal; the Russian Federation; Singapore; Slovak Republic; Slovenia; Spain; Sweden; Switzerland; United Kingdom; United States; and Uruguay.

Figure II.1. Selected High-Income Countries, External Debt to GDP Ratio, 2010–12

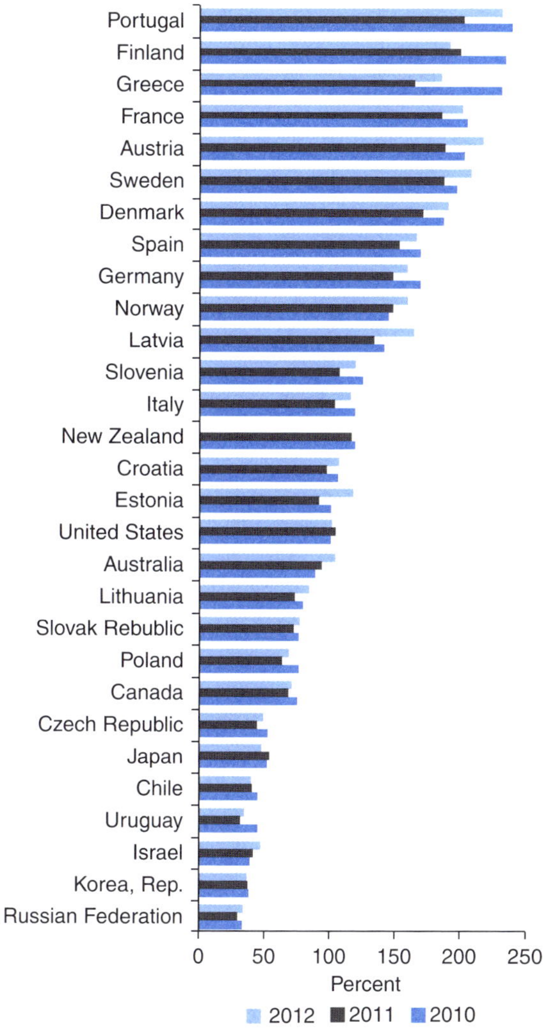

Source: World Bank Quarterly External Debt Statistics Database.

Figure II.2. G7 Countries, External Debt to GDP Ratio, 2008–12

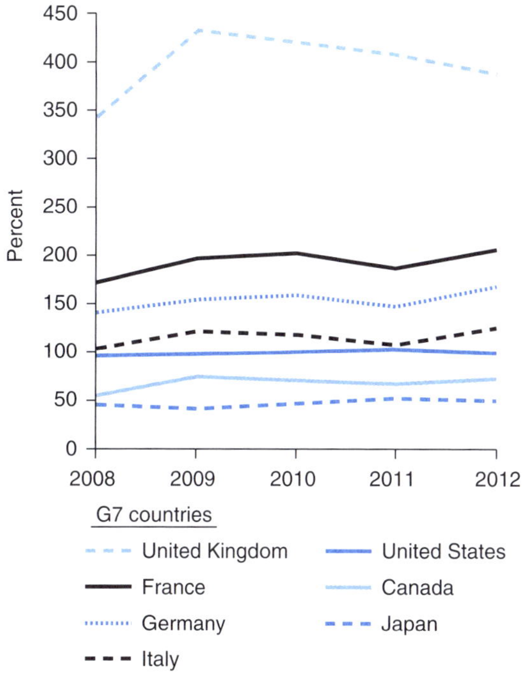

Source: World Bank Quarterly External Debt Statistics Database.

The United Kingdom saw the most significant change with the ratio of external debt to GDP falling to 388 percent, from 407 percent in 2011, and there was a marginal improvement in Japan and in the United States. Conversely, France, Germany, and Italy all saw a marked jump in their external debt burden relative to GDP in 2012. The United Kingdom has far and away the highest level of external debt to GDP among G7 countries, but the external debt of France moved above 200 percent in 2012, and that of Germany climbed to 168 percent.

Table II.1. G7 Countries, External Debt Stock, 2008–12
$ billion

	2008	2009	2010	2011	2012
Canada	839.6	998.7	1,105.8	1,191.5	1,331.3
France	4,879.5	5,164.3	5,145.2	5,172.7	5,370.7
Germany	5,123.4	5,110.3	5,227.6	5,332.8	5,716.5
Italy	2,395.3	2,551.2	2,435.2	2,349.7	2,516.0
Japan	2,230.6	2,086.4	2,588.6	3,115.2	3,016.8
United Kingdom	9,106.7	9,409.5	9,483.0	9,960.6	9,457.2
United States	13,749.6	13,661.8	14,516.5	15,508.2	15,680.5
Total G7 countries	38,324.8	38,982.2	40,501.8	42,630.6	43,089.0

Source: World Bank Quarterly External Debt Statistics Database.
Note: G7 = Group of Seven (Canada, France, Germany, Italy, Japan, the United Kingdom, and the United States).

III. Public Sector Debt

About the Data

The global economic and financial crisis of 2008 revealed the absence of transparent and comprehensive data on public sector debt (both domestic and external). Without this data, it is difficult to assess and anticipate fiscal risk and the impact of financial shocks on macroeconomic outcomes and costs to the public sector. To address and rectify these shortcomings, the Inter-Agency Group (IAG) recommended the creation of a public sector debt database consistent with the methodological framework of the Public Sector Debt Statistics Guide for Compilers (GFSM 2001, SNA 2008).

As part of the Open Data Initiative, the World Bank, in partnership with the IMF, launched an online, quarterly, Public Sector Debt database in December 2010. It aims to address the demand for comprehensive, high frequency data measuring countries' government and public sector debt obligations, domestic and external, to complement the external debt information captured through the World Bank Debtor Reporting System (DRS) and the joint IMF–World Bank Quarterly External Debt Statistics (QEDS). Currently, 72 developing and high-income countries report to the Public Sector Debt database. The Public Sector Debt database provides data on debt of both the central government and the broad public sector and includes the maturity structure.

Trends in 2012

Government debt levels in many advanced economies continued to rise in 2012 despite programs of fiscal austerity and, in some cases, debt restructuring. This rise is clearly illustrated by the European Union (EU), where the persistence of the economic slowdown throughout 2012, and the fiscal measures to contain the economic and social impact, impeded efforts to rein in public debt levels. Twelve of the EU-15 countries saw the level of government debt rise, or remain static, relative to GDP in 2012 (see table III.1). The average government debt to GDP ratio rose to 79.5 percent (it was 75.9 percent in 2011), and two-thirds of these countries had a government debt to GDP ratio above 60 percent. High government debt levels were not restricted to countries in the Euro zone. Japan recorded a government debt to GDP ratio of 195 percent at the end of 2012, while in the United States and the United Kingdom, it stood at 94 percent and 89 percent, respectively.

The four most heavily indebted European countries, Greece, Ireland, Italy, and Portugal, had a government debt to GDP ratio of 120 percent or more in 2012. Moreover, with the exception of Greece, debt levels in these countries continued on a rising trajectory. Ireland has experienced the sharpest rise in government debt, from a precrisis level of 28 percent of GDP in 2007 to 120 percent in 2012. Over the same period, Portugal's

Table III.1 EU-15, Government Debt to GDP, 2007–12
Percent

	2007	2008	2009	2010	2011	2012
Luxembourg	5	13	14	18	17	19
Sweden	39	36	40	37	35	34
Denmark	24	30	36	39	43	41
Finland	32	31	39	44	45	48
Germany	40	41	45	53	51	51
Netherlands	44	57	59	61	62	68
Austria	56	60	65	66	66	68
Spain	32	35	49	55	61	77
France	56	60	69	72	74	80
United Kingdom	43	52	68	79	85	89
Belgium	82	87	91	91	93	94
Italy	97	100	109	112	114	120
Ireland	28	47	67	94	108	120
Portugal	69	72	85	96	108	125
Greece	107	112	129	153	177	158

Source: World Bank Public Sector Debt Database.

Figure III.1 **Government Debt to GDP, 2007–12**

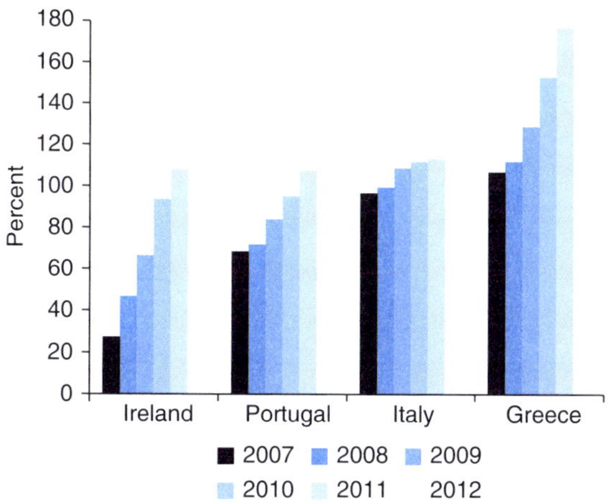

Source: World Bank Public Sector Debt Database.

Figure III.2 **Government Debt to GDP, 2009 and 2012**

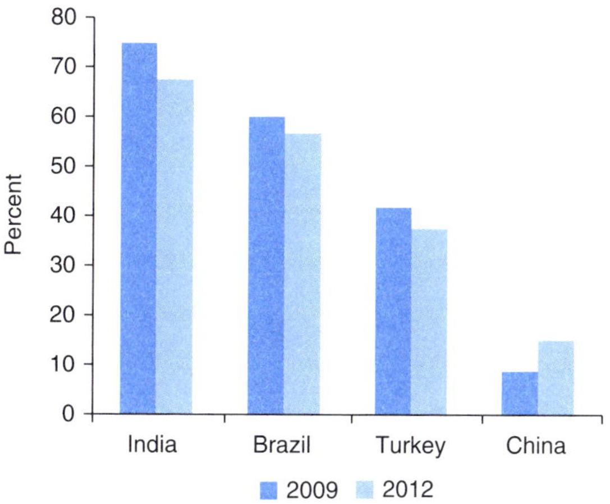

Source: World Bank Public Sector Debt Database.

Figure III.3 **Government Debt, Currency Composition**

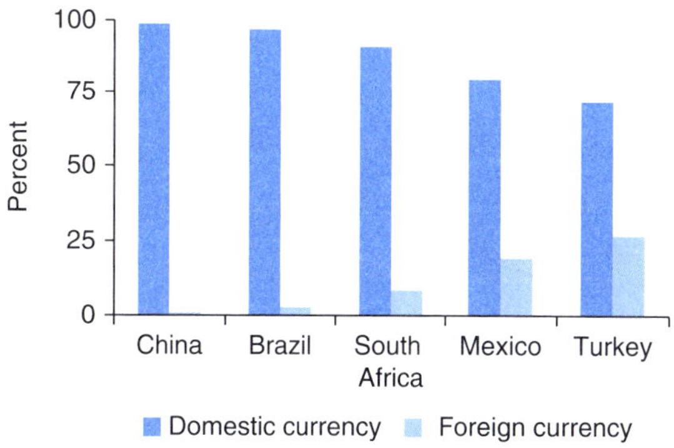

Source: World Bank Public Sector Debt Database.

government debt rose from 69 percent to 125 percent of GDP. Italy entered the crisis with an elevated level of government debt, which has continued to rise in each successive year. In Greece, restructuring in late 2011 and early 2012 reduced the level of government debt, but it remained the highest of all EU-15 countries at the end of 2012, 158 percent (see figure III.1).

Government debt to GDP levels in developing countries are, on average, much lower than those of high-income countries, and on a downward trajectory. For developing countries reporting to the Public Sector Debt database, the government debt to GDP ratio ranged from 10 percent to 70 percent in 2012 and was, in most instances, lower than the comparable ratio for 2008. At the upper end of the spectrum, Brazil and India saw government debt fall from 60 percent and 74.7 percent of GDP, respectively, in 2009 to 56.7 percent and 68.5 percent, respectively, in 2012. In Turkey, the comparable ratio fell from 46.3 percent in 2009 to 37.6 percent in 2012, and at the lower end, China has seen its government debt fall from 17.7 percent to 14.9 percent of GDP over the same period (see figure III.2).

In developing countries, a remarkable feature of the past few years has been the substantial jump in the domestic currency component of government debt. As options for borrowing in domestic markets have expanded, governments in developing countries have looked to debt issued in domestic currency as a mechanism to reduce exposure to exchange rate fluctuations and to correct currency and maturity mismatches. Brazil and China now raise virtually all (on average 98 percent) of central government financing requirements in domestic markets, and countries like Mexico, South Africa, and Turkey also finance a comparable share of central government financing in domestic markets. At the end of 2012, the domestic currency component of the central government debt of developing countries reporting to the Public Sector Debt database averaged 57 percent of the total, after excluding Brazil and China (see figure III.3).

Summary Tables

Summary Table 1. **Present Value of Debt, 2012**

Country name	Total external debt stocks $ million	Present value of external debt $ million	Ratio of present value of debt to exports (%)	Ratio of present value of debt to GNI (%)
Afghanistan	2,709	668	16	..
Albania	6,934	5,556	146	43
Algeria	5,643	3,389	4	..
Angola	22,171	19,147	27	19
Argentina	121,013	101,478	103	22
Armenia	7,608	5,886	157	56
Azerbaijan	9,712	11,469	30	19
Bangladesh	26,130	15,908	57	13
Belarus	34,173	29,254	55	47
Belize	1,241	952	91	..
Benin	2,055	365	..	5
Bhutan	1,459	1,216	171	73
Bolivia	6,909	1,840	15	7
Bosnia and Herzegovina	10,577	8,028	139	46
Botswana	2,488	1,629	25	12
Brazil	440,478	390,445	133	18
Bulgaria	50,750	46,321	133	94
Burkina Faso	2,506	769	..	7
Burundi	663	310	130	13
Cambodia	5,716	3,985	46	30
Cameroon	3,672	1,762	23	7
Cape Verde	1,261	695	88	37
Central African Republic	552	682	..	32
Chad	1,831	231	..	2
China	754,009	734,316	32	9
Colombia	79,051	68,403	97	19
Comoros	251	157	..	26
Congo, Dem. Rep.	5,651	3,868	44	24
Congo, Rep.	2,829	1,906	..	18
Costa Rica	14,458	12,698	95	29
Côte d'Ivoire	9,871	3,471	..	15
Djibouti	808	540	111	..
Dominica	284	203	103	44
Dominican Republic	16,851	13,433	107	24
Ecuador	16,931	13,757	52	17
Egypt, Arab Rep.	40,000	32,487	67	13
El Salvador	13,279	11,314	184	50
Eritrea	994	567	..	19
Ethiopia	10,462	2,618	44	6
Fiji	732	539	..	14
Gabon	2,870	2,322	..	14
Gambia, The	513	93	27	11
Georgia	13,426	12,041	170	77
Ghana	12,436	2,959	18	8
Grenada	591	681	341	91

(table continues next page)

Summary Table 1. Present Value of Debt, 2012 *(continued)*

Country name	Total external debt stocks $ million	Present value of external debt $ million	Ratio of present value of debt to exports (%)	Ratio of present value of debt to GNI (%)
Guatemala	14,975	12,466	97	25
Guinea	1,097	889	42	14
Guinea-Bissau	279	232	..	78
Guyana	1,974	849	49	30
Haiti	1,154	166	15	2
Honduras	4,987	773	12	5
Hungary	203,757	166,449	132	142
India	379,099	324,340	71	18
Indonesia	254,899	226,355	106	27
Iran, Islamic Rep.	11,477	7,607	..	..
Jamaica	14,333	13,625	290	95
Jordan	18,632	17,004	119	55
Kazakhstan	137,014	114,443	116	66
Kenya	11,569	7,833	70	21
Kosovo	2,002	982	66	15
Kyrgyz Republic	6,026	4,446	140	73
Lao PDR	6,372	4,595	158	53
Lebanon	28,950	26,575	90	63
Lesotho	860	510	31	19
Liberia	487	215	..	13
Macedonia, FYR	6,678	6,025	133	63
Madagascar	2,896	1,163	..	12
Malawi	1,314	1,306	93	32
Malaysia	103,950	94,789	34	32
Maldives	1,027	806	34	43
Mali	3,073	750	..	8
Mauritania	3,348	865	30	21
Mauritius	4,459	3,934	52	37
Mexico	354,897	320,189	80	28
Moldova	6,135	5,325	139	68
Mongolia	5,080	3,694	68	39
Montenegro	2,833	2,468	125	59
Morocco	33,816	28,089	85	30
Mozambique	4,788	2,980	58	20
Myanmar	2,563	903	..	..
Nepal	3,818	2,351	108	12
Nicaragua	8,858	4,602	92	45
Niger	2,340	896	..	14
Nigeria	10,077	4,330	4	2
Pakistan	61,867	46,279	145	19
Panama	12,294	10,297	35	26
Papua New Guinea	23,128	19,061	..	127
Paraguay	6,331	5,421	43	23
Peru	54,148	49,847	97	27
Philippines	61,390	52,331	87	25
Romania	131,889	111,675	173	67

Summary Table 1. Present Value of Debt, 2012 *(continued)*

Country name	Total external debt stocks $ million	Present value of external debt $ million	Ratio of present value of debt to exports (%)	Ratio of present value of debt to GNI (%)
Rwanda	1,269	905	88	..
Samoa	423	245	98	38
São Tomé and Príncipe	202	163	529	62
Senegal	4,900	679	..	5
Serbia	34,438	29,178	182	80
Seychelles	2,024	1,872	2693	190
Sierra Leone	1,121	889	66	23
Solomon Islands	228	148	22	21
Somalia	3,055	3,814	..	..
South Africa	137,501	68,480	60	18
Sri Lanka	25,382	19,287	140	33
St. Lucia	473	363	60	31
St. Vincent and the Grenadines	267	179	89	26
Sudan	21,840	25,583	564	47
Swaziland	460	373	16	11
Syrian Arab Republic	4,736	4,098	..	6
Tajikistan	3,648	2,611	155	38
Tanzania	11,581	2,818	32	10
Thailand	134,223	112,750	40	32
Togo	754	315	..	9
Tonga	197	129	159	27
Tunisia	25,475	21,192	94	49
Turkey	337,492	307,872	145	39
Turkmenistan	492	347	..	1
Uganda	3,769	1,429	30	9
Ukraine	135,067	124,585	133	72
Uzbekistan	8,853	6,579	..	12
Vanuatu	369	316	76	41
Venezuela, RB	72,097	69,381	68	19
Vietnam	59,133	46,519	37	35
Yemen, Rep.	7,555	4,445	..	13
Zambia	5,385	3,476	35	18
Zimbabwe	7,713	7,509	..	83

Note: GNI = gross national income; .. = not available. For definition of indicators, see "About the Data" section at the back of the book. Country names in bold italics are based on the latest available Debt Sustainability Analysis for Low-Income Countries (LIC DSA) and include the effects of traditional relief, debt relief under the Heavily Indebted Poor Country (HIPC) Initiative as well as relief under the Multilateral Debt Relief Initiative (MDRI). Under the MDRI, the International Development Association (IDA), the International Monetary Fund (IMF), and the African Development Fund (AfDF) provide debt stock cancellation to post-completion point HIPC countries on debt owed to the three institutions. The Inter-American Development Bank (IDB) provides similar debt stock cancellation under the IDB 2007 Debt Initiative. MDRI debt relief provides 100 percent stock cancellation on debt disbursed before end-2004 (for the IMF, AfDF, and IDB) or end-2003 (for IDA), and still outstanding at the time the country reaches the completion point under the HIPC Initiative. In line with the Debt Sustainability Framework for low-income countries, only the conditional debt relief under HIPC is included for countries in the interim period (between decision and completion point of the HIPC initiative).

Summary Table 2. Public and Publicly Guaranteed Debt, Multilateral Creditors, 2012
US$ million

Country name	Multilateral (excluding IMF)	IBRD	IDA	Other multilateral	Use of IMF credit
Afghanistan	1,121	0	422	699	388
Albania	1,871	59	874	937	107
Algeria	7	7	0	0	1,842
Angola	491	0	420	70	1,740
Argentina	18,351	5,625	0	12,726	3,105
Armenia	1,861	236	1,235	390	911
Azerbaijan	2,804	808	833	1,163	252
Bangladesh	19,512	0	11,159	8,353	1,213
Belarus	2,205	424	0	1,780	3,588
Belize	267	11	0	256	32
Benin	1,097	0	435	661	210
Bhutan	434	0	175	260	9
Bolivia	3,013	0	443	2,570	252
Bosnia and Herzegovina	2,876	455	1,193	1,228	888
Botswana	1,848	97	3	1,747	88
Brazil	27,860	11,439	0	16,422	4,437
Bulgaria	2,453	1,210	0	1,243	939
Burkina Faso	1,896	0	898	998	301
Burundi	336	0	175	162	249
Cambodia	1,631	0	589	1,041	129
Cameroon	1,127	13	498	615	440
Cape Verde	637	1	313	323	18
Central African Republic	42	0	23	19	183
Chad	1,478	0	830	649	87
China	34,614	12,913	6,777	14,923	10,743
Colombia	16,184	7,706	0	8,478	1,135
Comoros	172	0	90	82	28
Congo, Dem. Rep.	2,353	0	962	1,391	1,260
Congo, Rep.	164	0	91	73	152
Costa Rica	1,857	585	0	1,271	241
Côte d'Ivoire	518	0	118	399	1,265
Djibouti	420	0	151	269	58
Dominica	128	0	27	101	27
Dominican Republic	3,537	910	6	2,621	1,513
Ecuador	5,137	296	7	4,834	443
Egypt, Arab Rep.	10,441	3,109	1,230	6,102	1,381
El Salvador	3,786	983	6	2,797	252
Eritrea	654	0	480	174	23
Ethiopia	4,112	0	2,801	1,311	484
Fiji	135	0	0	135	103
Gabon	476	34	0	443	225
Gambia, The	278	0	63	215	94
Georgia	2,308	350	1,295	664	965
Ghana	3,698	0	2,523	1,175	1,253
Grenada	189	11	48	129	45
Guatemala	4,492	1,395	0	3,097	309

Summary Table 2. **Public and Publicly Guaranteed Debt, Multilateral Creditors, 2012 *(continued)***
US$ million

Country name	Multilateral (excluding IMF)	IBRD	IDA	Other multilateral	Use of IMF credit
Guinea	611	0	159	452	215
Guinea-Bissau	111	0	56	55	32
Guyana	605	0	11	594	171
Haiti	78	0	0	78	169
Honduras	2,753	0	809	1,944	209
Hungary	15,469	8	0	15,462	8,311
India	52,632	11,779	26,384	14,469	6,114
Indonesia	23,077	10,468	2,200	10,409	3,044
Iran, Islamic Rep.	714	702	0	12	2,136
Jamaica	2,460	659	0	1,801	1,235
Jordan	2,553	1,092	27	1,435	642
Kazakhstan	4,164	2,641	0	1,523	528
Kenya	4,930	0	3,586	1,344	1,293
Kosovo	295	283	11	0	234
Kyrgyz Republic	1,386	0	675	711	321
Lao PDR	1,845	0	620	1,225	79
Lebanon	1,138	253	0	886	317
Lesotho	652	0	316	336	115
Liberia	81	0	37	44	267
Macedonia, FYR	1,222	353	346	523	404
Madagascar	1,682	0	1,246	435	267
Malawi	706	0	323	383	283
Malaysia	178	0	0	178	2,069
Maldives	322	0	105	217	28
Mali	2,150	0	1,051	1,099	237
Mauritania	1,609	0	384	1,224	211
Mauritius	629	274	6	349	149
Mexico	25,273	14,706	0	10,567	4,382
Moldova	717	55	506	156	793
Mongolia	1,133	0	467	665	234
Montenegro	788	313	86	389	40
Morocco	12,052	2,952	10	9,090	863
Mozambique	2,607	0	1,808	798	353
Myanmar	615	0	445	170	368
Nepal	3,145	0	1,459	1,686	204
Nicaragua	2,076	0	498	1,577	361
Niger	962	0	447	515	164
Nigeria	5,349	0	4,686	663	2,575
Pakistan	25,102	1,486	11,136	12,480	7,684
Panama	2,391	489	0	1,902	303
Papua New Guinea	782	114	123	546	193
Paraguay	1,597	331	11	1,255	146
Peru	7,594	2,435	0	5,159	937
Philippines	9,395	3,333	154	5,909	1,288
Romania	16,796	3,550	0	13,246	15,748
Rwanda	877	0	430	447	131

(table continues next page)

Summary Table 2. Public and Publicly Guaranteed Debt, Multilateral Creditors, 2012 *(continued)*
US$ million

Country name	Multilateral (excluding IMF)	IBRD	IDA	Other multilateral	Use of IMF credit
Samoa	240	0	103	137	26
São Tomé and Príncipe	38	0	14	24	16
Senegal	2,526	0	1,320	1,207	442
Serbia	6,072	1,915	708	3,449	2,517
Seychelles	90	24	0	65	54
Sierra Leone	482	0	226	255	274
Solomon Islands	94	0	39	55	35
Somalia	798	0	442	356	243
South Africa	2,782	1,077	0	1,705	2,744
Sri Lanka	6,624	3	2,750	3,872	3,118
St. Lucia	226	15	64	147	41
St. Vincent and the Grenadines	201	6	23	173	23
Sudan	3,467	0	1,288	2,178	645
Swaziland	213	2	2	209	74
Syrian Arab Republic	1,641	0	14	1,627	429
Tajikistan	981	0	372	609	287
Tanzania	5,443	0	4,030	1,413	641
Thailand	503	162	0	340	1,491
Togo	205	0	14	191	254
Tonga	65	0	23	42	10
Tunisia	8,752	2,197	14	6,541	419
Turkey	23,177	13,152	30	9,995	2,510
Turkmenistan	44	8	0	35	107
Uganda	3,035	0	2,033	1,002	272
Ukraine	13,316	3,224	0	10,092	12,795
Uzbekistan	1,710	222	198	1,290	404
Vanuatu	62	0	10	51	25
Venezuela, RB	5,637	0	0	5,637	3,909
Vietnam	16,025	984	9,059	5,982	484
Yemen, Rep.	3,350	0	2,104	1,246	504
Zambia	1,077	0	565	512	1,126
Zimbabwe	1,626	463	512	651	520
All developing countries	**544,673**	**130,407**	**123,772**	**290,493**	**145,690**
East Asia and Pacific	90,392	27,973	20,611	41,809	20,320
Europe and Central Asia	102,514	29,267	8,362	64,884	52,649
Latin America and the Caribbean	135,693	47,602	1,954	86,137	23,676
Middle East and North Africa	41,068	10,312	3,549	27,208	8,590
South Asia	108,893	13,267	53,590	42,036	18,757
Sub-Saharan Africa	66,113	1,986	35,707	28,420	21,698
Low income	67,192	463	38,280	28,449	11,443
Middle income	477,481	129,945	85,493	262,044	134,248

Source: World Bank data.
Note: IBRD = International Bank for Reconstruction and Development; IDA = International Development Association; IMF = International Monetary Fund.

Aggregate Tables

ALL DEVELOPING COUNTRIES

(US$ million, unless otherwise indicated)

	2000	2005	2007	2008	2009	2010	2011	2012
Summary external debt data								
External debt stocks	**1,965,563**	**2,338,008**	**2,993,499**	**3,262,148**	**3,542,115**	**3,987,451**	**4,437,779**	**4,829,608**
Long-term external debt	1,635,351	1,793,999	2,260,296	2,510,831	2,643,040	2,828,045	3,106,276	3,406,325
Short-term external debt	269,418	481,229	700,067	702,784	749,435	1,000,336	1,172,469	1,277,593
interest arrears on long-term	27,342	25,509	27,254	27,049	26,278	21,569	18,582	20,330
Use of IMF credit	60,795	62,779	33,136	48,533	149,640	159,069	159,034	145,690
Long-term external debt								
Debt outstanding and disbursed	**1,635,351**	**1,793,999**	**2,260,296**	**2,510,831**	**2,643,040**	**2,828,045**	**3,106,276**	**3,406,325**
Public and publicly guaranteed	1,183,745	1,229,396	1,271,577	1,320,813	1,410,065	1,528,942	1,609,434	1,765,598
Official creditors	678,002	678,720	658,122	707,037	780,195	836,500	868,409	889,816
Private creditors	505,742	550,676	613,455	613,776	629,870	692,442	741,025	875,782
Private nonguaranteed	449,889	564,604	988,719	1,190,018	1,232,976	1,299,103	1,496,842	1,640,727
Disbursements	**225,799**	**336,484**	**584,151**	**615,503**	**545,603**	**649,364**	**750,573**	**777,737**
Public and publicly guaranteed	135,446	137,343	156,264	162,378	193,554	249,495	217,739	269,517
Official creditors	51,105	45,710	59,587	74,739	107,314	113,470	92,653	94,616
Private creditors	84,341	91,633	96,677	87,639	86,240	136,025	125,086	174,901
Private nonguaranteed	90,353	199,141	427,888	453,125	352,050	399,869	532,833	508,220
Principal repayments	**200,211**	**264,440**	**335,368**	**386,620**	**418,044**	**437,242**	**474,346**	**455,955**
Public and publicly guaranteed	103,334	123,957	115,411	128,617	107,976	105,289	125,620	101,357
Official creditors	46,179	50,646	51,204	48,579	45,262	46,778	61,187	53,338
Private creditors	57,154	73,311	64,207	80,038	62,715	58,511	64,433	48,019
Private nonguaranteed	96,848	140,462	219,957	258,003	310,068	331,952	348,726	354,598
Interest payments	**88,685**	**76,039**	**97,276**	**104,133**	**98,975**	**98,742**	**117,128**	**135,681**
Public and publicly guaranteed	60,591	55,907	56,367	54,494	50,351	50,234	55,617	80,976
Official creditors	24,498	21,388	19,636	18,748	16,947	15,848	16,741	18,591
Private creditors	36,093	34,519	36,731	35,746	33,404	34,386	38,876	62,384
Private nonguaranteed	28,094	20,132	40,909	49,639	48,624	48,508	61,511	54,705
Debt resource inflows								
Net debt inflows	8,024	120,684	382,125	248,430	206,749	481,172	451,869	411,814
Official creditors (incl. IMF)	-2,637	-41,511	3,242	42,784	93,829	80,130	31,989	27,935
Private creditors	10,691	162,216	378,883	205,647	112,920	401,006	419,880	383,880
Long-term	20,692	77,001	240,400	202,724	65,507	145,431	244,760	280,505
Public and publicly guaranteed	27,186	18,322	32,470	7,601	23,525	77,515	60,653	126,882
Private nonguaranteed	-6,495	58,679	207,930	195,123	41,982	67,916	184,107	153,622
Short-term	-10,001	85,216	138,483	2,923	47,413	255,575	175,120	103,375
Non-debt resource inflows								
Foreign direct investment	142,604	293,437	558,636	623,429	380,309	511,562	654,719	612,165
Portfolio equity	14,105	66,142	109,023	-40,623	110,947	123,378	2,687	97,585
Currency composition (%)								
Euro	..	15.1	17.2	16.0	16.7	14.5	13.5	13.0
U.S.dollars	60.9	62.4	61.2	61.5	60.5	61.4	62.1	63.2
Major economic aggregates								
Gross national income (GNI)	5,318,897	8,607,066	12,518,653	14,895,209	14,925,222	17,918,429	20,788,294	21,874,356
Exports of goods, services & prim. income	1,540,449	2,903,914	4,315,450	5,182,295	4,244,891	5,290,258	6,400,996	6,716,046
Personal transfers & comp. of employees	76,314	177,793	255,226	294,531	280,447	310,124	342,869	348,130
Imports of goods, services & prim. income	1,638,802	2,951,570	4,260,702	5,198,829	4,349,794	5,515,524	6,785,809	7,093,344
Primary income on FDI	64,228	177,122	285,499	331,745	317,104	432,676	514,713	486,302
Current account balance	-3,231	160,521	310,454	268,936	160,650	79,459	-77,059	-106,054
International reserves	568,313	1,737,316	3,137,717	3,644,614	4,277,422	4,950,847	5,426,656	5,679,420
Ratios								
External debt stocks to exports (%)	127.6	80.5	69.4	62.9	83.4	75.4	69.3	71.9
External debt stocks to GNI (%)	37.0	27.2	23.9	21.9	23.7	22.3	21.3	22.1
Debt service to exports (%)	21.1	13.8	10.8	9.9	12.5	11.0	10.0	9.8
Short-term to external debt stocks (%)	13.7	20.6	23.4	21.5	21.2	25.1	26.4	26.5
Multilateral to external debt stocks (%)	16.1	15.7	12.3	12.1	12.8	12.5	11.7	11.3
Reserves to external debt stocks (%)	28.9	74.3	104.8	111.7	120.8	124.2	122.3	117.6
Reserves to imports (months)	4.2	7.1	8.8	8.4	11.8	10.8	9.6	9.6

EAST ASIA AND PACIFIC

(US$ million, unless otherwise indicated)

	2000	2005	2007	2008	2009	2010	2011	2012
Summary external debt data								
External debt stocks	**497,305**	**628,126**	**746,652**	**775,278**	**883,306**	**1,080,620**	**1,286,637**	**1,412,411**
Long-term external debt	418,094	419,294	467,760	509,717	533,571	582,217	643,173	713,134
Short-term external debt	61,429	198,827	277,061	263,827	328,912	477,939	623,102	678,958
interest arrears on long-term	5,336	1,090	1,125	1,155	1,226	1,347	1,371	548
Use of IMF credit	17,781	10,005	1,832	1,734	20,823	20,464	20,362	20,320
Long-term external debt								
Debt outstanding and disbursed	**418,094**	**419,294**	**467,760**	**509,717**	**533,571**	**582,217**	**643,173**	**713,134**
Public and publicly guaranteed	270,939	264,726	271,582	290,873	312,413	338,574	341,214	354,456
Official creditors	171,436	172,448	177,117	193,734	202,972	210,822	215,391	208,140
Private creditors	99,504	92,278	94,465	97,139	109,441	127,752	125,823	146,316
Private nonguaranteed	147,155	154,568	196,178	218,844	221,158	243,643	301,959	358,678
Disbursements	**42,165**	**73,934**	**87,962**	**89,189**	**91,545**	**132,280**	**144,865**	**167,642**
Public and publicly guaranteed	28,719	24,904	20,620	23,740	39,777	53,462	41,310	48,722
Official creditors	15,620	9,059	11,827	13,040	16,705	16,850	14,604	17,920
Private creditors	13,099	15,845	8,793	10,700	23,072	36,612	26,705	30,801
Private nonguaranteed	13,446	49,030	67,341	65,448	51,768	78,818	103,556	118,920
Principal repayments	**47,006**	**66,906**	**73,888**	**71,278**	**82,369**	**83,078**	**90,221**	**90,056**
Public and publicly guaranteed	22,798	24,410	22,350	22,125	25,478	25,641	29,688	23,672
Official creditors	10,243	10,767	15,001	13,384	12,893	12,868	14,996	14,581
Private creditors	12,555	13,643	7,349	8,741	12,584	12,773	14,692	9,091
Private nonguaranteed	24,208	42,495	51,538	49,153	56,892	57,437	60,533	66,385
Interest payments	**20,429**	**12,633**	**17,060**	**16,415**	**14,091**	**17,076**	**20,232**	**22,144**
Public and publicly guaranteed	12,889	8,524	10,431	10,000	9,373	9,605	10,904	12,068
Official creditors	7,237	4,043	5,109	4,676	4,005	3,739	3,839	4,626
Private creditors	5,652	4,481	5,322	5,325	5,369	5,865	7,066	7,442
Private nonguaranteed	7,539	4,109	6,630	6,415	4,718	7,471	9,327	10,076
Debt resource inflows								
Net debt inflows	-14,461	42,319	66,966	4,599	74,313	198,093	199,752	134,214
Official creditors (incl. IMF)	6,602	-3,305	-3,209	-392	3,936	3,967	-423	3,289
Private creditors	-21,064	45,624	70,175	4,991	70,377	194,126	200,175	130,925
Long-term	-10,217	8,736	17,247	18,255	5,364	45,220	55,035	74,246
Public and publicly guaranteed	544	2,202	1,444	1,959	10,488	23,839	12,013	21,711
Private nonguaranteed	-10,761	6,534	15,803	16,296	-5,124	21,381	43,022	52,535
Short-term	-10,846	36,888	52,927	-13,263	65,013	148,906	145,140	56,679
Non-debt resource inflows								
Foreign direct investment	45,168	129,086	196,378	211,229	154,486	291,149	339,908	313,660
Portfolio equity	6,589	25,907	35,063	-7,583	30,185	40,324	6,707	37,899
Currency composition (%)								
Euro	..	7.8	8.6	7.1	6.3	5.5	5.0	4.4
U.S.dollars	55.9	57.1	58.0	58.2	61.2	63.3	64.0	69.3
Major economic aggregates								
Gross national income (GNI)	1,672,410	3,005,319	4,608,485	5,839,188	6,290,913	7,509,222	9,174,014	10,179,934
Exports of goods, services & prim. income	636,053	1,295,787	1,999,301	2,361,754	2,013,086	2,600,615	3,104,085	3,338,605
Personal transfers & comp. of employees	15,799	34,114	50,190	59,000	60,163	75,556	85,671	77,940
Imports of goods, services & prim. income	606,291	1,193,887	1,654,910	1,982,132	1,764,719	2,388,479	2,990,423	3,187,721
Primary income on FDI	31,677	80,019	101,896	117,334	144,470	212,274	265,310	251,635
Current account balance	45,054	146,684	409,990	454,109	309,130	283,182	177,153	197,431
International reserves	275,532	1,003,800	1,834,401	2,265,585	2,779,443	3,315,596	3,708,780	3,870,923
Ratios								
External debt stocks to exports (%)	78.2	48.5	37.3	32.8	43.9	41.6	41.4	42.3
External debt stocks to GNI (%)	29.7	20.9	16.2	13.3	14.0	14.4	14.0	13.9
Debt service to exports (%)	11.4	6.7	5.0	4.0	5.0	5.0	4.6	4.5
Short-term to external debt stocks (%)	12.4	31.7	37.1	34.0	37.2	44.2	48.4	48.1
Multilateral to external debt stocks (%)	13.2	10.2	9.3	9.5	9.2	8.0	6.9	6.4
Reserves to external debt stocks (%)	55.4	159.8	245.7	292.2	314.7	306.8	288.3	274.1
Reserves to imports (months)	5.5	10.1	13.3	13.7	18.9	16.7	14.9	14.6

EUROPE AND CENTRAL ASIA

(US$ million, unless otherwise indicated)

	2000	2005	2007	2008	2009	2010	2011	2012
Summary external debt data								
External debt stocks	**234,145**	**442,448**	**806,116**	**966,619**	**1,023,159**	**1,060,465**	**1,095,349**	**1,149,505**
Long-term external debt	173,585	317,558	617,545	760,144	796,002	782,946	806,577	862,896
Short-term external debt	44,075	98,893	172,076	177,904	168,353	210,692	223,155	233,960
interest arrears on long-term	3,979	947	980	1,118	1,463	2,219	621	2,462
Use of IMF credit	16,485	25,996	16,496	28,570	58,804	66,826	65,617	52,649
Long-term external debt								
Debt outstanding and disbursed	**173,585**	**317,558**	**617,545**	**760,144**	**796,002**	**782,946**	**806,577**	**862,896**
Public and publicly guaranteed	118,495	152,281	199,733	205,125	226,269	246,713	261,014	297,290
Official creditors	44,822	53,234	65,262	77,121	102,327	118,022	124,081	131,040
Private creditors	73,673	99,047	134,471	128,004	123,942	128,690	136,933	166,250
Private nonguaranteed	55,090	165,277	417,812	555,019	569,733	536,234	545,563	565,606
Disbursements	**40,350**	**116,049**	**243,015**	**315,574**	**245,787**	**233,682**	**281,170**	**265,581**
Public and publicly guaranteed	20,730	20,745	31,333	29,330	36,555	43,009	41,157	53,429
Official creditors	6,054	5,321	8,977	17,320	28,390	24,200	18,569	14,834
Private creditors	14,676	15,424	22,355	12,009	8,165	18,809	22,588	38,595
Private nonguaranteed	19,620	95,304	211,682	286,244	209,232	190,673	240,013	212,152
Principal repayments	**28,368**	**72,850**	**107,795**	**174,755**	**214,851**	**226,556**	**231,980**	**212,759**
Public and publicly guaranteed	12,822	19,237	13,337	22,817	17,877	14,928	21,489	17,893
Official creditors	4,773	5,082	4,875	5,576	4,806	5,227	10,634	8,771
Private creditors	8,050	14,155	8,462	17,241	13,072	9,701	10,855	9,122
Private nonguaranteed	15,546	53,613	94,458	151,938	196,974	211,628	210,491	194,866
Interest payments	**9,304**	**13,422**	**24,378**	**31,653**	**32,797**	**28,519**	**35,459**	**27,868**
Public and publicly guaranteed	6,477	7,587	9,305	9,596	8,933	8,430	9,773	10,449
Official creditors	1,832	1,739	2,309	2,610	2,499	2,296	2,964	3,073
Private creditors	4,645	5,848	6,996	6,986	6,434	6,134	6,809	7,377
Private nonguaranteed	2,827	5,835	15,073	22,057	23,864	20,089	25,686	17,418
Debt resource inflows								
Net debt inflows	21,521	57,849	171,910	159,331	46,500	57,687	62,222	48,826
Official creditors (incl. IMF)	3,658	-6,143	-933	24,565	49,047	27,950	6,905	-6,896
Private creditors	17,863	63,992	172,843	134,766	-2,547	29,736	55,318	55,722
Long-term	10,701	42,960	131,117	129,075	7,351	-11,847	41,255	46,759
Public and publicly guaranteed	6,626	1,269	13,893	-5,232	-4,907	9,108	11,733	29,472
Private nonguaranteed	4,075	41,691	117,224	134,306	12,258	-20,955	29,523	17,286
Short-term	7,162	21,032	41,726	5,691	-9,898	41,584	14,062	8,963
Non-debt resource inflows								
Foreign direct investment	9,063	49,444	158,815	165,952	51,141	23,842	75,806	64,424
Portfolio equity	721	6,621	3,495	-413	3,666	3,745	-659	7,988
Currency composition (%)								
Euro	..	31.2	34.7	36.8	40.0	38.3	37.4	35.9
U.S.dollars	52.9	58.5	56.0	52.9	48.1	48.6	50.0	53.6
Major economic aggregates								
Gross national income (GNI)	468,478	985,945	1,427,968	1,697,849	1,418,514	1,604,022	1,791,461	1,802,269
Exports of goods, services & prim. income	163,315	364,180	570,026	720,048	544,651	626,766	773,107	794,673
Personal transfers & comp. of employees	7,900	19,296	34,983	40,639	32,479	32,225	37,850	38,731
Imports of goods, services & prim. income	191,590	427,855	697,412	852,675	605,341	706,593	876,650	872,792
Primary income on FDI	1,998	18,044	48,751	57,336	43,628	51,891	61,246	57,237
Current account balance	-11,922	-43,345	-105,808	-107,409	-36,770	-57,515	-81,736	-60,149
International reserves	34,995	137,926	237,076	242,713	261,632	283,432	290,662	299,719
Ratios								
External debt stocks to exports (%)	143.4	121.5	141.4	134.2	187.9	169.2	141.7	144.7
External debt stocks to GNI (%)	50.0	44.9	56.5	56.9	72.1	66.1	61.1	63.8
Debt service to exports (%)	26.1	27.5	25.5	29.7	46.5	41.9	35.8	32.9
Short-term to external debt stocks (%)	18.8	22.4	21.3	18.4	16.5	19.9	20.4	20.4
Multilateral to external debt stocks (%)	9.7	7.7	5.5	5.5	7.4	8.4	8.6	8.9
Reserves to external debt stocks (%)	14.9	31.2	29.4	25.1	25.6	26.7	26.5	26.1
Reserves to imports (months)	2.2	3.9	4.1	3.4	5.2	4.8	4.0	4.1

LATIN AMERICA AND CARIBBEAN

(US$ million, unless otherwise indicated)

	2000	2005	2007	2008	2009	2010	2011	2012
Summary external debt data								
External debt stocks	**714,327**	**694,158**	**782,254**	**831,084**	**866,260**	**1,000,859**	**1,133,485**	**1,257,876**
Long-term external debt	600,829	569,719	648,907	694,619	717,579	810,941	948,638	1,060,622
Short-term external debt	102,426	111,012	129,659	132,829	125,712	166,312	161,071	173,577
interest arrears on long-term	1,693	8,855	10,319	10,887	11,667	6,350	7,018	7,235
Use of IMF credit	11,073	13,426	3,688	3,636	22,969	23,607	23,776	23,676
Long-term external debt								
Debt outstanding and disbursed	**600,829**	**569,719**	**648,907**	**694,619**	**717,579**	**810,941**	**948,638**	**1,060,622**
Public and publicly guaranteed	385,299	404,317	408,517	421,802	437,590	477,758	509,092	577,458
Official creditors	135,904	129,844	117,664	126,821	144,550	166,297	169,856	181,212
Private creditors	249,395	274,473	290,852	294,981	293,040	311,462	339,236	396,247
Private nonguaranteed	215,530	165,402	240,391	272,817	279,989	333,183	439,547	483,164
Disbursements	**110,430**	**91,383**	**142,928**	**138,685**	**138,495**	**189,066**	**227,699**	**232,448**
Public and publicly guaranteed	57,129	55,218	52,402	61,837	69,488	87,575	75,794	99,257
Official creditors	15,752	12,308	14,494	18,704	29,929	34,941	22,741	24,421
Private creditors	41,377	42,910	37,908	43,133	39,559	52,634	53,054	74,836
Private nonguaranteed	53,301	36,165	90,526	76,848	69,008	101,491	151,905	133,191
Principal repayments	**96,331**	**76,259**	**92,289**	**88,124**	**83,085**	**82,989**	**101,866**	**102,995**
Public and publicly guaranteed	41,549	40,685	46,367	45,900	36,973	39,024	44,345	30,121
Official creditors	16,458	15,865	15,512	12,313	13,125	13,627	18,116	12,451
Private creditors	25,091	24,820	30,855	33,586	23,847	25,397	26,229	17,670
Private nonguaranteed	54,782	35,574	45,922	42,224	46,113	43,965	57,520	72,874
Interest payments	**45,465**	**32,208**	**39,761**	**40,037**	**37,567**	**37,856**	**44,156**	**65,663**
Public and publicly guaranteed	29,178	23,935	25,575	24,075	22,171	22,398	24,596	46,281
Official creditors	8,198	5,330	5,754	5,261	4,725	4,501	4,635	4,678
Private creditors	20,980	18,605	19,821	18,814	17,446	17,898	19,961	41,603
Private nonguaranteed	16,287	8,273	14,186	15,961	15,396	15,458	19,560	19,382
Debt resource inflows								
Net debt inflows	-1,521	8,561	72,224	53,203	47,906	153,301	120,173	141,619
Official creditors (incl. IMF)	-11,433	-30,966	-989	6,431	17,196	22,621	4,872	11,848
Private creditors	9,913	39,527	73,213	46,772	30,710	130,680	115,302	129,771
Long-term	14,805	18,681	51,657	44,170	38,607	84,764	121,210	117,483
Public and publicly guaranteed	16,286	18,090	7,053	9,547	15,712	27,238	26,825	57,166
Private nonguaranteed	-1,481	591	44,604	34,624	22,895	57,526	94,385	60,317
Short-term	-4,892	20,846	21,556	2,601	-7,897	45,916	-5,908	12,288
Non-debt resource inflows								
Foreign direct investment	73,827	67,027	112,463	121,502	71,230	110,858	144,952	150,327
Portfolio equity	-139	10,641	28,430	-11,596	41,249	39,284	2,552	20,214
Currency composition (%)								
Euro	..	9.5	11.1	9.9	10.8	8.3	7.0	6.6
U.S.dollars	71.6	79.4	77.5	79.2	76.7	76.8	76.4	73.8
Major economic aggregates								
Gross national income (GNI)	1,875,306	2,425,882	3,396,608	3,973,632	3,718,127	4,619,946	5,170,855	5,145,954
Exports of goods, services & prim. income	413,611	599,656	812,781	944,012	741,007	917,744	1,133,537	1,161,214
Personal transfers & comp. of employees	20,124	48,748	61,637	62,621	55,073	55,698	59,023	57,917
Imports of goods, services & prim. income	481,150	622,140	879,432	1,046,328	829,472	1,041,430	1,267,460	1,314,097
Primary income on FDI	20,128	42,841	68,647	78,543	64,636	78,499	96,454	92,252
Current account balance	-46,664	28,749	-3,324	-38,592	-32,822	-67,124	-74,118	-93,556
International reserves	135,977	227,963	414,989	455,826	502,129	583,528	671,417	727,216
Ratios								
External debt stocks to exports (%)	172.7	115.8	96.2	88.0	116.9	109.1	100.0	108.3
External debt stocks to GNI (%)	38.1	28.6	23.0	20.9	23.3	21.7	21.9	24.4
Debt service to exports (%)	39.5	23.9	17.1	14.0	16.6	13.7	13.3	15.0
Short-term to external debt stocks (%)	14.3	16.0	16.6	16.0	14.5	16.6	14.2	13.8
Multilateral to external debt stocks (%)	12.6	14.3	11.8	11.8	12.8	12.8	11.4	10.8
Reserves to external debt stocks (%)	19.0	32.8	53.1	54.8	58.0	58.3	59.2	57.8
Reserves to imports (months)	3.4	4.4	5.7	5.2	7.3	6.7	6.4	6.6

MIDDLE EAST AND NORTH AFRICA

(US$ million, unless otherwise indicated)

	2000	2005	2007	2008	2009	2010	2011	2012
Summary external debt data								
External debt stocks	**143,802**	**150,613**	**156,269**	**148,707**	**160,566**	**166,620**	**162,918**	**177,092**
Long-term external debt	116,467	122,225	123,213	117,710	119,472	121,067	120,045	129,761
Short-term external debt	23,870	26,814	31,556	29,647	32,752	37,225	34,674	38,740
interest arrears on long-term	2,629	298	256	259	326	342	351	458
Use of IMF credit	3,465	1,574	1,501	1,350	8,342	8,328	8,199	8,590
Long-term external debt								
Debt outstanding and disbursed	**116,467**	**122,225**	**123,213**	**117,710**	**119,472**	**121,067**	**120,045**	**129,761**
Public and publicly guaranteed	112,496	115,440	116,479	110,320	112,587	114,033	112,740	121,235
Official creditors	88,137	77,719	76,967	74,764	78,274	78,123	78,754	82,438
Private creditors	24,359	37,721	39,512	35,556	34,313	35,910	33,986	38,797
Private nonguaranteed	3,970	6,785	6,734	7,390	6,885	7,034	7,304	8,526
Disbursements	**9,222**	**14,875**	**15,052**	**12,025**	**13,641**	**14,842**	**13,755**	**21,848**
Public and publicly guaranteed	7,941	12,955	13,216	9,677	12,024	13,472	12,267	18,960
Official creditors	3,411	5,493	7,173	6,337	8,167	7,246	7,772	10,446
Private creditors	4,530	7,462	6,042	3,340	3,857	6,226	4,494	8,514
Private nonguaranteed	1,281	1,920	1,837	2,348	1,617	1,370	1,489	2,888
Principal repayments	**10,613**	**14,162**	**14,218**	**16,190**	**13,250**	**12,162**	**13,967**	**11,583**
Public and publicly guaranteed	10,377	13,328	11,767	14,188	11,000	10,333	12,653	9,591
Official creditors	5,915	7,863	5,857	7,968	5,636	5,963	6,514	6,148
Private creditors	4,462	5,465	5,910	6,220	5,364	4,371	6,139	3,444
Private nonguaranteed	237	834	2,452	2,001	2,250	1,829	1,314	1,992
Interest payments	**4,888**	**4,749**	**4,728**	**4,768**	**4,382**	**4,297**	**4,257**	**4,006**
Public and publicly guaranteed	4,734	4,458	4,451	4,501	4,113	4,045	4,023	3,779
Official creditors	3,130	2,507	2,153	2,247	2,039	2,128	1,945	1,848
Private creditors	1,603	1,951	2,298	2,254	2,073	1,917	2,078	1,931
Private nonguaranteed	154	291	278	266	270	253	234	227
Debt resource inflows								
Net debt inflows	792	536	4,088	-6,164	3,367	7,135	-2,831	14,679
Official creditors (incl. IMF)	-2,718	-3,115	1,229	-1,719	2,470	1,283	1,198	4,753
Private creditors	3,510	3,651	2,859	-4,444	898	5,853	-4,029	9,926
Long-term	1,112	3,083	-483	-2,534	-2,140	1,397	-1,470	5,967
Public and publicly guaranteed	69	1,997	132	-2,881	-1,507	1,855	-1,645	5,071
Private nonguaranteed	1,044	1,086	-615	347	-633	-459	175	896
Short-term	2,398	568	3,342	-1,910	3,038	4,456	-2,559	3,959
Non-debt resource inflows								
Foreign direct investment	3,720	16,879	28,111	29,553	26,320	22,282	13,672	19,299
Portfolio equity	252	2,410	-2,096	422	1,200	1,964	-625	-1,293
Currency composition (%)								
Euro	..	30.9	35.6	33.9	34.5	33.0	32.0	30.9
U.S.dollars	49.5	43.0	38.7	38.4	37.6	38.5	38.6	42.0
Major economic aggregates								
Gross national income (GNI)	364,785	543,094	765,656	931,557	925,575	..	..	..
Exports of goods, services & prim. income	119,254	206,905	299,170	379,767	314,723	328,768	381,681	420,426
Personal transfers & comp. of employees	10,460	21,757	28,899	32,525	30,303	36,052	36,921	38,748
Imports of goods, services & prim. income	110,478	206,726	282,584	361,231	341,314	362,655	400,847	417,998
Primary income on FDI	1,721	10,685	11,376	13,463	13,976	17,349	18,349	17,823
Current account balance	12,620	19,948	24,304	19,624	-20,804	-9,520	-8,708	-15,548
International reserves	44,145	138,225	217,792	260,567	280,516	298,452	274,618	279,229
Ratios								
External debt stocks to exports (%)	120.6	72.8	52.2	39.2	51.0	50.7	42.7	42.1
External debt stocks to GNI (%)	39.4	27.7	20.4	16.0	17.3	..	..	..
Debt service to exports (%)	14.2	10.2	6.9	5.8	5.8	5.2	5.0	3.9
Short-term to external debt stocks (%)	16.6	17.8	20.2	19.9	20.4	22.3	21.3	21.9
Multilateral to external debt stocks (%)	16.1	17.3	19.8	21.0	21.8	21.8	23.5	23.2
Reserves to external debt stocks (%)	30.7	91.8	139.4	175.2	174.7	179.1	168.6	157.7
Reserves to imports (months)	4.8	8.0	9.2	8.7	9.9	9.9	8.2	8.0

SOUTH ASIA

(US$ million, unless otherwise indicated)

	2000	2005	2007	2008	2009	2010	2011	2012
Summary external debt data								
External debt stocks	**162,540**	**190,109**	**289,188**	**322,747**	**363,098**	**409,810**	**461,791**	**501,491**
Long-term external debt	153,202	174,607	243,710	266,344	292,328	325,598	354,726	382,503
Short-term external debt	6,067	11,851	41,606	49,471	52,107	63,894	86,776	100,230
interest arrears on long-term	128	30	24	20	22	72	213	224
Use of IMF credit	3,270	3,652	3,871	6,933	18,663	20,319	20,289	18,757
Long-term external debt								
Debt outstanding and disbursed	**153,202**	**174,607**	**243,710**	**266,344**	**292,328**	**325,598**	**354,726**	**382,503**
Public and publicly guaranteed	134,688	116,576	144,679	156,292	169,701	190,074	203,847	215,440
Official creditors	102,021	109,867	127,452	138,006	145,980	157,433	165,987	167,706
Private creditors	32,668	6,708	17,227	18,287	23,721	32,641	37,860	47,734
Private nonguaranteed	18,514	58,031	99,031	110,051	122,627	135,525	150,879	167,063
Disbursements	**13,995**	**24,451**	**71,454**	**45,659**	**35,240**	**55,914**	**51,876**	**58,514**
Public and publicly guaranteed	13,409	10,989	22,230	24,659	17,877	31,910	21,824	25,718
Official creditors	6,130	7,407	9,325	11,284	12,785	14,910	13,711	12,448
Private creditors	7,279	3,582	12,905	13,375	5,092	16,999	8,113	13,269
Private nonguaranteed	586	13,462	49,224	21,000	17,363	24,004	30,052	32,796
Principal repayments	**9,315**	**21,758**	**34,937**	**27,120**	**15,156**	**23,747**	**26,021**	**25,118**
Public and publicly guaranteed	8,607	14,498	11,362	16,341	8,721	8,862	10,176	10,078
Official creditors	5,352	4,475	4,821	5,600	5,433	6,051	7,128	6,921
Private creditors	3,256	10,023	6,541	10,741	3,288	2,811	3,048	3,156
Private nonguaranteed	707	7,260	23,575	10,779	6,435	14,884	15,845	15,041
Interest payments	**5,277**	**5,219**	**6,944**	**7,333**	**6,472**	**6,455**	**7,862**	**9,829**
Public and publicly guaranteed	4,396	3,946	2,742	2,950	2,702	2,732	2,728	3,363
Official creditors	2,275	1,913	2,259	2,312	2,159	2,042	2,133	2,540
Private creditors	2,121	2,033	483	638	544	690	595	824
Private nonguaranteed	881	1,272	4,202	4,383	3,769	3,723	5,134	6,466
Debt resource inflows								
Net debt inflows	3,454	4,958	49,380	29,582	26,339	45,880	48,630	45,295
Official creditors (incl. IMF)	489	2,912	4,435	8,859	10,973	10,835	6,617	3,983
Private creditors	2,964	2,045	44,945	20,723	15,366	35,010	42,013	41,312
Long-term	3,903	-239	32,013	12,854	12,732	23,308	19,272	27,869
Public and publicly guaranteed	4,024	-6,441	6,363	2,633	1,803	14,188	5,065	10,113
Private nonguaranteed	-121	6,202	25,649	10,221	10,928	9,120	14,207	17,756
Short-term	-938	2,284	12,932	7,869	2,634	11,702	22,741	13,443
Non-debt resource inflows								
Foreign direct investment	4,368	10,889	32,474	50,879	39,473	31,210	40,369	27,405
Portfolio equity	2,518	12,406	33,970	-15,823	24,103	29,907	-4,273	23,386
Currency composition (%)								
Euro	..	7.5	7.3	6.4	6.1	5.1	4.6	4.6
U.S.dollars	56.6	54.9	57.3	56.2	58.9	60.5	61.4	65.0
Major economic aggregates								
Gross national income (GNI)	616,558	1,043,828	1,507,666	1,536,201	1,691,078	2,070,169	2,298,444	2,293,742
Exports of goods, services & prim. income	88,760	201,378	305,078	381,176	329,570	427,327	538,341	535,452
Personal transfers & comp. of employees	17,206	33,909	54,029	71,723	74,925	81,954	96,464	108,112
Imports of goods, services & prim. income	117,568	260,015	385,933	511,244	440,138	574,556	715,523	752,557
Primary income on FDI	721	7,979	15,434	16,798	16,405	25,743	27,888	21,097
Current account balance	-6,218	-14,836	-17,039	-51,106	-28,948	-58,101	-73,673	-102,511
International reserves	43,326	149,529	292,620	268,668	298,771	315,374	310,608	310,799
Ratios								
External debt stocks to exports (%)	183.1	94.4	94.8	84.7	110.2	95.9	85.8	93.7
External debt stocks to GNI (%)	26.4	18.2	19.2	21.0	21.5	19.8	20.1	21.9
Debt service to exports (%)	17.5	13.8	14.5	9.6	6.9	7.4	6.6	7.3
Short-term to external debt stocks (%)	3.7	6.2	14.4	15.3	14.4	15.6	18.8	20.0
Multilateral to external debt stocks (%)	37.5	36.6	28.8	27.6	26.2	24.8	23.1	21.7
Reserves to external debt stocks (%)	26.7	78.7	101.2	83.2	82.3	77.0	67.3	62.0
Reserves to imports (months)	4.4	6.9	9.1	6.3	8.1	6.6	5.2	5.0

SUB-SAHARAN AFRICA

(US$ million, unless otherwise indicated)

	2000	2005	2007	2008	2009	2010	2011	2012
Summary external debt data								
External debt stocks	**213,444**	**232,554**	**213,020**	**217,714**	**245,726**	**269,077**	**297,599**	**331,234**
Long-term external debt	173,174	190,596	159,161	162,298	184,089	205,275	233,117	257,409
Short-term external debt	31,550	33,833	48,110	49,105	41,599	44,276	43,689	52,127
interest arrears on long-term	13,578	14,289	14,550	13,610	11,572	11,239	9,008	9,403
Use of IMF credit	8,720	8,125	5,749	6,311	20,039	19,526	20,792	21,698
Long-term external debt								
Debt outstanding and disbursed	**173,174**	**190,596**	**159,161**	**162,298**	**184,089**	**205,275**	**233,117**	**257,409**
Public and publicly guaranteed	161,826	176,056	130,588	136,400	151,505	161,790	181,527	199,718
Official creditors	135,683	135,608	93,661	96,592	106,092	105,803	114,340	119,280
Private creditors	26,143	40,449	36,928	39,808	45,413	55,988	67,187	80,438
Private nonguaranteed	9,631	14,540	28,573	25,898	32,584	43,485	51,590	57,691
Disbursements	**9,637**	**15,792**	**23,740**	**14,372**	**20,895**	**23,580**	**31,207**	**31,703**
Public and publicly guaranteed	7,518	12,532	16,463	13,135	17,833	20,067	25,388	23,432
Official creditors	4,139	6,122	7,790	8,053	11,338	15,323	15,256	14,547
Private creditors	3,379	6,410	8,673	5,082	6,495	4,745	10,132	8,886
Private nonguaranteed	2,119	3,260	7,278	1,236	3,062	3,513	5,819	8,271
Principal repayments	**8,578**	**12,504**	**12,240**	**9,154**	**9,332**	**8,711**	**10,291**	**13,442**
Public and publicly guaranteed	7,180	11,798	10,228	7,246	7,928	6,501	7,268	10,003
Official creditors	3,440	6,593	5,139	3,738	3,369	3,043	3,798	4,466
Private creditors	3,741	5,205	5,089	3,508	4,559	3,458	3,470	5,536
Private nonguaranteed	1,368	685	2,012	1,907	1,405	2,210	3,023	3,440
Interest payments	**3,323**	**7,808**	**4,405**	**3,928**	**3,666**	**4,539**	**5,162**	**6,171**
Public and publicly guaranteed	2,918	7,456	3,864	3,371	3,059	3,025	3,593	5,035
Official creditors	1,826	5,856	2,052	1,642	1,521	1,142	1,226	1,827
Private creditors	1,092	1,600	1,812	1,729	1,538	1,882	2,367	3,208
Private nonguaranteed	405	352	541	556	607	1,514	1,569	1,137
Debt resource inflows								
Net debt inflows	-1,761	6,462	17,557	7,879	8,323	19,075	23,922	27,182
Official creditors (incl. IMF)	765	-895	2,708	5,040	10,207	13,475	12,820	10,958
Private creditors	-2,495	7,378	14,849	2,839	-1,883	5,601	11,102	16,224
Long-term	389	3,780	8,850	903	3,594	2,590	9,458	8,181
Public and publicly guaranteed	-362	1,206	3,584	1,574	1,937	1,286	6,662	3,349
Private nonguaranteed	751	2,574	5,266	-671	1,657	1,303	2,796	4,831
Short-term	-2,885	3,598	5,999	1,936	-5,477	3,011	1,644	8,043
Non-debt resource inflows								
Foreign direct investment	6,458	20,112	30,395	44,314	37,659	32,222	40,012	37,049
Portfolio equity	4,164	8,157	10,161	-5,629	10,544	8,155	-1,015	9,392
Currency composition (%)								
Euro	..	19.3	21.2	18.6	18.7	13.1	11.7	10.6
U.S.dollars	61.3	52.3	49.5	51.3	49.9	48.8	51.2	46.9
Major economic aggregates								
Gross national income (GNI)	320,365	602,767	812,355	918,253	884,219	1,068,853	1,181,588	1,216,845
Exports of goods, services & prim. income	114,847	238,161	332,477	400,682	303,067	390,004	470,482	463,470
Personal transfers & comp. of employees	4,825	19,969	25,487	28,022	27,504	28,639	26,942	26,682
Imports of goods, services & prim. income	118,757	242,006	366,394	453,437	374,028	445,898	536,202	547,429
Primary income on FDI	7,983	17,553	39,396	48,271	33,989	46,920	45,466	46,257
Current account balance	3,898	23,322	2,331	-7,690	-29,137	-11,463	-15,976	-31,720
International reserves	34,337	79,872	140,839	151,256	154,931	154,464	170,570	191,534
Ratios								
External debt stocks to exports (%)	185.9	97.6	64.1	54.3	81.1	69.0	63.3	71.5
External debt stocks to GNI (%)	66.6	38.6	26.2	23.7	27.8	25.2	25.2	27.2
Debt service to exports (%)	11.8	9.2	5.5	3.8	4.7	3.7	3.5	4.5
Short-term to external debt stocks (%)	14.8	14.5	22.6	22.6	16.9	16.5	14.7	15.7
Multilateral to external debt stocks (%)	25.6	31.2	22.6	23.1	22.3	21.7	21.0	20.0
Reserves to external debt stocks (%)	16.1	34.3	66.1	69.5	63.1	57.4	57.3	57.8
Reserves to imports (months)	3.5	4.0	4.6	4.0	5.0	4.2	3.8	4.2

Country Tables

AFGHANISTAN

(US$ million, unless otherwise indicated)

	2000	2005	2007	2008	2009	2010	2011	2012
Summary external debt data								
External debt stocks	..	..	**2,013**	**2,134**	**2,470**	**2,423**	**2,627**	**2,709**
Long-term external debt	..	..	1,893	1,985	2,097	1,966	2,023	2,071
Short-term external debt	..	..	21	17	20	102	232	250
interest arrears on long-term	..	..	21	17	20	67	210	219
Use of IMF credit	..	..	99	131	353	355	373	388
Long-term external debt								
Debt outstanding and disbursed	..	..	**1,893**	**1,985**	**2,097**	**1,966**	**2,023**	**2,071**
Public and publicly guaranteed	..	..	1,893	1,985	2,097	1,966	2,023	2,071
Official creditors	..	..	1,893	1,985	2,097	1,966	2,023	2,071
Private creditors	..	..	0	0	0	0	0	0
Private nonguaranteed	..	..	..	..	..	..	..	..
Disbursements	..	..	**147**	**96**	**109**	**76**	**62**	**52**
Public and publicly guaranteed	..	..	147	96	109	76	62	52
Official creditors	..	..	147	96	109	76	62	52
Private creditors	..	..	0	0	0	0	0	0
Private nonguaranteed	..	..	..	..	..	..	..	..
Principal repayments	..	..	**1**	**1**	**3**	**1**	**1**	**1**
Public and publicly guaranteed	..	..	1	1	3	1	1	1
Official creditors	..	..	1	1	3	1	1	1
Private creditors	..	..	0	0	0	0	0	0
Private nonguaranteed	..	..	..	..	..	..	..	..
Interest payments	..	..	**3**	**6**	**7**	**7**	**9**	**8**
Public and publicly guaranteed	..	..	3	6	7	7	9	8
Official creditors	..	..	3	6	7	7	9	8
Private creditors	..	..	0	0	0	0	0	0
Private nonguaranteed	..	..	..	..	..	..	..	..
Debt resource inflows								
Net debt inflows	..	..	201	131	123	119	67	75
Official creditors (incl. IMF)	..	..	201	131	123	84	80	66
Private creditors	..	..	0	0	0	0	-13	9
Long-term	..	..	0	0	0	0	0	0
Public and publicly guaranteed	..	..	0	0	0	0	0	0
Private nonguaranteed	..	..	..	..	..	..	..	..
Short-term	..	..	..	..	..	0	-13	9
Non-debt resource inflows								
Foreign direct investment	..	..	189	87	214	76	91	94
Portfolio equity	..	..	..	-1	..	0	0	2
Currency composition (%)								
Euro	..	..	..	..	..	..	..	..
U.S.dollars	..	..	78.7	82.2	81.2	77.7	74.5	73.4
Major economic aggregates								
Gross national income (GNI)	..	..	9,844	10,192	12,487	15,937	18,034	..
Exports of goods, services & prim. income	..	..	..	1,935	2,546	3,920	4,300	4,238
Personal transfers & comp. of employees	..	..	..	104	152	331	247	385
Imports of goods, services & prim. income	..	..	..	3,752	4,467	6,840	8,204	11,885
Primary income on FDI	..	..	..	0	0	0	0	2
Current account balance	..	..	..	-1,673	-1,893	-2,795	-3,583	-7,286
International reserves	..	..	..	2,431	3,501	4,174	5,268	5,983
Ratios								
External debt stocks to exports (%)	..	..	..	110.3	97.0	61.8	61.1	63.9
External debt stocks to GNI (%)	..	..	20.4	20.9	19.8	15.2	14.6	..
Debt service to exports (%)	..	..	..	0.4	0.4	0.3	0.3	0.3
Short-term to external debt stocks (%)	..	..	1.0	0.8	0.8	4.2	8.8	9.2
Multilateral to external debt stocks (%)	..	..	40.7	42.3	41.2	41.9	40.8	41.4
Reserves to external debt stocks (%)	..	..	..	113.9	141.8	172.3	200.5	220.9
Reserves to imports (months)	..	..	..	7.8	9.4	7.3	7.7	6.0

Notes:

Short-term debt is based on data from the BIS. Data include the effects of Paris Club debt restructuring agreements signed in 2010 and HIPC and MDRI debt relief.

ALBANIA

(US$ million, unless otherwise indicated)

	2000	2005	2007	2008	2009	2010	2011	2012
Summary external debt data								
External debt stocks	**1,122**	**2,101**	**2,898**	**4,238**	**4,309**	**5,004**	**6,038**	**6,934**
Long-term external debt	937	1,788	2,224	2,936	3,485	4,328	5,019	5,349
Short-term external debt	37	155	511	1,150	680	547	903	1,478
interest arrears on long-term	3	1	1	0	0	0	0	0
Use of IMF credit	148	158	163	152	144	129	117	107
Long-term external debt								
Debt outstanding and disbursed	**937**	**1,788**	**2,224**	**2,936**	**3,485**	**4,328**	**5,019**	**5,349**
Public and publicly guaranteed	921	1,375	1,789	2,298	2,602	3,043	3,286	3,552
Official creditors	895	1,343	1,757	1,868	2,122	2,151	2,289	2,504
Private creditors	26	32	32	431	480	893	997	1,049
Private nonguaranteed	16	413	435	638	884	1,285	1,732	1,796
Disbursements	**119**	**489**	**291**	**870**	**457**	**820**	**755**	**537**
Public and publicly guaranteed	119	119	165	650	291	631	418	336
Official creditors	119	119	163	210	256	184	274	302
Private creditors	0	0	1	440	34	447	144	34
Private nonguaranteed	0	370	127	220	167	189	336	202
Principal repayments	**9**	**41**	**74**	**74**	**112**	**127**	**143**	**161**
Public and publicly guaranteed	9	40	55	58	80	89	102	108
Official creditors	8	39	51	56	78	86	99	105
Private creditors	1	1	5	1	2	3	3	3
Private nonguaranteed	0	1	19	17	32	38	41	53
Interest payments	**8**	**25**	**33**	**48**	**58**	**47**	**85**	**84**
Public and publicly guaranteed	7	23	31	44	50	39	77	74
Official creditors	7	23	31	35	35	31	36	37
Private creditors	0	0	0	9	14	7	41	38
Private nonguaranteed	1	1	2	5	8	8	8	9
Debt resource inflows								
Net debt inflows	130	605	334	1,428	-135	548	956	942
Official creditors (incl. IMF)	122	83	105	146	168	85	163	187
Private creditors	7	522	229	1,283	-303	463	793	755
Long-term	-1	368	105	642	167	596	437	180
Public and publicly guaranteed	-1	-1	-3	439	33	444	141	31
Private nonguaranteed	0	369	108	203	134	151	295	149
Short-term	8	154	124	640	-470	-133	356	575
Non-debt resource inflows								
Foreign direct investment	143	262	652	1,241	1,343	1,089	1,368	1,265
Portfolio equity	..	..	..	23	-4	7	23	13
Currency composition (%)								
Euro	..	28.4	35.2	48.6	50.8	57.5	59.5	59.4
U.S.dollars	73.2	58.4	51.2	39.2	36.8	30.6	29.0	29.3
Major economic aggregates								
Gross national income (GNI)	3,790	8,541	11,006	13,135	12,009	11,759	12,893	13,051
Exports of goods, services & prim. income	819	1,687	2,847	3,751	3,439	3,704	4,083	3,797
Personal transfers & comp. of employees	598	1,290	1,468	1,495	1,318	1,156	1,126	1,027
Imports of goods, services & prim. income	1,509	3,553	5,429	7,149	6,598	6,280	6,985	6,232
Primary income on FDI	0	2	9	301	448	381	115	212
Current account balance	-156	-571	-1,151	-2,018	-1,851	-1,353	-1,650	-1,314
International reserves	616	1,404	2,104	2,320	2,314	2,470	2,394	2,516
Ratios								
External debt stocks to exports (%)	137.0	124.5	101.8	113.0	125.3	135.1	147.9	182.6
External debt stocks to GNI (%)	29.6	24.6	26.3	32.3	35.9	42.6	46.8	53.1
Debt service to exports (%)	3.7	4.8	5.3	4.5	5.7	5.2	6.2	7.1
Short-term to external debt stocks (%)	3.3	7.4	17.6	27.1	15.8	10.9	14.9	21.3
Multilateral to external debt stocks (%)	38.0	41.1	40.5	30.5	34.0	30.3	27.6	27.0
Reserves to external debt stocks (%)	54.9	66.8	72.6	54.7	53.7	49.4	39.6	36.3
Reserves to imports (months)	4.9	4.7	4.7	3.9	4.2	4.7	4.1	4.8

ALGERIA

(US$ million, unless otherwise indicated)

	2000	2005	2007	2008	2009	2010	2011	2012
Summary external debt data								
External debt stocks	**25,477**	**17,092**	**6,135**	**6,246**	**7,405**	**7,246**	**6,045**	**5,643**
Long-term external debt	23,369	16,393	5,182	4,745	4,035	3,623	3,064	2,597
Short-term external debt	222	516	750	1,304	1,492	1,778	1,142	1,205
interest arrears on long-term	0	0	0	0	0	0	0	0
Use of IMF credit	1,886	184	203	198	1,878	1,845	1,840	1,842
Long-term external debt								
Debt outstanding and disbursed	**23,369**	**16,393**	**5,182**	**4,745**	**4,035**	**3,623**	**3,064**	**2,597**
Public and publicly guaranteed	23,369	15,527	4,033	3,301	3,053	2,655	2,246	1,627
Official creditors	17,518	12,500	2,340	2,127	2,092	1,889	1,643	1,198
Private creditors	5,851	3,027	1,693	1,174	961	766	603	429
Private nonguaranteed	..	866	1,148	1,444	982	968	818	970
Disbursements	**1,219**	**1,240**	**624**	**675**	**211**	**43**	**30**	**29**
Public and publicly guaranteed	1,219	777	320	268	88	41	30	28
Official creditors	799	446	147	197	86	40	26	28
Private creditors	420	331	173	71	2	1	4	0
Private nonguaranteed	..	463	304	407	123	2	0	0
Principal repayments	**2,721**	**4,448**	**1,137**	**1,058**	**910**	**557**	**536**	**742**
Public and publicly guaranteed	2,721	4,219	606	914	388	324	415	589
Official creditors	1,055	3,014	214	370	155	167	255	488
Private creditors	1,666	1,205	391	544	233	157	160	101
Private nonguaranteed	..	229	532	144	522	234	121	153
Interest payments	**1,552**	**889**	**202**	**161**	**124**	**95**	**80**	**103**
Public and publicly guaranteed	1,552	864	146	113	75	64	58	85
Official creditors	1,132	719	61	50	34	35	32	67
Private creditors	421	145	84	63	41	29	26	18
Private nonguaranteed	..	25	57	48	49	31	22	18
Debt resource inflows								
Net debt inflows	-1,568	-3,734	-305	171	-510	-229	-1,142	-650
Official creditors (incl. IMF)	-349	-3,180	-68	-173	-69	-127	-229	-460
Private creditors	-1,219	-555	-237	345	-441	-101	-914	-190
Long-term	-1,246	-640	-446	-210	-629	-387	-277	-253
Public and publicly guaranteed	-1,246	-874	-218	-473	-231	-155	-157	-101
Private nonguaranteed	..	234	-228	264	-398	-232	-121	-152
Short-term	27	85	209	554	189	286	-637	63
Non-debt resource inflows								
Foreign direct investment	280	1,156	1,834	2,675	3,053	2,331	2,721	1,602
Portfolio equity	..	..	..	..	..	..	..	..
Currency composition (%)								
Euro	..	40.5	60.1	59.5	60.5	58.1	59.0	72.6
U.S.dollars	44.6	40.8	28.6	29.2	29.0	30.1	32.4	16.0
Major economic aggregates								
Gross national income (GNI)	52,080	97,259	134,004	169,689	139,577	155,538	181,167	..
Exports of goods, services & prim. income	..	50,268	67,230	87,212	52,915	65,253	80,960	79,453
Personal transfers & comp. of employees	790	170	98	104	150	196	203	213
Imports of goods, services & prim. income	..	31,155	38,818	55,546	55,146	55,757	65,917	70,371
Primary income on FDI	..	5,485	5,405	6,206	5,892	4,855	6,313	7,453
Current account balance	..	21,180	30,631	34,440	401	12,146	17,690	12,247
International reserves	12,024	56,303	110,318	143,243	149,041	162,614	182,822	191,297
Ratios								
External debt stocks to exports (%)	..	34.0	9.1	7.2	14.0	11.1	7.5	7.1
External debt stocks to GNI (%)	48.9	17.6	4.6	3.7	5.3	4.7	3.3	..
Debt service to exports (%)	..	11.9	2.0	1.4	2.0	1.0	0.8	1.1
Short-term to external debt stocks (%)	0.9	3.0	12.2	20.9	20.2	24.5	18.9	21.4
Multilateral to external debt stocks (%)	16.2	14.3	2.2	0.2	0.2	0.1	0.1	0.1
Reserves to external debt stocks (%)	47.2	329.4	1,798.3	2,293.2	2,012.6	2,244.2	3,024.5	3,389.7
Reserves to imports (months)	..	21.7	34.1	30.9	32.4	35.0	33.3	32.6

ANGOLA

(US$ million, unless otherwise indicated)

	2000	2005	2007	2008	2009	2010	2011	2012
Summary external debt data								
External debt stocks	**9,763**	**12,224**	**11,932**	**15,502**	**17,014**	**19,004**	**21,122**	**22,171**
Long-term external debt	8,085	9,518	9,231	12,690	13,635	15,466	17,525	18,203
Short-term external debt	1,323	2,316	2,270	2,391	2,593	2,236	1,992	2,228
interest arrears on long-term	874	577	89	70	85	68	62	58
Use of IMF credit	356	390	431	421	787	1,302	1,606	1,740
Long-term external debt								
Debt outstanding and disbursed	**8,085**	**9,518**	**9,231**	**12,690**	**13,635**	**15,466**	**17,525**	**18,203**
Public and publicly guaranteed	8,085	9,518	9,231	12,690	13,635	15,466	17,525	18,203
Official creditors	2,703	3,174	3,210	4,008	4,822	8,161	9,687	9,615
Private creditors	5,382	6,344	6,021	8,682	8,813	7,305	7,837	8,588
Private nonguaranteed	..	..	..	..	..	..	..	..
Disbursements	**1,045**	**3,676**	**5,647**	**4,622**	**3,543**	**3,951**	**4,793**	**4,215**
Public and publicly guaranteed	1,045	3,676	5,647	4,622	3,543	3,951	4,793	4,215
Official creditors	34	321	952	1,101	1,111	3,658	2,353	1,103
Private creditors	1,011	3,355	4,695	3,521	2,432	293	2,440	3,112
Private nonguaranteed	..	..	..	..	..	..	..	..
Principal repayments	**1,530**	**2,289**	**3,779**	**1,130**	**3,131**	**2,110**	**2,681**	**3,554**
Public and publicly guaranteed	1,530	2,289	3,779	1,130	3,131	2,110	2,681	3,554
Official creditors	268	505	352	276	310	283	820	1,164
Private creditors	1,262	1,784	3,427	854	2,821	1,827	1,862	2,390
Private nonguaranteed	..	..	..	..	..	..	..	..
Interest payments	**149**	**257**	**579**	**443**	**392**	**176**	**154**	**640**
Public and publicly guaranteed	149	257	579	443	392	176	154	640
Official creditors	36	61	162	118	143	114	79	321
Private creditors	113	195	416	325	250	63	75	319
Private nonguaranteed	..	..	..	..	..	..	..	..
Debt resource inflows								
Net debt inflows	-733	2,603	2,079	3,632	952	2,025	2,190	1,032
Official creditors (incl. IMF)	-234	-185	600	825	1,155	3,900	1,849	70
Private creditors	-499	2,788	1,479	2,807	-203	-1,874	341	962
Long-term	-251	1,572	1,269	2,667	-390	-1,534	579	722
Public and publicly guaranteed	-251	1,572	1,269	2,667	-390	-1,534	579	722
Private nonguaranteed	..	..	..	..	..	..	..	..
Short-term	-248	1,216	210	140	187	-340	-238	240
Non-debt resource inflows								
Foreign direct investment	879	-1,304	-893	1,679	2,205	-3,227	-3,024	-6,898
Portfolio equity	..	..	..	..	..	..	..	..
Currency composition (%)								
Euro	..	8.2	6.4	7.6	9.7	8.6	8.1	8.7
U.S.dollars	86.3	87.8	91.0	90.5	88.5	89.8	90.2	89.0
Major economic aggregates								
Gross national income (GNI)	7,449	24,203	52,850	70,461	68,669	74,299	92,035	102,658
Exports of goods, services & prim. income	8,222	24,312	45,329	64,666	41,582	51,586	68,252	72,131
Personal transfers & comp. of employees	..	..	..	82	0	18	0	0
Imports of goods, services & prim. income	7,454	19,201	34,526	57,261	48,784	43,642	53,805	56,518
Primary income on FDI	929	3,406	7,268	13,185	6,130	7,526	9,040	9,722
Current account balance	796	5,138	10,581	7,194	-7,572	7,506	13,085	13,851
International reserves	1,198	3,197	11,197	17,869	13,664	19,749	28,786	33,415
Ratios								
External debt stocks to exports (%)	118.7	50.3	26.3	24.0	40.9	36.8	30.9	30.7
External debt stocks to GNI (%)	131.1	50.5	22.6	22.0	24.8	25.6	23.0	21.6
Debt service to exports (%)	20.9	10.8	9.9	2.5	8.5	4.5	4.2	5.9
Short-term to external debt stocks (%)	13.5	18.9	19.0	15.4	15.2	11.8	9.4	10.1
Multilateral to external debt stocks (%)	3.0	3.0	3.6	2.8	2.6	2.3	2.1	2.2
Reserves to external debt stocks (%)	12.3	26.2	93.8	115.3	80.3	103.9	136.3	150.7
Reserves to imports (months)	1.9	2.0	3.9	3.7	3.4	5.4	6.4	7.1

Notes:

Short-term debt is based on data from the BIS.

ARGENTINA

(US$ million, unless otherwise indicated)

	2000	2005	2007	2008	2009	2010	2011	2012
Summary external debt data								
External debt stocks	**147,029**	**127,452**	**120,418**	**122,497**	**127,335**	**117,357**	**122,978**	**121,013**
Long-term external debt	113,234	82,640	100,643	102,024	104,324	100,355	103,064	103,930
Short-term external debt	28,325	34,844	19,272	19,983	19,844	13,891	16,813	13,978
interest arrears on long-term	10	7,738	9,462	10,009	10,774	5,464	6,115	6,312
Use of IMF credit	5,470	9,968	503	490	3,167	3,111	3,101	3,105
Long-term external debt								
Debt outstanding and disbursed	**113,234**	**82,640**	**100,643**	**102,024**	**104,324**	**100,355**	**103,064**	**103,930**
Public and publicly guaranteed	87,324	56,279	70,614	71,123	75,953	69,253	68,339	67,597
Official creditors	20,822	20,564	20,681	20,785	22,539	23,109	23,804	23,855
Private creditors	66,503	35,715	49,934	50,339	53,414	46,144	44,535	43,742
Private nonguaranteed	25,909	26,361	30,028	30,900	28,371	31,102	34,725	36,332
Disbursements	**18,794**	**4,727**	**9,572**	**7,036**	**7,547**	**6,893**	**10,774**	**7,667**
Public and publicly guaranteed	14,312	3,219	6,131	4,046	3,602	2,592	2,612	2,377
Official creditors	1,971	993	2,383	2,020	3,499	2,455	2,588	2,341
Private creditors	12,341	2,227	3,747	2,026	103	137	23	36
Private nonguaranteed	4,482	1,507	3,441	2,990	3,946	4,300	8,163	5,290
Principal repayments	**11,689**	**3,450**	**5,192**	**4,651**	**11,225**	**10,693**	**11,967**	**9,658**
Public and publicly guaranteed	6,185	1,684	3,251	2,383	5,511	5,038	5,256	3,351
Official creditors	1,871	1,501	2,697	2,380	1,796	1,923	1,907	2,148
Private creditors	4,314	183	554	3	3,715	3,115	3,349	1,203
Private nonguaranteed	5,503	1,766	1,941	2,268	5,714	5,655	6,712	6,307
Interest payments	**9,837**	**2,154**	**2,948**	**2,947**	**3,356**	**3,524**	**3,382**	**3,205**
Public and publicly guaranteed	7,797	1,438	1,665	1,741	2,022	2,436	2,444	2,298
Official creditors	1,600	756	874	768	661	614	571	544
Private creditors	6,196	682	792	973	1,361	1,821	1,872	1,754
Private nonguaranteed	2,041	716	1,282	1,206	1,335	1,089	938	907
Debt resource inflows								
Net debt inflows	6,820	14,812	-6,657	2,548	-4,581	-4,444	1,078	-5,023
Official creditors (incl. IMF)	915	-4,079	-314	-360	1,703	532	681	194
Private creditors	5,905	18,891	-6,343	2,908	-6,284	-4,976	397	-5,217
Long-term	7,005	1,785	4,694	2,744	-5,380	-4,333	-1,874	-2,185
Public and publicly guaranteed	8,026	2,044	3,193	2,022	-3,612	-2,978	-3,325	-1,167
Private nonguaranteed	-1,021	-259	1,501	722	-1,768	-1,355	1,451	-1,017
Short-term	-1,100	17,106	-11,037	164	-904	-643	2,271	-3,032
Non-debt resource inflows								
Foreign direct investment	10,418	5,265	6,473	9,726	4,017	7,846	10,720	12,128
Portfolio equity	-3,227	-48	1,785	-531	-212	-208	-174	876
Currency composition (%)								
Euro	..	35.4	37.7	35.7	34.7	29.2	28.5	29.3
U.S.dollars	57.1	54.7	54.5	56.8	58.2	63.9	65.4	65.2
Major economic aggregates								
Gross national income (GNI)	276,656	176,985	255,510	319,416	297,710	358,619	435,223	460,533
Exports of goods, services & prim. income	38,697	51,204	72,794	87,609	69,991	84,380	102,761	98,182
Personal transfers & comp. of employees	86	432	606	698	621	639	692	573
Imports of goods, services & prim. income	48,076	46,414	65,793	81,023	61,706	82,615	104,370	97,842
Primary income on FDI	3,086	5,456	7,283	7,902	8,360	9,964	10,811	9,271
Current account balance	-8,981	5,274	7,354	6,756	8,338	1,360	-2,173	-56
International reserves	25,147	27,179	44,682	44,855	46,093	49,734	43,227	39,920
Ratios								
External debt stocks to exports (%)	380.0	248.9	165.4	139.8	181.9	139.1	119.7	123.3
External debt stocks to GNI (%)	53.1	72.0	47.1	38.4	42.8	32.7	28.3	26.3
Debt service to exports (%)	64.0	19.6	12.0	9.0	21.0	17.0	15.1	13.2
Short-term to external debt stocks (%)	19.3	27.3	16.0	16.3	15.6	11.8	13.7	11.6
Multilateral to external debt stocks (%)	11.2	12.3	12.5	12.2	12.8	14.5	14.6	15.2
Reserves to external debt stocks (%)	17.1	21.3	37.1	36.6	36.2	42.4	35.2	33.0
Reserves to imports (months)	6.3	7.0	8.1	6.6	9.0	7.2	5.0	4.9

Notes:

Long-term private nonguaranteed debt data from 2009 are reported by the country. Historical data are World Bank staff estimates. Long-term provincial debt data are World Bank staff estimates. Short-term debt is based on data from the BIS.

ARMENIA

(US$ million, unless otherwise indicated)

	2000	2005	2007	2008	2009	2010	2011	2012
Summary external debt data								
External debt stocks	**1,010**	**1,968**	**3,037**	**3,541**	**5,023**	**6,241**	**7,383**	**7,608**
Long-term external debt	675	1,368	2,281	2,818	3,778	4,744	5,551	5,889
Short-term external debt	44	298	459	453	521	621	869	807
interest arrears on long-term	6	0	0	0	0	0	0	0
Use of IMF credit	290	302	297	270	725	876	963	911
Long-term external debt								
Debt outstanding and disbursed	**675**	**1,368**	**2,281**	**2,818**	**3,778**	**4,744**	**5,551**	**5,889**
Public and publicly guaranteed	675	923	1,282	1,446	2,376	2,557	2,736	2,956
Official creditors	658	921	1,281	1,444	2,375	2,556	2,733	2,942
Private creditors	17	1	1	1	1	1	4	14
Private nonguaranteed	..	446	999	1,373	1,401	2,187	2,815	2,933
Disbursements	**63**	**168**	**751**	**776**	**1,247**	**1,734**	**1,488**	**1,626**
Public and publicly guaranteed	63	50	207	164	941	198	206	280
Official creditors	62	50	207	164	941	198	203	270
Private creditors	1	0	0	0	0	0	2	10
Private nonguaranteed	..	117	544	612	306	1,536	1,282	1,346
Principal repayments	**15**	**69**	**58**	**253**	**300**	**857**	**735**	**842**
Public and publicly guaranteed	15	16	17	15	21	24	28	30
Official creditors	13	16	17	15	21	24	28	30
Private creditors	2	0	0	0	0	0	0	0
Private nonguaranteed	..	53	42	238	279	833	707	812
Interest payments	**9**	**23**	**91**	**70**	**79**	**60**	**126**	**124**
Public and publicly guaranteed	9	9	10	11	23	35	38	43
Official creditors	9	9	10	11	23	35	38	43
Private creditors	0	0	0	0	0	0	0	0
Private nonguaranteed	..	14	81	58	56	25	88	81
Debt resource inflows								
Net debt inflows	21	-38	831	497	1,458	1,139	1,093	670
Official creditors (incl. IMF)	34	10	177	130	1,362	337	266	188
Private creditors	-13	-48	655	367	96	802	827	482
Long-term	-2	64	502	374	28	703	578	544
Public and publicly guaranteed	-2	0	0	0	0	0	2	10
Private nonguaranteed	..	64	503	374	28	703	576	533
Short-term	-11	-112	152	-6	68	99	249	-62
Non-debt resource inflows								
Foreign direct investment	104	239	699	935	777	570	663	489
Portfolio equity	0	1	0	-1	1	0	0	2
Currency composition (%)								
Euro	..	8.0	9.0	8.7	6.3	5.8	7.8	10.7
U.S.dollars	93.3	86.3	71.2	62.9	66.0	62.8	60.8	59.1
Major economic aggregates								
Gross national income (GNI)	1,964	5,033	9,485	12,133	8,815	9,599	10,693	10,431
Exports of goods, services & prim. income	551	1,873	2,587	2,751	2,053	2,896	3,639	3,749
Personal transfers & comp. of employees	87	487	837	1,053	763	991	1,994	2,123
Imports of goods, services & prim. income	1,017	2,448	4,121	5,271	4,236	4,833	5,497	5,580
Primary income on FDI	22	170	332	279	332	364	377	335
Current account balance	-278	-52	-590	-1,383	-1,369	-1,373	-1,136	-1,108
International reserves	302	669	1,659	1,407	2,004	1,866	1,932	1,799
Ratios								
External debt stocks to exports (%)	183.4	105.1	117.4	128.7	244.7	215.5	202.9	203.0
External debt stocks to GNI (%)	51.4	39.1	32.0	29.2	57.0	65.0	69.0	72.9
Debt service to exports (%)	9.2	7.6	7.5	13.3	20.6	33.4	25.4	30.9
Short-term to external debt stocks (%)	4.4	15.1	15.1	12.8	10.4	9.9	11.8	10.6
Multilateral to external debt stocks (%)	48.0	41.1	34.3	31.4	28.4	24.2	22.3	24.5
Reserves to external debt stocks (%)	29.9	34.0	54.6	39.7	39.9	29.9	26.2	23.7
Reserves to imports (months)	3.6	3.3	4.8	3.2	5.7	4.6	4.2	3.9

Notes:

Long-term private nonguaranteed debt data from 2011 are World Bank staff estimates.

AZERBAIJAN

(US$ million, unless otherwise indicated)

	2000	2005	2007	2008	2009	2010	2011	2012
Summary external debt data								
External debt stocks	**1,524**	**2,119**	**3,729**	**4,467**	**4,755**	**7,094**	**8,370**	**9,712**
Long-term external debt	832	1,550	2,341	2,982	3,642	5,933	7,214	8,608
Short-term external debt	156	186	1,043	1,169	810	878	891	852
interest arrears on long-term	0	0	0	0	0	0	0	0
Use of IMF credit	536	383	346	316	303	282	265	252
Long-term external debt								
Debt outstanding and disbursed	**832**	**1,550**	**2,341**	**2,982**	**3,642**	**5,933**	**7,214**	**8,608**
Public and publicly guaranteed	734	1,362	2,197	2,656	3,329	3,775	4,597	5,856
Official creditors	643	1,103	1,517	1,839	2,172	2,626	3,428	4,192
Private creditors	90	260	681	816	1,157	1,149	1,170	1,664
Private nonguaranteed	99	187	143	327	314	2,158	2,616	2,752
Disbursements	**269**	**431**	**489**	**741**	**870**	**2,607**	**2,159**	**2,401**
Public and publicly guaranteed	263	307	442	526	820	693	1,096	1,583
Official creditors	204	71	232	283	431	513	916	993
Private creditors	59	236	210	242	389	180	180	590
Private nonguaranteed	6	124	47	216	50	1,914	1,063	818
Principal repayments	**22**	**134**	**51**	**148**	**231**	**300**	**855**	**940**
Public and publicly guaranteed	14	37	40	125	178	228	247	256
Official creditors	12	34	24	46	102	97	116	144
Private creditors	2	3	16	80	76	131	131	111
Private nonguaranteed	7	97	11	23	53	72	608	684
Interest payments	**37**	**24**	**77**	**88**	**67**	**80**	**948**	**952**
Public and publicly guaranteed	32	17	70	77	55	67	77	103
Official creditors	31	15	33	30	35	33	42	50
Private creditors	1	2	37	47	21	35	35	53
Private nonguaranteed	5	7	7	11	12	13	871	848
Debt resource inflows								
Net debt inflows	323	316	924	697	262	2,360	1,300	1,409
Official creditors (incl. IMF)	141	8	171	216	311	401	784	835
Private creditors	182	308	753	481	-49	1,959	517	574
Long-term	55	260	230	355	310	1,891	504	613
Public and publicly guaranteed	57	233	193	162	312	50	49	479
Private nonguaranteed	-2	27	36	193	-2	1,842	455	134
Short-term	127	48	523	126	-359	68	13	-39
Non-debt resource inflows								
Foreign direct investment	130	4,476	4,594	3,987	2,900	3,353	4,485	5,293
Portfolio equity	..	..	2	..	..	1	0	0
Currency composition (%)								
Euro	..	14.0	22.7	21.4	27.1	27.2	26.2	23.3
U.S.dollars	64.4	51.4	50.9	51.5	51.4	50.5	50.0	56.0
Major economic aggregates								
Gross national income (GNI)	4,987	11,599	27,970	43,586	40,772	49,437	56,402	59,543
Exports of goods, services & prim. income	2,174	8,341	22,683	32,484	23,311	28,910	38,058	37,837
Personal transfers & comp. of employees	57	623	1,268	1,518	1,255	1,410	1,893	1,990
Imports of goods, services & prim. income	2,415	8,658	14,669	17,082	13,858	14,379	21,586	22,811
Primary income on FDI	317	1,582	4,995	5,401	3,664	3,815	5,488	4,906
Current account balance	-168	167	9,019	16,453	10,175	15,040	17,145	14,977
International reserves	680	1,178	4,273	6,467	5,364	6,409	10,274	11,277
Ratios								
External debt stocks to exports (%)	70.1	25.4	16.4	13.8	20.4	24.5	22.0	25.7
External debt stocks to GNI (%)	30.6	18.3	13.3	10.2	11.7	14.3	14.8	16.3
Debt service to exports (%)	6.4	2.7	0.8	0.9	1.4	1.4	4.8	5.1
Short-term to external debt stocks (%)	10.2	8.8	28.0	26.2	17.0	12.4	10.6	8.8
Multilateral to external debt stocks (%)	20.4	28.5	25.2	25.1	30.6	24.7	26.6	28.9
Reserves to external debt stocks (%)	44.6	55.6	114.6	144.8	112.8	90.3	122.8	116.1
Reserves to imports (months)	3.4	1.6	3.5	4.5	4.6	5.3	5.7	5.9

Notes:

Long-term private nonguaranteed debt data are World Bank staff estimates based on the market data. Short-term debt is based on data from the BIS.

BANGLADESH

(US$ million, unless otherwise indicated)

	2000	2005	2007	2008	2009	2010	2011	2012
Summary external debt data								
External debt stocks	**15,596**	**18,449**	**21,373**	**22,952**	**24,619**	**25,752**	**27,326**	**26,130**
Long-term external debt	14,985	17,385	19,428	20,300	21,210	21,400	22,350	23,251
Short-term external debt	334	688	1,370	1,894	1,934	2,949	3,705	1,667
interest arrears on long-term	0	16	4	1	1	2	2	2
Use of IMF credit	277	376	575	758	1,475	1,403	1,271	1,213
Long-term external debt								
Debt outstanding and disbursed	**14,985**	**17,385**	**19,428**	**20,300**	**21,210**	**21,400**	**22,350**	**23,251**
Public and publicly guaranteed	14,985	17,385	19,428	20,300	21,210	21,400	22,350	23,251
Official creditors	14,809	17,209	19,288	20,237	21,160	21,367	22,328	23,237
Private creditors	176	176	140	63	50	33	22	13
Private nonguaranteed	..	..	..	..	..	..	..	..
Disbursements	**861**	**878**	**1,080**	**1,732**	**1,499**	**982**	**1,028**	**2,091**
Public and publicly guaranteed	861	878	1,080	1,732	1,499	982	1,028	2,091
Official creditors	794	878	1,080	1,732	1,499	982	1,028	2,091
Private creditors	67	0	0	0	0	0	0	0
Private nonguaranteed	..	..	..	..	..	..	..	..
Principal repayments	**487**	**566**	**735**	**632**	**703**	**743**	**1,050**	**988**
Public and publicly guaranteed	487	566	735	632	703	743	1,050	988
Official creditors	465	551	719	612	691	732	1,039	980
Private creditors	22	16	17	20	13	11	11	9
Private nonguaranteed	..	..	..	..	..	..	..	..
Interest payments	**165**	**197**	**180**	**203**	**197**	**201**	**258**	**296**
Public and publicly guaranteed	165	197	180	203	197	201	258	296
Official creditors	156	195	178	200	196	199	257	295
Private creditors	9	2	2	2	1	2	1	1
Private nonguaranteed	..	..	..	..	..	..	..	..
Debt resource inflows								
Net debt inflows	368	370	532	1,826	812	1,207	603	-995
Official creditors (incl. IMF)	244	425	361	1,319	785	204	-142	1,052
Private creditors	125	-56	171	507	27	1,003	745	-2,047
Long-term	45	-16	-17	-20	-13	-11	-11	-9
Public and publicly guaranteed	45	-16	-17	-20	-13	-11	-11	-9
Private nonguaranteed	..	..	..	..	..	..	..	..
Short-term	80	-40	188	527	40	1,014	756	-2,039
Non-debt resource inflows								
Foreign direct investment	280	813	653	1,010	733	918	1,138	1,178
Portfolio equity	1	20	153	-48	-153	0	-16	91
Currency composition (%)								
Euro	..	0.7	0.9	0.7	0.7	0.6	0.5	0.6
U.S.dollars	44.3	50.7	51.9	52.4	53.4	52.6	50.5	51.7
Major economic aggregates								
Gross national income (GNI)	48,857	63,355	73,523	86,607	97,485	109,695	122,091	126,976
Exports of goods, services & prim. income	7,293	10,537	14,150	17,654	17,083	21,764	27,145	27,764
Personal transfers & comp. of employees	1,968	4,315	6,562	8,941	10,521	10,850	12,071	14,085
Imports of goods, services & prim. income	10,018	15,487	20,581	26,286	24,507	31,037	39,553	39,609
Primary income on FDI	149	661	903	840	1,105	1,210	1,298	1,572
Current account balance	-306	-176	857	986	3,556	2,106	-165	2,648
International reserves	1,486	2,767	5,183	5,689	10,219	10,564	8,510	12,031
Ratios								
External debt stocks to exports (%)	213.9	175.1	151.0	130.0	144.1	118.3	100.7	94.1
External debt stocks to GNI (%)	31.9	29.1	29.1	26.5	25.3	23.5	22.4	20.6
Debt service to exports (%)	10.5	7.6	7.0	5.0	5.6	4.7	5.5	5.4
Short-term to external debt stocks (%)	2.1	3.7	6.4	8.3	7.9	11.5	13.6	6.4
Multilateral to external debt stocks (%)	70.5	76.1	76.3	75.4	74.6	71.7	68.4	74.7
Reserves to external debt stocks (%)	9.5	15.0	24.3	24.8	41.5	41.0	31.1	46.0
Reserves to imports (months)	1.8	2.1	3.0	2.6	5.0	4.1	2.6	3.6

Notes:

Historical short-term debt until 2011 is based on data from the BIS.

BELARUS

(US$ million, unless otherwise indicated)

	2000	2005	2007	2008	2009	2010	2011	2012
Summary external debt data								
External debt stocks	**2,604**	**5,284**	**12,488**	**15,122**	**22,054**	**28,397**	**33,926**	**34,173**
Long-term external debt	771	1,254	4,544	6,996	9,528	12,470	16,430	18,511
Short-term external debt	1,239	3,503	7,361	7,558	9,076	11,864	13,446	12,075
interest arrears on long-term	14	1	2	2	3	4	4	4
Use of IMF credit	594	527	583	568	3,449	4,063	4,050	3,588
Long-term external debt								
Debt outstanding and disbursed	**771**	**1,254**	**4,544**	**6,996**	**9,528**	**12,470**	**16,430**	**18,511**
Public and publicly guaranteed	673	769	3,419	5,407	6,217	7,999	10,609	12,559
Official creditors	384	552	2,066	3,539	4,689	5,725	8,380	7,303
Private creditors	289	217	1,354	1,868	1,529	2,274	2,228	5,256
Private nonguaranteed	98	485	1,125	1,589	3,311	4,471	5,821	5,952
Disbursements	**237**	**647**	**3,632**	**3,306**	**1,984**	**3,810**	**5,406**	**3,542**
Public and publicly guaranteed	131	252	2,817	2,165	1,264	2,679	3,926	2,223
Official creditors	13	188	1,596	1,563	1,254	1,580	2,826	1,050
Private creditors	118	64	1,220	602	10	1,099	1,100	1,173
Private nonguaranteed	106	395	815	1,141	720	1,132	1,479	1,320
Principal repayments	**193**	**508**	**755**	**850**	**1,275**	**1,257**	**2,339**	**3,412**
Public and publicly guaranteed	121	175	250	175	450	455	1,310	2,649
Official creditors	39	92	96	95	97	108	167	2,551
Private creditors	82	83	154	80	352	347	1,143	97
Private nonguaranteed	71	333	505	675	825	802	1,029	763
Interest payments	**37**	**53**	**80**	**236**	**185**	**208**	**572**	**851**
Public and publicly guaranteed	36	37	48	180	114	127	460	729
Official creditors	17	16	29	158	96	114	312	431
Private creditors	19	21	18	21	17	14	148	298
Private nonguaranteed	1	15	33	56	71	80	112	121
Debt resource inflows								
Net debt inflows	-87	696	5,858	2,654	5,051	6,008	4,648	-1,704
Official creditors (incl. IMF)	-81	87	1,501	1,468	3,982	2,141	2,659	-1,965
Private creditors	-6	608	4,357	1,185	1,069	3,867	1,990	262
Long-term	70	42	1,376	988	-448	1,081	408	1,632
Public and publicly guaranteed	36	-19	1,066	521	-343	752	-42	1,075
Private nonguaranteed	35	61	311	466	-105	329	450	556
Short-term	-76	566	2,981	198	1,517	2,786	1,582	-1,370
Non-debt resource inflows								
Foreign direct investment	119	307	1,807	2,188	1,877	1,393	4,002	1,464
Portfolio equity	1	1	5	1	1	1	0	-4
Currency composition (%)								
Euro	..	14.4	6.0	2.4	5.7	5.3	3.9	3.1
U.S.dollars	47.7	71.5	90.9	95.8	92.1	81.2	85.7	95.3
Major economic aggregates								
Gross national income (GNI)	12,690	30,220	44,865	59,976	48,157	54,058	63,537	61,751
Exports of goods, services & prim. income	7,667	17,705	27,149	36,878	24,818	29,805	47,242	52,777
Personal transfers & comp. of employees	139	199	288	583	504	575	891	1,053
Imports of goods, services & prim. income	8,160	17,411	30,331	42,007	31,224	38,402	49,812	51,242
Primary income on FDI	5	135	435	682	872	1,039	1,186	1,258
Current account balance	-338	459	-3,013	-4,959	-6,133	-8,280	-5,053	-1,688
International reserves	350	1,137	3,952	2,687	4,831	3,431	6,011	5,809
Ratios								
External debt stocks to exports (%)	34.0	29.8	46.0	41.0	88.9	95.3	71.8	64.8
External debt stocks to GNI (%)	20.5	17.5	27.8	25.2	45.8	52.5	53.4	55.3
Debt service to exports (%)	4.9	3.9	4.0	3.3	6.5	5.8	6.8	9.5
Short-term to external debt stocks (%)	47.6	66.3	58.9	50.0	41.2	41.8	39.6	35.3
Multilateral to external debt stocks (%)	7.7	1.3	0.3	0.3	1.2	1.0	7.8	6.5
Reserves to external debt stocks (%)	13.5	21.5	31.6	17.8	21.9	12.1	17.7	17.0
Reserves to imports (months)	0.5	0.8	1.6	0.8	1.9	1.1	1.4	1.4

BELIZE

(US$ million, unless otherwise indicated)

	2000	2005	2007	2008	2009	2010	2011	2012
Summary external debt data								
External debt stocks	**528**	**989**	**1,049**	**1,252**	**1,271**	**1,287**	**1,261**	**1,241**
Long-term external debt	455	956	1,013	1,217	1,226	1,245	1,219	1,190
Short-term external debt	50	7	7	7	10	7	8	19
interest arrears on long-term	0	7	7	7	10	7	8	19
Use of IMF credit	23	26	28	28	35	35	35	32
Long-term external debt								
Debt outstanding and disbursed	**455**	**956**	**1,013**	**1,217**	**1,226**	**1,245**	**1,219**	**1,190**
Public and publicly guaranteed	455	956	1,013	998	1,017	1,002	1,001	984
Official creditors	228	348	391	386	412	402	406	412
Private creditors	226	608	622	612	605	600	595	573
Private nonguaranteed	..	..	..	219	209	243	218	206
Disbursements	**195**	**213**	**604**	**109**	**79**	**39**	**54**	**38**
Public and publicly guaranteed	195	213	604	41	66	32	36	37
Official creditors	27	48	63	40	65	32	36	37
Private creditors	169	165	541	2	1	0	0	0
Private nonguaranteed	..	..	..	68	13	7	18	1
Principal repayments	**41**	**152**	**582**	**84**	**66**	**66**	**69**	**67**
Public and publicly guaranteed	41	152	582	49	47	46	37	54
Official creditors	20	21	88	38	39	41	32	31
Private creditors	21	131	493	11	9	5	5	22
Private nonguaranteed	..	..	..	35	18	20	32	13
Interest payments	**22**	**70**	**61**	**57**	**54**	**56**	**57**	**49**
Public and publicly guaranteed	22	70	61	45	43	45	46	40
Official creditors	12	15	19	17	15	13	10	9
Private creditors	11	54	42	28	28	32	36	31
Private nonguaranteed	..	..	..	12	11	11	11	9
Debt resource inflows								
Net debt inflows	153	61	23	25	21	-26	-15	-31
Official creditors (incl. IMF)	7	27	-26	2	33	-9	3	3
Private creditors	146	34	48	23	-13	-17	-18	-35
Long-term	147	34	48	23	-13	-17	-18	-35
Public and publicly guaranteed	147	34	48	-10	-7	-5	-5	-22
Private nonguaranteed	..	..	..	33	-6	-12	-14	-12
Short-term	-1	..	..	..	..	..	..	..
Non-debt resource inflows								
Foreign direct investment	23	127	140	170	109	96	95	194
Portfolio equity	..	..	..	2	..	..	..	..
Currency composition (%)								
Euro	..	1.7	1.6	1.1	1.0	0.9	0.8	0.7
U.S.dollars	90.9	96.3	96.8	97.4	97.7	97.9	97.8	98.0
Major economic aggregates								
Gross national income (GNI)	775	1,000	1,118	1,198	1,241	1,240	1,322	..
Exports of goods, services & prim. income	441	622	823	872	733	834	949	1,047
Personal transfers & comp. of employees	26	45	73	76	79	78	75	76
Imports of goods, services & prim. income	661	824	969	1,129	895	972	1,052	1,150
Primary income on FDI	31	35	87	107	56	102	40	68
Current account balance	-162	-151	-52	-145	-83	-46	-20	-27
International reserves	123	71	109	166	214	218	237	289
Ratios								
External debt stocks to exports (%)	119.6	159.0	127.4	143.5	173.4	154.3	132.9	118.5
External debt stocks to GNI (%)	68.1	98.8	93.8	104.5	102.4	103.8	95.4	..
Debt service to exports (%)	15.3	35.7	78.1	16.2	16.3	14.6	13.3	11.3
Short-term to external debt stocks (%)	9.5	0.7	0.7	0.6	0.7	0.5	0.6	1.5
Multilateral to external debt stocks (%)	26.3	22.7	23.2	18.4	19.7	19.7	20.5	21.5
Reserves to external debt stocks (%)	23.3	7.2	10.3	13.3	16.8	16.9	18.8	23.3
Reserves to imports (months)	2.2	1.0	1.3	1.8	2.9	2.7	2.7	3.0

Notes:

Long-term private nonguaranteed debt data are revised from 2008 based on reports obtained from the Central Bank.

BENIN

(US$ million, unless otherwise indicated)

	2000	2005	2007	2008	2009	2010	2011	2012
Summary external debt data								
External debt stocks	**1,400**	**1,552**	**771**	**976**	**1,319**	**1,599**	**1,870**	**2,055**
Long-term external debt	1,237	1,445	747	850	974	1,113	1,196	1,304
Short-term external debt	66	41	5	89	213	341	497	542
interest arrears on long-term	1	2	5	4	32	25	28	47
Use of IMF credit	96	66	19	37	132	146	177	210
Long-term external debt								
Debt outstanding and disbursed	**1,237**	**1,445**	**747**	**850**	**974**	**1,113**	**1,196**	**1,304**
Public and publicly guaranteed	1,237	1,445	747	850	974	1,113	1,196	1,304
Official creditors	1,234	1,445	747	850	974	1,113	1,196	1,304
Private creditors	3	0	0	0	0	0	0	0
Private nonguaranteed	..	..	..	..	..	..	..	..
Disbursements	**39**	**97**	**159**	**143**	**142**	**184**	**116**	**116**
Public and publicly guaranteed	39	97	159	143	142	184	116	116
Official creditors	39	97	159	143	142	184	116	116
Private creditors	0	0	0	0	0	0	0	0
Private nonguaranteed	..	..	..	..	..	..	..	..
Principal repayments	**43**	**24**	**18**	**16**	**25**	**25**	**29**	**39**
Public and publicly guaranteed	43	24	18	16	25	25	29	39
Official creditors	43	20	18	16	25	25	29	39
Private creditors	0	4	0	0	0	0	0	0
Private nonguaranteed	..	..	..	..	..	..	..	..
Interest payments	**16**	**14**	**10**	**41**	**12**	**13**	**13**	**16**
Public and publicly guaranteed	16	14	10	41	12	13	13	16
Official creditors	16	14	10	41	12	13	13	16
Private creditors	0	0	0	0	0	0	0	0
Private nonguaranteed	..	..	..	..	..	..	..	..
Debt resource inflows								
Net debt inflows	-54	82	103	231	229	309	274	135
Official creditors (incl. IMF)	-6	71	142	146	133	175	120	109
Private creditors	-48	11	-39	85	96	134	154	26
Long-term	0	-4	0	0	0	0	0	0
Public and publicly guaranteed	0	-4	0	0	0	0	0	0
Private nonguaranteed	..	..	..	..	..	..	..	..
Short-term	-48	15	-39	85	96	134	154	26
Non-debt resource inflows								
Foreign direct investment	60	-9	139	48	-19	53	161	159
Portfolio equity	0	2	5	-2	9	5	..	..
Currency composition (%)								
Euro	..	4.4	3.9	3.2	5.4	9.9	9.5	10.1
U.S.dollars	54.8	50.6	28.0	24.5	21.9	20.3	19.3	18.0
Major economic aggregates								
Gross national income (GNI)	2,347	4,340	5,497	6,622	6,552	6,505	7,260	7,512
Exports of goods, services & prim. income	552	797	1,386	1,675	1,489	1,707	..	..
Personal transfers & comp. of employees	87	147	240	207	126	139	..	..
Imports of goods, services & prim. income	744	1,188	2,188	2,456	2,310	2,393	..	..
Primary income on FDI	-1	9	53	30	32	55	..	..
Current account balance	-81	-226	-534	-536	-649	-530	-512	..
International reserves	459	655	1,209	1,263	1,230	1,200	887	713
Ratios								
External debt stocks to exports (%)	253.6	194.6	55.7	58.3	88.6	93.7	..	..
External debt stocks to GNI (%)	59.6	35.8	14.0	14.7	20.1	24.6	25.8	27.4
Debt service to exports (%)	13.6	6.0	2.2	3.7	3.6	3.3	..	..
Short-term to external debt stocks (%)	4.7	2.6	0.6	9.2	16.2	21.3	26.6	26.4
Multilateral to external debt stocks (%)	69.2	87.4	77.3	70.9	61.0	58.3	53.3	53.4
Reserves to external debt stocks (%)	32.8	42.2	156.8	129.4	93.2	75.0	47.5	34.7
Reserves to imports (months)	7.4	6.6	6.6	6.2	6.4	6.0	..	..

Notes:

Data include the effects of Paris Club debt restructuring agreement and HIPC and MDRI debt relief.

BHUTAN

(US$ million, unless otherwise indicated)

	2000	2005	2007	2008	2009	2010	2011	2012
Summary external debt data								
External debt stocks	**212**	**658**	**803**	**695**	**761**	**907**	**1,048**	**1,459**
Long-term external debt	202	637	775	678	747	892	1,031	1,350
Short-term external debt	2	12	18	8	5	6	8	100
interest arrears on long-term	0	4	0	0	0	0	0	0
Use of IMF credit	8	9	9	9	9	9	9	9
Long-term external debt								
Debt outstanding and disbursed	**202**	**637**	**775**	**678**	**747**	**892**	**1,031**	**1,350**
Public and publicly guaranteed	202	637	775	678	747	892	1,021	1,342
Official creditors	202	637	775	678	747	892	1,021	1,342
Private creditors	0	0	0	0	0	0	0	0
Private nonguaranteed	..	..	..	..	..	..	10	8
Disbursements	**35**	**82**	**32**	**32**	**92**	**178**	**270**	**409**
Public and publicly guaranteed	35	82	32	32	92	178	260	409
Official creditors	35	82	32	32	92	178	260	409
Private creditors	0	0	0	0	0	0	0	0
Private nonguaranteed	..	..	..	..	..	..	10	0
Principal repayments	**5**	**5**	**24**	**43**	**41**	**47**	**45**	**69**
Public and publicly guaranteed	5	5	24	43	41	47	45	67
Official creditors	5	5	24	43	41	47	45	67
Private creditors	0	0	0	0	0	0	0	0
Private nonguaranteed	..	..	..	..	..	..	0	2
Interest payments	**2**	**2**	**7**	**38**	**34**	**37**	**37**	**58**
Public and publicly guaranteed	2	2	7	38	34	37	37	57
Official creditors	2	2	7	38	34	37	37	57
Private creditors	0	0	0	0	0	0	0	0
Private nonguaranteed	..	..	..	..	..	..	0	0
Debt resource inflows								
Net debt inflows	30	85	10	-22	48	132	227	432
Official creditors (incl. IMF)	30	77	8	-12	51	131	215	342
Private creditors	0	8	2	-10	-3	1	12	90
Long-term	0	0	0	0	0	0	10	-2
Public and publicly guaranteed	0	0	0	0	0	0	0	0
Private nonguaranteed	..	..	..	..	..	..	10	-2
Short-term	0	8	2	-10	-3	1	2	92
Non-debt resource inflows								
Foreign direct investment	..	6	74	3	7	19	26	10
Portfolio equity	..	..	..	..	..	..	..	..
Currency composition (%)								
Euro	..	9.6	11.1	11.6	11.5	10.1	8.9	7.2
U.S.dollars	17.7	18.2	19.0	22.9	24.0	22.3	23.4	17.9
Major economic aggregates								
Gross national income (GNI)	439	807	1,180	1,222	1,219	1,497	1,729	1,675
Exports of goods, services & prim. income	..	..	658	686	591	625	761	711
Personal transfers & comp. of employees	..	..	3	4	5	8	10	18
Imports of goods, services & prim. income	..	..	608	832	731	1,006	1,395	1,304
Primary income on FDI	..	..	1	3	-1	4	4	0
Current account balance	..	..	145	-28	-14	-142	-410	-350
International reserves	318	467	699	765	891	1,002	790	955
Ratios								
External debt stocks to exports (%)	..	..	122.0	101.2	128.7	145.2	137.8	205.2
External debt stocks to GNI (%)	48.2	81.5	68.0	56.8	62.4	60.6	60.6	87.1
Debt service to exports (%)	..	..	4.9	11.9	12.8	13.5	10.8	17.8
Short-term to external debt stocks (%)	0.7	1.9	2.2	1.2	0.7	0.7	0.8	6.9
Multilateral to external debt stocks (%)	47.6	26.9	27.9	34.3	37.6	36.5	36.7	29.8
Reserves to external debt stocks (%)	150.1	71.1	87.1	110.1	117.0	110.4	75.3	65.4
Reserves to imports (months)	..	..	13.8	11.0	14.6	12.0	6.8	8.8

Notes:

Short-term debt is based on data from the BIS.

BOLIVIA, PLURINATIONAL STATE OF

(US$ million, unless otherwise indicated)

	2000	2005	2007	2008	2009	2010	2011	2012
Summary external debt data								
External debt stocks	**5,885**	**6,961**	**5,421**	**5,936**	**6,021**	**6,050**	**6,474**	**6,909**
Long-term external debt	5,228	6,497	4,823	5,377	5,196	5,170	5,587	5,937
Short-term external debt	402	182	555	518	568	628	635	720
interest arrears on long-term	2	0	0	0	0	0	0	0
Use of IMF credit	255	282	42	41	257	253	252	252
Long-term external debt								
Debt outstanding and disbursed	**5,228**	**6,497**	**4,823**	**5,377**	**5,196**	**5,170**	**5,587**	**5,937**
Public and publicly guaranteed	4,201	4,583	2,202	2,409	2,549	2,812	3,414	4,142
Official creditors	4,168	4,556	2,166	2,312	2,457	2,788	3,325	3,622
Private creditors	33	27	36	97	92	24	89	520
Private nonguaranteed	1,026	1,914	2,621	2,969	2,647	2,358	2,173	1,795
Disbursements	**745**	**880**	**912**	**1,263**	**512**	**552**	**776**	**1,250**
Public and publicly guaranteed	277	434	319	590	415	522	776	1,250
Official creditors	264	429	308	524	408	519	709	683
Private creditors	13	4	10	67	7	3	67	567
Private nonguaranteed	468	447	593	673	97	30	0	0
Principal repayments	**438**	**316**	**525**	**767**	**454**	**568**	**358**	**548**
Public and publicly guaranteed	157	185	166	376	197	247	173	402
Official creditors	153	183	162	371	184	177	171	400
Private creditors	4	2	4	5	13	70	2	2
Private nonguaranteed	281	131	360	392	257	322	185	146
Interest payments	**160**	**159**	**194**	**175**	**119**	**76**	**78**	**80**
Public and publicly guaranteed	113	100	103	98	71	54	57	65
Official creditors	112	100	103	98	67	50	54	65
Private creditors	1	0	0	1	4	4	4	0
Private nonguaranteed	47	59	91	77	48	22	20	14
Debt resource inflows								
Net debt inflows	291	448	707	459	108	44	425	787
Official creditors (incl. IMF)	105	220	132	153	224	342	538	283
Private creditors	186	227	575	306	-116	-299	-113	504
Long-term	196	318	240	343	-166	-359	-120	419
Public and publicly guaranteed	9	2	6	62	-6	-67	65	564
Private nonguaranteed	187	316	233	281	-161	-292	-185	-146
Short-term	-10	-91	335	-37	50	60	7	85
Non-debt resource inflows								
Foreign direct investment	736	-239	366	512	423	622	859	1,060
Portfolio equity	..	..	..	..	..	..	..	..
Currency composition (%)								
Euro	..	1.5	4.2	3.6	3.1	2.7	2.2	1.8
U.S.dollars	44.3	75.1	76.2	79.4	81.8	84.6	86.7	89.1
Major economic aggregates								
Gross national income (GNI)	8,172	9,173	12,631	16,138	16,666	18,786	22,788	25,406
Exports of goods, services & prim. income	1,610	3,401	5,325	7,369	5,663	6,919	9,260	12,332
Personal transfers & comp. of employees	127	337	1,055	1,135	1,058	960	1,043	1,111
Imports of goods, services & prim. income	2,443	3,362	4,999	6,661	6,062	7,126	9,900	11,460
Primary income on FDI	148	271	644	681	769	863	977	1,649
Current account balance	-446	622	1,591	1,993	814	874	537	2,138
International reserves	926	1,328	4,554	6,927	7,584	8,134	9,911	11,659
Ratios								
External debt stocks to exports (%)	365.6	204.7	101.8	80.6	106.3	87.4	69.9	56.0
External debt stocks to GNI (%)	72.0	75.9	42.9	36.8	36.1	32.2	28.4	27.2
Debt service to exports (%)	39.8	15.7	14.1	13.0	10.5	9.6	4.9	5.3
Short-term to external debt stocks (%)	6.8	2.6	10.2	8.7	9.4	10.4	9.8	10.4
Multilateral to external debt stocks (%)	48.7	60.6	31.3	30.5	32.8	37.4	40.1	43.6
Reserves to external debt stocks (%)	15.7	19.1	84.0	116.7	126.0	134.4	153.1	168.7
Reserves to imports (months)	4.6	4.7	10.9	12.5	15.0	13.7	12.0	12.2

Notes:

Data include the effects of HIPC and MDRI debt relief.

BOSNIA AND HERZEGOVINA

(US$ million, unless otherwise indicated)

	2000	2005	2007	2008	2009	2010	2011	2012
Summary external debt data								
External debt stocks	**2,800**	**6,378**	**9,250**	**9,815**	**11,328**	**9,935**	**10,165**	**10,577**
Long-term external debt	2,619	5,326	7,528	8,876	9,111	8,128	8,091	8,427
Short-term external debt	49	960	1,687	907	1,678	1,038	1,308	1,262
interest arrears on long-term	1	0	0	0	0	0	0	0
Use of IMF credit	131	91	35	32	539	769	766	888
Long-term external debt								
Debt outstanding and disbursed	**2,619**	**5,326**	**7,528**	**8,876**	**9,111**	**8,128**	**8,091**	**8,427**
Public and publicly guaranteed	1,957	2,559	2,967	3,008	3,570	3,733	3,874	4,202
Official creditors	1,832	2,404	2,772	2,808	3,042	3,267	3,451	3,798
Private creditors	125	155	195	200	527	466	423	404
Private nonguaranteed	663	2,767	4,561	5,868	5,541	4,395	4,216	4,225
Disbursements	**103**	**540**	**1,023**	**471**	**394**	**510**	**491**	**526**
Public and publicly guaranteed	98	153	150	189	321	441	382	449
Official creditors	98	153	138	163	309	427	370	432
Private creditors	0	0	12	26	12	14	12	17
Private nonguaranteed	5	386	873	282	73	69	108	77
Principal repayments	**170**	**95**	**109**	**137**	**171**	**537**	**594**	**758**
Public and publicly guaranteed	170	54	79	91	110	145	171	167
Official creditors	170	51	72	82	97	108	129	124
Private creditors	0	3	7	9	13	37	43	43
Private nonguaranteed	1	41	30	46	61	392	423	591
Interest payments	**119**	**136**	**217**	**257**	**217**	**177**	**186**	**183**
Public and publicly guaranteed	89	53	70	80	63	55	66	65
Official creditors	86	48	63	70	56	47	55	56
Private creditors	2	6	6	10	8	9	11	9
Private nonguaranteed	30	83	147	176	153	121	120	118
Debt resource inflows								
Net debt inflows	-41	1,052	1,411	-448	1,276	-429	166	-158
Official creditors (incl. IMF)	-56	63	47	79	494	556	241	428
Private creditors	15	989	1,364	-526	782	-985	-75	-586
Long-term	4	342	848	254	11	-345	-345	-540
Public and publicly guaranteed	..	-3	5	17	-1	-23	-30	-26
Private nonguaranteed	4	346	843	236	12	-322	-315	-514
Short-term	11	647	516	-780	771	-640	270	-46
Non-debt resource inflows								
Foreign direct investment	146	624	1,804	1,005	139	444	469	350
Portfolio equity	..	..	..	..	..	..	..	..
Currency composition (%)								
Euro	..	34.0	38.2	39.1	48.8	50.8	53.0	57.5
U.S.dollars	27.6	41.2	40.0	39.0	32.8	30.9	29.4	26.7
Major economic aggregates								
Gross national income (GNI)	6,096	11,416	15,740	19,213	17,661	17,054	18,470	17,323
Exports of goods, services & prim. income	2,247	4,227	5,181	6,190	5,189	5,492	6,386	5,783
Personal transfers & comp. of employees	1,607	2,038	2,686	2,718	2,127	1,822	1,958	1,849
Imports of goods, services & prim. income	4,234	8,103	9,336	11,706	8,704	8,910	10,681	9,775
Primary income on FDI	..	97	345	187	-104	79	272	205
Current account balance	-396	-1,844	-1,412	-2,640	-1,136	-1,029	-1,803	-1,633
International reserves	497	2,548	5,042	4,480	4,529	4,366	4,150	4,283
Ratios								
External debt stocks to exports (%)	124.6	150.9	178.5	158.6	218.3	180.9	159.2	182.9
External debt stocks to GNI (%)	45.9	55.9	58.8	51.1	64.1	58.3	55.0	61.1
Debt service to exports (%)	14.2	7.3	8.3	7.7	9.1	14.6	13.6	18.4
Short-term to external debt stocks (%)	1.8	15.1	18.2	9.2	14.8	10.4	12.9	11.9
Multilateral to external debt stocks (%)	45.2	26.8	21.0	20.2	19.4	24.3	25.1	27.2
Reserves to external debt stocks (%)	17.7	39.9	54.5	45.6	40.0	43.9	40.8	40.5
Reserves to imports (months)	1.4	3.8	6.5	4.6	6.2	5.9	4.7	5.3

Notes:

Long-term private nonguaranteed debt data from 2005 are World Bank staff estimates. Short-term debt is based on data from the BIS.

BOTSWANA

(US$ million, unless otherwise indicated)

	2000	2005	2007	2008	2009	2010	2011	2012
Summary external debt data								
External debt stocks	**458**	**454**	**420**	**440**	**1,707**	**1,797**	**2,396**	**2,488**
Long-term external debt	438	412	391	391	1,388	1,352	1,897	2,015
Short-term external debt	15	35	22	43	229	357	411	385
interest arrears on long-term	0	0	0	0	0	0	0	0
Use of IMF credit	6	6	7	7	90	88	88	88
Long-term external debt								
Debt outstanding and disbursed	**438**	**412**	**391**	**391**	**1,388**	**1,352**	**1,897**	**2,015**
Public and publicly guaranteed	438	412	391	391	1,388	1,352	1,897	2,015
Official creditors	410	401	384	389	1,387	1,351	1,896	1,935
Private creditors	28	12	7	2	2	1	1	80
Private nonguaranteed	..	..	..	..	..	..	..	..
Disbursements	**28**	**11**	**50**	**54**	**1,006**	**17**	**595**	**149**
Public and publicly guaranteed	28	11	50	54	1,006	17	595	149
Official creditors	24	11	50	54	1,006	17	595	69
Private creditors	4	0	0	0	0	0	0	80
Private nonguaranteed	..	..	..	..	..	..	..	..
Principal repayments	**52**	**40**	**37**	**61**	**36**	**56**	**51**	**28**
Public and publicly guaranteed	52	40	37	61	36	56	51	28
Official creditors	45	38	35	56	35	55	51	27
Private creditors	7	2	2	5	1	1	0	1
Private nonguaranteed	..	..	..	..	..	..	..	..
Interest payments	**15**	**12**	**9**	**7**	**9**	**16**	**16**	**20**
Public and publicly guaranteed	15	12	9	7	9	16	16	20
Official creditors	14	11	9	7	9	16	16	20
Private creditors	1	0	0	0	0	0	0	0
Private nonguaranteed	..	..	..	..	..	..	..	..
Debt resource inflows								
Net debt inflows	-29	-17	11	15	1,156	89	598	94
Official creditors (incl. IMF)	-21	-27	16	-1	971	-38	544	42
Private creditors	-8	11	-4	16	186	128	54	53
Long-term	-3	-2	-2	-5	-1	-1	0	79
Public and publicly guaranteed	-3	-2	-2	-5	-1	-1	0	79
Private nonguaranteed	..	..	..	..	..	..	..	..
Short-term	-5	13	-2	21	186	128	54	-26
Non-debt resource inflows								
Foreign direct investment	57	279	495	521	129	-6	414	293
Portfolio equity	-6	27	9	-37	18	11	-17	-9
Currency composition (%)								
Euro	..	6.9	8.0	7.2	2.0	0.3	0.2	0.2
U.S.dollars	18.0	20.5	18.3	24.9	7.7	8.1	8.1	13.3
Major economic aggregates								
Gross national income (GNI)	5,280	9,420	10,201	10,481	10,077	13,690	15,811	14,020
Exports of goods, services & prim. income	3,378	5,739	6,536	5,475	3,989	5,172	7,198	6,574
Personal transfers & comp. of employees	26	118	92	47	15	22	20	16
Imports of goods, services & prim. income	3,050	4,737	5,995	6,637	5,549	6,533	7,931	9,045
Primary income on FDI	658	1,066	1,075	1,045	207	204	-125	428
Current account balance	545	1,634	1,654	54	-708	-192	359	-795
International reserves	6,318	6,309	9,790	9,119	8,704	7,885	8,082	7,628
Ratios								
External debt stocks to exports (%)	13.6	7.9	6.4	8.0	42.8	34.7	33.3	37.8
External debt stocks to GNI (%)	8.7	4.8	4.1	4.2	16.9	13.1	15.2	17.7
Debt service to exports (%)	2.0	0.9	0.7	1.3	1.2	1.5	1.0	0.8
Short-term to external debt stocks (%)	3.3	7.7	5.2	9.8	13.4	19.9	17.2	15.5
Multilateral to external debt stocks (%)	64.9	57.8	57.2	56.2	73.3	68.0	74.9	74.3
Reserves to external debt stocks (%)	1,378.2	1,391.1	2,331.0	2,070.1	509.8	438.8	337.3	306.6
Reserves to imports (months)	24.9	16.0	19.6	16.5	18.8	14.5	12.2	10.1

Notes:

Short-term debt is based on data from the BIS.

BRAZIL

(US$ million, unless otherwise indicated)

	2000	2005	2007	2008	2009	2010	2011	2012
Summary external debt data								
External debt stocks	**242,512**	**188,365**	**238,444**	**262,951**	**281,648**	**352,364**	**404,046**	**440,478**
Long-term external debt	209,303	163,859	198,632	225,755	237,336	282,425	357,473	403,458
Short-term external debt	30,973	23,993	39,246	36,644	39,786	65,492	42,140	32,583
interest arrears on long-term	176	0	0	0	0	0	0	0
Use of IMF credit	2,235	513	567	552	4,526	4,446	4,432	4,437
Long-term external debt								
Debt outstanding and disbursed	**209,303**	**163,859**	**198,632**	**225,755**	**237,336**	**282,425**	**357,473**	**403,458**
Public and publicly guaranteed	96,622	94,354	79,870	79,912	87,510	97,485	94,712	116,628
Official creditors	29,845	26,160	26,406	29,269	32,595	41,460	36,516	38,959
Private creditors	66,776	68,194	53,464	50,643	54,916	56,025	58,195	77,669
Private nonguaranteed	112,682	69,505	118,762	145,842	149,826	184,940	262,761	286,830
Disbursements	**44,079**	**27,414**	**59,915**	**69,559**	**57,675**	**85,379**	**111,458**	**79,610**
Public and publicly guaranteed	19,664	13,207	6,285	16,696	13,732	19,957	13,655	27,958
Official creditors	5,272	3,327	2,065	4,353	6,845	11,317	3,250	4,985
Private creditors	14,391	9,880	4,220	12,342	6,887	8,640	10,405	22,973
Private nonguaranteed	24,415	14,207	53,630	52,863	43,943	65,422	97,803	51,652
Principal repayments	**34,746**	**25,788**	**40,466**	**40,353**	**30,470**	**32,024**	**41,777**	**30,597**
Public and publicly guaranteed	10,932	9,481	14,124	16,351	7,784	9,626	15,851	6,696
Official creditors	7,093	3,334	2,294	2,402	3,447	2,662	8,349	2,316
Private creditors	3,839	6,147	11,829	13,949	4,338	6,965	7,502	4,379
Private nonguaranteed	23,813	16,306	26,343	24,002	22,685	22,398	25,925	23,901
Interest payments	**15,297**	**10,314**	**13,034**	**15,046**	**13,554**	**13,157**	**16,615**	**14,259**
Public and publicly guaranteed	6,943	6,700	7,078	6,057	5,656	5,172	5,446	5,019
Official creditors	1,932	1,058	1,361	1,291	1,083	967	1,012	962
Private creditors	5,010	5,642	5,717	4,766	4,573	4,205	4,434	4,057
Private nonguaranteed	8,355	3,614	5,956	8,989	7,898	7,985	11,169	9,240
Debt resource inflows								
Net debt inflows	4,471	-23,457	38,372	26,604	30,347	79,061	46,329	39,456
Official creditors (incl. IMF)	-8,514	-23,817	-230	1,951	3,399	8,655	-5,099	2,668
Private creditors	12,985	360	38,602	24,653	26,948	70,406	51,428	36,787
Long-term	11,154	1,634	19,679	27,255	23,806	44,699	74,780	46,345
Public and publicly guaranteed	10,552	3,733	-7,609	-1,606	2,549	1,675	2,902	18,594
Private nonguaranteed	602	-2,099	27,288	28,861	21,257	43,024	71,878	27,750
Short-term	1,831	-1,274	18,923	-2,602	3,142	25,706	-23,352	-9,557
Non-debt resource inflows								
Foreign direct investment	32,779	15,460	44,579	50,716	31,481	53,345	71,539	76,111
Portfolio equity	3,076	6,451	26,217	-7,565	37,071	37,671	7,174	5,600
Currency composition (%)								
Euro	..	9.4	9.8	9.0	7.2	6.1	4.3	5.1
U.S.dollars	70.0	79.1	80.5	80.3	84.0	85.2	88.2	87.5
Major economic aggregates								
Gross national income (GNI)	626,889	856,883	1,338,704	1,614,398	1,588,117	2,104,366	2,429,947	2,217,452
Exports of goods, services & prim. income	68,205	136,200	196,096	240,904	189,564	240,920	305,002	293,331
Personal transfers & comp. of employees	1,649	2,805	3,306	3,643	2,889	2,754	2,798	2,583
Imports of goods, services & prim. income	93,950	125,773	198,574	273,320	217,207	291,094	360,466	350,424
Primary income on FDI	4,238	11,035	19,692	28,773	21,029	26,584	31,716	24,564
Current account balance	-24,225	13,985	1,551	-28,192	-24,306	-47,273	-52,480	-54,246
International reserves	32,434	53,245	179,433	192,844	237,364	287,056	350,356	369,566
Ratios								
External debt stocks to exports (%)	355.6	138.3	121.6	109.2	148.6	146.3	132.5	150.2
External debt stocks to GNI (%)	38.7	22.0	17.8	16.3	17.7	16.7	16.6	19.9
Debt service to exports (%)	85.9	46.2	28.1	23.5	23.5	19.0	19.4	15.5
Short-term to external debt stocks (%)	12.8	12.7	16.5	13.9	14.1	18.6	10.4	7.4
Multilateral to external debt stocks (%)	7.8	10.4	9.6	9.4	8.9	8.5	6.2	6.3
Reserves to external debt stocks (%)	13.4	28.3	75.3	73.3	84.3	81.5	86.7	83.9
Reserves to imports (months)	4.1	5.1	10.8	8.5	13.1	11.8	11.7	12.7

BULGARIA

(US$ million, unless otherwise indicated)

	2000	2005	2007	2008	2009	2010	2011	2012
Summary external debt data								
External debt stocks	**12,009**	**16,573**	**33,958**	**49,544**	**54,456**	**49,018**	**47,235**	**50,750**
Long-term external debt	8,440	10,597	18,957	30,269	34,921	32,704	33,391	36,050
Short-term external debt	1,451	4,442	14,036	18,334	18,578	15,373	12,907	13,761
interest arrears on long-term	1	0	0	0	0	0	0	0
Use of IMF credit	2,118	1,533	965	941	958	941	938	939
Long-term external debt								
Debt outstanding and disbursed	**8,440**	**10,597**	**18,957**	**30,269**	**34,921**	**32,704**	**33,391**	**36,050**
Public and publicly guaranteed	7,671	5,075	5,268	4,397	4,772	4,466	4,138	5,210
Official creditors	2,603	3,045	3,362	3,019	3,322	3,152	3,141	3,096
Private creditors	5,068	2,030	1,906	1,378	1,450	1,314	997	2,114
Private nonguaranteed	769	5,522	13,689	25,871	30,148	28,238	29,253	30,840
Disbursements	**719**	**3,710**	**7,740**	**15,545**	**8,191**	**1,499**	**10,804**	**5,987**
Public and publicly guaranteed	405	402	368	370	520	200	292	1,439
Official creditors	381	383	361	362	520	200	292	229
Private creditors	24	19	7	8	0	0	0	1,211
Private nonguaranteed	313	3,308	7,372	15,175	7,671	1,299	10,511	4,547
Principal repayments	**573**	**2,909**	**2,686**	**3,641**	**3,817**	**3,381**	**3,597**	**3,715**
Public and publicly guaranteed	345	1,761	404	733	404	268	258	263
Official creditors	297	255	299	715	266	261	251	263
Private creditors	48	1,507	105	19	138	7	7	0
Private nonguaranteed	229	1,147	2,282	2,908	3,413	3,113	3,338	3,452
Interest payments	**456**	**445**	**618**	**864**	**770**	**586**	**785**	**749**
Public and publicly guaranteed	424	327	300	292	208	177	188	161
Official creditors	139	93	129	148	106	71	83	82
Private creditors	285	234	171	144	102	106	105	79
Private nonguaranteed	32	118	318	572	562	408	598	587
Debt resource inflows								
Net debt inflows	465	1,564	10,704	16,202	4,617	-5,087	4,741	3,126
Official creditors (incl. IMF)	221	-315	-285	-352	254	-61	41	-34
Private creditors	244	1,879	10,989	16,554	4,363	-5,025	4,700	3,160
Long-term	61	673	4,992	12,257	4,119	-1,820	7,166	2,306
Public and publicly guaranteed	-24	-1,488	-98	-11	-138	-7	-7	1,211
Private nonguaranteed	85	2,161	5,090	12,267	4,258	-1,813	7,173	1,095
Short-term	183	1,206	5,996	4,298	244	-3,205	-2,466	855
Non-debt resource inflows								
Foreign direct investment	1,002	4,098	13,875	10,297	3,897	1,867	2,124	2,095
Portfolio equity	5	449	89	-106	8	9	-42	5
Currency composition (%)								
Euro	..	48.4	51.7	51.7	56.8	56.1	58.5	72.0
U.S.dollars	80.1	44.9	40.0	34.6	30.4	29.2	26.2	18.0
Major economic aggregates								
Gross national income (GNI)	12,580	28,979	38,878	49,257	46,903	46,226	51,024	49,304
Exports of goods, services & prim. income	7,321	17,674	27,487	31,897	24,384	27,944	36,606	34,905
Personal transfers & comp. of employees	58	1,613	1,694	1,919	1,592	1,333	1,483	1,449
Imports of goods, services & prim. income	8,314	22,034	39,909	45,096	29,966	30,711	38,836	38,311
Primary income on FDI	107	912	3,742	2,725	1,823	1,573	2,521	2,054
Current account balance	-703	-3,347	-11,437	-11,875	-4,256	-796	133	-735
International reserves	3,155	8,041	16,478	16,816	17,127	15,421	15,252	18,371
Ratios								
External debt stocks to exports (%)	164.0	93.8	123.5	155.3	223.3	175.4	129.0	145.4
External debt stocks to GNI (%)	95.5	57.2	87.3	100.6	116.1	106.0	92.6	102.9
Debt service to exports (%)	18.2	22.6	15.4	16.5	21.9	14.4	12.2	13.0
Short-term to external debt stocks (%)	12.1	26.8	41.3	37.0	34.1	31.4	27.3	27.1
Multilateral to external debt stocks (%)	12.8	14.8	7.9	4.4	4.6	4.8	5.0	4.8
Reserves to external debt stocks (%)	26.3	48.5	48.5	33.9	31.5	31.5	32.3	36.2
Reserves to imports (months)	4.6	4.4	5.0	4.5	6.9	6.0	4.7	5.8

Notes:

Long-term private nonguaranteed debt data from 2008 are World Bank staff estimates based on reports provided by the country. The data may include long-term public and publicly guaranteed debt owed by the state-owned railway. Short-term debt is based on Central Bank data.

BURKINA FASO

(US$ million, unless otherwise indicated)

	2000	2005	2007	2008	2009	2010	2011	2012
Summary external debt data								
External debt stocks	**1,435**	**2,000**	**1,465**	**1,685**	**1,917**	**2,173**	**2,414**	**2,506**
Long-term external debt	1,226	1,861	1,258	1,506	1,716	1,931	2,050	2,205
Short-term external debt	84	22	155	110	0	25	131	0
interest arrears on long-term	5	0	0	0	0	0	0	0
Use of IMF credit	124	117	52	69	201	217	233	301
Long-term external debt								
Debt outstanding and disbursed	**1,226**	**1,861**	**1,258**	**1,506**	**1,716**	**1,931**	**2,050**	**2,205**
Public and publicly guaranteed	1,226	1,861	1,258	1,506	1,716	1,931	2,050	2,205
Official creditors	1,223	1,861	1,232	1,484	1,694	1,913	2,035	2,192
Private creditors	3	0	26	22	22	18	15	13
Private nonguaranteed	..	..	..	..	..	..	..	..
Disbursements	**91**	**208**	**231**	**293**	**217**	**276**	**162**	**154**
Public and publicly guaranteed	91	208	231	293	217	276	162	154
Official creditors	91	208	217	293	217	276	162	154
Private creditors	0	0	14	0	0	0	0	0
Private nonguaranteed	..	..	..	..	..	..	..	..
Principal repayments	**26**	**24**	**25**	**27**	**28**	**30**	**43**	**43**
Public and publicly guaranteed	26	24	25	27	28	30	43	43
Official creditors	26	24	22	24	28	27	40	41
Private creditors	0	0	3	3	0	2	3	2
Private nonguaranteed	..	..	..	..	..	..	..	..
Interest payments	**12**	**16**	**12**	**14**	**15**	**18**	**21**	**21**
Public and publicly guaranteed	12	16	12	14	15	18	21	21
Official creditors	12	16	12	14	15	18	21	21
Private creditors	0	0	0	0	0	0	0	0
Private nonguaranteed	..	..	..	..	..	..	..	..
Debt resource inflows								
Net debt inflows	47	194	273	239	134	291	242	48
Official creditors (incl. IMF)	66	196	196	287	244	269	139	181
Private creditors	-19	-2	77	-48	-110	23	103	-133
Long-term	0	0	11	-3	0	-2	-3	-2
Public and publicly guaranteed	0	0	11	-3	0	-2	-3	-2
Private nonguaranteed	..	..	..	..	..	..	..	..
Short-term	-19	-2	66	-45	-110	25	106	-131
Non-debt resource inflows								
Foreign direct investment	23	52	22	33	56	39	42	40
Portfolio equity	-3	-4	-1	-2	0	3	..	..
Currency composition (%)								
Euro	..	1.5	6.4	12.7	12.4	12.0	11.9	11.8
U.S.dollars	59.4	56.9	40.0	36.8	36.0	34.0	32.8	31.5
Major economic aggregates								
Gross national income (GNI)	2,606	5,442	6,754	8,348	8,343	9,203	10,392	10,454
Exports of goods, services & prim. income	251	583	804	1,069	1,140	1,981	..	..
Personal transfers & comp. of employees	67	57	84	99	96	120	..	..
Imports of goods, services & prim. income	691	1,452	1,767	2,442	2,035	2,655	..	..
Primary income on FDI	3	7	11	38	35	26	..	..
Current account balance	-319	-634	-560	-963	-380	-181	..	..
International reserves	243	438	1,029	928	1,296	1,068	957	1,025
Ratios								
External debt stocks to exports (%)	572.8	343.0	182.3	157.6	168.1	109.7	..	..
External debt stocks to GNI (%)	55.1	36.8	21.7	20.2	23.0	23.6	23.2	24.0
Debt service to exports (%)	18.8	7.8	5.2	4.2	3.8	2.5	..	..
Short-term to external debt stocks (%)	5.9	1.1	10.6	6.5	..	1.2	5.4	..
Multilateral to external debt stocks (%)	71.4	84.6	66.9	71.1	73.2	74.1	72.1	75.7
Reserves to external debt stocks (%)	16.9	21.9	70.2	55.1	67.6	49.1	39.6	40.9
Reserves to imports (months)	4.2	3.6	7.0	4.6	7.6	4.8	..	..

Notes:

Short-term debt is based on data from the BIS. Data include HIPC and MDRI debt relief.

BURUNDI

(US$ million, unless otherwise indicated)

	2000	2005	2007	2008	2009	2010	2011	2012
Summary external debt data								
External debt stocks	**1,125.9**	**1,287.9**	**1,409.7**	**1,390.3**	**602.2**	**615.8**	**599.1**	**662.7**
Long-term external debt	1,036.0	1,176.1	1,276.1	1,234.3	388.5	376.8	358.2	407.0
Short-term external debt	65.0	34.1	13.8	18.0	7.0	15.6	0.1	7.0
interest arrears on long-term	19.7	33.1	12.8	4.0	0.0	0.6	0.1	0.0
Use of IMF credit	24.9	77.7	119.9	138.0	206.7	223.4	240.7	248.7
Long-term external debt								
Debt outstanding and disbursed	**1,036.0**	**1,176.1**	**1,276.1**	**1,234.3**	**388.5**	**376.8**	**358.2**	**407.0**
Public and publicly guaranteed	1,036.0	1,176.1	1,276.1	1,234.3	388.5	376.8	358.2	407.0
Official creditors	1,032.0	1,174.0	1,275.4	1,234.3	388.5	376.8	358.2	407.0
Private creditors	4.0	2.1	0.7	0.0	0.0	0.0	0.0	0.0
Private nonguaranteed	..	..	..	..	..	..	..	..
Disbursements	**41.3**	**42.1**	**31.3**	**24.8**	**24.3**	**31.6**	**28.0**	**60.2**
Public and publicly guaranteed	41.3	42.1	31.3	24.8	24.3	31.6	28.0	60.2
Official creditors	38.2	42.1	31.3	24.8	24.3	31.6	28.0	60.2
Private creditors	3.0	0.0	0.0	0.0	0.0	0.0	0.0	0.0
Private nonguaranteed	..	..	..	..	..	..	..	..
Principal repayments	**9.4**	**27.2**	**11.3**	**11.3**	**8.5**	**2.4**	**5.8**	**9.6**
Public and publicly guaranteed	9.4	27.2	11.3	11.3	8.5	2.4	5.8	9.6
Official creditors	9.4	22.6	11.3	11.3	8.5	2.4	5.8	9.6
Private creditors	0.0	4.6	0.0	0.0	0.0	0.0	0.0	0.0
Private nonguaranteed	..	..	..	..	..	..	..	..
Interest payments	**4.5**	**11.9**	**5.7**	**7.4**	**3.6**	**1.4**	**2.0**	**3.0**
Public and publicly guaranteed	4.5	11.9	5.7	7.4	3.6	1.4	2.0	3.0
Official creditors	4.5	11.9	5.7	7.4	3.6	1.4	2.0	3.0
Private creditors	0.0	0.0	0.0	0.0	0.0	0.0	0.0	0.0
Private nonguaranteed	..	..	..	..	..	..	..	..
Debt resource inflows								
Net debt inflows	18.4	34.1	30.9	48.3	22.2	57.3	25.8	65.2
Official creditors (incl. IMF)	24.3	40.7	30.9	35.3	29.2	49.3	40.8	58.2
Private creditors	-5.9	-6.6	0.0	13.0	-7.0	8.0	-15.0	7.0
Long-term	3.0	-4.6	0.0	0.0	0.0	0.0	0.0	0.0
Public and publicly guaranteed	3.0	-4.6	0.0	0.0	0.0	0.0	0.0	0.0
Private nonguaranteed	..	..	..	..	..	..	..	..
Short-term	-8.9	-2.0	..	13.0	-7.0	8.0	-15.0	7.0
Non-debt resource inflows								
Foreign direct investment	11.7	0.6	0.5	3.8	0.3	0.8	3.4	0.6
Portfolio equity	..	..	..	..	..	..	..	..
Currency composition (%)								
Euro	..	7.6	8.0	6.0	18.2	10.1	0.3	..
U.S.dollars	59.4	64.6	63.5	63.4	35.0	37.0	42.9	46.2
Major economic aggregates								
Gross national income (GNI)	882.6	1,135.0	1,336.0	1,603.3	1,721.4	2,015.0	2,336.5	2,455.6
Exports of goods, services & prim. income	55.4	98.7	98.3	163.9	119.7	181.9	243.1	239.0
Personal transfers & comp. of employees	..	0.1	0.2	3.6	28.2	34.5	45.5	46.4
Imports of goods, services & prim. income	164.9	343.9	450.8	609.4	538.0	618.7	790.3	940.6
Primary income on FDI	0.4	2.1	4.8	..	..	..	..	..
Current account balance	-50.2	-5.7	-111.3	-259.4	-161.2	-301.0	-283.6	-255.1
International reserves	32.9	100.1	176.3	265.7	322.0	330.7	294.0	307.2
Ratios								
External debt stocks to exports (%)	2031.9	1304.3	1434.1	848.5	503.0	338.6	246.4	277.3
External debt stocks to GNI (%)	127.6	113.5	105.5	86.7	35.0	30.6	25.6	27.0
Debt service to exports (%)	40.9	40.5	18.5	12.0	16.6	2.4	4.2	8.5
Short-term to external debt stocks (%)	5.8	2.6	1.0	1.3	1.2	2.5	0.0	1.1
Multilateral to external debt stocks (%)	79.1	81.9	82.8	82.4	50.4	52.8	51.5	50.8
Reserves to external debt stocks (%)	2.9	7.8	12.5	19.1	53.5	53.7	49.1	46.4
Reserves to imports (months)	2.4	3.5	4.7	5.2	7.2	6.4	4.5	3.9

Notes:

Short-term debt is based on data from the BIS. Data include the effects of Paris Club debt restructuring agreement and HIPC and MDRI debt relief.

CAMBODIA

(US$ million, unless otherwise indicated)

	2000	2005	2007	2008	2009	2010	2011	2012
Summary external debt data								
External debt stocks	**2,648**	**3,538**	**2,815**	**3,269**	**3,530**	**3,852**	**4,430**	**5,716**
Long-term external debt	2,328	3,155	2,565	2,920	3,127	3,442	3,815	4,549
Short-term external debt	227	280	226	325	272	281	486	1,038
interest arrears on long-term	131	243	164	197	208	215	221	209
Use of IMF credit	93	103	24	24	132	129	129	129
Long-term external debt								
Debt outstanding and disbursed	**2,328**	**3,155**	**2,565**	**2,920**	**3,127**	**3,442**	**3,815**	**4,549**
Public and publicly guaranteed	2,328	3,155	2,565	2,920	3,127	3,442	3,815	4,549
Official creditors	2,328	3,155	2,565	2,920	3,127	3,442	3,815	4,549
Private creditors	0	0	0	0	0	0	0	0
Private nonguaranteed	..	..	..	..	..	..	..	..
Disbursements	**79**	**168**	**154**	**383**	**211**	**347**	**404**	**779**
Public and publicly guaranteed	79	168	154	383	211	347	404	779
Official creditors	79	168	154	383	211	347	404	779
Private creditors	0	0	0	0	0	0	0	0
Private nonguaranteed	..	..	..	..	..	..	..	..
Principal repayments	**7**	**8**	**13**	**19**	**26**	**33**	**41**	**47**
Public and publicly guaranteed	7	8	13	19	26	33	41	47
Official creditors	7	8	13	19	26	33	41	47
Private creditors	0	0	0	0	0	0	0	0
Private nonguaranteed	..	..	..	..	..	..	..	..
Interest payments	**12**	**12**	**15**	**21**	**22**	**28**	**34**	**44**
Public and publicly guaranteed	12	12	15	21	22	28	34	44
Official creditors	12	12	15	21	22	28	34	44
Private creditors	0	0	0	0	0	0	0	0
Private nonguaranteed	..	..	..	..	..	..	..	..
Debt resource inflows								
Net debt inflows	128	155	171	430	121	315	562	1,296
Official creditors (incl. IMF)	76	152	141	364	185	313	363	732
Private creditors	52	3	30	66	-64	2	199	564
Long-term	0	0	0	0	0	0	0	0
Public and publicly guaranteed	0	0	0	0	0	0	0	0
Private nonguaranteed	..	..	..	..	..	..	..	..
Short-term	52	3	30	66	-64	2	199	564
Non-debt resource inflows								
Foreign direct investment	149	379	867	815	539	783	902	1,557
Portfolio equity	..	..	..	..	..	..	..	..
Currency composition (%)								
Euro	..	0.8	1.2	1.1	1.2	1.1	1.0	0.8
U.S.dollars	36.9	48.5	86.2	84.8	84.2	82.2	77.9	76.3
Major economic aggregates								
Gross national income (GNI)	3,534	6,006	8,263	9,844	9,918	10,711	12,108	13,327
Exports of goods, services & prim. income	1,893	4,094	4,793	5,129	4,576	5,612	7,493	8,629
Personal transfers & comp. of employees	121	164	186	188	142	153	160	256
Imports of goods, services & prim. income	2,453	4,921	5,809	6,560	5,932	7,026	8,789	10,320
Primary income on FDI	123	227	353	403	358	399	586	707
Current account balance	-136	-307	-423	-820	-785	-772	-712	-1,208
International reserves	502	953	1,807	2,292	2,851	3,255	3,450	4,267
Ratios								
External debt stocks to exports (%)	139.9	86.4	58.7	63.7	77.2	68.6	59.1	66.2
External debt stocks to GNI (%)	74.9	58.9	34.1	33.2	35.6	36.0	36.6	42.9
Debt service to exports (%)	1.7	0.8	0.7	0.9	1.1	1.2	1.2	1.5
Short-term to external debt stocks (%)	8.6	7.9	8.0	9.9	7.7	7.3	11.0	18.2
Multilateral to external debt stocks (%)	14.4	29.9	46.1	43.5	42.5	39.7	35.8	28.5
Reserves to external debt stocks (%)	18.9	26.9	64.2	70.1	80.8	84.5	77.9	74.7
Reserves to imports (months)	2.5	2.3	3.7	4.2	5.8	5.6	4.7	5.0

Notes:

Short-term debt is based on data from the BIS. Data include MDRI debt relief.

CAMEROON

(US$ million, unless otherwise indicated)

	2000	2005	2007	2008	2009	2010	2011	2012
Summary external debt data								
External debt stocks	**10,561**	**7,700**	**3,087**	**2,827**	**3,239**	**3,195**	**3,074**	**3,672**
Long-term external debt	9,070	7,059	2,794	2,724	2,784	2,741	2,562	3,074
Short-term external debt	1,224	334	238	41	3	9	70	157
interest arrears on long-term	205	280	39	41	3	9	2	24
Use of IMF credit	267	307	55	62	453	445	442	440
Long-term external debt								
Debt outstanding and disbursed	**9,070**	**7,059**	**2,794**	**2,724**	**2,784**	**2,741**	**2,562**	**3,074**
Public and publicly guaranteed	8,753	6,467	2,158	2,089	2,168	2,164	2,101	2,706
Official creditors	8,436	6,384	2,152	2,083	2,154	2,144	2,078	2,662
Private creditors	317	83	6	6	14	20	23	45
Private nonguaranteed	317	592	636	636	615	577	461	368
Disbursements	**286**	**227**	**242**	**276**	**356**	**278**	**141**	**564**
Public and publicly guaranteed	247	130	160	189	147	278	141	564
Official creditors	247	130	160	189	139	272	137	542
Private creditors	0	0	0	0	8	6	5	22
Private nonguaranteed	39	98	82	87	209	0	0	0
Principal repayments	**253**	**537**	**366**	**352**	**334**	**154**	**233**	**174**
Public and publicly guaranteed	166	396	182	160	104	116	122	81
Official creditors	162	396	163	160	104	116	121	80
Private creditors	4	0	19	0	0	0	1	1
Private nonguaranteed	86	141	183	192	229	38	111	93
Interest payments	**215**	**228**	**114**	**91**	**57**	**42**	**86**	**60**
Public and publicly guaranteed	198	178	71	47	26	27	57	35
Official creditors	198	177	49	47	26	27	56	34
Private creditors	1	1	23	0	0	0	1	1
Private nonguaranteed	17	51	42	44	31	15	28	25
Debt resource inflows								
Net debt inflows	-21	-683	16	-267	169	124	-25	452
Official creditors (incl. IMF)	136	-301	5	37	182	156	15	460
Private creditors	-157	-382	11	-304	-12	-32	-39	-8
Long-term	-52	-44	-120	-105	-12	-32	-107	-73
Public and publicly guaranteed	-4	..	-19	0	8	6	4	20
Private nonguaranteed	-48	-44	-102	-105	-20	-38	-111	-93
Short-term	-105	-339	131	-199	..	..	68	65
Non-debt resource inflows								
Foreign direct investment	159	244	189	21	740	538	652	526
Portfolio equity	0	-4	-14	-1	0	0	0	0
Currency composition (%)								
Euro	..	68.0	73.2	66.6	64.4	54.7	50.9	42.9
U.S.dollars	23.8	19.5	12.3	14.0	13.6	18.7	18.9	21.2
Major economic aggregates								
Gross national income (GNI)	8,694	16,099	19,931	23,323	22,075	22,224	25,018	24,747
Exports of goods, services & prim. income	2,694	4,248	6,314	7,372	5,438	5,692	7,648	7,582
Personal transfers & comp. of employees	30	77	167	162	184	115	219	210
Imports of goods, services & prim. income	3,021	4,977	6,472	8,419	6,835	6,694	8,654	8,801
Primary income on FDI	41	289	385	165	436	166	282	503
Current account balance	-218	-493	286	-450	-1,119	-856	-748	-956
International reserves	212	949	2,907	3,087	3,676	3,643	3,199	3,381
Ratios								
External debt stocks to exports (%)	392.0	181.3	48.9	38.4	59.6	56.1	40.2	48.4
External debt stocks to GNI (%)	121.5	47.8	15.5	12.1	14.7	14.4	12.3	14.8
Debt service to exports (%)	20.8	19.3	7.7	6.1	7.2	3.5	4.2	3.1
Short-term to external debt stocks (%)	11.6	4.3	7.7	1.4	0.1	0.3	2.3	4.3
Multilateral to external debt stocks (%)	13.4	20.6	18.2	21.5	21.2	24.6	28.0	30.7
Reserves to external debt stocks (%)	2.0	12.3	94.2	109.2	113.5	114.0	104.0	92.1
Reserves to imports (months)	0.8	2.3	5.4	4.4	6.5	6.5	4.4	4.6

Notes:

Short-term debt is based on data from the BIS. Data include the effects of HIPC and MDRI debt relief.

CAPE VERDE

(US$ million, unless otherwise indicated)

	2000	2005	2007	2008	2009	2010	2011	2012
Summary external debt data								
External debt stocks	**320**	**477**	**581**	**626**	**727**	**892**	**1,039**	**1,261**
Long-term external debt	315	463	565	611	700	868	1,017	1,242
Short-term external debt	4	1	1	1	2	2	2	2
interest arrears on long-term	4	1	1	1	2	2	2	2
Use of IMF credit	1	13	14	13	25	23	20	18
Long-term external debt								
Debt outstanding and disbursed	**315**	**463**	**565**	**611**	**700**	**868**	**1,017**	**1,242**
Public and publicly guaranteed	315	463	565	611	700	868	1,017	1,242
Official creditors	308	442	550	601	693	816	944	1,124
Private creditors	7	22	15	10	6	53	73	118
Private nonguaranteed	..	..	..	..	..	..	..	..
Disbursements	**29**	**74**	**51**	**75**	**102**	**208**	**191**	**223**
Public and publicly guaranteed	29	74	51	75	102	208	191	223
Official creditors	29	65	51	75	102	158	165	180
Private creditors	0	9	0	0	0	50	25	43
Private nonguaranteed	..	..	..	..	..	..	..	..
Principal repayments	**11**	**29**	**23**	**24**	**25**	**26**	**26**	**20**
Public and publicly guaranteed	11	29	23	24	25	26	26	20
Official creditors	10	23	19	20	21	22	24	20
Private creditors	2	5	4	4	4	3	2	0
Private nonguaranteed	..	..	..	..	..	..	..	..
Interest payments	**5**	**7**	**6**	**7**	**7**	**8**	**10**	**13**
Public and publicly guaranteed	5	7	6	7	7	8	10	13
Official creditors	4	6	6	6	7	8	9	12
Private creditors	1	1	0	0	0	0	1	2
Private nonguaranteed	..	..	..	..	..	..	..	..
Debt resource inflows								
Net debt inflows	2	49	28	50	76	180	162	200
Official creditors (incl. IMF)	19	45	32	54	79	134	138	158
Private creditors	-18	4	-4	-4	-4	46	23	43
Long-term	-2	4	-4	-4	-4	46	23	43
Public and publicly guaranteed	-2	4	-4	-4	-4	46	23	43
Private nonguaranteed	..	..	..	..	..	..	..	..
Short-term	-16	..	..	..	..	..	..	..
Non-debt resource inflows								
Foreign direct investment	33	80	192	211	127	116	102	74
Portfolio equity	..	..	2	..	2	..	..	..
Currency composition (%)								
Euro	..	13.4	16.1	18.1	19.5	27.3	33.9	43.6
U.S.dollars	56.2	54.3	49.7	48.5	43.1	37.5	31.5	26.1
Major economic aggregates								
Gross national income (GNI)	525	938	1,300	1,515	1,557	1,586	1,846	1,858
Exports of goods, services & prim. income	151	373	593	738	590	644	796	790
Personal transfers & comp. of employees	87	137	139	155	137	131	177	167
Imports of goods, services & prim. income	344	695	1,092	1,259	1,149	1,207	1,459	1,265
Primary income on FDI	5	11	28	38	26	56	42	23
Current account balance	-58	-41	-198	-205	-247	-223	-304	-209
International reserves	28	174	364	361	398	382	339	376
Ratios								
External debt stocks to exports (%)	211.8	128.0	97.9	84.8	123.1	138.6	130.5	159.7
External debt stocks to GNI (%)	60.9	50.9	44.7	41.3	46.7	56.3	56.3	67.9
Debt service to exports (%)	10.7	9.6	5.0	4.2	5.7	5.6	4.9	4.6
Short-term to external debt stocks (%)	1.2	0.2	0.2	0.2	0.2	0.2	0.1	0.1
Multilateral to external debt stocks (%)	72.4	78.8	78.5	77.2	73.5	67.0	58.8	50.5
Reserves to external debt stocks (%)	8.8	36.4	62.8	57.7	54.8	42.8	32.6	29.8
Reserves to imports (months)	1.0	3.0	4.0	3.4	4.2	3.8	2.8	3.6

CENTRAL AFRICAN REPUBLIC

(US$ million, unless otherwise indicated)

	2000	2005	2007	2008	2009	2010	2011	2012
Summary external debt data								
External debt stocks	**872.1**	**1,033.0**	**997.4**	**990.0**	**537.6**	**614.2**	**547.3**	**551.5**
Long-term external debt	797.3	877.2	860.7	827.0	293.8	361.9	271.2	288.3
Short-term external debt	41.2	106.6	72.7	85.6	81.7	79.7	104.1	80.3
interest arrears on long-term	26.1	97.6	72.7	73.6	77.7	77.7	71.1	73.3
Use of IMF credit	33.6	49.2	64.1	77.4	162.1	172.6	172.0	182.9
Long-term external debt								
Debt outstanding and disbursed	**797.3**	**877.2**	**860.7**	**827.0**	**293.8**	**361.9**	**271.2**	**288.3**
Public and publicly guaranteed	797.3	877.2	860.7	827.0	293.8	361.9	271.2	288.3
Official creditors	764.8	843.1	826.0	792.5	259.4	325.3	244.1	261.2
Private creditors	32.6	34.1	34.7	34.5	34.4	36.6	27.1	27.1
Private nonguaranteed	0.0	0.0	0.0	0.0	0.0	0.0	0.0	0.0
Disbursements	**16.1**	**0.0**	**3.2**	**1.9**	**18.7**	**19.2**	**17.1**	**18.4**
Public and publicly guaranteed	16.1	0.0	3.2	1.9	18.7	19.2	17.1	18.4
Official creditors	16.1	0.0	3.2	1.9	18.7	19.2	17.1	18.4
Private creditors	0.0	0.0	0.0	0.0	0.0	0.0	0.0	0.0
Private nonguaranteed	0.0	0.0	0.0	0.0	0.0	0.0	0.0	0.0
Principal repayments	**7.5**	**0.7**	**42.4**	**11.3**	**8.4**	**1.0**	**0.8**	**2.1**
Public and publicly guaranteed	7.5	0.7	42.4	11.3	8.4	1.0	0.8	2.1
Official creditors	7.4	0.7	42.4	11.3	8.4	1.0	0.7	2.1
Private creditors	0.0	0.0	0.0	0.0	0.0	0.0	0.1	0.1
Private nonguaranteed	0.0	0.0	0.0	0.0	0.0	0.0	0.0	0.0
Interest payments	**4.3**	**0.2**	**19.6**	**6.1**	**3.0**	**1.2**	**0.2**	**1.9**
Public and publicly guaranteed	4.3	0.2	19.6	6.1	3.0	1.2	0.2	1.9
Official creditors	4.3	0.2	19.6	6.1	3.0	1.2	0.2	1.9
Private creditors	0.0	0.0	0.0	0.0	0.0	0.0	0.0	0.0
Private nonguaranteed	0.0	0.0	0.0	0.0	0.0	0.0	0.0	0.0
Debt resource inflows								
Net debt inflows	-13.8	-5.6	-43.2	17.9	22.6	29.4	47.3	0.9
Official creditors (incl. IMF)	7.8	-5.6	-34.2	5.9	30.6	31.4	16.4	26.9
Private creditors	-21.6	0.0	-9.0	12.0	-8.0	-2.0	30.9	-26.1
Long-term	0.0	0.0	0.0	0.0	0.0	0.0	-0.1	-0.1
Public and publicly guaranteed	0.0	0.0	0.0	0.0	0.0	0.0	-0.1	-0.1
Private nonguaranteed	0.0	0.0	0.0	0.0	0.0	0.0	0.0	0.0
Short-term	-21.6	..	-9.0	12.0	-8.0	-2.0	31.0	-26.0
Non-debt resource inflows								
Foreign direct investment	0.9	10.1	56.8	117.1	42.3	61.5	36.9	71.2
Portfolio equity	..	..	..	..	..	..	..	..
Currency composition (%)								
Euro	..	5.9	6.0	5.7	10.4	12.3	14.9	15.2
U.S.dollars	61.2	59.6	61.0	62.5	53.0	50.3	49.5	48.0
Major economic aggregates								
Gross national income (GNI)	901.3	1,339.8	1,686.6	1,960.3	1,960.6	1,981.5	2,162.9	2,136.6
Exports of goods, services & prim. income	..	..	..	..	..	..	..	..
Personal transfers & comp. of employees	..	..	..	..	..	..	..	..
Imports of goods, services & prim. income	..	..	..	..	..	..	..	..
Primary income on FDI	..	..	..	..	..	..	..	..
Current account balance	-10.7	-91.3	-109.3	-197.8	-142.8	..	..	..
International reserves	133.3	139.2	82.6	121.8	210.6	181.2	154.5	157.9
Ratios								
External debt stocks to exports (%)	..	..	..	..	..	..	..	..
External debt stocks to GNI (%)	96.8	77.1	59.1	50.5	27.4	31.0	25.3	25.8
Debt service to exports (%)	..	..	..	..	..	..	..	..
Short-term to external debt stocks (%)	4.7	10.3	7.3	8.6	15.2	13.0	19.0	14.6
Multilateral to external debt stocks (%)	66.9	60.8	60.4	57.7	9.3	6.7	6.4	7.7
Reserves to external debt stocks (%)	15.3	13.5	8.3	12.3	39.2	29.5	28.2	28.6
Reserves to imports (months)	..	..	..	..	..	..	..	..

Notes:

Short-term debt is based on data from the BIS. Data include the effects of HIPC and MDRI debt relief.

CHAD

(US$ million, unless otherwise indicated)

	2000	2005	2007	2008	2009	2010	2011	2012
Summary external debt data								
External debt stocks	**1,101**	**1,598**	**1,812**	**1,765**	**1,830**	**1,816**	**1,821**	**1,831**
Long-term external debt	986	1,494	1,712	1,705	1,714	1,708	1,710	1,717
Short-term external debt	25	11	29	4	4	8	19	27
interest arrears on long-term	10	6	6	4	4	7	7	8
Use of IMF credit	90	93	71	55	113	99	91	87
Long-term external debt								
Debt outstanding and disbursed	**986**	**1,494**	**1,712**	**1,705**	**1,714**	**1,708**	**1,710**	**1,717**
Public and publicly guaranteed	986	1,494	1,712	1,705	1,714	1,708	1,710	1,717
Official creditors	971	1,462	1,679	1,672	1,682	1,679	1,681	1,688
Private creditors	15	32	33	33	32	30	29	29
Private nonguaranteed	..	..	..	..	..	..	..	..
Disbursements	**46**	**110**	**50**	**97**	**38**	**57**	**55**	**73**
Public and publicly guaranteed	46	110	50	97	38	57	55	73
Official creditors	46	110	50	97	38	57	55	73
Private creditors	0	0	0	0	0	0	0	0
Private nonguaranteed	..	..	..	..	..	..	..	..
Principal repayments	**13**	**24**	**34**	**105**	**43**	**46**	**53**	**57**
Public and publicly guaranteed	13	24	34	105	43	46	53	57
Official creditors	13	23	33	105	42	44	52	56
Private creditors	1	1	1	0	1	2	1	1
Private nonguaranteed	..	..	..	..	..	..	..	..
Interest payments	**9**	**16**	**19**	**18**	**23**	**17**	**17**	**16**
Public and publicly guaranteed	9	16	19	18	23	17	17	16
Official creditors	9	16	18	18	23	17	17	16
Private creditors	0	0	0	0	0	0	0	0
Private nonguaranteed	..	..	..	..	..	..	..	..
Debt resource inflows								
Net debt inflows	44	75	21	-44	-17	2	5	19
Official creditors (incl. IMF)	46	80	2	-21	-16	3	-5	12
Private creditors	-2	-4	18	-23	-1	-1	10	6
Long-term	-1	-1	-1	..	-1	-2	-1	-1
Public and publicly guaranteed	-1	-1	-1	..	-1	-2	-1	-1
Private nonguaranteed	..	..	..	..	..	..	..	..
Short-term	-2	-3	19	-23	..	1	11	7
Non-debt resource inflows								
Foreign direct investment	115	-99	-322	466	376	313	282	323
Portfolio equity	..	..	..	..	..	..	..	..
Currency composition (%)								
Euro	..	3.3	3.6	3.3	3.3	3.2	3.2	3.4
U.S.dollars	58.7	66.1	64.4	60.2	59.8	58.3	56.9	55.4
Major economic aggregates								
Gross national income (GNI)	1,368	4,277	5,808	6,690	6,676	7,850	9,592	9,752
Exports of goods, services & prim. income	..	..	..	..	..	..	..	..
Personal transfers & comp. of employees	..	..	..	..	..	..	..	..
Imports of goods, services & prim. income	..	..	..	..	..	..	..	..
Primary income on FDI	..	..	..	..	..	..	..	..
Current account balance	-214	140	-298	258	-1,339	..	..	..
International reserves	111	226	955	1,345	617	632	951	1,156
Ratios								
External debt stocks to exports (%)	..	..	..	..	..	..	..	..
External debt stocks to GNI (%)	80.5	37.3	31.2	26.4	27.4	23.1	19.0	18.8
Debt service to exports (%)	..	..	..	..	..	..	..	..
Short-term to external debt stocks (%)	2.2	0.7	1.6	0.2	0.2	0.5	1.1	1.5
Multilateral to external debt stocks (%)	75.8	83.9	84.3	83.3	81.0	81.7	81.9	80.7
Reserves to external debt stocks (%)	10.1	14.1	52.7	76.2	33.7	34.8	52.2	63.1
Reserves to imports (months)	..	..	..	..	..	..	..	..

Notes:

Long-term public and publicly guaranteed debt data from 2011 are World Bank staff estimates. Short-term debt is based on data from the BIS. Data include the effects of HIPC debt relief.

CHINA

(US$ million, unless otherwise indicated)

	2000	2005	2007	2008	2009	2010	2011	2012
Summary external debt data								
External debt stocks	**145,648**	**281,114**	**371,721**	**378,469**	**445,942**	**559,772**	**710,234**	**754,009**
Long-term external debt	132,259	132,508	167,649	190,916	194,475	201,484	222,592	233,674
Short-term external debt	13,080	148,267	203,698	187,188	240,509	347,524	476,911	509,592
interest arrears on long-term	0	0	0	0	0	0	0	0
Use of IMF credit	309	338	374	365	10,958	10,764	10,731	10,743
Long-term external debt								
Debt outstanding and disbursed	**132,259**	**132,508**	**167,649**	**190,916**	**194,475**	**201,484**	**222,592**	**233,674**
Public and publicly guaranteed	94,470	82,016	85,365	89,142	92,318	90,637	75,176	74,004
Official creditors	50,374	52,421	58,323	63,349	68,358	67,204	67,684	69,464
Private creditors	44,096	29,595	27,042	25,793	23,960	23,433	7,492	4,540
Private nonguaranteed	37,789	50,492	82,284	101,774	102,157	110,847	147,416	159,671
Disbursements	**19,006**	**28,228**	**36,907**	**38,188**	**23,648**	**42,423**	**46,950**	**40,638**
Public and publicly guaranteed	11,924	8,776	7,130	5,449	6,481	10,125	7,785	6,893
Official creditors	5,790	2,170	3,403	3,893	3,310	4,348	3,848	6,671
Private creditors	6,133	6,606	3,727	1,556	3,171	5,777	3,937	222
Private nonguaranteed	7,082	19,452	29,777	32,739	17,167	32,298	39,165	33,746
Principal repayments	**19,362**	**20,936**	**20,405**	**23,959**	**33,448**	**27,237**	**36,277**	**35,519**
Public and publicly guaranteed	10,235	6,659	5,342	6,750	6,473	8,400	12,199	8,132
Official creditors	4,270	1,413	2,949	2,809	2,594	3,643	5,301	4,491
Private creditors	5,965	5,246	2,393	3,940	3,878	4,757	6,898	3,641
Private nonguaranteed	9,127	14,277	15,063	17,209	26,976	18,837	24,078	27,387
Interest payments	**6,064**	**3,157**	**5,358**	**4,733**	**3,045**	**5,316**	**6,920**	**7,329**
Public and publicly guaranteed	4,140	2,140	3,131	2,513	2,030	1,651	1,792	2,141
Official creditors	2,386	1,375	1,701	1,407	1,090	944	1,070	1,832
Private creditors	1,754	765	1,431	1,106	940	707	722	309
Private nonguaranteed	1,924	1,017	2,227	2,220	1,015	3,665	5,127	5,188
Debt resource inflows								
Net debt inflows	-2,457	39,789	46,823	-2,280	43,521	122,201	140,060	37,801
Official creditors (incl. IMF)	1,520	757	454	1,084	716	705	-1,453	2,180
Private creditors	-3,977	39,032	46,369	-3,364	42,805	121,496	141,513	35,621
Long-term	-1,877	6,535	16,048	13,146	-10,516	14,481	12,126	2,940
Public and publicly guaranteed	168	1,360	1,334	-2,384	-707	1,020	-2,961	-3,419
Private nonguaranteed	-2,045	5,175	14,714	15,530	-9,809	13,461	15,087	6,359
Short-term	-2,100	32,497	30,321	-16,510	53,321	107,015	129,387	32,681
Non-debt resource inflows								
Foreign direct investment	38,399	104,109	156,249	171,535	131,057	243,703	280,072	253,475
Portfolio equity	6,912	20,569	18,478	8,464	29,117	31,357	5,308	29,903
Currency composition (%)								
Euro	..	7.1	7.7	6.1	5.7	6.1	6.6	6.0
U.S.dollars	71.3	74.9	80.6	82.2	84.2	84.8	84.4	87.6
Major economic aggregates								
Gross national income (GNI)	1,183,809	2,240,803	3,501,856	4,539,527	4,998,556	5,904,632	7,310,070	8,203,602
Exports of goods, services & prim. income	292,111	809,731	1,338,833	1,605,353	1,368,583	1,790,140	2,134,931	2,327,689
Personal transfers & comp. of employees	5,237	8,832	17,513	22,694	22,903	33,440	40,483	39,221
Imports of goods, services & prim. income	277,904	701,218	1,022,752	1,227,941	1,156,985	1,593,015	2,023,344	2,137,983
Primary income on FDI	20,198	47,566	61,893	72,637	105,948	159,637	204,476	187,502
Current account balance	20,518	132,378	353,183	420,569	243,257	237,810	136,097	193,139
International reserves	168,278	821,514	1,530,282	1,949,260	2,416,044	2,866,079	3,202,789	3,331,120
Ratios								
External debt stocks to exports (%)	49.9	34.7	27.8	23.6	32.6	31.3	33.3	32.4
External debt stocks to GNI (%)	12.3	12.5	10.6	8.3	8.9	9.5	9.7	9.2
Debt service to exports (%)	9.1	3.4	2.4	2.1	2.9	3.4	3.5	3.3
Short-term to external debt stocks (%)	9.0	52.7	54.8	49.5	53.9	62.1	67.1	67.6
Multilateral to external debt stocks (%)	17.7	9.4	7.9	8.1	7.4	6.3	4.9	4.6
Reserves to external debt stocks (%)	115.5	292.2	411.7	515.0	541.8	512.0	450.9	441.8
Reserves to imports (months)	7.3	14.1	18.0	19.0	25.1	21.6	19.0	18.7

Notes:

Long-term private nonguaranteed and short-term debt data are World Bank staff estimates based on creditors and market data.

COLOMBIA

(US$ million, unless otherwise indicated)

	2000	2005	2007	2008	2009	2010	2011	2012
Summary external debt data								
External debt stocks	**33,159**	**37,162**	**43,391**	**46,246**	**53,047**	**63,815**	**76,782**	**79,051**
Long-term external debt	30,139	30,823	38,050	40,437	47,876	54,766	65,052	67,229
Short-term external debt	2,871	6,176	5,161	5,633	4,013	7,912	10,596	10,687
interest arrears on long-term	0	0	0	0	0	0	0	0
Use of IMF credit	149	163	181	176	1,157	1,137	1,134	1,135
Long-term external debt								
Debt outstanding and disbursed	**30,139**	**30,823**	**38,050**	**40,437**	**47,876**	**54,766**	**65,052**	**67,229**
Public and publicly guaranteed	19,880	21,834	26,938	28,625	35,127	36,688	39,124	43,184
Official creditors	6,805	9,834	11,515	13,386	14,985	16,152	16,684	19,495
Private creditors	13,075	12,000	15,423	15,239	20,142	20,536	22,440	23,689
Private nonguaranteed	10,259	8,989	11,112	11,812	12,749	18,078	25,928	24,045
Disbursements	**3,753**	**6,518**	**8,800**	**7,083**	**13,148**	**12,831**	**16,410**	**17,197**
Public and publicly guaranteed	2,889	4,397	4,434	3,851	8,107	3,491	4,571	6,749
Official creditors	610	1,469	1,581	2,555	2,415	2,125	1,559	3,840
Private creditors	2,279	2,928	2,853	1,296	5,691	1,365	3,012	2,909
Private nonguaranteed	865	2,121	4,366	3,232	5,041	9,340	11,839	10,448
Principal repayments	**2,882**	**7,272**	**5,456**	**4,733**	**5,769**	**6,431**	**6,404**	**11,362**
Public and publicly guaranteed	2,049	4,580	2,729	2,028	1,643	2,183	2,211	2,789
Official creditors	543	2,095	1,234	742	793	981	1,022	1,067
Private creditors	1,507	2,486	1,495	1,286	850	1,202	1,189	1,722
Private nonguaranteed	832	2,692	2,727	2,705	4,126	4,248	4,193	8,573
Interest payments	**1,948**	**2,513**	**2,696**	**2,722**	**2,694**	**2,824**	**3,187**	**3,638**
Public and publicly guaranteed	1,330	1,875	1,896	2,066	1,976	2,117	2,087	2,143
Official creditors	458	502	629	615	573	540	516	531
Private creditors	872	1,374	1,267	1,451	1,403	1,578	1,571	1,611
Private nonguaranteed	618	637	800	656	718	707	1,100	1,495
Debt resource inflows								
Net debt inflows	-222	302	3,743	2,823	5,759	10,300	12,690	5,925
Official creditors (incl. IMF)	67	-626	347	1,813	1,622	1,144	537	2,773
Private creditors	-290	928	3,395	1,009	4,137	9,155	12,153	3,153
Long-term	804	-128	2,997	537	5,757	5,256	9,469	3,062
Public and publicly guaranteed	772	443	1,358	10	4,841	163	1,823	1,187
Private nonguaranteed	32	-571	1,639	527	916	5,093	7,646	1,875
Short-term	-1,094	1,056	398	472	-1,620	3,900	2,684	91
Non-debt resource inflows								
Foreign direct investment	2,436	10,252	9,487	10,158	7,137	6,753	13,403	15,649
Portfolio equity	17	86	790	-86	67	1,351	1,969	3,778
Currency composition (%)								
Euro	..	4.3	3.5	1.4	1.2	1.0	0.1	0.1
U.S.dollars	72.6	84.4	89.4	93.4	94.1	94.7	96.3	97.7
Major economic aggregates								
Gross national income (GNI)	97,597	141,059	199,462	233,826	224,541	274,994	320,353	353,123
Exports of goods, services & prim. income	16,850	25,289	35,844	44,285	39,355	46,346	65,561	70,387
Personal transfers & comp. of employees	1,610	3,346	4,523	4,827	4,125	4,031	4,101	4,019
Imports of goods, services & prim. income	17,728	31,257	47,050	56,604	48,994	59,713	80,234	87,040
Primary income on FDI	655	3,565	6,598	8,706	7,628	9,959	14,755	15,318
Current account balance	795	-1,886	-5,977	-6,865	-5,081	-8,919	-9,839	-12,173
International reserves	8,916	14,787	20,767	23,479	24,748	27,766	31,386	36,444
Ratios								
External debt stocks to exports (%)	196.8	147.0	121.1	104.4	134.8	137.7	117.1	112.3
External debt stocks to GNI (%)	34.0	26.3	21.8	19.8	23.6	23.2	24.0	22.4
Debt service to exports (%)	29.7	39.7	16.6	23.4	17.4	22.0	20.8	15.4	22.0
Short-term to external debt stocks (%)	8.7	16.6	11.9	12.2	7.6	12.4	13.8	13.5
Multilateral to external debt stocks (%)	17.4	24.6	25.3	27.9	27.4	24.7	20.8	20.5
Reserves to external debt stocks (%)	26.9	39.8	47.9	50.8	46.7	43.5	40.9	46.1
Reserves to imports (months)	6.0	5.7	5.3	5.0	6.1	5.6	4.7	5.0

COMOROS

(US$ million, unless otherwise indicated)

	2000	2005	2007	2008	2009	2010	2011	2012
Summary external debt data								
External debt stocks	**226.7**	**280.8**	**289.2**	**278.8**	**288.4**	**280.6**	**277.9**	**251.2**
Long-term external debt	204.0	255.3	276.5	267.4	260.2	250.7	245.5	219.0
Short-term external debt	20.3	24.5	11.6	5.2	4.7	4.4	4.7	4.1
interest arrears on long-term	11.3	21.5	7.6	5.2	4.7	4.4	4.7	4.1
Use of IMF credit	2.4	1.0	1.1	6.2	23.4	25.4	27.7	28.0
Long-term external debt								
Debt outstanding and disbursed	**204.0**	**255.3**	**276.5**	**267.4**	**260.2**	**250.7**	**245.5**	**219.0**
Public and publicly guaranteed	204.0	255.3	276.5	267.4	260.2	250.7	245.5	219.0
Official creditors	204.0	255.3	276.5	267.4	260.2	250.7	245.5	219.0
Private creditors	0.0	0.0	0.0	0.0	0.0	0.0	0.0	0.0
Private nonguaranteed	..	..	..	..	..	..	..	..
Disbursements	**2.1**	**3.3**	**4.8**	**1.4**	**0.3**	**0.0**	**0.0**	**0.0**
Public and publicly guaranteed	2.1	3.3	4.8	1.4	0.3	0.0	0.0	0.0
Official creditors	2.1	3.3	4.8	1.4	0.3	0.0	0.0	0.0
Private creditors	0.0	0.0	0.0	0.0	0.0	0.0	0.0	0.0
Private nonguaranteed	..	..	..	..	..	..	..	..
Principal repayments	**1.2**	**2.6**	**12.8**	**8.1**	**7.2**	**3.1**	**2.2**	**5.1**
Public and publicly guaranteed	1.2	2.6	12.8	8.1	7.2	3.1	2.2	5.1
Official creditors	1.2	2.6	12.8	8.1	7.2	3.1	2.2	5.1
Private creditors	0.0	0.0	0.0	0.0	0.0	0.0	0.0	0.0
Private nonguaranteed	..	..	..	..	..	..	..	..
Interest payments	**0.8**	**1.3**	**13.1**	**4.2**	**2.9**	**1.1**	**1.7**	**2.3**
Public and publicly guaranteed	0.8	1.3	13.1	4.2	2.9	1.1	1.7	2.3
Official creditors	0.8	1.3	13.1	4.2	2.9	1.1	1.7	2.3
Private creditors	0.0	0.0	0.0	0.0	0.0	0.0	0.0	0.0
Private nonguaranteed	..	..	..	..	..	..	..	..
Debt resource inflows								
Net debt inflows	2.3	0.7	-8.0	-5.5	-2.1	-0.7	0.2	-4.9
Official creditors (incl. IMF)	0.3	0.7	-8.0	-1.5	-2.1	-0.7	0.2	-4.9
Private creditors	2.0	0.0	0.0	-4.0	0.0	0.0	0.0	0.0
Long-term	0.0	0.0	0.0	0.0	0.0	0.0	0.0	0.0
Public and publicly guaranteed	0.0	0.0	0.0	0.0	0.0	0.0	0.0	0.0
Private nonguaranteed	..	..	..	..	..	..	..	..
Short-term	2.0	..	..	-4.0	..	..	..	..
Non-debt resource inflows								
Foreign direct investment	0.1	0.6	7.7	4.6	13.8	8.3	23.1	17.0
Portfolio equity	..	..	..	..	..	..	..	..
Currency composition (%)								
Euro	..	12.5	11.7	11.6	11.6	11.6	11.3	12.3
U.S.dollars	32.4	41.1	43.1	43.7	44.3	45.0	45.0	41.0
Major economic aggregates								
Gross national income (GNI)	202.2	385.9	466.9	528.4	534.7	541.1	608.6	595.4
Exports of goods, services & prim. income	..	59.6	76.9	79.4	81.1	91.1	102.7	..
Personal transfers & comp. of employees	..	..	..	..	..	..	..	..
Imports of goods, services & prim. income	..	144.5	195.4	263.9	258.7	275.9	308.4	..
Primary income on FDI	..	..	..	..	..	..	..	..
Current account balance	..	-26.9	-31.6	-69.7	-39.3	-39.4	-56.3	..
International reserves	43.2	85.8	117.2	112.2	150.3	145.3	155.2	194.1
Ratios								
External debt stocks to exports (%)	..	470.7	376.0	351.4	355.6	308.2	270.7	..
External debt stocks to GNI (%)	112.1	72.8	61.9	52.8	53.9	51.9	45.7	42.2
Debt service to exports (%)	..	6.8	34.0	15.6	14.6	4.7	3.8	..
Short-term to external debt stocks (%)	9.0	8.7	4.0	1.9	1.6	1.6	1.7	1.6
Multilateral to external debt stocks (%)	73.2	73.8	78.9	78.7	74.4	72.7	71.4	68.6
Reserves to external debt stocks (%)	19.1	30.6	40.5	40.2	52.1	51.8	55.8	77.3
Reserves to imports (months)	..	7.1	7.2	5.1	7.0	6.3	6.0	..

Notes:

Data include the effects of Paris Club debt restructuring agreements signed in 2010 and the HIPC debt relief.

CONGO, DEMOCRATIC REPUBLIC OF

(US$ million, unless otherwise indicated)

	2000	2005	2007	2008	2009	2010	2011	2012
Summary external debt data								
External debt stocks	**11,805**	**10,715**	**12,485**	**12,336**	**13,097**	**6,202**	**5,544**	**5,651**
Long-term external debt	7,880	9,403	10,918	10,876	10,893	4,611	4,036	4,163
Short-term external debt	3,421	397	622	673	603	481	250	229
interest arrears on long-term	3,042	359	442	467	489	267	73	71
Use of IMF credit	503	914	945	787	1,601	1,110	1,258	1,260
Long-term external debt								
Debt outstanding and disbursed	**7,880**	**9,403**	**10,918**	**10,876**	**10,893**	**4,611**	**4,036**	**4,163**
Public and publicly guaranteed	7,880	9,403	10,918	10,876	10,893	4,611	4,036	4,163
Official creditors	7,384	9,033	10,561	10,524	10,561	4,485	4,021	4,140
Private creditors	496	370	357	351	332	126	14	23
Private nonguaranteed	..	..	..	..	..	..	..	..
Disbursements	**0**	**249**	**116**	**110**	**131**	**78**	**152**	**289**
Public and publicly guaranteed	0	249	116	110	131	78	152	289
Official creditors	0	249	115	110	131	58	152	276
Private creditors	0	0	1	0	0	20	0	12
Private nonguaranteed	..	..	..	..	..	..	..	..
Principal repayments	**0**	**112**	**155**	**170**	**226**	**89**	**133**	**108**
Public and publicly guaranteed	0	112	155	170	226	89	133	108
Official creditors	0	110	150	163	205	85	128	105
Private creditors	0	2	5	7	21	4	5	4
Private nonguaranteed	..	..	..	..	..	..	..	..
Interest payments	**0**	**97**	**266**	**275**	**242**	**125**	**120**	**168**
Public and publicly guaranteed	0	97	266	275	242	125	120	168
Official creditors	0	95	264	272	240	124	120	168
Private creditors	0	1	2	3	2	0	0	0
Private nonguaranteed	..	..	..	..	..	..	..	..
Debt resource inflows								
Net debt inflows	20	95	-65	-171	-55	107	138	161
Official creditors (incl. IMF)	0	178	-99	-191	58	-8	180	172
Private creditors	20	-83	34	19	-113	116	-42	-11
Long-term	0	-2	-4	-7	-21	16	-5	8
Public and publicly guaranteed	0	-2	-4	-7	-21	16	-5	8
Private nonguaranteed	..	..	..	..	..	..	..	..
Short-term	20	-81	38	26	-92	100	-37	-19
Non-debt resource inflows								
Foreign direct investment	72	167	1,794	1,673	-278	2,729	1,596	2,892
Portfolio equity	..	..	..	..	..	..	..	..
Currency composition (%)								
Euro	..	30.1	31.0	28.9	29.3	8.0	3.4	3.1
U.S.dollars	44.6	45.8	41.7	41.9	41.4	44.5	53.3	54.6
Major economic aggregates								
Gross national income (GNI)	3,917	6,684	9,380	10,345	5,604	12,197	14,379	15,801
Exports of goods, services & prim. income	..	2,756	6,566	7,716	5,047	8,915	10,379	8,840
Personal transfers & comp. of employees	..	9	9	15	20	16	115	12
Imports of goods, services & prim. income	..	3,892	6,901	8,863	7,571	11,931	13,071	11,703
Primary income on FDI	..	..	..	..	..	131	..	..
Current account balance	..	-389	527	-151	-1,123	-2,174	-1,281	-1,696
International reserves	83	131	181	78	1,035	1,300	1,268	1,633
Ratios								
External debt stocks to exports (%)	..	388.8	190.1	159.9	259.5	69.6	53.4	63.9
External debt stocks to GNI (%)	301.4	160.3	133.1	119.2	233.7	50.8	38.6	35.8
Debt service to exports (%)	..	7.9	7.6	7.7	12.4	3.1	2.5	3.2
Short-term to external debt stocks (%)	29.0	3.7	5.0	5.5	4.6	7.8	4.5	4.0
Multilateral to external debt stocks (%)	18.3	28.5	32.5	33.7	32.1	42.0	43.5	41.6
Reserves to external debt stocks (%)	0.7	1.2	1.4	0.6	7.9	21.0	22.9	28.9
Reserves to imports (months)	..	0.4	0.3	0.1	1.6	1.3	1.2	1.7

Notes:

Short-term debt is based on data from the BIS. Data include the effects of Paris Club debt restructuring agreement and HIPC and MDRI debt relief.

CONGO, REPUBLIC OF

(US$ million, unless otherwise indicated)

	2000	2005	2007	2008	2009	2010	2011	2012
Summary external debt data								
External debt stocks	**4,865**	**6,258**	**5,280**	**5,488**	**4,939**	**2,406**	**2,638**	**2,829**
Long-term external debt	3,735	5,471	4,898	5,071	4,610	2,063	2,329	2,492
Short-term external debt	1,076	747	330	364	162	193	155	185
interest arrears on long-term	655	736	225	227	95	76	61	60
Use of IMF credit	54	40	53	53	168	150	155	152
Long-term external debt								
Debt outstanding and disbursed	**3,735**	**5,471**	**4,898**	**5,071**	**4,610**	**2,063**	**2,329**	**2,492**
Public and publicly guaranteed	3,735	5,471	4,898	5,071	4,610	2,063	2,329	2,492
Official creditors	2,920	3,293	3,863	3,964	3,656	1,224	1,402	1,479
Private creditors	815	2,179	1,035	1,107	954	840	927	1,013
Private nonguaranteed	..	..	..	..	..	..	..	..
Disbursements	**1**	**183**	**28**	**19**	**7**	**504**	**356**	**472**
Public and publicly guaranteed	1	183	28	19	7	504	356	472
Official creditors	1	183	28	14	7	502	244	251
Private creditors	0	0	0	5	0	2	112	221
Private nonguaranteed	..	..	..	..	..	..	..	..
Principal repayments	**6**	**65**	**74**	**107**	**114**	**116**	**114**	**141**
Public and publicly guaranteed	6	65	74	107	114	116	114	141
Official creditors	6	65	72	79	80	104	92	106
Private creditors	0	0	1	27	34	12	22	35
Private nonguaranteed	..	..	..	..	..	..	..	..
Interest payments	**7**	**34**	**29**	**57**	**63**	**23**	**20**	**23**
Public and publicly guaranteed	7	34	29	57	63	23	20	23
Official creditors	7	34	29	57	48	9	6	7
Private creditors	0	0	0	0	14	14	14	16
Private nonguaranteed	..	..	..	..	..	..	..	..
Debt resource inflows								
Net debt inflows	-52	128	-3	-54	-174	439	224	359
Official creditors (incl. IMF)	9	117	-45	-64	-70	400	158	142
Private creditors	-61	11	42	10	-104	39	66	217
Long-term	0	0	-1	-22	-34	-11	89	186
Public and publicly guaranteed	0	0	-1	-22	-34	-11	89	186
Private nonguaranteed	..	..	..	..	..	..	..	..
Short-term	-61	11	43	32	-70	50	-23	31
Non-debt resource inflows								
Foreign direct investment	166	801	2,638	2,526	1,862	2,211	3,056	2,758
Portfolio equity	0	..	..	..	..	..	..	..
Currency composition (%)								
Euro	..	36.7	46.6	39.9	38.9	5.9	4.9	4.5
U.S.dollars	29.5	52.0	38.2	48.0	48.2	83.8	85.2	86.4
Major economic aggregates								
Gross national income (GNI)	2,275	4,032	5,774	8,768	6,979	9,024	10,713	10,832
Exports of goods, services & prim. income	2,642	4,983	6,151	..	..	..	..	..
Personal transfers & comp. of employees	10	11	15	..	..	..	..	..
Imports of goods, services & prim. income	2,013	4,318	8,294	..	..	..	..	..
Primary income on FDI	466	1,296	1,651	..	..	..	..	..
Current account balance	648	696	-2,181	..	..	..	..	..
International reserves	222	732	2,174	3,872	3,806	4,447	5,641	5,550
Ratios								
External debt stocks to exports (%)	184.1	125.6	85.8	..	..	..	..	..
External debt stocks to GNI (%)	213.8	155.2	91.4	62.6	70.8	26.7	24.6	26.1
Debt service to exports (%)	1.7	2.3	1.8	..	..	..	..	..
Short-term to external debt stocks (%)	22.1	11.9	6.2	6.6	3.3	8.0	5.9	6.5
Multilateral to external debt stocks (%)	10.3	8.2	9.5	8.1	8.8	7.9	6.3	5.8
Reserves to external debt stocks (%)	4.6	11.7	41.2	70.5	77.1	184.8	213.8	196.1
Reserves to imports (months)	1.3	2.0	3.1	..	..	..	..	..

Notes:

Long-term public and publicly guaranteed debt data from 2011 are World Bank staff estimates based on reports provided by the country. Short-term debt is based on data from the BIS. Data include the effects of Paris Club debt restructuring agreement and HIPC and MDRI debt relief.

COSTA RICA

(US$ million, unless otherwise indicated)

	2000	2005	2007	2008	2009	2010	2011	2012
Summary external debt data								
External debt stocks	**4,736**	**6,524**	**8,450**	**9,251**	**8,164**	**8,552**	**10,723**	**14,458**
Long-term external debt	3,742	4,393	5,178	5,226	5,675	5,880	7,673	11,379
Short-term external debt	962	2,097	3,234	3,989	2,243	2,431	2,810	2,839
interest arrears on long-term	27	2	0	0	0	0	0	0
Use of IMF credit	31	34	37	37	245	241	240	241
Long-term external debt								
Debt outstanding and disbursed	**3,742**	**4,393**	**5,178**	**5,226**	**5,675**	**5,880**	**7,673**	**11,379**
Public and publicly guaranteed	3,506	3,162	3,657	3,232	3,216	3,827	3,968	4,983
Official creditors	1,915	1,371	1,483	1,420	1,586	2,201	2,196	2,198
Private creditors	1,591	1,791	2,174	1,812	1,630	1,626	1,773	2,786
Private nonguaranteed	236	1,231	1,521	1,994	2,459	2,053	3,704	6,396
Disbursements	**758**	**986**	**610**	**1,178**	**1,329**	**1,458**	**1,878**	**3,846**
Public and publicly guaranteed	749	75	118	394	559	928	773	1,790
Official creditors	249	75	118	383	419	845	269	357
Private creditors	500	0	0	11	141	82	504	1,433
Private nonguaranteed	9	910	492	785	770	531	1,105	2,056
Principal repayments	**391**	**570**	**562**	**1,124**	**858**	**625**	**1,176**	**1,698**
Public and publicly guaranteed	374	365	266	848	574	343	641	742
Official creditors	337	306	224	475	251	257	283	323
Private creditors	37	59	42	373	323	86	357	420
Private nonguaranteed	17	204	296	276	284	282	536	956
Interest payments	**206**	**180**	**208**	**352**	**366**	**329**	**415**	**581**
Public and publicly guaranteed	190	106	116	249	219	213	200	202
Official creditors	105	63	43	81	77	86	85	77
Private creditors	86	43	73	168	142	127	115	125
Private nonguaranteed	16	74	92	104	147	116	215	379
Debt resource inflows								
Net debt inflows	545	841	928	809	-1,274	1,021	1,081	2,177
Official creditors (incl. IMF)	-89	-231	-106	-92	168	588	-14	35
Private creditors	634	1,072	1,035	902	-1,441	433	1,095	2,142
Long-term	455	647	154	147	304	246	716	2,113
Public and publicly guaranteed	463	-59	-42	-362	-182	-4	147	1,013
Private nonguaranteed	-8	706	196	509	486	249	569	1,100
Short-term	179	425	880	755	-1,745	188	379	29
Non-debt resource inflows								
Foreign direct investment	409	861	1,896	2,078	1,347	1,466	2,156	2,636
Portfolio equity	..	..	..	..	..	..	..	..
Currency composition (%)								
Euro	..	1.7	1.7	1.7	1.6	1.2	0.9	0.6
U.S.dollars	68.8	77.1	82.8	86.3	87.7	87.8	89.5	94.2
Major economic aggregates								
Gross national income (GNI)	14,697	19,184	25,574	29,084	28,489	35,317	40,050	43,886
Exports of goods, services & prim. income	7,992	7,535	10,184	10,863	9,890	10,797	12,061	13,397
Personal transfers & comp. of employees	136	420	618	605	513	531	520	562
Imports of goods, services & prim. income	8,793	8,787	12,300	14,092	10,825	12,445	14,587	16,106
Primary income on FDI	1,141	743	1,131	749	986	606	753	1,046
Current account balance	-707	-981	-1,646	-2,787	-576	-1,281	-2,203	-2,376
International reserves	1,318	2,313	4,114	3,799	4,066	4,627	4,756	6,857
Ratios								
External debt stocks to exports (%)	59.3	86.6	83.0	85.2	82.5	79.2	88.9	107.9
External debt stocks to GNI (%)	32.2	34.0	33.0	31.8	28.7	24.2	26.8	32.9
Debt service to exports (%)	8.2	11.2	8.9	14.6	13.0	9.5	13.8	17.6
Short-term to external debt stocks (%)	20.3	32.1	38.3	43.1	27.5	28.4	26.2	19.6
Multilateral to external debt stocks (%)	28.7	18.0	14.2	11.9	14.6	20.7	16.7	12.8
Reserves to external debt stocks (%)	27.8	35.5	48.7	41.1	49.8	54.1	44.4	47.4
Reserves to imports (months)	1.8	3.2	4.0	3.2	4.5	4.5	3.9	5.1

Notes:

Long-term private nonguaranteed debt data are World Bank staff estimates based on reports provided by the country.

COTE D'IVOIRE

(US$ million, unless otherwise indicated)

	2000	2005	2007	2008	2009	2010	2011	2012
Summary external debt data								
External debt stocks	**12,187**	**11,966**	**13,925**	**12,956**	**14,499**	**11,532**	**13,043**	**9,871**
Long-term external debt	10,546	10,866	12,237	11,365	13,561	10,357	11,132	8,428
Short-term external debt	1,043	848	1,455	1,344	98	314	821	178
interest arrears on long-term	79	848	1,455	1,344	98	7	5	5
Use of IMF credit	599	252	233	247	839	861	1,090	1,265
Long-term external debt								
Debt outstanding and disbursed	**10,546**	**10,866**	**12,237**	**11,365**	**13,561**	**10,357**	**11,132**	**8,428**
Public and publicly guaranteed	9,063	9,965	11,646	10,628	12,713	9,339	9,800	5,937
Official creditors	6,669	7,673	9,062	8,129	10,647	9,227	9,670	5,809
Private creditors	2,394	2,292	2,584	2,499	2,066	112	131	129
Private nonguaranteed	1,482	900	591	738	848	1,018	1,332	2,490
Disbursements	**148**	**55**	**77**	**310**	**405**	**539**	**1,083**	**981**
Public and publicly guaranteed	148	21	57	35	85	185	681	161
Official creditors	148	21	57	35	85	159	646	147
Private creditors	0	0	0	0	0	26	34	13
Private nonguaranteed	0	34	20	275	320	355	402	820
Principal repayments	**442**	**164**	**298**	**782**	**698**	**625**	**569**	**929**
Public and publicly guaranteed	329	21	112	586	533	440	349	663
Official creditors	283	21	112	586	533	440	340	646
Private creditors	46	0	0	0	0	0	9	16
Private nonguaranteed	113	143	187	196	165	185	220	266
Interest payments	**462**	**46**	**82**	**216**	**289**	**115**	**140**	**380**
Public and publicly guaranteed	342	3	41	183	241	59	69	261
Official creditors	189	3	41	183	241	59	69	261
Private creditors	153	0	0	0	0	0	0	0
Private nonguaranteed	120	43	41	33	48	56	70	119
Debt resource inflows								
Net debt inflows	-617	-308	-206	-452	-135	266	1,261	-419
Official creditors (incl. IMF)	-174	-91	-39	-531	-290	-237	545	-326
Private creditors	-442	-217	-167	79	155	503	716	-92
Long-term	-159	-109	-167	79	155	196	207	551
Public and publicly guaranteed	-46	0	0	0	0	26	25	-3
Private nonguaranteed	-113	-109	-167	79	155	170	182	554
Short-term	-283	-108	..	0	..	307	509	-643
Non-debt resource inflows								
Foreign direct investment	235	349	443	466	396	358	286	478
Portfolio equity	1	14	2	2	2	2	..	..
Currency composition (%)								
Euro	..	51.9	55.6	56.2	63.7	59.9	55.3	72.8
U.S.dollars	53.7	37.7	34.1	33.0	29.8	30.8	35.5	21.7
Major economic aggregates								
Gross national income (GNI)	9,715	15,643	18,913	22,434	22,055	21,923	23,035	23,683
Exports of goods, services & prim. income	4,512	8,717	9,813	11,643	12,562	12,811	..	..
Personal transfers & comp. of employees	119	163	185	199	315	373	..	..
Imports of goods, services & prim. income	4,423	8,215	9,608	10,859	10,845	11,907	..	..
Primary income on FDI	284	370	531	581	572	562	..	..
Current account balance	-241	40	-139	452	1,618	465	..	..
International reserves	674	1,367	2,519	2,253	3,267	3,624	4,316	3,928
Ratios								
External debt stocks to exports (%)	270.1	137.3	141.9	111.3	115.4	90.0	..	..
External debt stocks to GNI (%)	125.4	76.5	73.6	57.7	65.7	52.6	56.6	41.7
Debt service to exports (%)	22.7	3.5	4.4	9.0	9.0	5.9	..	..
Short-term to external debt stocks (%)	8.6	7.1	10.4	10.4	0.7	2.7	6.3	1.8
Multilateral to external debt stocks (%)	24.3	25.8	24.9	22.4	16.7	20.3	17.9	5.2
Reserves to external debt stocks (%)	5.5	11.4	18.1	17.4	22.5	31.4	33.1	39.8
Reserves to imports (months)	1.8	2.0	3.1	2.5	3.6	3.7	..	..

Notes:

Long-term public and publicly guaranteed debt data and long-term private nonguaranteed debt data for 2012 are World Bank staff estimates based on reports provided by the country. Data include the effects of Paris Club agreement signed in 2011, 2012 and HIPC and MDRI debt relief.

DJIBOUTI

(US$ million, unless otherwise indicated)

	2000	2005	2007	2008	2009	2010	2011	2012
Summary external debt data								
External debt stocks	**298.6**	**485.1**	**821.2**	**843.3**	**894.1**	**769.7**	**775.9**	**807.7**
Long-term external debt	238.3	376.9	651.4	678.3	735.3	619.7	650.6	641.9
Short-term external debt	45.4	87.9	151.8	145.7	119.3	114.5	85.6	108.3
interest arrears on long-term	6.4	8.9	5.8	0.7	2.3	0.5	0.6	1.3
Use of IMF credit	14.9	20.4	17.9	19.2	39.5	35.5	39.7	57.5
Long-term external debt								
Debt outstanding and disbursed	**238.3**	**376.9**	**651.4**	**678.3**	**735.3**	**619.7**	**650.6**	**641.9**
Public and publicly guaranteed	238.3	376.9	651.4	678.3	735.3	619.7	650.6	641.9
Official creditors	238.3	371.3	620.6	651.0	711.1	599.3	633.4	628.1
Private creditors	0.0	5.6	30.8	27.4	24.2	20.4	17.2	13.8
Private nonguaranteed	..	..	..	..	..	..	..	..
Disbursements	**7.7**	**26.5**	**39.0**	**45.9**	**67.4**	**35.2**	**55.7**	**25.2**
Public and publicly guaranteed	7.7	26.5	39.0	45.9	67.4	35.2	55.7	25.2
Official creditors	7.7	26.5	39.0	45.9	67.4	35.2	55.7	25.2
Private creditors	0.0	0.0	0.0	0.0	0.0	0.0	0.0	0.0
Private nonguaranteed	..	..	..	..	..	..	..	..
Principal repayments	**8.4**	**11.0**	**14.3**	**17.5**	**22.3**	**22.2**	**24.8**	**30.8**
Public and publicly guaranteed	8.4	11.0	14.3	17.5	22.3	22.2	24.8	30.8
Official creditors	8.4	11.0	13.2	13.6	17.3	19.8	21.9	27.3
Private creditors	0.0	0.0	1.1	3.9	5.1	2.4	2.9	3.5
Private nonguaranteed	..	..	..	..	..	..	..	..
Interest payments	**2.2**	**3.7**	**6.5**	**7.7**	**8.1**	**8.2**	**9.2**	**9.3**
Public and publicly guaranteed	2.2	3.7	6.5	7.7	8.1	8.2	9.2	9.3
Official creditors	2.2	3.7	6.5	7.2	7.6	7.5	8.5	8.8
Private creditors	0.0	0.0	0.0	0.5	0.6	0.6	0.7	0.5
Private nonguaranteed	..	..	..	..	..	..	..	..
Debt resource inflows								
Net debt inflows	39.7	56.7	71.0	29.2	15.1	6.6	6.2	34.1
Official creditors (incl. IMF)	0.7	14.7	23.0	34.1	48.2	12.0	38.2	15.7
Private creditors	39.0	42.0	47.9	-4.9	-33.1	-5.4	-31.9	18.5
Long-term	0.0	0.0	-1.1	-3.9	-5.1	-2.4	-2.9	-3.5
Public and publicly guaranteed	0.0	0.0	-1.1	-3.9	-5.1	-2.4	-2.9	-3.5
Private nonguaranteed	..	..	..	..	..	..	..	..
Short-term	39.0	42.0	49.0	-1.0	-28.0	-3.0	-29.0	22.0
Non-debt resource inflows								
Foreign direct investment	3.3	22.2	195.4	227.7	96.9	36.5	79.0	110.0
Portfolio equity	..	..	..	..	..	..	..	..
Currency composition (%)								
Euro	..	13.2	34.0	31.7	30.5	13.9	14.1	13.8
U.S.dollars	16.2	33.9	25.6	25.3	24.5	29.1	28.1	28.7
Major economic aggregates								
Gross national income (GNI)	567.0	775.8	..	..	..	..	..	..
Exports of goods, services & prim. income	218.4	319.8	329.4	398.3	422.7	439.0	440.3	487.7
Personal transfers & comp. of employees	12.3	25.8	28.6	30.3	32.5	32.6	32.4	33.3
Imports of goods, services & prim. income	287.1	372.3	579.9	703.5	580.0	493.8	686.3	700.7
Primary income on FDI	4.2	5.9	4.2	5.0	6.5	6.8	18.0	7.2
Current account balance	-19.0	20.1	-171.4	-225.4	-71.1	50.5	-171.8	-121.7
International reserves	67.8	89.3	132.1	175.5	241.8	249.0	244.1	248.6
Ratios								
External debt stocks to exports (%)	136.7	151.7	249.3	211.7	211.5	175.3	176.2	165.6
External debt stocks to GNI (%)	52.7	62.5	..	..	..	..	..	..
Debt service to exports (%)	6.9	5.6	8.4	8.4	8.5	8.1	8.6	8.8
Short-term to external debt stocks (%)	15.2	18.1	18.5	17.3	13.3	14.9	11.0	13.4
Multilateral to external debt stocks (%)	46.3	55.0	42.0	42.8	44.5	52.5	55.2	52.0
Reserves to external debt stocks (%)	22.7	18.4	16.1	20.8	27.0	32.4	31.5	30.8
Reserves to imports (months)	2.8	2.9	2.7	3.0	5.0	6.1	4.3	4.3

Notes:

Short-term debt is based on data from the BIS. Data include the effects of Paris Club debt restructuring agreement signed in 2008.

DOMINICA

(US$ million, unless otherwise indicated)

	2000	2005	2007	2008	2009	2010	2011	2012
Summary external debt data								
External debt stocks	**183.3**	**277.3**	**291.8**	**303.9**	**270.1**	**249.7**	**260.0**	**284.3**
Long-term external debt	163.6	224.4	215.7	204.9	200.3	217.9	227.1	252.2
Short-term external debt	19.0	40.6	63.0	83.0	37.9	1.5	5.6	5.6
interest arrears on long-term	0.0	8.6	14.0	17.0	17.9	1.5	1.5	1.5
Use of IMF credit	0.8	12.4	13.1	15.9	31.9	30.2	27.3	26.6
Long-term external debt								
Debt outstanding and disbursed	**163.6**	**224.4**	**215.7**	**204.9**	**200.3**	**217.9**	**227.1**	**252.2**
Public and publicly guaranteed	163.6	224.4	215.7	204.9	200.3	217.9	227.1	252.2
Official creditors	114.3	174.0	165.4	157.8	156.3	174.0	183.3	217.6
Private creditors	49.2	50.4	50.4	47.1	44.0	44.0	43.8	34.5
Private nonguaranteed	..	..	..	..	..	..	..	..
Disbursements	**56.2**	**4.5**	**4.9**	**7.9**	**8.6**	**29.7**	**18.3**	**36.3**
Public and publicly guaranteed	56.2	4.5	4.9	7.9	8.6	29.7	18.3	36.3
Official creditors	25.7	4.5	4.9	6.2	8.6	29.7	18.3	36.3
Private creditors	30.5	0.0	0.0	1.7	0.0	0.0	0.0	0.0
Private nonguaranteed	..	..	..	..	..	..	..	..
Principal repayments	**6.8**	**9.6**	**10.5**	**12.9**	**14.8**	**9.8**	**9.4**	**7.8**
Public and publicly guaranteed	6.8	9.6	10.5	12.9	14.8	9.8	9.4	7.8
Official creditors	6.8	9.6	10.5	12.9	12.9	9.8	9.2	7.6
Private creditors	0.0	0.0	0.0	0.0	1.9	0.1	0.2	0.2
Private nonguaranteed	..	..	..	..	..	..	..	..
Interest payments	**3.1**	**4.7**	**4.9**	**4.3**	**4.5**	**4.3**	**4.2**	**7.8**
Public and publicly guaranteed	3.1	4.7	4.9	4.3	4.5	4.3	4.2	7.8
Official creditors	2.9	4.3	4.5	4.1	4.0	3.9	3.9	4.2
Private creditors	0.2	0.4	0.5	0.2	0.6	0.4	0.3	3.6
Private nonguaranteed	..	..	..	..	..	..	..	..
Debt resource inflows								
Net debt inflows	49.5	-37.0	29.9	15.2	-47.9	-1.2	10.0	27.7
Official creditors (incl. IMF)	18.8	-2.0	-8.1	-3.5	0.0	18.8	6.1	27.9
Private creditors	30.7	-35.0	38.0	18.7	-47.9	-20.1	3.9	-0.2
Long-term	30.5	0.0	0.0	1.7	-1.9	-0.1	-0.2	-0.2
Public and publicly guaranteed	30.5	0.0	0.0	1.7	-1.9	-0.1	-0.2	-0.2
Private nonguaranteed	..	..	..	..	..	..	..	..
Short-term	0.2	-35.0	38.0	17.0	-46.0	-20.0	4.1	..
Non-debt resource inflows								
Foreign direct investment	17.6	19.2	40.5	56.5	42.4	24.3	14.2	19.6
Portfolio equity	..	..	..	..	..	..	..	..
Currency composition (%)								
Euro	..	5.3	3.4	2.7	3.4	3.0	3.2	7.9
U.S.dollars	72.3	84.9	86.1	86.2	83.6	79.4	77.8	59.8
Major economic aggregates								
Gross national income (GNI)	285.1	332.6	393.1	433.8	468.5	465.4	465.9	462.5
Exports of goods, services & prim. income	149.2	135.3	156.4	165.1	156.3	178.9	190.2	196.7
Personal transfers & comp. of employees	16.3	21.8	22.5	22.7	22.1	22.9	22.9	23.2
Imports of goods, services & prim. income	227.1	231.0	264.5	314.1	284.7	280.1	278.0	268.2
Primary income on FDI	33.0	22.7	13.0	12.5	13.4	7.8	5.0	5.2
Current account balance	-59.8	-76.1	-86.9	-129.9	-109.3	-81.4	-71.3	-54.9
International reserves	29.4	49.2	60.5	55.2	75.5	76.1	81.1	94.6
Ratios								
External debt stocks to exports (%)	122.9	205.0	186.6	184.0	172.8	139.5	136.7	144.5
External debt stocks to GNI (%)	64.3	83.4	74.2	70.0	57.7	53.6	55.8	61.5
Debt service to exports (%)	7.4	12.1	12.6	11.6	13.3	8.6	8.8	10.0
Short-term to external debt stocks (%)	10.4	14.6	21.6	27.3	14.0	0.6	2.1	2.0
Multilateral to external debt stocks (%)	45.5	45.4	41.5	38.5	43.8	46.9	47.0	45.0
Reserves to external debt stocks (%)	16.0	17.7	20.7	18.1	27.9	30.5	31.2	33.3
Reserves to imports (months)	1.6	2.6	2.7	2.1	3.2	3.3	3.5	4.2

DOMINICAN REPUBLIC

(US$ million, unless otherwise indicated)

	2000	2005	2007	2008	2009	2010	2011	2012
Summary external debt data								
External debt stocks	**4,652**	**7,739**	**10,739**	**10,603**	**11,490**	**13,465**	**15,426**	**16,851**
Long-term external debt	3,381	6,406	7,662	8,122	8,999	10,281	11,673	13,180
Short-term external debt	1,178	887	2,480	1,940	1,397	1,723	2,130	2,157
interest arrears on long-term	28	20	9	3	0	0	0	0
Use of IMF credit	93	446	598	541	1,094	1,461	1,623	1,513
Long-term external debt								
Debt outstanding and disbursed	**3,381**	**6,406**	**7,662**	**8,122**	**8,999**	**10,281**	**11,673**	**13,180**
Public and publicly guaranteed	3,381	6,405	6,817	7,279	8,156	9,439	10,760	11,982
Official creditors	2,625	3,257	3,748	4,458	5,505	6,376	7,119	8,159
Private creditors	756	3,147	3,068	2,821	2,651	3,063	3,641	3,823
Private nonguaranteed	0	2	845	843	843	843	913	1,198
Disbursements	**314**	**657**	**1,252**	**1,310**	**1,481**	**2,111**	**2,165**	**2,393**
Public and publicly guaranteed	314	656	821	1,310	1,481	2,111	2,120	1,843
Official creditors	150	372	459	1,023	1,392	1,176	1,117	1,458
Private creditors	164	284	362	287	89	935	1,003	385
Private nonguaranteed	0	2	431	0	0	0	45	550
Principal repayments	**264**	**460**	**942**	**821**	**893**	**794**	**796**	**1,056**
Public and publicly guaranteed	264	460	942	821	893	794	788	624
Official creditors	223	184	370	311	354	311	376	407
Private creditors	40	276	572	510	539	483	412	217
Private nonguaranteed	0	0	0	1	0	0	8	432
Interest payments	**211**	**212**	**332**	**446**	**431**	**443**	**584**	**543**
Public and publicly guaranteed	211	212	275	338	323	335	473	448
Official creditors	159	109	148	136	150	156	176	198
Private creditors	53	103	127	202	173	179	297	250
Private nonguaranteed	0	0	57	108	108	108	111	95
Debt resource inflows								
Net debt inflows	316	394	1,457	-87	309	2,025	1,947	1,254
Official creditors (incl. IMF)	-73	407	152	670	1,299	1,247	912	941
Private creditors	389	-13	1,305	-757	-990	778	1,035	313
Long-term	124	10	221	-223	-450	452	628	286
Public and publicly guaranteed	124	8	-210	-222	-449	452	591	168
Private nonguaranteed	..	2	430	-1	0	0	37	118
Short-term	265	-23	1,084	-534	-540	326	407	27
Non-debt resource inflows								
Foreign direct investment	953	1,118	2,253	2,728	1,695	2,094	2,196	3,857
Portfolio equity	..	..	..	..	..	..	..	..
Currency composition (%)								
Euro	..	2.3	5.6	7.3	8.3	6.2	4.7	5.9
U.S.dollars	73.2	88.2	87.1	86.2	86.1	89.2	91.6	91.3
Major economic aggregates								
Gross national income (GNI)	22,955	32,102	39,044	43,964	44,989	49,968	53,579	56,760
Exports of goods, services & prim. income	9,264	8,013	10,314	9,999	8,444	9,940	11,556	12,564
Personal transfers & comp. of employees	1,839	2,719	3,397	3,606	3,415	3,430	3,651	3,615
Imports of goods, services & prim. income	12,193	11,183	15,882	18,031	13,986	17,393	19,369	19,974
Primary income on FDI	1,068	1,765	2,194	1,669	1,518	1,528	1,802	1,884
Current account balance	-1,027	-473	-2,166	-4,520	-2,303	-4,330	-4,379	-4,037
International reserves	627	1,920	3,030	2,679	3,560	3,849	4,086	3,548
Ratios								
External debt stocks to exports (%)	50.2	96.6	104.1	106.0	136.1	135.5	133.5	134.1
External debt stocks to GNI (%)	20.3	24.1	27.5	24.1	25.5	26.9	28.8	29.7
Debt service to exports (%)	5.7	9.1	15.1	15.0	16.6	14.3	13.9	14.0
Short-term to external debt stocks (%)	25.3	11.5	23.1	18.3	12.2	12.8	13.8	12.8
Multilateral to external debt stocks (%)	25.0	23.4	17.6	17.8	22.8	22.9	21.7	21.0
Reserves to external debt stocks (%)	13.5	24.8	28.2	25.3	31.0	28.6	26.5	21.1
Reserves to imports (months)	0.6	2.1	2.3	1.8	3.1	2.7	2.5	2.1

Notes:

Long-term private nonguaranteed debt data only cover Inter-American Development Bank and Bonds. Short-term debt is based on data from the BIS. Data include the effects of Paris Club debt restructuring agreement signed in 2005.

ECUADOR

(US$ million, unless otherwise indicated)

	2000	2005	2007	2008	2009	2010	2011	2012
Summary external debt data								
External debt stocks	**13,338**	**17,408**	**17,868**	**15,818**	**13,263**	**14,963**	**16,497**	**16,931**
Long-term external debt	12,350	15,564	15,946	14,084	11,426	13,715	15,309	15,815
Short-term external debt	797	1,719	1,870	1,683	1,386	804	745	673
interest arrears on long-term	3	1	0	31	37	37	46	44
Use of IMF credit	191	125	52	51	452	444	443	443
Long-term external debt								
Debt outstanding and disbursed	**12,350**	**15,564**	**15,946**	**14,084**	**11,426**	**13,715**	**15,309**	**15,815**
Public and publicly guaranteed	10,915	10,896	10,763	10,095	6,960	8,633	9,929	10,065
Official creditors	5,922	5,993	6,635	6,006	5,895	7,610	8,939	9,106
Private creditors	4,993	4,902	4,128	4,088	1,065	1,023	990	959
Private nonguaranteed	1,435	4,668	5,183	3,990	4,466	5,082	5,380	5,750
Disbursements	**983**	**3,154**	**3,048**	**1,369**	**1,180**	**2,977**	**3,370**	**2,322**
Public and publicly guaranteed	602	991	1,357	353	384	2,307	2,342	1,336
Official creditors	531	318	1,333	343	382	2,305	2,342	1,336
Private creditors	71	674	24	10	2	2	1	0
Private nonguaranteed	381	2,162	1,691	1,016	796	670	1,028	986
Principal repayments	**1,067**	**3,048**	**2,340**	**1,485**	**4,187**	**1,260**	**1,837**	**1,894**
Public and publicly guaranteed	550	923	1,029	964	3,529	637	1,048	1,174
Official creditors	399	803	964	915	503	593	1,015	1,143
Private creditors	151	120	65	49	3,025	44	33	31
Private nonguaranteed	517	2,125	1,311	521	659	623	789	720
Interest payments	**708**	**843**	**1,228**	**847**	**521**	**464**	**534**	**674**
Public and publicly guaranteed	536	658	736	656	330	326	361	481
Official creditors	296	275	327	311	227	255	292	414
Private creditors	240	383	409	345	103	71	69	67
Private nonguaranteed	172	185	492	191	191	139	174	193
Debt resource inflows								
Net debt inflows	-189	-235	557	-334	-3,310	1,135	1,466	358
Official creditors (incl. IMF)	282	-680	346	-572	-121	1,712	1,326	194
Private creditors	-471	445	211	238	-3,189	-577	139	164
Long-term	-216	590	339	456	-2,886	5	207	235
Public and publicly guaranteed	-80	553	-41	-39	-3,023	-42	-33	-31
Private nonguaranteed	-136	37	380	495	138	47	239	266
Short-term	-254	-145	-128	-218	-303	-582	-68	-71
Non-debt resource inflows								
Foreign direct investment	-23	493	194	1,006	321	167	641	591
Portfolio equity	0	2	0	1	2	0	2	5
Currency composition (%)								
Euro	..	3.4	3.3	3.0	4.0	2.8	2.1	1.5
U.S.dollars	83.0	87.1	88.4	89.6	86.2	89.9	92.2	89.6
Major economic aggregates								
Gross national income (GNI)	16,916	39,692	49,063	60,312	61,147	66,585	76,476	83,221
Exports of goods, services & prim. income	6,163	11,693	16,431	21,218	15,854	19,686	24,754	26,569
Personal transfers & comp. of employees	1,322	2,460	3,341	3,089	2,742	2,599	2,681	2,456
Imports of goods, services & prim. income	6,403	13,880	17,924	22,692	18,366	23,757	27,700	29,231
Primary income on FDI	329	1,004	1,160	785	821	546	701	676
Current account balance	1,113	474	1,938	1,648	136	-1,623	-225	-177
International reserves	947	1,714	2,816	3,738	2,873	1,435	1,664	1,080
Ratios								
External debt stocks to exports (%)	216.4	148.9	108.7	74.6	83.7	76.0	66.6	63.7
External debt stocks to GNI (%)	78.8	43.9	36.4	26.2	21.7	22.5	21.6	20.3
Debt service to exports (%)	30.6	35.9	22.7	11.1	30.2	9.1	9.7	9.8
Short-term to external debt stocks (%)	6.0	9.9	10.5	10.6	10.4	5.4	4.5	4.0
Multilateral to external debt stocks (%)	27.8	21.0	26.3	27.4	33.1	34.8	31.5	30.3
Reserves to external debt stocks (%)	7.1	9.8	15.8	23.6	21.7	9.6	10.1	6.4
Reserves to imports (months)	1.8	1.5	1.9	2.0	1.9	0.7	0.7	0.4

Notes:

Short-term debt is World Bank staff estimates based on Central Bank data.

EGYPT, ARAB REPUBLIC OF

(US$ million, unless otherwise indicated)

	2000	2005	2007	2008	2009	2010	2011	2012
Summary external debt data								
External debt stocks	**29,178**	**29,948**	**34,224**	**33,571**	**35,062**	**36,544**	**35,150**	**40,000**
Long-term external debt	24,897	28,098	31,774	30,519	31,093	32,011	30,745	31,962
Short-term external debt	4,104	1,656	2,236	2,842	2,561	3,149	3,026	6,657
interest arrears on long-term	0	2	1	0	0	0	0	0
Use of IMF credit	177	194	215	209	1,408	1,384	1,379	1,381
Long-term external debt								
Debt outstanding and disbursed	**24,897**	**28,098**	**31,774**	**30,519**	**31,093**	**32,011**	**30,745**	**31,962**
Public and publicly guaranteed	24,325	28,005	31,754	30,439	31,019	31,957	30,729	31,942
Official creditors	23,785	25,777	29,039	28,098	28,669	28,238	27,457	28,689
Private creditors	540	2,228	2,715	2,341	2,350	3,719	3,272	3,253
Private nonguaranteed	573	93	21	80	74	54	16	20
Disbursements	**569**	**3,090**	**3,188**	**1,133**	**2,131**	**3,617**	**1,510**	**3,681**
Public and publicly guaranteed	362	3,090	3,188	1,063	2,122	3,612	1,480	3,656
Official creditors	218	1,114	2,445	962	2,016	1,903	1,459	3,601
Private creditors	144	1,976	743	101	107	1,709	21	55
Private nonguaranteed	207	0	0	70	9	5	30	25
Principal repayments	**1,098**	**1,573**	**1,976**	**2,333**	**2,053**	**2,155**	**2,649**	**2,247**
Public and publicly guaranteed	982	1,573	1,915	2,322	2,033	2,130	2,582	2,225
Official creditors	861	1,344	1,824	1,847	1,914	2,056	2,121	2,151
Private creditors	121	229	90	476	119	74	460	74
Private nonguaranteed	116	0	61	11	20	25	68	22
Interest payments	**619**	**569**	**776**	**802**	**779**	**735**	**757**	**719**
Public and publicly guaranteed	603	565	774	799	776	734	757	719
Official creditors	572	547	680	714	654	581	563	557
Private creditors	31	18	94	85	123	152	194	161
Private nonguaranteed	16	4	2	3	2	1	0	0
Debt resource inflows								
Net debt inflows	-718	1,453	1,728	-593	-203	2,050	-1,262	5,066
Official creditors (incl. IMF)	-643	-230	621	-885	102	-153	-662	1,450
Private creditors	-75	1,683	1,107	292	-305	2,203	-600	3,616
Long-term	115	1,747	591	-315	-24	1,615	-477	-15
Public and publicly guaranteed	23	1,747	652	-375	-13	1,635	-439	-19
Private nonguaranteed	91	..	-61	59	-11	-20	-38	4
Short-term	-189	-64	516	607	-281	588	-123	3,632
Non-debt resource inflows								
Foreign direct investment	1,235	5,376	11,578	9,495	6,712	6,386	-483	2,798
Portfolio equity	269	729	-3,199	-674	393	1,724	-711	-983
Currency composition (%)								
Euro	..	33.6	36.3	35.1	35.9	31.8	30.5	29.2
U.S.dollars	39.8	36.6	35.3	34.3	33.9	37.7	37.2	40.5
Major economic aggregates								
Gross national income (GNI)	100,770	89,432	132,930	165,655	191,178	217,727	232,593	254,233
Exports of goods, services & prim. income	18,735	32,141	47,707	57,826	45,601	49,365	47,371	48,834
Personal transfers & comp. of employees	2,852	5,017	7,656	8,694	7,150	12,453	14,324	19,236
Imports of goods, services & prim. income	23,878	35,787	55,618	68,999	56,910	66,308	68,076	75,597
Primary income on FDI	92	647	1,015	680	2,101	5,268	5,079	5,704
Current account balance	-971	2,103	412	-1,415	-3,349	-4,504	-5,484	-6,972
International reserves	13,118	20,609	30,188	32,216	32,253	33,612	14,916	11,628
Ratios								
External debt stocks to exports (%)	155.7	93.2	71.7	58.1	76.9	74.0	74.2	81.9
External debt stocks to GNI (%)	29.0	33.5	25.7	20.3	18.3	16.8	15.1	15.7
Debt service to exports (%)	9.8	6.9	6.0	5.6	6.4	6.1	7.4	6.6
Short-term to external debt stocks (%)	14.1	5.5	6.5	8.5	7.3	8.6	8.6	16.6
Multilateral to external debt stocks (%)	13.4	17.4	22.5	22.9	24.7	25.3	27.3	26.1
Reserves to external debt stocks (%)	45.0	68.8	88.2	96.0	92.0	92.0	42.4	29.1
Reserves to imports (months)	6.6	6.9	6.5	5.6	6.8	6.1	2.6	1.8

EL SALVADOR

(US$ million, unless otherwise indicated)

	2000	2005	2007	2008	2009	2010	2011	2012
Summary external debt data								
External debt stocks	**4,535**	**9,317**	**9,855**	**10,651**	**10,368**	**11,328**	**11,995**	**13,279**
Long-term external debt	2,858	7,425	8,523	9,070	9,248	9,971	10,521	11,411
Short-term external debt	1,645	1,856	1,292	1,542	863	1,105	1,223	1,616
interest arrears on long-term	0	0	0	0	0	0	0	0
Use of IMF credit	33	36	39	38	257	252	251	252
Long-term external debt								
Debt outstanding and disbursed	**2,858**	**7,425**	**8,523**	**9,070**	**9,248**	**9,971**	**10,521**	**11,411**
Public and publicly guaranteed	2,746	4,802	5,444	5,754	6,109	6,402	6,537	7,371
Official creditors	2,541	3,083	3,169	3,487	3,845	4,182	4,301	4,338
Private creditors	205	1,719	2,275	2,267	2,264	2,220	2,237	3,033
Private nonguaranteed	111	2,622	3,079	3,316	3,139	3,569	3,983	4,040
Disbursements	**372**	**1,222**	**246**	**1,042**	**1,216**	**1,055**	**874**	**917**
Public and publicly guaranteed	321	682	246	666	910	707	476	522
Official creditors	201	337	246	601	910	707	476	522
Private creditors	120	345	0	65	0	0	0	0
Private nonguaranteed	51	540	0	376	306	348	398	395
Principal repayments	**163**	**406**	**551**	**490**	**687**	**604**	**757**	**630**
Public and publicly guaranteed	130	245	341	351	559	455	587	453
Official creditors	126	230	282	347	555	388	367	452
Private creditors	4	16	60	4	4	68	220	1
Private nonguaranteed	33	160	210	139	127	149	170	177
Interest payments	**140**	**344**	**466**	**484**	**475**	**465**	**515**	**504**
Public and publicly guaranteed	133	257	349	369	374	350	386	373
Official creditors	124	119	138	136	139	117	119	121
Private creditors	9	139	211	232	235	233	267	252
Private nonguaranteed	7	87	117	116	102	115	129	131
Debt resource inflows								
Net debt inflows	802	892	-302	803	-150	693	234	680
Official creditors (incl. IMF)	75	107	-35	254	354	320	109	70
Private creditors	726	785	-267	548	-504	373	126	610
Long-term	134	709	-270	298	175	131	8	217
Public and publicly guaranteed	116	329	-59	61	-4	-68	-220	-1
Private nonguaranteed	18	380	-210	237	178	199	229	218
Short-term	592	77	3	250	-679	242	117	393
Non-debt resource inflows								
Foreign direct investment	173	511	1,551	903	369	248	306	467
Portfolio equity	..	..	..	..	..	..	..	..
Currency composition (%)								
Euro	..	3.5	3.8	3.4	3.2	2.8	2.6	2.4
U.S.dollars	67.4	81.2	83.1	83.4	85.1	86.4	87.5	90.1
Major economic aggregates								
Gross national income (GNI)	12,881	16,604	19,649	21,042	20,105	20,877	22,463	22,854
Exports of goods, services & prim. income	3,803	3,517	4,657	4,989	4,293	5,035	5,946	6,142
Personal transfers & comp. of employees	1,765	3,029	3,709	3,755	3,402	3,447	3,665	3,927
Imports of goods, services & prim. income	6,031	7,173	9,620	10,268	8,047	9,203	10,924	11,404
Primary income on FDI	60	181	159	39	175	209	276	515
Current account balance	-431	-622	-1,217	-1,532	-312	-570	-1,137	-1,257
International reserves	1,773	1,723	2,110	2,443	2,869	2,570	2,153	2,806
Ratios								
External debt stocks to exports (%)	119.3	264.9	211.6	213.5	241.5	225.0	201.7	216.2
External debt stocks to GNI (%)	35.2	56.1	50.2	50.6	51.6	54.3	53.4	58.1
Debt service to exports (%)	9.9	24.2	23.5	20.2	27.4	21.5	21.6	18.7
Short-term to external debt stocks (%)	36.3	19.9	13.1	14.5	8.3	9.8	10.2	12.2
Multilateral to external debt stocks (%)	42.7	26.3	25.5	26.1	30.7	31.2	30.7	28.5
Reserves to external debt stocks (%)	39.1	18.5	21.4	22.9	27.7	22.7	17.9	21.1
Reserves to imports (months)	3.5	2.9	2.6	2.9	4.3	3.4	2.4	3.0

Notes:

Long-term private nonguaranteed debt data from 2005 are World Bank staff estimates based on reports provided by the country.

ERITREA

(US$ million, unless otherwise indicated)

	2000	2005	2007	2008	2009	2010	2011	2012
Summary external debt data								
External debt stocks	**329.7**	**757.2**	**896.4**	**997.8**	**1,050.7**	**1,041.5**	**1,055.2**	**994.1**
Long-term external debt	298.0	723.0	855.7	957.0	1,013.0	1,002.0	1,013.6	952.1
Short-term external debt	12.0	12.6	16.7	17.5	13.9	16.2	18.4	18.6
interest arrears on long-term	2.0	1.6	3.7	4.5	5.9	6.2	7.4	12.6
Use of IMF credit	19.8	21.7	24.0	23.3	23.8	23.3	23.3	23.3
Long-term external debt								
Debt outstanding and disbursed	**298.0**	**723.0**	**855.7**	**957.0**	**1,013.0**	**1,002.0**	**1,013.6**	**952.1**
Public and publicly guaranteed	298.0	723.0	855.7	957.0	1,013.0	1,002.0	1,013.6	952.1
Official creditors	298.0	690.1	814.7	917.4	972.1	964.1	976.9	914.7
Private creditors	0.0	32.9	41.0	39.5	40.9	38.0	36.8	37.5
Private nonguaranteed	..	..	..	..	..	..	..	..
Disbursements	**50.7**	**70.6**	**42.1**	**104.9**	**57.6**	**8.6**	**24.2**	**26.8**
Public and publicly guaranteed	50.7	70.6	42.1	104.9	57.6	8.6	24.2	26.8
Official creditors	50.7	70.6	42.1	104.1	57.6	8.6	24.2	26.8
Private creditors	0.0	0.0	0.0	0.8	0.0	0.0	0.0	0.0
Private nonguaranteed	..	..	..	..	..	..	..	..
Principal repayments	**0.5**	**11.8**	**1.7**	**6.5**	**11.3**	**13.3**	**14.0**	**86.0**
Public and publicly guaranteed	0.5	11.8	1.7	6.5	11.3	13.3	14.0	86.0
Official creditors	0.5	11.8	1.7	6.5	11.3	13.3	14.0	86.0
Private creditors	0.0	0.0	0.0	0.0	0.0	0.0	0.0	0.0
Private nonguaranteed	..	..	..	..	..	..	..	..
Interest payments	**2.5**	**8.4**	**4.1**	**9.1**	**10.3**	**9.3**	**7.9**	**8.5**
Public and publicly guaranteed	2.5	8.4	4.1	9.1	10.3	9.3	7.9	8.5
Official creditors	2.5	8.4	4.1	9.1	10.3	9.3	7.9	8.3
Private creditors	0.0	0.0	0.0	0.0	0.0	0.0	0.0	0.2
Private nonguaranteed	..	..	..	..	..	..	..	..
Debt resource inflows								
Net debt inflows	60.2	38.9	38.4	98.3	41.3	-2.7	11.2	-64.3
Official creditors (incl. IMF)	50.2	58.9	40.4	97.5	46.3	-4.7	10.2	-59.3
Private creditors	10.0	-20.0	-2.0	0.8	-5.0	2.0	1.0	-5.0
Long-term	0.0	0.0	0.0	0.8	0.0	0.0	0.0	0.0
Public and publicly guaranteed	0.0	0.0	0.0	0.8	0.0	0.0	0.0	0.0
Private nonguaranteed	..	..	..	..	..	..	..	..
Short-term	10.0	-20.0	-2.0	..	-5.0	2.0	1.0	-5.0
Non-debt resource inflows								
Foreign direct investment	27.9	1.4	7.2	39.0	91.0	91.0	39.0	73.7
Portfolio equity	..	..	..	..	..	..	..	..
Currency composition (%)								
Euro	..	5.3	5.5	4.7	4.4	4.0	3.7	4.0
U.S.dollars	57.0	68.5	67.9	66.6	67.8	67.3	67.2	66.5
Major economic aggregates								
Gross national income (GNI)	706.8	1,089.0	1,310.7	1,368.4	1,840.5	2,097.4	2,584.2	3,063.9
Exports of goods, services & prim. income	106.9	..	..	..	..	..	..	..
Personal transfers & comp. of employees	3.3	..	..	..	..	..	..	..
Imports of goods, services & prim. income	510.3	..	..	..	..	..	..	..
Primary income on FDI	4.4	..	..	..	..	..	..	..
Current account balance	-104.7	..	..	..	..	..	..	..
International reserves	25.5	27.9	34.3	57.9	90.0	114.1	114.8	..
Ratios								
External debt stocks to exports (%)	308.5	..	..	..	..	..	..	..
External debt stocks to GNI (%)	46.6	69.5	68.4	72.9	57.1	49.7	40.8	32.4
Debt service to exports (%)	4.3	..	..	..	..	..	..	..
Short-term to external debt stocks (%)	3.6	1.7	1.9	1.8	1.3	1.6	1.7	1.9
Multilateral to external debt stocks (%)	46.1	67.4	68.4	64.5	62.6	62.5	63.1	65.8
Reserves to external debt stocks (%)	7.7	3.7	3.8	5.8	8.6	11.0	10.9	..
Reserves to imports (months)	0.6	..	..	..	..	..	..	..

Notes:

Long-term public and publicly guaranteed debt from 2010 are World Bank staff estimates. Short-term debt is based on data from the BIS.

ETHIOPIA

(US$ million, unless otherwise indicated)

	2000	2005	2007	2008	2009	2010	2011	2012
Summary external debt data								
External debt stocks	**5,509**	**6,224**	**2,638**	**2,896**	**5,232**	**7,347**	**8,604**	**10,462**
Long-term external debt	5,339	5,928	2,571	2,829	4,819	6,547	7,945	9,941
Short-term external debt	79	120	49	50	45	314	175	37
interest arrears on long-term	65	36	32	32	32	30	30	26
Use of IMF credit	92	176	18	17	368	485	484	484
Long-term external debt								
Debt outstanding and disbursed	**5,339**	**5,928**	**2,571**	**2,829**	**4,819**	**6,547**	**7,945**	**9,941**
Public and publicly guaranteed	5,339	5,928	2,571	2,829	4,819	6,547	7,945	9,941
Official creditors	5,226	5,564	2,299	2,590	3,556	4,638	5,685	7,218
Private creditors	113	364	272	239	1,263	1,909	2,259	2,723
Private nonguaranteed	..	..	..	..	..	..	..	..
Disbursements	**185**	**527**	**376**	**379**	**2,148**	**1,760**	**1,693**	**2,309**
Public and publicly guaranteed	185	527	376	379	2,148	1,760	1,693	2,309
Official creditors	184	400	376	379	1,098	1,021	1,157	1,645
Private creditors	2	127	0	0	1,050	739	537	664
Private nonguaranteed	..	..	..	..	..	..	..	..
Principal repayments	**72**	**36**	**88**	**72**	**62**	**130**	**259**	**328**
Public and publicly guaranteed	72	36	88	72	62	130	259	328
Official creditors	62	25	44	39	34	39	80	122
Private creditors	10	11	44	33	27	91	179	206
Private nonguaranteed	..	..	..	..	..	..	..	..
Interest payments	**52**	**49**	**44**	**39**	**40**	**50**	**91**	**103**
Public and publicly guaranteed	52	49	44	39	40	50	91	103
Official creditors	48	40	29	27	33	35	52	58
Private creditors	4	10	15	11	8	15	38	46
Private nonguaranteed	..	..	..	..	..	..	..	..
Debt resource inflows								
Net debt inflows	90	478	265	309	2,246	2,023	1,295	1,847
Official creditors (incl. IMF)	109	371	333	340	1,228	1,105	1,077	1,524
Private creditors	-19	107	-68	-32	1,018	918	219	324
Long-term	-8	116	-44	-33	1,023	647	358	458
Public and publicly guaranteed	-8	116	-44	-33	1,023	647	358	458
Private nonguaranteed	..	..	..	..	..	..	..	..
Short-term	-11	-9	-23	1	-5	271	-139	-134
Non-debt resource inflows								
Foreign direct investment	135	265	222	109	221	288	627	279
Portfolio equity	..	..	..	..	..	..	..	..
Currency composition (%)								
Euro	..	5.6	17.5	16.9	8.5	10.1	8.0	6.9
U.S.dollars	75.8	72.4	58.3	55.3	68.9	70.3	72.3	74.1
Major economic aggregates								
Gross national income (GNI)	8,119	12,271	19,571	26,881	32,147	29,598	31,639	43,037
Exports of goods, services & prim. income	1,008	1,973	2,726	3,533	3,436	4,652	5,824	6,003
Personal transfers & comp. of employees	53	174	358	387	262	345	513	624
Imports of goods, services & prim. income	1,673	4,943	6,941	9,634	9,086	9,982	11,736	14,235
Primary income on FDI	9	21	18	17	18	35	23	6
Current account balance	13	-1,568	-828	-1,806	-2,191	-425	-783	-2,985
International reserves	306	1,043	1,290	871	1,781	..	..	..
Ratios								
External debt stocks to exports (%)	546.3	315.5	96.8	82.0	152.3	157.9	147.7	174.3
External debt stocks to GNI (%)	67.9	50.7	13.5	10.8	16.3	24.8	27.2	24.3
Debt service to exports (%)	13.7	4.8	4.9	3.1	3.0	3.9	6.1	7.2
Short-term to external debt stocks (%)	1.4	1.9	1.8	1.7	0.9	4.3	2.0	0.4
Multilateral to external debt stocks (%)	50.0	75.6	52.2	55.3	44.2	38.3	39.6	39.3
Reserves to external debt stocks (%)	5.6	16.8	48.9	30.1	34.0	..	..	..
Reserves to imports (months)	2.2	2.5	2.2	1.1	2.4	..	..	..

Notes:

Short-term debt is based on data from the BIS. Data include the effects of HIPC and MDRI debt relief.

FIJI

(US$ million, unless otherwise indicated)

	2000	2005	2007	2008	2009	2010	2011	2012
Summary external debt data								
External debt stocks	**181.7**	**195.7**	**380.3**	**390.6**	**536.2**	**554.6**	**860.6**	**731.7**
Long-term external debt	172.4	185.4	347.0	360.5	360.9	390.2	545.5	610.4
Short-term external debt	0.2	0.4	22.3	19.4	70.1	61.1	212.1	18.1
interest arrears on long-term	0.2	0.4	0.3	0.4	0.1	0.1	0.1	0.1
Use of IMF credit	9.1	9.9	11.0	10.7	105.2	103.3	103.0	103.1
Long-term external debt								
Debt outstanding and disbursed	**172.4**	**185.4**	**347.0**	**360.5**	**360.9**	**390.2**	**545.5**	**610.4**
Public and publicly guaranteed	172.4	185.4	347.0	360.1	360.4	389.7	545.0	610.0
Official creditors	172.4	185.4	197.0	210.1	210.4	239.7	295.0	360.0
Private creditors	0.0	0.0	150.0	150.0	150.0	150.0	250.0	250.0
Private nonguaranteed	..	..	..	0.4	0.5	0.5	0.5	0.5
Disbursements	**7.1**	**14.1**	**12.6**	**13.4**	**15.2**	**32.6**	**315.4**	**78.3**
Public and publicly guaranteed	7.1	14.1	12.6	13.2	15.0	32.6	315.4	78.2
Official creditors	7.1	14.1	12.6	13.2	15.0	32.6	65.4	78.2
Private creditors	0.0	0.0	0.0	0.0	0.0	0.0	250.0	0.0
Private nonguaranteed	..	..	..	0.2	0.3	0.0	0.0	0.0
Principal repayments	**16.9**	**8.5**	**10.4**	**7.8**	**10.4**	**7.9**	**163.8**	**11.4**
Public and publicly guaranteed	16.9	8.5	10.4	7.7	10.3	7.9	163.8	11.3
Official creditors	16.9	8.5	10.4	7.7	10.3	7.9	13.8	11.3
Private creditors	0.0	0.0	0.0	0.0	0.0	0.0	150.0	0.0
Private nonguaranteed	..	..	..	0.0	0.0	0.0	0.1	0.1
Interest payments	**7.7**	**5.5**	**16.1**	**15.8**	**14.4**	**13.3**	**24.9**	**26.7**
Public and publicly guaranteed	7.7	5.5	16.1	15.8	14.4	13.3	24.9	26.7
Official creditors	7.7	5.5	5.8	5.5	4.1	3.0	3.3	4.2
Private creditors	0.0	0.0	10.3	10.3	10.3	10.3	21.6	22.5
Private nonguaranteed	..	..	..	0.0	0.0	0.0	0.0	0.0
Debt resource inflows								
Net debt inflows	-9.8	-47.5	13.2	2.6	55.9	15.6	302.6	-127.1
Official creditors (incl. IMF)	-9.8	5.5	2.2	5.5	4.6	24.6	51.7	66.9
Private creditors	0.0	-53.0	11.0	-2.9	51.2	-9.0	251.0	-194.0
Long-term	0.0	0.0	0.0	0.1	0.2	0.0	100.0	0.0
Public and publicly guaranteed	0.0	0.0	0.0	0.0	0.0	0.0	100.0	0.0
Private nonguaranteed	..	..	..	0.1	0.2	0.0	0.0	0.0
Short-term	..	-53.0	11.0	-3.0	51.0	-9.0	151.0	-194.0
Non-debt resource inflows								
Foreign direct investment	0.6	159.6	377.0	350.3	134.7	196.2	417.2	267.9
Portfolio equity	..	1.7	4.8	1.4	-1.1	0.1	..	..
Currency composition (%)								
Euro	..	2.3	1.3	1.1	0.6	0.5	..	..
U.S.dollars	49.0	64.2	83.4	82.7	83.5	80.8	81.4	76.3
Major economic aggregates								
Gross national income (GNI)	1,717.4	3,050.1	3,329.5	3,503.4	2,870.6	3,072.1	3,698.9	3,829.6
Exports of goods, services & prim. income	1,023.2	1,600.7	1,631.3	1,913.4	1,375.0	1,755.3	..	..
Personal transfers & comp. of employees	44.0	203.7	183.2	146.7	171.2	173.8	..	..
Imports of goods, services & prim. income	1,136.4	2,038.7	2,258.1	2,752.7	1,783.5	2,236.0	..	..
Primary income on FDI	7.5	132.8	127.1	122.3	48.0	143.4	..	..
Current account balance	-25.5	-257.5	-436.2	-647.3	-224.8	-360.3	-152.4	70.2
International reserves	411.8	320.9	527.6	321.5	569.1	719.4	832.2	920.0
Ratios								
External debt stocks to exports (%)	17.8	12.2	23.3	20.4	39.0	31.6	..	..
External debt stocks to GNI (%)	10.6	6.4	11.4	11.1	18.7	18.1	23.3	19.1
Debt service to exports (%)	2.4	0.9	1.7	1.3	1.9	1.3	..	..
Short-term to external debt stocks (%)	0.1	0.2	5.9	5.0	13.1	11.0	24.6	2.5
Multilateral to external debt stocks (%)	48.9	46.9	26.7	27.8	19.2	20.7	14.6	18.4
Reserves to external debt stocks (%)	226.7	164.0	138.7	82.3	106.1	129.7	96.7	125.7
Reserves to imports (months)	4.3	1.9	2.8	1.4	3.8	3.9	..	..

Notes:

Long-term private nonguaranteed debt data for 2012 are World Bank staff estimates. Short-term debt is based on data from the BIS.

GABON

(US$ million, unless otherwise indicated)

	2000	2005	2007	2008	2009	2010	2011	2012
Summary external debt data								
External debt stocks	**3,920**	**3,898**	**2,883**	**2,153**	**2,324**	**2,517**	**2,783**	**2,870**
Long-term external debt	3,457	3,564	2,611	2,016	1,991	2,121	2,372	2,534
Short-term external debt	355	246	225	115	104	170	185	111
interest arrears on long-term	63	186	10	5	1	0	0	0
Use of IMF credit	107	88	47	22	230	226	225	225
Long-term external debt								
Debt outstanding and disbursed	**3,457**	**3,564**	**2,611**	**2,016**	**1,991**	**2,121**	**2,372**	**2,534**
Public and publicly guaranteed	3,457	3,564	2,611	2,016	1,991	2,121	2,372	2,534
Official creditors	3,338	3,444	1,476	954	893	877	913	981
Private creditors	119	119	1,135	1,062	1,098	1,244	1,459	1,553
Private nonguaranteed	..	..	..	..	..	..	..	..
Disbursements	**34**	**18**	**1,089**	**107**	**261**	**466**	**540**	**401**
Public and publicly guaranteed	34	18	1,089	107	261	466	540	401
Official creditors	13	18	41	62	147	189	207	180
Private creditors	21	0	1,048	45	114	276	333	221
Private nonguaranteed	..	..	..	..	..	..	..	..
Principal repayments	**188**	**112**	**2,234**	**552**	**261**	**298**	**257**	**260**
Public and publicly guaranteed	188	112	2,234	552	261	298	257	260
Official creditors	160	63	2,195	492	222	177	165	119
Private creditors	27	48	39	61	39	120	91	142
Private nonguaranteed	..	..	..	..	..	..	..	..
Interest payments	**124**	**52**	**366**	**218**	**141**	**131**	**127**	**129**
Public and publicly guaranteed	124	52	366	218	141	131	127	129
Official creditors	118	46	361	133	49	32	30	28
Private creditors	7	7	5	85	91	99	97	102
Private nonguaranteed	..	..	..	..	..	..	..	..
Debt resource inflows								
Net debt inflows	-363	-58	-1,054	-575	-7	235	298	67
Official creditors (incl. IMF)	-140	-70	-2,188	-454	-75	12	42	61
Private creditors	-223	12	1,134	-121	69	223	257	5
Long-term	-7	-48	1,009	-16	76	156	242	79
Public and publicly guaranteed	-7	-48	1,009	-16	76	156	242	79
Private nonguaranteed	..	..	..	..	..	..	..	..
Short-term	-216	60	125	-105	-7	67	15	-74
Non-debt resource inflows								
Foreign direct investment	-43	326	269	773	573	499	696	702
Portfolio equity	..	..	..	..	..	..	..	..
Currency composition (%)								
Euro	..	47.5	34.9	25.8	23.9	25.2	28.1	29.1
U.S.dollars	29.1	36.2	44.5	55.5	56.0	55.4	52.1	50.4
Major economic aggregates								
Gross national income (GNI)	4,289	7,708	10,082	13,882	11,068	12,732	16,298	16,577
Exports of goods, services & prim. income	3,547	5,639	..	..	..	..	..	..
Personal transfers & comp. of employees	6	11	..	..	..	..	..	..
Imports of goods, services & prim. income	2,483	3,387	..	..	..	..	..	..
Primary income on FDI	473	765	..	..	..	..	..	..
Current account balance	1,001	1,983	2,046	3,402	1,625	..	..	..
International reserves	190	669	1,227	1,923	1,993	1,736	2,157	2,352
Ratios								
External debt stocks to exports (%)	110.5	69.1	..	..	..	..	..	..
External debt stocks to GNI (%)	91.4	50.6	28.6	15.5	21.0	19.8	17.1	17.3
Debt service to exports (%)	9.9	3.4	..	..	..	..	..	..
Short-term to external debt stocks (%)	9.1	6.3	7.8	5.3	4.5	6.8	6.6	3.9
Multilateral to external debt stocks (%)	11.9	10.1	14.1	17.7	17.2	15.3	15.9	16.6
Reserves to external debt stocks (%)	4.8	17.2	42.6	89.3	85.8	69.0	77.5	81.9
Reserves to imports (months)	0.9	2.4	..	..	..	..	..	..

Notes:

Long-term public and publicly guaranteed debt data before 2008 are World Bank staff estimates based on reports provided by the country. Short-term debt is based on data from the BIS. Data include the effects of Paris Club debt buyback agreement signed in 2007.

GAMBIA, THE

(US$ million, unless otherwise indicated)

	2000	2005	2007	2008	2009	2010	2011	2012
Summary external debt data								
External debt stocks	**490.1**	**667.1**	**700.1**	**373.0**	**506.2**	**512.3**	**475.8**	**512.9**
Long-term external debt	438.0	616.5	664.0	336.8	387.6	391.0	394.4	395.8
Short-term external debt	27.3	22.4	21.6	15.9	43.4	44.3	1.1	22.6
interest arrears on long-term	0.0	1.4	0.6	1.9	2.4	2.3	1.1	1.6
Use of IMF credit	24.8	28.1	14.4	20.2	75.2	77.0	80.3	94.4
Long-term external debt								
Debt outstanding and disbursed	**438.0**	**616.5**	**664.0**	**336.8**	**387.6**	**391.0**	**394.4**	**395.8**
Public and publicly guaranteed	438.0	616.5	664.0	336.8	387.6	391.0	394.4	395.8
Official creditors	437.0	616.5	664.0	334.3	384.2	384.6	390.3	386.2
Private creditors	1.0	0.0	0.0	2.5	3.4	6.4	4.1	9.6
Private nonguaranteed	..	..	..	..	..	..	..	..
Disbursements	**20.7**	**54.3**	**39.9**	**37.3**	**33.5**	**43.2**	**24.3**	**25.2**
Public and publicly guaranteed	20.7	54.3	39.9	37.3	33.5	43.2	24.3	25.2
Official creditors	20.7	54.3	39.9	35.8	32.7	36.8	24.3	17.8
Private creditors	0.0	0.0	0.0	1.5	0.8	6.4	0.0	7.3
Private nonguaranteed	..	..	..	..	..	..	..	..
Principal repayments	**12.7**	**16.1**	**20.1**	**10.3**	**11.3**	**15.8**	**18.4**	**17.8**
Public and publicly guaranteed	12.7	16.1	20.1	10.3	11.3	15.8	18.4	17.8
Official creditors	12.3	15.8	20.1	10.3	11.3	12.6	16.2	15.7
Private creditors	0.4	0.3	0.0	0.0	0.0	3.2	2.2	2.1
Private nonguaranteed	..	..	..	..	..	..	..	..
Interest payments	**6.0**	**9.4**	**8.8**	**5.8**	**7.0**	**6.6**	**6.3**	**6.1**
Public and publicly guaranteed	6.0	9.4	8.8	5.8	7.0	6.6	6.3	6.1
Official creditors	5.9	9.4	8.8	5.8	7.0	6.6	6.2	5.9
Private creditors	0.1	0.0	0.0	0.0	0.0	0.0	0.1	0.2
Private nonguaranteed	..	..	..	..	..	..	..	..
Debt resource inflows								
Net debt inflows	20.6	33.2	26.2	26.3	64.9	31.5	-32.5	42.4
Official creditors (incl. IMF)	15.8	36.5	22.2	31.8	37.1	27.3	11.7	16.1
Private creditors	4.8	-3.3	4.0	-5.5	27.8	4.2	-44.2	26.3
Long-term	-0.4	-0.3	..	1.5	0.8	3.2	-2.2	5.3
Public and publicly guaranteed	-0.4	-0.3	..	1.5	0.8	3.2	-2.2	5.3
Private nonguaranteed	..	..	..	..	..	..	..	..
Short-term	5.2	-3.0	4.0	-7.0	27.0	1.0	-42.0	21.0
Non-debt resource inflows								
Foreign direct investment	..	53.7	78.1	78.6	39.4	37.4	36.2	33.5
Portfolio equity	..	..	..	..	..	..	..	..
Currency composition (%)								
Euro	..	3.5	3.6	5.2	5.0	5.1	3.5	4.9
U.S.dollars	51.2	55.2	48.0	50.8	46.6	46.9	45.7	43.0
Major economic aggregates								
Gross national income (GNI)	752.7	601.7	773.0	940.1	872.6	922.3	867.6	874.5
Exports of goods, services & prim. income	..	189.8	271.3	335.8	290.1	284.9	318.9	343.8
Personal transfers & comp. of employees	..	59.3	55.7	64.8	79.8	115.7	107.9	141.0
Imports of goods, services & prim. income	..	305.0	419.8	407.4	362.3	341.3	392.8	468.0
Primary income on FDI	..	26.9	38.4	42.8	11.7	11.5	11.3	10.2
Current account balance	..	-43.4	-58.4	10.9	63.0	56.3	109.8	57.6
International reserves	109.4	98.3	142.8	116.5	224.2	201.6	223.2	236.2
Ratios								
External debt stocks to exports (%)	..	351.5	258.1	111.1	174.5	179.8	149.2	149.2
External debt stocks to GNI (%)	65.1	110.9	90.6	39.7	58.0	55.5	54.8	58.7
Debt service to exports (%)	..	15.1	12.5	5.1	6.5	8.1	7.9	7.1
Short-term to external debt stocks (%)	5.6	3.4	3.1	4.3	8.6	8.7	0.2	4.4
Multilateral to external debt stocks (%)	70.1	75.3	78.0	58.1	53.1	51.6	57.8	54.2
Reserves to external debt stocks (%)	22.3	14.7	20.4	31.2	44.3	39.4	46.9	46.1
Reserves to imports (months)	..	3.9	4.1	3.4	7.4	7.1	6.8	6.1

Notes:

Short-term debt is based on data from the BIS. Data include the effects of HIPC and MDRI debt relief.

GEORGIA

(US$ million, unless otherwise indicated)

	2000	2005	2007	2008	2009	2010	2011	2012
Summary external debt data								
External debt stocks	**1,826**	**2,151**	**2,897**	**7,633**	**8,556**	**9,519**	**11,359**	**13,426**
Long-term external debt	1,316	1,663	1,844	6,003	6,736	7,284	8,605	10,302
Short-term external debt	44	50	574	948	808	963	1,545	2,159
interest arrears on long-term	1	11	7	7	7	7	84	389
Use of IMF credit	466	438	479	682	1,012	1,272	1,210	965
Long-term external debt								
Debt outstanding and disbursed	**1,316**	**1,663**	**1,844**	**6,003**	**6,736**	**7,284**	**8,605**	**10,302**
Public and publicly guaranteed	1,274	1,531	1,604	2,974	3,529	4,141	4,343	4,876
Official creditors	1,272	1,529	1,602	1,780	2,155	2,450	2,706	3,097
Private creditors	2	2	2	1,194	1,375	1,691	1,637	1,778
Private nonguaranteed	42	132	241	3,029	3,207	3,143	4,262	5,426
Disbursements	**65**	**146**	**193**	**893**	**1,147**	**1,190**	**1,785**	**2,652**
Public and publicly guaranteed	37	76	100	725	678	815	843	690
Official creditors	37	76	100	225	427	401	343	431
Private creditors	0	0	0	500	250	414	500	258
Private nonguaranteed	28	69	93	168	469	375	942	1,963
Principal repayments	**42**	**103**	**103**	**423**	**474**	**510**	**1,199**	**956**
Public and publicly guaranteed	41	80	86	110	140	169	620	165
Official creditors	41	80	85	40	70	71	67	48
Private creditors	0	0	0	70	70	97	553	118
Private nonguaranteed	2	23	17	314	334	342	579	790
Interest payments	**43**	**28**	**33**	**225**	**251**	**247**	**307**	**410**
Public and publicly guaranteed	42	24	25	54	77	87	139	112
Official creditors	42	24	25	28	31	39	35	38
Private creditors	0	0	0	27	45	47	104	73
Private nonguaranteed	1	4	8	171	174	160	167	298
Debt resource inflows								
Net debt inflows	33	-30	231	1,065	846	1,111	1,031	1,762
Official creditors (incl. IMF)	-29	-17	17	406	670	605	216	139
Private creditors	62	-14	213	659	176	505	815	1,622
Long-term	26	46	75	285	316	350	310	1,313
Public and publicly guaranteed	0	0	0	430	181	316	-53	141
Private nonguaranteed	26	47	75	-145	136	34	363	1,172
Short-term	36	-60	138	374	-140	156	505	309
Non-debt resource inflows								
Foreign direct investment	131	453	1,878	1,591	653	869	1,084	831
Portfolio equity	..	3	34	115	12	-22	-7	74
Currency composition (%)								
Euro	..	19.7	16.7	9.0	7.9	8.0	9.7	12.5
U.S.dollars	82.3	73.3	73.1	81.7	80.3	80.7	78.4	73.5
Major economic aggregates								
Gross national income (GNI)	3,175	6,473	10,209	12,680	10,679	11,416	14,012	15,723
Exports of goods, services & prim. income	1,007	2,415	3,645	4,245	3,672	4,591	6,000	7,099
Personal transfers & comp. of employees	274	446	883	1,065	1,112	1,184	1,547	1,770
Imports of goods, services & prim. income	1,433	3,469	6,325	8,115	5,779	6,885	9,168	10,357
Primary income on FDI	36	116	298	358	262	470	800	747
Current account balance	-177	-695	-1,991	-2,810	-1,139	-1,196	-1,840	-1,850
International reserves	116	479	1,361	1,480	2,110	2,264	2,818	2,873
Ratios								
External debt stocks to exports (%)	181.3	89.1	79.5	179.8	233.0	207.4	189.3	189.1
External debt stocks to GNI (%)	57.5	33.2	28.4	60.2	80.1	83.4	81.1	85.4
Debt service to exports (%)	12.5	8.1	6.0	16.7	21.0	17.5	26.8	23.3
Short-term to external debt stocks (%)	2.4	2.3	19.8	12.4	9.4	10.1	13.6	16.1
Multilateral to external debt stocks (%)	26.2	38.1	35.0	15.6	17.9	18.9	17.8	17.2
Reserves to external debt stocks (%)	6.4	22.2	47.0	19.4	24.7	23.8	24.8	21.4
Reserves to imports (months)	1.0	1.7	2.6	2.2	4.4	3.9	3.7	3.3

GHANA

(US$ million, unless otherwise indicated)

	2000	2005	2007	2008	2009	2010	2011	2012
Summary external debt data								
External debt stocks	**6,261**	**7,182**	**5,113**	**5,689**	**7,190**	**9,316**	**11,296**	**12,436**
Long-term external debt	5,314	6,059	3,565	4,084	5,032	6,116	7,400	8,606
Short-term external debt	572	616	1,282	1,346	1,332	2,264	2,795	2,577
interest arrears on long-term	10	38	27	8	50	28	105	106
Use of IMF credit	375	507	266	259	826	937	1,101	1,253
Long-term external debt								
Debt outstanding and disbursed	**5,314**	**6,059**	**3,565**	**4,084**	**5,032**	**6,116**	**7,400**	**8,606**
Public and publicly guaranteed	5,057	6,059	3,565	4,084	5,032	6,116	7,400	8,606
Official creditors	4,705	5,496	2,137	2,600	3,329	4,220	5,133	5,979
Private creditors	352	563	1,428	1,485	1,703	1,895	2,267	2,627
Private nonguaranteed	257	0	0	0	0	0	0	0
Disbursements	**425**	**560**	**1,312**	**757**	**1,005**	**1,310**	**1,534**	**1,597**
Public and publicly guaranteed	425	560	1,312	757	1,005	1,310	1,534	1,597
Official creditors	342	485	436	600	726	998	1,025	1,060
Private creditors	82	74	876	156	279	312	509	537
Private nonguaranteed	0	0	0	0	0	0	0	0
Principal repayments	**217**	**190**	**134**	**137**	**138**	**151**	**199**	**440**
Public and publicly guaranteed	214	190	134	137	138	151	199	440
Official creditors	141	127	64	64	56	75	90	244
Private creditors	73	63	70	73	82	76	108	196
Private nonguaranteed	3	0	0	0	0	0	0	0
Interest payments	**95**	**88**	**66**	**130**	**107**	**160**	**98**	**192**
Public and publicly guaranteed	80	88	66	130	107	160	98	192
Official creditors	64	57	31	34	46	72	61	87
Private creditors	16	30	35	96	61	88	37	104
Private nonguaranteed	14	0	0	0	0	0	0	0
Debt resource inflows								
Net debt inflows	70	268	1,309	702	916	2,238	1,961	1,088
Official creditors (incl. IMF)	199	366	372	537	775	1,048	1,106	965
Private creditors	-129	-98	937	166	141	1,190	855	123
Long-term	6	11	806	83	197	236	401	342
Public and publicly guaranteed	9	11	806	83	197	236	401	342
Private nonguaranteed	-3	..	..	..	..	..	..	..
Short-term	-136	-109	131	83	-56	954	454	-219
Non-debt resource inflows								
Foreign direct investment	166	145	1,383	2,715	2,373	2,527	3,222	3,295
Portfolio equity	..	..	..	..	535	18	1	..
Currency composition (%)								
Euro	..	4.7	16.5	18.7	21.1	19.2	18.6	17.6
U.S.dollars	68.0	77.4	56.1	54.0	51.7	54.0	55.4	56.3
Major economic aggregates								
Gross national income (GNI)	4,836	10,601	24,617	28,412	25,885	31,765	37,922	38,564
Exports of goods, services & prim. income	2,456	3,952	6,088	7,156	7,735	9,490	14,712	16,858
Personal transfers & comp. of employees	32	99	117	126	114	136	152	138
Imports of goods, services & prim. income	3,473	6,851	10,510	12,695	11,710	14,560	20,813	24,186
Primary income on FDI	17	94	334	-80	495	396	1,062	1,915
Current account balance	-386	-1,105	-2,379	-3,327	-1,897	-2,747	-3,504	-4,778
International reserves	232	1,753	1,984	1,770	3,386	4,763	5,483	5,368
Ratios								
External debt stocks to exports (%)	254.9	181.7	84.0	79.5	93.0	98.2	76.8	73.8
External debt stocks to GNI (%)	129.5	67.7	20.8	20.0	27.8	29.3	29.8	32.2
Debt service to exports (%)	16.0	8.5	3.9	4.2	3.6	3.9	2.3	4.2
Short-term to external debt stocks (%)	9.1	8.6	25.1	23.6	18.5	24.3	24.7	20.7
Multilateral to external debt stocks (%)	58.5	70.2	30.2	33.4	32.4	29.5	29.0	29.7
Reserves to external debt stocks (%)	3.7	24.4	38.8	31.1	47.1	51.1	48.5	43.2
Reserves to imports (months)	0.8	3.1	2.3	1.7	3.5	3.9	3.2	2.7

Notes:

Long-term public and publicly guaranteed debt data for 2012 are World Bank staff estimates. Long-term private nonguaranteed debt data only cover bonds. Short-term debt is based on data from the BIS. Data include the effects of MDRI debt relief.

GRENADA

(US$ million, unless otherwise indicated)

	2000	2005	2007	2008	2009	2010	2011	2012
Summary external debt data								
External debt stocks	**203.5**	**407.2**	**537.6**	**551.8**	**571.4**	**578.1**	**566.9**	**590.6**
Long-term external debt	180.7	391.3	479.5	477.2	494.6	493.3	487.2	489.9
Short-term external debt	21.6	6.3	49.0	60.2	36.3	38.6	33.8	55.2
interest arrears on long-term	4.5	4.3	12.0	11.2	13.3	14.6	15.8	39.2
Use of IMF credit	1.2	9.7	9.1	14.4	40.5	46.3	45.9	45.5
Long-term external debt								
Debt outstanding and disbursed	**180.7**	**391.3**	**479.5**	**477.2**	**494.6**	**493.3**	**487.2**	**489.9**
Public and publicly guaranteed	180.7	391.3	479.5	477.2	494.6	493.3	487.2	489.9
Official creditors	116.8	172.4	231.6	257.2	274.6	277.7	273.2	275.8
Private creditors	63.9	218.9	247.9	219.9	219.9	215.6	214.0	214.0
Private nonguaranteed	..	..	..	..	..	..	..	..
Disbursements	**77.6**	**38.5**	**24.3**	**30.5**	**25.7**	**21.1**	**6.3**	**8.7**
Public and publicly guaranteed	77.6	38.5	24.3	30.5	25.7	21.1	6.3	8.7
Official creditors	19.8	38.5	24.3	30.5	25.7	21.1	6.3	8.7
Private creditors	57.8	0.0	0.0	0.0	0.0	0.0	0.0	0.0
Private nonguaranteed	..	..	..	..	..	..	..	..
Principal repayments	**10.1**	**5.6**	**7.2**	**8.9**	**9.4**	**15.4**	**13.5**	**6.3**
Public and publicly guaranteed	10.1	5.6	7.2	8.9	9.4	15.4	13.5	6.3
Official creditors	6.3	5.3	7.2	8.9	9.4	11.0	10.6	6.3
Private creditors	3.7	0.4	0.0	0.0	0.0	4.4	2.9	0.0
Private nonguaranteed	..	..	..	..	..	..	..	..
Interest payments	**3.4**	**3.3**	**8.6**	**8.3**	**11.1**	**10.9**	**11.5**	**8.2**
Public and publicly guaranteed	3.4	3.3	8.6	8.3	11.1	10.9	11.5	8.2
Official creditors	2.3	3.3	5.6	5.6	5.8	5.7	6.4	3.6
Private creditors	1.1	0.0	3.0	2.6	5.4	5.2	5.1	4.6
Private nonguaranteed	..	..	..	..	..	..	..	..
Debt resource inflows								
Net debt inflows	63.4	-28.1	22.8	39.3	0.0	13.1	-13.4	-0.1
Official creditors (incl. IMF)	13.4	33.2	14.8	27.3	26.0	16.5	-4.5	1.9
Private creditors	50.0	-61.4	8.0	12.0	-26.0	-3.4	-8.9	-2.0
Long-term	54.1	-0.4	0.0	0.0	0.0	-4.4	-2.9	0.0
Public and publicly guaranteed	54.1	-0.4	0.0	0.0	0.0	-4.4	-2.9	0.0
Private nonguaranteed	..	..	..	..	..	..	..	..
Short-term	-4.1	-61.0	8.0	12.0	-26.0	1.0	-6.0	-2.0
Non-debt resource inflows								
Foreign direct investment	37.4	70.2	156.6	134.8	102.6	60.4	42.6	30.2
Portfolio equity	..	..	..	..	..	..	..	..
Currency composition (%)								
Euro	..	0.4	0.3	0.3	0.3	0.3	0.3	0.3
U.S.dollars	78.4	91.3	92.1	91.0	90.3	91.0	91.3	91.3
Major economic aggregates								
Gross national income (GNI)	489.5	672.1	717.6	783.3	708.2	729.8	748.6	751.3
Exports of goods, services & prim. income	240.8	160.3	223.2	215.9	195.3	190.8	199.5	199.5
Personal transfers & comp. of employees	46.4	26.8	28.6	28.9	27.7	28.5	28.9	29.4
Imports of goods, services & prim. income	349.0	435.9	491.1	502.5	432.1	425.3	428.1	438.3
Primary income on FDI	27.8	22.7	35.7	31.7	55.4	30.8	20.6	21.0
Current account balance	-88.1	-193.3	-241.7	-251.9	-197.2	-202.6	-204.5	-214.4
International reserves	57.7	94.3	110.6	105.3	129.1	119.2	120.7	119.5
Ratios								
External debt stocks to exports (%)	84.5	254.0	240.9	255.6	292.7	303.0	284.2	296.0
External debt stocks to GNI (%)	41.6	60.6	74.9	70.4	80.7	79.2	75.7	78.6
Debt service to exports (%)	6.0	6.6	8.8	10.0	12.0	14.0	12.8	7.7
Short-term to external debt stocks (%)	10.6	1.5	9.1	10.9	6.4	6.7	6.0	9.3
Multilateral to external debt stocks (%)	31.1	27.2	28.0	30.6	32.0	32.5	32.8	32.0
Reserves to external debt stocks (%)	28.3	23.1	20.6	19.1	22.6	20.6	21.3	20.2
Reserves to imports (months)	2.0	2.6	2.7	2.5	3.6	3.4	3.4	3.3

GUATEMALA

(US$ million, unless otherwise indicated)

	2000	2005	2007	2008	2009	2010	2011	2012
Summary external debt data								
External debt stocks	**3,948**	**9,506**	**12,676**	**13,821**	**14,822**	**15,039**	**16,286**	**14,975**
Long-term external debt	2,740	8,014	10,629	11,627	13,281	13,144	13,712	12,697
Short-term external debt	1,172	1,453	2,004	2,151	1,226	1,585	2,265	1,970
interest arrears on long-term	317	414	0	0	0	0	0	0
Use of IMF credit	36	40	44	43	315	309	308	309
Long-term external debt								
Debt outstanding and disbursed	**2,740**	**8,014**	**10,629**	**11,627**	**13,281**	**13,144**	**13,712**	**12,697**
Public and publicly guaranteed	2,598	3,720	4,220	4,383	4,923	5,555	5,358	6,145
Official creditors	2,156	2,484	3,265	3,427	3,968	4,600	4,728	4,815
Private creditors	442	1,237	955	955	955	955	630	1,330
Private nonguaranteed	142	4,294	6,408	7,245	8,358	7,589	8,354	6,551
Disbursements	**220**	**1,639**	**2,237**	**958**	**941**	**1,471**	**1,031**	**1,373**
Public and publicly guaranteed	220	144	599	396	807	879	399	1,071
Official creditors	220	144	599	396	807	879	399	371
Private creditors	0	0	0	0	0	0	0	700
Private nonguaranteed	0	1,495	1,638	562	135	592	633	302
Principal repayments	**192**	**570**	**875**	**917**	**1,086**	**949**	**1,343**	**839**
Public and publicly guaranteed	172	200	360	260	269	264	600	259
Official creditors	139	199	210	260	269	264	275	259
Private creditors	32	1	150	0	0	0	325	0
Private nonguaranteed	20	371	515	656	817	685	743	580
Interest payments	**153**	**420**	**570**	**621**	**657**	**636**	**684**	**528**
Public and publicly guaranteed	134	203	249	257	258	284	284	210
Official creditors	112	102	149	169	170	196	196	177
Private creditors	23	101	101	88	88	88	88	34
Private nonguaranteed	19	217	321	365	399	352	401	318
Debt resource inflows								
Net debt inflows	62	906	1,892	188	-1,070	881	368	239
Official creditors (incl. IMF)	80	-56	390	136	537	615	123	111
Private creditors	-18	961	1,503	52	-1,607	266	245	127
Long-term	-52	1,124	973	-95	-682	-93	-435	422
Public and publicly guaranteed	-32	-1	-150	0	0	0	-325	700
Private nonguaranteed	-20	1,125	1,123	-95	-682	-93	-110	-278
Short-term	34	-163	530	147	-925	359	680	-295
Non-debt resource inflows								
Foreign direct investment	230	540	859	751	696	921	1,140	1,150
Portfolio equity	..	..	..	..	..	..	..	..
Currency composition (%)								
Euro	..	2.5	2.1	1.9	1.7	1.3	1.3	1.2
U.S.dollars	73.3	85.0	87.4	87.9	89.5	90.7	90.7	92.5
Major economic aggregates								
Gross national income (GNI)	19,065	26,726	33,270	38,199	36,632	40,129	45,330	49,426
Exports of goods, services & prim. income	4,077	7,069	9,270	10,264	9,572	11,108	13,106	12,809
Personal transfers & comp. of employees	596	3,067	4,236	4,460	4,019	4,232	4,524	5,035
Imports of goods, services & prim. income	5,991	11,886	15,910	17,052	14,190	16,680	19,838	19,963
Primary income on FDI	248	370	819	886	951	1,001	1,453	1,192
Current account balance	-1,050	-1,241	-1,786	-1,681	8	-626	-1,599	-1,447
International reserves	1,746	3,664	4,130	4,462	4,964	5,637	5,835	6,325
Ratios								
External debt stocks to exports (%)	96.8	134.5	136.7	134.7	154.8	135.4	124.3	116.9
External debt stocks to GNI (%)	20.7	35.6	38.1	36.2	40.5	37.5	35.9	30.3
Debt service to exports (%)	9.7	14.8	16.4	15.7	18.4	14.4	15.7	10.9
Short-term to external debt stocks (%)	29.7	15.3	15.8	15.6	8.3	10.5	13.9	13.2
Multilateral to external debt stocks (%)	38.5	21.5	22.9	22.2	24.4	28.2	26.9	30.0
Reserves to external debt stocks (%)	44.2	38.5	32.6	32.3	33.5	37.5	35.8	42.2
Reserves to imports (months)	3.5	3.7	3.1	3.1	4.2	4.1	3.5	3.8

Notes:

Long-term public and publicly guaranteed debt data for 2012 are World Bank staff estimates based on the original terms of the loans. Long-term private nonguaranteed debt data are World Bank staff estimates based on reports provided by the country. Short-term debt is based on data from the BIS.

GUINEA

(US$ million, unless otherwise indicated)

	2000	2005	2007	2008	2009	2010	2011	2012
Summary external debt data								
External debt stocks	**3,083**	**2,968**	**3,224**	**3,165**	**3,128**	**3,127**	**3,139**	**1,097**
Long-term external debt	2,650	2,771	2,992	2,873	2,868	2,798	2,849	842
Short-term external debt	298	84	139	194	40	124	91	40
interest arrears on long-term	81	84	95	38	38	56	80	40
Use of IMF credit	136	113	92	98	220	205	199	215
Long-term external debt								
Debt outstanding and disbursed	**2,650**	**2,771**	**2,992**	**2,873**	**2,868**	**2,798**	**2,849**	**842**
Public and publicly guaranteed	2,650	2,771	2,992	2,873	2,868	2,798	2,849	842
Official creditors	2,621	2,740	2,957	2,855	2,850	2,780	2,831	830
Private creditors	29	31	35	18	19	18	18	12
Private nonguaranteed	..	..	..	..	..	..	..	..
Disbursements	**71**	**93**	**74**	**63**	**42**	**32**	**33**	**39**
Public and publicly guaranteed	71	93	74	63	42	32	33	39
Official creditors	71	92	72	63	42	32	33	39
Private creditors	0	1	2	0	0	0	0	0
Private nonguaranteed	..	..	..	..	..	..	..	..
Principal repayments	**91**	**84**	**78**	**78**	**77**	**45**	**133**	**90**
Public and publicly guaranteed	91	84	78	78	77	45	133	90
Official creditors	91	84	78	78	77	45	133	90
Private creditors	0	0	0	0	0	0	0	0
Private nonguaranteed	..	..	..	..	..	..	..	..
Interest payments	**41**	**45**	**44**	**27**	**24**	**17**	**31**	**17**
Public and publicly guaranteed	41	45	44	27	24	17	31	17
Official creditors	41	45	44	27	24	17	31	17
Private creditors	0	0	0	0	0	0	0	0
Private nonguaranteed	..	..	..	..	..	..	..	..
Debt resource inflows								
Net debt inflows	-41	-17	-32	105	-202	42	-163	-47
Official creditors (incl. IMF)	-28	-18	-16	-7	-48	-24	-106	-36
Private creditors	-13	1	-16	112	-154	66	-57	-11
Long-term	0	1	2	0	0	0	0	0
Public and publicly guaranteed	0	1	2	0	0	0	0	0
Private nonguaranteed	..	..	..	..	..	..	..	..
Short-term	-12	..	-18	112	-154	66	-57	-11
Non-debt resource inflows								
Foreign direct investment	10	105	386	382	141	101	956	605
Portfolio equity	..	..	..	..	..	..	..	..
Currency composition (%)								
Euro	..	10.7	13.2	12.7	13.3	12.5	11.8	5.8
U.S.dollars	60.0	62.9	62.1	65.0	64.4	64.4	65.5	60.1
Major economic aggregates								
Gross national income (GNI)	2,922	2,658	3,832	3,341	3,711	4,302	4,651	6,237
Exports of goods, services & prim. income	758	929	1,313	1,455	1,144	1,549	1,528	2,118
Personal transfers & comp. of employees	1	42	15	62	52	46	65	66
Imports of goods, services & prim. income	973	1,079	1,637	1,911	1,581	1,892	2,829	3,289
Primary income on FDI	8	..	54	14	88	0	26	39
Current account balance	-140	-160	-455	-438	-403	-327	-1,161	-1,039
International reserves	148	95	..	..	..	..	103	..
Ratios								
External debt stocks to exports (%)	406.9	319.5	245.6	217.5	273.4	201.9	205.4	51.8
External debt stocks to GNI (%)	105.5	111.7	84.1	94.7	84.3	72.7	67.5	17.6
Debt service to exports (%)	20.7	16.8	11.2	8.8	10.1	4.7	11.2	7.0
Short-term to external debt stocks (%)	9.7	2.8	4.3	6.1	1.3	4.0	2.9	3.6
Multilateral to external debt stocks (%)	52.2	60.4	60.1	60.4	60.5	59.6	61.0	55.7
Reserves to external debt stocks (%)	4.8	3.2	..	..	..	..	3.3	..
Reserves to imports (months)	1.8	1.1	..	..	..	..	0.4	..

Notes:

Long-term public and publicly guaranteed debt data are World Bank staff estimates based on the original terms of the loans. Short-term debt is based on data from the BIS. Data include the effects of Paris Club debt restructuring agreement signed in 2010, 2012 and HIPC debt relief.

GUINEA-BISSAU

(US$ million, unless otherwise indicated)

	2000	2005	2007	2008	2009	2010	2011	2012
Summary external debt data								
External debt stocks	**947.8**	**1,021.7**	**1,091.3**	**1,098.3**	**1,149.0**	**1,128.6**	**283.7**	**279.5**
Long-term external debt	821.1	887.8	934.8	941.4	963.3	977.3	218.5	213.4
Short-term external debt	100.4	120.7	149.4	146.5	154.5	126.6	33.1	34.1
interest arrears on long-term	87.4	118.7	142.4	144.5	147.5	125.6	33.1	33.1
Use of IMF credit	26.3	13.2	7.1	10.5	31.3	24.7	32.0	32.0
Long-term external debt								
Debt outstanding and disbursed	**821.1**	**887.8**	**934.8**	**941.4**	**963.3**	**977.3**	**218.5**	**213.4**
Public and publicly guaranteed	821.1	887.8	934.8	941.4	963.3	977.3	218.5	213.4
Official creditors	821.1	887.8	934.8	941.4	963.3	977.3	218.5	213.4
Private creditors	0.0	0.0	0.0	0.0	0.0	0.0	0.0	0.0
Private nonguaranteed	..	..	..	..	..	..	..	..
Disbursements	**13.6**	**15.6**	**16.1**	**7.6**	**6.0**	**4.0**	**9.1**	**2.7**
Public and publicly guaranteed	13.6	15.6	16.1	7.6	6.0	4.0	9.1	2.7
Official creditors	13.6	15.6	16.1	7.6	6.0	4.0	9.1	2.7
Private creditors	0.0	0.0	0.0	0.0	0.0	0.0	0.0	0.0
Private nonguaranteed	..	..	..	..	..	..	..	..
Principal repayments	**2.6**	**1.0**	**3.6**	**4.1**	**4.7**	**5.8**	**4.5**	**6.3**
Public and publicly guaranteed	2.6	1.0	3.6	4.1	4.7	5.8	4.5	6.3
Official creditors	2.4	1.0	3.6	4.1	4.7	5.8	4.5	6.3
Private creditors	0.2	0.0	0.0	0.0	0.0	0.0	0.0	0.0
Private nonguaranteed	..	..	..	..	..	..	..	..
Interest payments	**1.6**	**2.0**	**3.3**	**3.4**	**3.7**	**3.3**	**0.5**	**0.6**
Public and publicly guaranteed	1.6	2.0	3.3	3.4	3.7	3.3	0.5	0.6
Official creditors	1.6	2.0	3.3	3.4	3.7	3.3	0.5	0.6
Private creditors	0.0	0.0	0.0	0.0	0.0	0.0	0.0	0.0
Private nonguaranteed	..	..	..	..	..	..	..	..
Debt resource inflows								
Net debt inflows	29.4	10.4	16.2	2.1	7.4	-0.2	11.2	-2.7
Official creditors (incl. IMF)	19.6	11.4	9.2	7.1	2.4	5.8	12.2	-3.7
Private creditors	9.8	-1.0	7.0	-5.0	5.0	-6.0	-1.0	1.0
Long-term	-0.2	0.0	0.0	0.0	0.0	0.0	0.0	0.0
Public and publicly guaranteed	-0.2	0.0	0.0	0.0	0.0	0.0	0.0	0.0
Private nonguaranteed	..	..	..	..	..	..	..	..
Short-term	10.0	-1.0	7.0	-5.0	5.0	-6.0	-1.0	1.0
Non-debt resource inflows								
Foreign direct investment	0.7	8.7	18.8	6.6	-1.3	1.5	25.0	16.2
Portfolio equity	..	..	0.2	..	-0.2	2.7	..	..
Currency composition (%)								
Euro	..	10.3	12.0	11.3	11.4	9.3	..	..
U.S.dollars	34.0	46.4	49.5	50.0	50.2	53.8	48.8	49.6
Major economic aggregates								
Gross national income (GNI)	203.1	561.4	686.8	829.4	822.4	834.5	967.3	896.0
Exports of goods, services & prim. income	..	95.2	140.9	172.1	163.4	183.8	..	..
Personal transfers & comp. of employees	8.0	19.9	43.0	49.5	48.9	45.9	..	..
Imports of goods, services & prim. income	..	156.9	246.5	298.9	308.9	314.6	..	..
Primary income on FDI	..	..	..	0.3	5.6	5.7	..	..
Current account balance	..	-10.5	-30.6	-28.8	-47.6	-70.8	-13.9	..
International reserves	66.8	79.8	112.9	124.6	168.6	156.4	220.0	164.6
Ratios								
External debt stocks to exports (%)	..	1072.9	774.7	638.2	703.2	614.0	..	..
External debt stocks to GNI (%)	466.8	182.0	158.9	132.4	139.7	135.2	29.3	31.2
Debt service to exports (%)	..	6.7	7.5	5.7	6.2	9.5	..	..
Short-term to external debt stocks (%)	10.6	11.8	13.7	13.3	13.4	11.2	11.7	12.2
Multilateral to external debt stocks (%)	41.8	45.4	47.7	47.2	45.3	44.8	40.4	39.6
Reserves to external debt stocks (%)	7.0	7.8	10.3	11.3	14.7	13.9	77.6	58.9
Reserves to imports (months)	..	6.1	5.5	5.0	6.5	6.0	..	..

Notes:

Long-term public and publicly guaranteed debt data are World Bank staff estimates. Short-term debt is based on data from the BIS. Data include the effects of Paris Club debt restructuring agreement and HIPC and MDRI debt relief.

GUYANA

(US$ million, unless otherwise indicated)

	2000	2005	2007	2008	2009	2010	2011	2012
Summary external debt data								
External debt stocks	**1,384**	**1,237**	**759**	**850**	**1,172**	**1,485**	**1,846**	**1,974**
Long-term external debt	1,129	1,043	584	675	781	885	1,054	1,215
Short-term external debt	119	82	93	96	196	410	609	588
interest arrears on long-term	67	82	93	96	97	103	107	111
Use of IMF credit	136	112	82	79	195	190	182	171
Long-term external debt								
Debt outstanding and disbursed	**1,129**	**1,043**	**584**	**675**	**781**	**885**	**1,054**	**1,215**
Public and publicly guaranteed	1,125	1,041	584	675	779	885	1,054	1,215
Official creditors	1,080	1,033	575	654	758	864	1,034	1,194
Private creditors	45	9	8	21	21	21	21	21
Private nonguaranteed	4	2	..	..	2	0	0	..
Disbursements	**64**	**104**	**101**	**138**	**105**	**123**	**188**	**279**
Public and publicly guaranteed	64	104	101	138	105	123	188	279
Official creditors	64	104	101	138	105	123	188	279
Private creditors	0	0	0	0	0	0	0	0
Private nonguaranteed	0	0	..	..	0	0	0	..
Principal repayments	**23**	**16**	**16**	**16**	**8**	**16**	**20**	**119**
Public and publicly guaranteed	22	15	16	16	8	16	20	119
Official creditors	22	15	16	16	8	16	20	119
Private creditors	0	0	0	0	0	0	0	0
Private nonguaranteed	0	0	..	..	0	0	0	..
Interest payments	**26**	**10**	**9**	**10**	**11**	**11**	**13**	**13**
Public and publicly guaranteed	26	10	9	10	10	11	13	13
Official creditors	26	10	9	10	10	11	13	13
Private creditors	0	0	0	0	0	0	0	0
Private nonguaranteed	0	0	..	..	0	0	0	..
Debt resource inflows								
Net debt inflows	21	76	9	122	195	314	355	124
Official creditors (incl. IMF)	34	108	85	122	96	106	160	149
Private creditors	-14	-32	-76	..	99	208	195	-25
Long-term	0	-1	..	..	0	0	0	..
Public and publicly guaranteed	0	0	..	..	..	..	..	..
Private nonguaranteed	0	0	..	..	0	0	0	..
Short-term	-13	-31	-76	..	99	208	195	-25
Non-debt resource inflows								
Foreign direct investment	67	77	152	178	164	198	247	276
Portfolio equity	..	..	..	..	..	..	..	..
Currency composition (%)								
Euro	..	2.1	4.6	3.5	2.9	2.2	1.7	1.4
U.S.dollars	69.3	74.3	86.5	88.8	90.2	90.3	89.9	88.9
Major economic aggregates								
Gross national income (GNI)	661	804	1,705	1,908	2,009	2,272	2,567	2,849
Exports of goods, services & prim. income	684	697	889	1,055	978	1,183	1,479	1,742
Personal transfers & comp. of employees	27	201	283	274	262	368	412	469
Imports of goods, services & prim. income	813	960	1,288	1,705	1,509	1,709	2,265	2,556
Primary income on FDI	6	7	-7	12	13	13	18	8
Current account balance	-82	-96	-112	-321	-231	-155	-372	-395
International reserves	305	252	313	356	631	782	802	864
Ratios								
External debt stocks to exports (%)	202.4	177.5	85.3	80.6	119.8	125.5	124.8	113.3
External debt stocks to GNI (%)	209.5	153.7	44.5	44.6	58.3	65.4	71.9	69.3
Debt service to exports (%)	10.2	5.0	3.2	2.5	2.1	2.7	3.1	8.7
Short-term to external debt stocks (%)	8.6	6.6	12.3	11.3	16.7	27.6	33.0	29.8
Multilateral to external debt stocks (%)	43.4	68.8	48.4	44.8	38.2	33.8	29.9	30.7
Reserves to external debt stocks (%)	22.0	20.4	41.3	41.9	53.9	52.7	43.4	43.8
Reserves to imports (months)	4.5	3.1	2.9	2.5	5.0	5.5	4.2	4.1

Notes:

Principal payment shown for 2012 include the price of rice exchanged under "Rice for oil". Data include the effects of HIPC and MDRI debt relief.

HAITI

(US$ million, unless otherwise indicated)

	2000	2005	2007	2008	2009	2010	2011	2012
Summary external debt data								
External debt stocks	**1,203**	**1,347**	**1,601**	**1,972**	**1,448**	**985**	**783**	**1,154**
Long-term external debt	1,056	1,278	1,525	1,846	1,158	850	635	985
Short-term external debt	90	28	0	0	0	0	0	0
interest arrears on long-term	1	15	0	0	0	0	0	0
Use of IMF credit	57	41	77	126	291	135	148	169
Long-term external debt								
Debt outstanding and disbursed	**1,056**	**1,278**	**1,525**	**1,846**	**1,158**	**850**	**635**	**985**
Public and publicly guaranteed	1,056	1,278	1,525	1,846	1,158	850	635	985
Official creditors	1,056	1,278	1,525	1,846	1,158	850	635	985
Private creditors	0	0	0	0	0	0	0	0
Private nonguaranteed	..	..	..	..	..	..	..	..
Disbursements	**51**	**77**	**97**	**356**	**212**	**284**	**341**	**346**
Public and publicly guaranteed	51	77	97	356	212	284	341	346
Official creditors	51	77	97	356	212	284	341	346
Private creditors	0	0	0	0	0	0	0	0
Private nonguaranteed	..	..	..	..	..	..	..	..
Principal repayments	**19**	**34**	**23**	**34**	**26**	**122**	**2**	**1**
Public and publicly guaranteed	19	34	23	34	26	122	2	1
Official creditors	19	34	23	34	26	122	2	1
Private creditors	0	0	0	0	0	0	0	0
Private nonguaranteed	..	..	..	..	..	..	..	..
Interest payments	**15**	**17**	**22**	**23**	**15**	**8**	**3**	**3**
Public and publicly guaranteed	15	17	22	23	15	8	3	3
Official creditors	15	17	22	23	15	8	3	3
Private creditors	0	0	0	0	0	0	0	0
Private nonguaranteed	..	..	..	..	..	..	..	..
Debt resource inflows								
Net debt inflows	20	21	-14	372	243	286	351	368
Official creditors (incl. IMF)	26	55	94	372	243	286	351	368
Private creditors	-6	-34	-108	0	0	0	0	0
Long-term	0	0	0	0	0	0	0	0
Public and publicly guaranteed	0	0	0	0	0	0	0	0
Private nonguaranteed	..	..	..	..	..	..	..	..
Short-term	-6	-34	-108	..	..	..	..	..
Non-debt resource inflows								
Foreign direct investment	13	26	75	30	38	150	181	179
Portfolio equity	..	..	..	..	..	..	..	..
Currency composition (%)								
Euro	..	3.4	5.7	5.0	4.0	3.6	..	..
U.S.dollars	81.1	80.4	80.9	84.1	87.3	88.6	89.8	93.4
Major economic aggregates								
Gross national income (GNI)	..	4,228	5,973	6,413	6,483	6,657	7,387	7,912
Exports of goods, services & prim. income	504	605	801	861	961	835	1,061	1,114
Personal transfers & comp. of employees	578	986	1,222	1,370	1,376	1,474	1,571	..
Imports of goods, services & prim. income	1,378	1,888	2,404	2,876	2,823	4,098	4,157	3,853
Primary income on FDI	..	..	..	..	..	..	..	..
Current account balance	-114	7	-86	-289	-226	-166	-339	-349
International reserves	182	133	452	541	789	1,335	1,195	1,284
Ratios								
External debt stocks to exports (%)	238.9	222.6	199.9	229.1	150.7	118.0	73.8	103.6
External debt stocks to GNI (%)	..	31.9	26.8	30.8	22.3	14.8	10.6	14.6
Debt service to exports (%)	9.2	9.5	10.4	6.7	4.7	15.7	0.5	0.3
Short-term to external debt stocks (%)	7.5	2.1	..	..	..	0.0	..	..
Multilateral to external debt stocks (%)	76.4	79.9	77.9	67.4	35.9	56.5	9.8	6.8
Reserves to external debt stocks (%)	15.1	9.9	28.2	27.5	54.4	135.5	152.6	111.3
Reserves to imports (months)	1.6	0.8	2.3	2.3	3.4	3.9	3.4	4.0

Notes:

Short-term debt is based on data from the BIS. Data include the effects of Paris Club restructuring agreements signed in 2006 and 2009 and HIPC and MDRI debt relief.

HONDURAS

(US$ million, unless otherwise indicated)

	2000	2005	2007	2008	2009	2010	2011	2012
Summary external debt data								
External debt stocks	**5,478**	**5,170**	**3,000**	**3,489**	**3,806**	**3,977**	**4,388**	**4,987**
Long-term external debt	4,863	4,654	2,621	2,963	3,330	3,382	3,905	4,433
Short-term external debt	374	321	317	466	249	374	267	345
interest arrears on long-term	35	12	5	3	10	11	6	6
Use of IMF credit	241	195	62	61	226	220	215	209
Long-term external debt								
Debt outstanding and disbursed	**4,863**	**4,654**	**2,621**	**2,963**	**3,330**	**3,382**	**3,905**	**4,433**
Public and publicly guaranteed	4,303	4,145	1,997	2,306	2,451	2,803	3,186	3,645
Official creditors	4,201	4,090	1,959	2,269	2,364	2,719	3,106	3,543
Private creditors	102	55	39	37	87	84	81	102
Private nonguaranteed	560	509	624	657	880	579	719	788
Disbursements	**347**	**481**	**385**	**649**	**703**	**904**	**1,453**	**1,416**
Public and publicly guaranteed	163	302	230	431	246	452	558	513
Official creditors	159	297	229	430	196	452	558	493
Private creditors	4	4	1	1	50	0	0	20
Private nonguaranteed	184	179	155	218	457	452	894	903
Principal repayments	**259**	**265**	**234**	**277**	**341**	**452**	**922**	**826**
Public and publicly guaranteed	93	139	105	54	107	62	65	60
Official creditors	91	138	103	53	106	61	63	60
Private creditors	1	1	2	1	1	1	2	0
Private nonguaranteed	166	126	130	223	234	390	856	767
Interest payments	**108**	**83**	**81**	**77**	**68**	**56**	**74**	**89**
Public and publicly guaranteed	77	64	53	49	41	46	59	70
Official creditors	76	63	53	49	41	46	58	70
Private creditors	0	0	0	0	0	0	0	0
Private nonguaranteed	31	20	28	27	27	10	15	19
Debt resource inflows								
Net debt inflows	42	155	182	523	139	575	424	662
Official creditors (incl. IMF)	84	159	126	377	90	389	490	427
Private creditors	-42	-4	56	146	49	185	-66	234
Long-term	20	57	25	-5	272	62	36	157
Public and publicly guaranteed	3	4	0	0	49	-1	-2	20
Private nonguaranteed	18	54	25	-6	223	62	38	136
Short-term	-63	-61	31	151	-223	124	-102	78
Non-debt resource inflows								
Foreign direct investment	382	601	967	1,201	494	485	1,043	1,068
Portfolio equity	..	..	..	..	..	..	..	..
Currency composition (%)								
Euro	..	5.7	8.8	9.3	10.0	8.3	7.2	7.0
U.S.dollars	64.9	72.4	68.0	69.1	69.0	73.3	76.2	78.1
Major economic aggregates								
Gross national income (GNI)	6,951	9,259	11,963	13,364	13,540	14,668	16,450	16,687
Exports of goods, services & prim. income	4,001	3,817	4,641	5,013	4,318	4,839	6,245	6,707
Personal transfers & comp. of employees	484	1,805	2,614	2,821	2,477	2,618	2,811	2,909
Imports of goods, services & prim. income	5,047	6,016	8,428	10,116	7,514	8,557	10,851	11,654
Primary income on FDI	160	479	535	534	602	681	910	1,218
Current account balance	-508	-304	-1,115	-2,129	-557	-836	-1,498	-1,744
International reserves	1,313	2,327	2,528	2,473	2,086	2,671	2,750	2,495
Ratios								
External debt stocks to exports (%)	136.9	135.5	64.6	69.6	88.1	82.2	70.3	74.4
External debt stocks to GNI (%)	78.8	55.8	25.1	26.1	28.1	27.1	26.7	29.9
Debt service to exports (%)	9.9	10.0	7.2	7.4	9.6	10.6	16.1	13.8
Short-term to external debt stocks (%)	6.8	6.2	10.6	13.3	6.5	9.4	6.1	6.9
Multilateral to external debt stocks (%)	50.7	61.7	42.6	41.2	40.0	47.7	53.2	55.2
Reserves to external debt stocks (%)	24.0	45.0	84.3	70.9	54.8	67.2	62.7	50.0
Reserves to imports (months)	3.1	4.6	3.6	2.9	3.3	3.7	3.0	2.6

Notes:

Data include the effects of HIPC and MDRI debt relief.

HUNGARY

(US$ million, unless otherwise indicated)

	2000	2005	2007	2008	2009	2010	2011	2012
Summary external debt data								
External debt stocks	**30,754**	**86,226**	**174,521**	**222,899**	**239,941**	**215,921**	**210,737**	**203,757**
Long-term external debt	25,310	66,184	139,622	186,755	197,704	169,836	165,850	172,700
Short-term external debt	4,152	18,626	33,333	28,125	28,711	32,798	31,641	22,745
interest arrears on long-term	0	0	0	0	0	0	0	0
Use of IMF credit	1,291	1,416	1,566	8,019	13,526	13,287	13,246	8,311
Long-term external debt								
Debt outstanding and disbursed	**25,310**	**66,184**	**139,622**	**186,755**	**197,704**	**169,836**	**165,850**	**172,700**
Public and publicly guaranteed	14,296	33,675	50,552	50,026	54,802	53,966	52,652	62,140
Official creditors	1,860	2,401	3,367	8,640	16,155	17,508	14,998	15,528
Private creditors	12,437	31,274	47,185	41,386	38,647	36,458	37,654	46,612
Private nonguaranteed	11,014	32,509	89,070	136,729	142,902	115,870	113,198	110,560
Disbursements	**6,283**	**26,467**	**52,795**	**112,009**	**105,860**	**67,411**	**113,838**	**99,030**
Public and publicly guaranteed	1,115	6,254	6,767	8,346	8,947	4,755	7,795	11,783
Official creditors	133	623	259	6,582	7,221	2,911	1,331	579
Private creditors	982	5,631	6,508	1,764	1,726	1,844	6,464	11,204
Private nonguaranteed	5,168	20,213	46,028	103,663	96,913	62,656	106,043	87,247
Principal repayments	**6,443**	**21,833**	**28,209**	**66,568**	**101,707**	**94,173**	**110,860**	**95,875**
Public and publicly guaranteed	2,512	4,209	1,618	9,605	5,612	3,060	8,217	2,814
Official creditors	343	214	190	952	226	374	3,363	382
Private creditors	2,169	3,995	1,428	8,653	5,386	2,686	4,854	2,432
Private nonguaranteed	3,931	17,624	26,591	56,964	96,095	91,113	102,644	93,062
Interest payments	**1,319**	**1,942**	**3,877**	**6,662**	**7,088**	**6,964**	**6,257**	**5,544**
Public and publicly guaranteed	937	893	1,233	1,497	1,468	1,531	1,831	1,701
Official creditors	126	87	145	291	343	437	568	481
Private creditors	811	806	1,088	1,207	1,124	1,094	1,263	1,220
Private nonguaranteed	382	1,049	2,644	5,165	5,620	5,433	4,426	3,844
Debt resource inflows								
Net debt inflows	449	6,114	35,269	46,895	10,017	-22,674	1,820	-10,659
Official creditors (incl. IMF)	-210	410	69	12,293	12,273	2,538	-2,032	-4,722
Private creditors	660	5,704	35,200	34,602	-2,256	-25,212	3,853	-5,938
Long-term	50	4,224	24,517	39,810	-2,842	-29,299	5,010	2,958
Public and publicly guaranteed	-1,187	1,636	5,080	-6,889	-3,660	-842	1,610	8,772
Private nonguaranteed	1,237	2,589	19,437	46,699	818	-28,457	3,399	-5,815
Short-term	609	1,480	10,683	-5,208	586	4,087	-1,157	-8,895
Non-debt resource inflows								
Foreign direct investment	2,770	8,505	70,631	74,992	-2,966	-20,659	11,311	8,586
Portfolio equity	..	-16	-5,010	-197	665	-206	-203	1,137
Currency composition (%)								
Euro	..	41.7	45.5	57.0	62.3	57.2	50.5	41.2
U.S.dollars	23.4	45.6	43.5	31.0	23.6	29.6	36.9	49.2
Major economic aggregates								
Gross national income (GNI)	44,085	104,367	126,596	144,346	121,031	122,372	131,829	117,509
Exports of goods, services & prim. income	..	74,311	119,237	139,525	113,546	125,137	135,733	126,013
Personal transfers & comp. of employees	..	1,913	2,309	2,509	2,137	2,162	2,441	2,302
Imports of goods, services & prim. income	..	82,180	128,517	149,801	114,299	124,218	135,159	124,410
Primary income on FDI	..	5,900	16,524	19,017	18,187	19,631	16,038	15,137
Current account balance	..	-8,238	-9,962	-11,119	-193	1,402	1,211	2,087
International reserves	..	18,552	23,970	33,788	44,074	44,849	48,681	44,506
Ratios								
External debt stocks to exports (%)	..	116.0	146.4	159.8	211.3	172.5	155.3	161.7
External debt stocks to GNI (%)	69.8	82.6	137.9	154.4	198.2	176.4	159.9	173.4
Debt service to exports (%)	..	32.9	27.9	52.5	96.0	81.1	86.5	84.6
Short-term to external debt stocks (%)	13.5	21.6	19.1	12.6	12.0	15.2	15.0	11.2
Multilateral to external debt stocks (%)	4.3	2.5	1.8	3.8	6.7	8.1	7.1	7.6
Reserves to external debt stocks (%)	..	21.5	13.7	15.2	18.4	20.8	23.1	21.8
Reserves to imports (months)	..	2.7	2.2	2.7	4.6	4.3	4.3	4.3

INDIA

(US$ million, unless otherwise indicated)

	2000	2005	2007	2008	2009	2010	2011	2012
Summary external debt data								
External debt stocks	**101,130**	**121,195**	**204,058**	**227,114**	**256,312**	**291,651**	**336,845**	**379,099**
Long-term external debt	96,781	111,406	166,888	182,243	203,473	229,076	252,685	279,636
Short-term external debt	3,462	8,816	36,093	43,821	46,603	56,448	78,052	93,349
interest arrears on long-term	0	0	0	0	0	0	0	0
Use of IMF credit	888	974	1,076	1,049	6,237	6,127	6,108	6,114
Long-term external debt								
Debt outstanding and disbursed	**96,781**	**111,406**	**166,888**	**182,243**	**203,473**	**229,076**	**252,685**	**279,636**
Public and publicly guaranteed	81,195	54,726	69,908	76,318	85,293	101,786	110,371	119,432
Official creditors	51,729	50,058	57,366	62,626	65,971	73,956	78,354	78,026
Private creditors	29,466	4,668	12,542	13,692	19,322	27,830	32,017	41,406
Private nonguaranteed	15,586	56,680	96,980	105,925	118,180	127,290	142,314	160,204
Disbursements	**10,556**	**19,380**	**64,526**	**38,712**	**26,646**	**44,629**	**44,073**	**50,065**
Public and publicly guaranteed	10,256	6,630	16,040	18,824	10,396	25,560	14,865	17,269
Official creditors	3,270	3,824	4,693	5,917	5,971	9,780	7,924	5,170
Private creditors	6,986	2,805	11,347	12,907	4,425	15,781	6,941	12,099
Private nonguaranteed	300	12,751	48,486	19,888	16,250	19,069	29,207	32,796
Principal repayments	**6,702**	**19,384**	**32,097**	**23,685**	**10,990**	**19,018**	**22,228**	**21,089**
Public and publicly guaranteed	6,454	12,469	8,842	13,447	5,336	5,164	6,823	6,183
Official creditors	3,494	2,701	2,392	3,001	2,923	3,159	3,908	3,696
Private creditors	2,959	9,769	6,450	10,446	2,413	2,005	2,915	2,488
Private nonguaranteed	249	6,914	23,255	10,238	5,654	13,854	15,405	14,906
Interest payments	**4,007**	**4,196**	**5,488**	**5,718**	**4,942**	**4,675**	**6,258**	**8,136**
Public and publicly guaranteed	3,378	3,022	1,450	1,524	1,322	1,063	1,262	1,758
Official creditors	1,436	1,062	1,173	1,164	1,012	798	926	1,265
Private creditors	1,941	1,960	276	360	310	265	335	493
Private nonguaranteed	630	1,174	4,038	4,194	3,620	3,612	4,996	6,378
Debt resource inflows								
Net debt inflows	3,358	1,949	43,425	22,755	18,437	35,456	43,449	44,272
Official creditors (incl. IMF)	-249	1,124	2,301	2,916	3,048	6,621	4,016	1,474
Private creditors	3,607	825	41,124	19,839	15,389	28,836	39,433	42,798
Long-term	4,078	-1,127	30,128	12,111	12,607	18,991	17,829	27,501
Public and publicly guaranteed	4,026	-6,964	4,897	2,461	2,011	13,776	4,026	9,611
Private nonguaranteed	51	5,837	25,231	9,650	10,596	5,215	13,803	17,890
Short-term	-471	1,952	10,996	7,728	2,782	9,845	21,604	15,297
Non-debt resource inflows								
Foreign direct investment	3,584	7,269	25,228	43,406	35,581	27,397	36,499	23,996
Portfolio equity	2,481	12,151	32,863	-15,030	24,689	30,442	-4,048	22,809
Currency composition (%)								
Euro	..	7.4	6.5	5.5	5.0	4.0	3.6	3.5
U.S.dollars	66.3	65.6	67.3	64.3	67.6	70.0	71.1	75.2
Major economic aggregates								
Gross national income (GNI)	469,716	828,318	1,233,605	1,216,938	1,357,363	1,692,962	1,856,813	1,824,735
Exports of goods, services & prim. income	62,453	160,228	252,732	320,713	274,580	357,996	456,523	453,744
Personal transfers & comp. of employees	12,883	22,125	37,217	49,977	49,204	53,480	62,499	68,821
Imports of goods, services & prim. income	80,489	194,154	297,951	400,437	349,529	464,622	579,253	610,650
Primary income on FDI	..	5,244	10,910	11,989	12,279	21,763	23,760	16,389
Current account balance	-4,601	-10,284	-8,076	-30,972	-26,186	-54,516	-62,518	-91,471
International reserves	37,902	131,924	266,988	247,419	265,182	275,277	271,285	270,587
Ratios								
External debt stocks to exports (%)	161.9	75.6	80.7	70.8	93.3	81.5	73.8	83.5
External debt stocks to GNI (%)	21.5	14.6	16.5	18.7	18.9	17.2	18.1	20.8
Debt service to exports (%)	17.5	14.9	15.6	9.7	6.0	6.8	6.4	6.8
Short-term to external debt stocks (%)	3.4	7.3	17.7	19.3	18.2	19.4	23.2	24.6
Multilateral to external debt stocks (%)	30.1	25.9	18.2	17.4	16.5	16.4	15.3	13.9
Reserves to external debt stocks (%)	37.5	108.9	130.8	108.9	103.5	94.4	80.5	71.4
Reserves to imports (months)	5.7	8.2	10.8	7.4	9.1	7.1	5.6	5.3

Notes:

External debt data prior to 2003 are revised from fiscal year to calendar year. Long-term public and publicly guaranteed bonds include Foreign Institutional Investor debt (FII) as reported by the Reserve Bank of India.

INDONESIA

(US$ million, unless otherwise indicated)

	2000	2005	2007	2008	2009	2010	2011	2012
Summary external debt data								
External debt stocks	**143,655**	**141,820**	**147,854**	**157,906**	**179,394**	**200,267**	**224,838**	**254,899**
Long-term external debt	110,818	122,649	128,821	137,050	152,240	164,170	183,624	207,091
Short-term external debt	21,688	11,023	18,655	20,488	24,050	33,047	38,173	44,764
interest arrears on long-term	4,632	0	0	0	0	0	0	0
Use of IMF credit	11,149	8,148	378	368	3,105	3,050	3,041	3,044
Long-term external debt								
Debt outstanding and disbursed	**110,818**	**122,649**	**128,821**	**137,050**	**152,240**	**164,170**	**183,624**	**207,091**
Public and publicly guaranteed	69,649	77,405	80,315	87,753	97,447	105,387	113,964	120,690
Official creditors	54,883	59,945	58,720	63,184	63,259	66,487	66,503	61,648
Private creditors	14,766	17,460	21,595	24,569	34,188	38,900	47,461	59,042
Private nonguaranteed	41,169	45,244	48,507	49,297	54,793	58,783	69,660	86,401
Disbursements	**5,651**	**13,881**	**18,272**	**22,932**	**31,425**	**36,335**	**42,930**	**52,967**
Public and publicly guaranteed	3,301	5,015	6,031	9,065	12,729	16,345	13,320	16,206
Official creditors	3,038	2,581	3,756	4,602	6,142	6,587	3,782	3,202
Private creditors	263	2,434	2,275	4,463	6,587	9,758	9,538	13,004
Private nonguaranteed	2,350	8,866	12,240	13,867	18,695	19,990	29,609	36,761
Principal repayments	**9,268**	**15,746**	**18,811**	**16,704**	**20,432**	**23,975**	**25,164**	**29,386**
Public and publicly guaranteed	3,868	6,232	8,062	6,482	7,063	5,846	6,132	6,289
Official creditors	1,586	3,539	6,781	5,729	6,134	5,214	5,156	5,012
Private creditors	2,282	2,692	1,281	753	929	632	976	1,276
Private nonguaranteed	5,400	9,515	10,749	10,221	13,368	18,129	19,032	23,097
Interest payments	**5,673**	**2,933**	**4,996**	**4,461**	**4,301**	**4,944**	**6,203**	**6,786**
Public and publicly guaranteed	3,738	1,921	2,730	2,718	2,802	3,034	4,156	4,310
Official creditors	2,575	1,189	2,042	1,968	1,693	1,586	1,508	1,376
Private creditors	1,163	732	689	751	1,109	1,448	2,648	2,933
Private nonguaranteed	1,935	1,012	2,266	1,743	1,499	1,910	2,048	2,477
Debt resource inflows								
Net debt inflows	-1,967	-6,611	5,908	8,061	14,554	21,358	22,891	30,171
Official creditors (incl. IMF)	2,575	-2,103	-3,024	-1,127	8	1,373	-1,374	-1,810
Private creditors	-4,542	-4,508	8,932	9,189	14,546	19,985	24,265	31,981
Long-term	-5,069	-906	2,485	7,356	10,985	10,987	19,139	25,391
Public and publicly guaranteed	-2,019	-258	994	3,710	5,658	9,127	8,562	11,728
Private nonguaranteed	-3,050	-649	1,491	3,646	5,327	1,861	10,577	13,663
Short-term	527	-3,602	6,447	1,833	3,561	8,998	5,126	6,591
Non-debt resource inflows								
Foreign direct investment	-4,550	8,336	6,928	9,318	4,877	13,771	19,241	19,618
Portfolio equity	-1,021	-165	3,559	322	787	2,132	-326	1,698
Currency composition (%)								
Euro	..	12.8	13.1	10.5	8.8	6.9	5.7	4.9
U.S.dollars	50.3	43.6	40.1	41.4	45.6	49.6	53.7	60.1
Major economic aggregates								
Gross national income (GNI)	150,317	271,958	414,441	492,112	520,694	689,283	822,205	852,561
Exports of goods, services & prim. income	73,079	97,565	127,333	151,202	128,433	168,862	215,469	213,601
Personal transfers & comp. of employees	1,190	5,420	6,174	6,794	6,793	6,916	6,924	7,212
Imports of goods, services & prim. income	66,903	102,080	121,945	156,440	122,382	168,348	217,995	241,704
Primary income on FDI	3,574	9,525	10,813	10,675	8,848	12,844	17,975	17,366
Current account balance	7,992	278	10,493	126	10,628	5,144	1,685	-24,074
International reserves	28,502	33,140	54,976	49,597	63,563	92,908	106,539	108,837
Ratios								
External debt stocks to exports (%)	196.6	145.4	116.1	104.4	139.7	118.6	104.3	119.3
External debt stocks to GNI (%)	95.6	52.1	35.7	32.1	34.5	29.1	27.3	29.9
Debt service to exports (%)	22.8	20.8	18.8	14.1	19.4	17.4	14.7	17.1
Short-term to external debt stocks (%)	15.1	7.8	12.6	13.0	13.4	16.5	17.0	17.6
Multilateral to external debt stocks (%)	13.9	13.1	12.6	12.6	11.7	11.3	10.2	9.1
Reserves to external debt stocks (%)	19.8	23.4	37.2	31.4	35.4	46.4	47.4	42.7
Reserves to imports (months)	5.1	3.9	5.4	3.8	6.2	6.6	5.9	5.4

IRAN, ISLAMIC REPUBLIC OF

(US$ million, unless otherwise indicated)

	2000	2005	2007	2008	2009	2010	2011	2012
Summary external debt data								
External debt stocks	**8,024**	**21,543**	**21,438**	**15,722**	**18,247**	**20,030**	**15,499**	**11,477**
Long-term external debt	4,709	10,506	11,145	8,758	7,295	6,156	4,814	4,003
Short-term external debt	3,008	10,686	9,891	6,599	8,787	11,613	8,475	5,337
interest arrears on long-term	0	0	0	0	0	0	0	0
Use of IMF credit	308	352	401	365	2,165	2,261	2,209	2,136
Long-term external debt								
Debt outstanding and disbursed	**4,709**	**10,506**	**11,145**	**8,758**	**7,295**	**6,156**	**4,814**	**4,003**
Public and publicly guaranteed	4,709	10,506	11,145	8,758	7,295	6,156	4,814	4,003
Official creditors	1,664	2,045	2,436	2,385	2,266	2,024	1,640	1,206
Private creditors	3,045	8,461	8,709	6,373	5,029	4,132	3,174	2,798
Private nonguaranteed	..	..	..	..	..	..	..	..
Disbursements	**1,469**	**2,740**	**1,140**	**787**	**400**	**252**	**216**	**18**
Public and publicly guaranteed	1,469	2,740	1,140	787	400	252	216	18
Official creditors	477	673	338	289	223	105	31	15
Private creditors	993	2,068	803	498	177	147	185	3
Private nonguaranteed	..	..	..	..	..	..	..	..
Principal repayments	**2,345**	**1,734**	**2,007**	**2,131**	**2,046**	**1,575**	**1,389**	**383**
Public and publicly guaranteed	2,345	1,734	2,007	2,131	2,046	1,575	1,389	383
Official creditors	1,785	329	302	328	379	321	420	117
Private creditors	561	1,405	1,705	1,802	1,667	1,255	970	267
Private nonguaranteed	..	..	..	..	..	..	..	..
Interest payments	**391**	**418**	**570**	**498**	**274**	**139**	**110**	**34**
Public and publicly guaranteed	391	418	570	498	274	139	110	34
Official creditors	190	103	114	89	73	53	46	15
Private creditors	202	316	456	410	201	86	64	19
Private nonguaranteed	..	..	..	..	..	..	..	..
Debt resource inflows								
Net debt inflows	-1,485	1,440	-75	-4,636	542	1,502	-4,311	-3,504
Official creditors (incl. IMF)	-1,308	344	35	-40	-156	-216	-389	-102
Private creditors	-177	1,096	-111	-4,596	698	1,718	-3,922	-3,402
Long-term	432	663	-902	-1,304	-1,490	-1,108	-784	-264
Public and publicly guaranteed	432	663	-902	-1,304	-1,490	-1,108	-784	-264
Private nonguaranteed	..	..	..	..	..	..	..	..
Short-term	-609	433	791	-3,292	2,188	2,826	-3,138	-3,138
Non-debt resource inflows								
Foreign direct investment	39	3,136	2,005	1,909	3,048	3,648	4,150	4,870
Portfolio equity	..	..	..	..	..	..	..	..
Currency composition (%)								
Euro	..	52.3	58.7	56.5	56.0	55.4	51.8	54.2
U.S.dollars	68.3	34.9	30.8	33.2	33.6	34.2	38.2	42.5
Major economic aggregates								
Gross national income (GNI)	101,335	188,503	283,000	335,654	328,593	..	..	..
Exports of goods, services & prim. income	30,131	50,757	83,968	107,760	112,334	98,191	123,593	155,666
Personal transfers & comp. of employees	536	1,032	1,115	1,115	1,072	1,181	1,330	..
Imports of goods, services & prim. income	18,107	50,115	63,866	75,808	89,859	88,815	96,224	96,707
Primary income on FDI	..	..	..	..	..	..	..	..
Current account balance	12,481	..	..	..	..	..	..	..
International reserves	..	..	..	..	..	..	..	..
Ratios								
External debt stocks to exports (%)	26.6	42.4	25.5	14.6	16.2	20.4	12.5	7.4
External debt stocks to GNI (%)	7.9	11.4	7.6	4.7	5.6	..	..	..
Debt service to exports (%)	9.7	5.5	3.5	2.6	2.2	1.9	1.3	0.3
Short-term to external debt stocks (%)	37.5	49.6	46.1	42.0	48.2	58.0	54.7	46.5
Multilateral to external debt stocks (%)	6.3	1.8	3.3	4.8	4.7	4.2	4.9	6.2
Reserves to external debt stocks (%)	..	..	..	..	..	..	..	..
Reserves to imports (months)	..	..	..	..	..	..	..	..

Notes:

Fiscal year-end for external debt data is March. Short-term debt is World Bank staff estimates.

JAMAICA

(US$ million, unless otherwise indicated)

	2000	2005	2007	2008	2009	2010	2011	2012
Summary external debt data								
External debt stocks	**4,746**	**6,490**	**10,424**	**10,350**	**11,082**	**14,157**	**14,326**	**14,333**
Long-term external debt	3,846	5,866	8,876	9,077	9,934	11,890	12,099	11,276
Short-term external debt	787	566	1,484	1,210	738	1,078	993	1,822
interest arrears on long-term	144	174	229	214	213	203	202	183
Use of IMF credit	113	58	64	63	410	1,188	1,234	1,235
Long-term external debt								
Debt outstanding and disbursed	**3,846**	**5,866**	**8,876**	**9,077**	**9,934**	**11,890**	**12,099**	**11,276**
Public and publicly guaranteed	3,743	5,476	6,703	6,913	6,693	7,583	7,756	7,383
Official creditors	2,423	2,096	2,252	2,285	2,403	3,256	3,215	3,181
Private creditors	1,320	3,380	4,451	4,629	4,290	4,327	4,542	4,202
Private nonguaranteed	103	390	2,173	2,164	3,241	4,307	4,343	3,894
Disbursements	**899**	**1,351**	**2,409**	**709**	**1,547**	**2,360**	**1,208**	**2,033**
Public and publicly guaranteed	899	1,044	1,009	709	462	1,285	1,170	266
Official creditors	306	91	284	281	358	1,075	418	226
Private creditors	593	953	725	428	104	210	753	39
Private nonguaranteed	0	307	1,400	0	1,085	1,075	37	1,767
Principal repayments	**422**	**544**	**575**	**459**	**729**	**341**	**714**	**1,075**
Public and publicly guaranteed	358	536	553	451	720	332	712	625
Official creditors	272	225	243	256	254	208	195	242
Private creditors	87	310	309	195	466	124	518	383
Private nonguaranteed	64	9	22	9	9	9	2	450
Interest payments	**207**	**387**	**657**	**674**	**746**	**828**	**899**	**687**
Public and publicly guaranteed	193	361	472	481	522	488	491	458
Official creditors	119	84	90	81	96	100	108	66
Private creditors	75	277	381	400	426	388	383	393
Private nonguaranteed	13	26	185	193	225	341	408	228
Debt resource inflows								
Net debt inflows	437	327	2,247	-10	347	3,148	460	1,806
Official creditors (incl. IMF)	15	-135	41	25	104	1,646	274	-16
Private creditors	421	462	2,206	-34	243	1,502	187	1,822
Long-term	443	941	1,793	225	714	1,152	271	974
Public and publicly guaranteed	506	642	415	233	-362	86	235	-343
Private nonguaranteed	-64	298	1,378	-9	1,076	1,066	36	1,317
Short-term	-21	-479	413	-259	-471	350	-84	848
Non-debt resource inflows								
Foreign direct investment	468	638	812	1,377	485	186	173	229
Portfolio equity	..	..	..	..	..	..	..	-1
Currency composition (%)								
Euro	..	18.2	22.3	20.3	17.3	14.8	10.3	7.1
U.S.dollars	61.6	70.0	69.8	72.7	76.3	79.5	84.4	88.3
Major economic aggregates								
Gross national income (GNI)	8,662	10,407	12,162	13,119	11,405	12,709	13,890	14,406
Exports of goods, services & prim. income	3,782	4,322	5,590	6,027	4,273	4,248	4,508	4,704
Personal transfers & comp. of employees	892	1,762	2,122	2,157	1,889	2,026	2,106	2,145
Imports of goods, services & prim. income	4,970	6,972	9,668	10,970	7,259	7,192	8,567	8,657
Primary income on FDI	290	454	533	376	232	127	112	..
Current account balance	-367	-1,071	-2,038	-2,793	-1,128	-934	-2,063	-1,905
International reserves	1,054	2,170	1,879	1,773	2,076	2,501	2,282	1,996
Ratios								
External debt stocks to exports (%)	125.5	150.2	186.5	171.7	259.3	333.3	317.8	304.7
External debt stocks to GNI (%)	54.8	62.4	85.7	78.9	97.2	111.4	103.1	99.5
Debt service to exports (%)	18.6	22.3	23.2	19.3	34.8	27.9	36.4	38.2
Short-term to external debt stocks (%)	16.6	8.7	14.2	11.7	6.7	7.6	6.9	12.7
Multilateral to external debt stocks (%)	25.9	20.6	12.1	12.9	13.7	16.6	17.6	17.2
Reserves to external debt stocks (%)	22.2	33.4	18.0	17.1	18.7	17.7	15.9	13.9
Reserves to imports (months)	2.5	3.7	2.3	1.9	3.4	4.2	3.2	2.8

Notes:

Short-term debt is based on data from the BIS.

JORDAN

(US$ million, unless otherwise indicated)

	2000	2005	2007	2008	2009	2010	2011	2012
Summary external debt data								
External debt stocks	**11,063**	**12,904**	**14,991**	**13,969**	**14,427**	**16,721**	**17,350**	**18,632**
Long-term external debt	6,183	6,901	7,433	5,319	5,643	7,025	7,111	7,395
Short-term external debt	4,396	5,742	7,444	8,596	8,518	9,439	9,983	10,595
interest arrears on long-term	102	0	0	0	0	1	1	1
Use of IMF credit	484	260	114	54	266	257	257	642
Long-term external debt								
Debt outstanding and disbursed	**6,183**	**6,901**	**7,433**	**5,319**	**5,643**	**7,025**	**7,111**	**7,395**
Public and publicly guaranteed	6,183	6,878	7,321	5,126	5,445	6,502	6,317	6,302
Official creditors	5,243	6,483	6,951	4,815	5,137	5,452	5,291	5,308
Private creditors	940	395	371	311	308	1,050	1,026	994
Private nonguaranteed	..	24	112	193	198	522	794	1,093
Disbursements	**176**	**434**	**272**	**330**	**787**	**1,538**	**475**	**1,010**
Public and publicly guaranteed	176	434	190	230	762	1,388	325	711
Official creditors	176	269	190	224	756	626	325	711
Private creditors	0	165	0	6	6	762	0	0
Private nonguaranteed	..	0	82	100	25	150	150	299
Principal repayments	**308**	**366**	**435**	**2,430**	**425**	**513**	**599**	**615**
Public and publicly guaranteed	308	341	409	2,412	405	487	574	585
Official creditors	238	323	394	2,341	396	463	548	557
Private creditors	70	19	16	71	9	25	26	28
Private nonguaranteed	..	25	25	19	20	26	25	30
Interest payments	**239**	**161**	**231**	**207**	**155**	**162**	**191**	**190**
Public and publicly guaranteed	239	160	227	200	147	147	171	165
Official creditors	162	157	212	185	134	124	130	126
Private creditors	77	4	15	15	12	22	41	39
Private nonguaranteed	..	1	4	7	8	15	20	25
Debt resource inflows								
Net debt inflows	3,371	325	605	-1,007	268	1,941	420	1,390
Official creditors (incl. IMF)	-73	-131	-280	-2,176	344	159	-223	537
Private creditors	3,445	456	885	1,169	-76	1,781	643	853
Long-term	-70	121	41	16	2	862	99	241
Public and publicly guaranteed	-70	146	-16	-65	-3	738	-26	-28
Private nonguaranteed	..	-25	57	82	5	124	125	269
Short-term	3,515	335	844	1,152	-78	920	544	612
Non-debt resource inflows								
Foreign direct investment	913	1,984	2,622	2,827	2,413	1,651	1,474	1,497
Portfolio equity	-17	169	346	521	-30	-21	109	53
Currency composition (%)								
Euro	..	21.1	24.1	12.6	12.0	9.3	9.0	11.0
U.S.dollars	29.3	26.4	25.3	24.8	31.1	37.1	37.4	39.9
Major economic aggregates								
Gross national income (GNI)	8,564	12,925	17,794	22,667	24,327	26,334	28,660	31,172
Exports of goods, services & prim. income	4,207	7,426	10,684	13,751	12,022	13,639	13,942	14,346
Personal transfers & comp. of employees	1,845	2,500	3,434	3,794	3,597	3,641	3,453	3,574
Imports of goods, services & prim. income	6,363	12,314	16,421	19,869	17,044	19,344	22,276	24,054
Primary income on FDI	33	74	160	256	313	814	713	821
Current account balance	27	-2,272	-2,875	-2,054	-1,244	-1,882	-3,468	-5,694
International reserves	3,331	5,250	7,542	8,562	11,689	13,057	11,467	8,090
Ratios								
External debt stocks to exports (%)	263.0	173.8	140.3	101.6	120.0	122.6	124.4	129.9
External debt stocks to GNI (%)	129.2	99.8	84.2	61.6	59.3	63.5	60.5	59.8
Debt service to exports (%)	20.1	11.9	10.6	20.9	6.0	5.8	6.8	6.9
Short-term to external debt stocks (%)	39.7	44.5	49.7	61.5	59.0	56.4	57.5	56.9
Multilateral to external debt stocks (%)	15.4	14.8	13.2	14.0	16.4	15.1	13.8	13.7
Reserves to external debt stocks (%)	30.1	40.7	50.3	61.3	81.0	78.1	66.1	43.4
Reserves to imports (months)	6.3	5.1	5.5	5.2	8.2	8.1	6.2	4.0

Notes:

Long-term private nonguaranteed debt data are revised from 2001 based on reports provided by the country. Historical short-term debt until 1999 is based on data from the BIS.

KAZAKHSTAN

(US$ million, unless otherwise indicated)

	2000	2005	2007	2008	2009	2010	2011	2012
Summary external debt data								
External debt stocks	**12,890**	**43,857**	**96,232**	**106,731**	**109,734**	**119,145**	**124,317**	**137,014**
Long-term external debt	11,481	35,263	84,159	96,715	102,210	109,751	115,033	127,141
Short-term external debt	961	8,102	11,530	9,487	6,985	8,864	8,756	9,345
interest arrears on long-term	0	0	0	0	0	0	0	0
Use of IMF credit	448	491	543	529	539	529	528	528
Long-term external debt								
Debt outstanding and disbursed	**11,481**	**35,263**	**84,159**	**96,715**	**102,210**	**109,751**	**115,033**	**127,141**
Public and publicly guaranteed	3,623	2,177	1,698	1,915	2,487	3,845	4,675	7,375
Official creditors	2,239	1,780	1,684	1,912	2,486	3,845	4,675	5,065
Private creditors	1,384	396	13	3	1	0	0	2,310
Private nonguaranteed	7,859	33,087	82,462	94,800	99,724	105,905	110,358	119,766
Disbursements	**3,063**	**17,207**	**44,651**	**40,803**	**30,471**	**45,054**	**32,740**	**32,654**
Public and publicly guaranteed	623	197	160	145	717	1,522	920	3,050
Official creditors	168	197	160	145	717	1,522	920	740
Private creditors	455	0	0	0	0	0	0	2,310
Private nonguaranteed	2,440	17,010	44,491	40,658	29,754	43,532	31,821	29,604
Principal repayments	**2,155**	**11,417**	**23,571**	**29,011**	**20,032**	**34,639**	**26,226**	**20,862**
Public and publicly guaranteed	216	1,090	640	131	131	278	134	254
Official creditors	133	1,018	279	120	130	278	134	254
Private creditors	83	72	361	11	2	1	0	0
Private nonguaranteed	1,939	10,327	22,931	28,881	19,901	34,360	26,092	20,607
Interest payments	**713**	**1,521**	**3,531**	**4,105**	**5,365**	**4,517**	**5,921**	**2,033**
Public and publicly guaranteed	235	146	96	67	58	54	61	75
Official creditors	124	102	74	66	58	54	61	75
Private creditors	112	44	22	1	0	0	0	0
Private nonguaranteed	478	1,376	3,435	4,039	5,307	4,463	5,860	1,957
Debt resource inflows								
Net debt inflows	1,061	9,950	20,165	9,749	7,937	12,295	6,406	12,381
Official creditors (incl. IMF)	-407	-820	-119	26	587	1,244	786	486
Private creditors	1,469	10,770	20,283	9,723	7,350	11,050	5,620	11,895
Long-term	873	6,610	21,199	11,766	9,851	9,171	5,729	11,306
Public and publicly guaranteed	373	-72	-361	-11	-2	-1	..	2,310
Private nonguaranteed	501	6,683	21,559	11,777	9,853	9,172	5,729	8,996
Short-term	595	4,160	-916	-2,043	-2,502	1,879	-109	589
Non-debt resource inflows								
Foreign direct investment	1,283	2,546	11,973	16,819	14,276	7,456	14,287	15,117
Portfolio equity	19	150	828	-1,280	38	134	17	-418
Currency composition (%)								
Euro	..	1.9	2.6	1.9	1.4	0.8	0.6	0.4
U.S.dollars	61.2	53.9	46.8	42.1	55.9	73.1	77.8	87.9
Major economic aggregates								
Gross national income (GNI)	17,038	51,757	91,893	114,115	102,688	128,701	160,413	173,489
Exports of goods, services & prim. income	10,480	31,209	55,379	79,637	50,660	67,530	93,943	98,899
Personal transfers & comp. of employees	122	62	143	126	198	226	180	171
Imports of goods, services & prim. income	10,362	31,852	61,541	72,327	54,051	65,655	81,407	90,178
Primary income on FDI	1,046	4,633	11,305	16,956	10,415	17,316	24,892	24,589
Current account balance	366	-1,056	-8,322	6,326	-4,114	1,393	12,281	7,716
International reserves	1,594	6,084	15,777	17,871	20,720	25,223	25,179	22,132
Ratios								
External debt stocks to exports (%)	123.0	140.5	173.8	134.0	216.6	176.4	132.3	138.5
External debt stocks to GNI (%)	75.7	84.7	104.7	93.5	106.9	92.6	77.5	79.0
Debt service to exports (%)	32.4	42.2	49.0	41.9	50.7	58.5	34.5	23.5
Short-term to external debt stocks (%)	7.5	18.5	12.0	8.9	6.4	7.4	7.0	6.8
Multilateral to external debt stocks (%)	11.5	2.0	0.7	0.7	1.2	2.3	2.9	3.0
Reserves to external debt stocks (%)	12.4	13.9	16.4	16.7	18.9	21.2	20.3	16.2
Reserves to imports (months)	1.8	2.3	3.1	3.0	4.6	4.6	3.7	2.9

KENYA

(US$ million, unless otherwise indicated)

	2000	2005	2007	2008	2009	2010	2011	2012
Summary external debt data								
External debt stocks	**6,189**	**6,483**	**7,523**	**7,607**	**8,589**	**8,801**	**10,287**	**11,569**
Long-term external debt	5,216	5,772	6,231	6,388	6,720	6,979	7,566	8,834
Short-term external debt	798	499	964	910	1,012	1,005	1,622	1,442
interest arrears on long-term	47	21	57	66	73	80	100	93
Use of IMF credit	175	212	327	309	858	817	1,100	1,293
Long-term external debt								
Debt outstanding and disbursed	**5,216**	**5,772**	**6,231**	**6,388**	**6,720**	**6,979**	**7,566**	**8,834**
Public and publicly guaranteed	5,041	5,772	6,231	6,388	6,720	6,979	7,566	8,834
Official creditors	4,559	5,409	5,892	6,070	6,369	6,668	7,246	7,896
Private creditors	482	363	339	319	352	311	320	938
Private nonguaranteed	175	0	0	0	0	0	0	0
Disbursements	**333**	**168**	**341**	**350**	**538**	**530**	**865**	**1,680**
Public and publicly guaranteed	333	168	341	350	538	530	865	1,680
Official creditors	248	140	341	343	510	518	841	1,003
Private creditors	85	28	0	7	27	12	23	677
Private nonguaranteed	0	0	0	0	0	0	0	0
Principal repayments	**407**	**439**	**336**	**288**	**258**	**259**	**289**	**337**
Public and publicly guaranteed	362	429	336	288	258	259	289	337
Official creditors	241	356	325	273	255	255	282	328
Private creditors	121	74	11	15	3	4	7	10
Private nonguaranteed	45	10	0	0	0	0	0	0
Interest payments	**100**	**72**	**78**	**91**	**85**	**90**	**93**	**171**
Public and publicly guaranteed	81	72	78	91	85	90	93	171
Official creditors	55	66	76	90	84	90	92	144
Private creditors	27	6	2	1	1	1	1	26
Private nonguaranteed	19	0	0	0	0	0	0	0
Debt resource inflows								
Net debt inflows	-31	-459	449	-12	566	232	1,466	1,361
Official creditors (incl. IMF)	9	-149	121	60	446	238	853	866
Private creditors	-40	-310	328	-71	119	-6	614	495
Long-term	-81	-56	-11	-8	24	8	17	668
Public and publicly guaranteed	-36	-46	-11	-8	24	8	17	668
Private nonguaranteed	-45	-10	..	..	..	..	..	..
Short-term	41	-254	339	-63	95	-14	597	-173
Non-debt resource inflows								
Foreign direct investment	111	21	729	96	116	178	335	259
Portfolio equity	-6	3	0	5	3	22	20	26
Currency composition (%)								
Euro	..	19.2	19.8	17.0	18.1	16.2	16.4	15.9
U.S.dollars	49.8	49.3	48.2	46.7	45.3	43.6	41.8	44.7
Major economic aggregates								
Gross national income (GNI)	12,576	18,732	27,093	30,419	30,542	32,040	33,628	37,248
Exports of goods, services & prim. income	2,821	5,416	7,223	8,467	7,567	9,127	10,130	11,205
Personal transfers & comp. of employees	538	425	645	667	631	686	934	1,214
Imports of goods, services & prim. income	3,941	6,921	10,364	12,781	11,514	13,823	16,631	18,270
Primary income on FDI	29	35	124	52	60	60	105	111
Current account balance	-199	-252	-1,032	-1,983	-1,689	-2,369	-3,830	-4,253
International reserves	898	1,799	3,355	2,879	3,849	4,320	4,264	5,711
Ratios								
External debt stocks to exports (%)	219.4	119.7	104.1	89.8	113.5	96.4	101.6	103.2
External debt stocks to GNI (%)	49.2	34.6	27.8	25.0	28.1	27.5	30.6	31.1
Debt service to exports (%)	21.0	10.0	6.3	4.9	5.1	4.4	4.3	5.1
Short-term to external debt stocks (%)	12.9	7.7	12.8	12.0	11.8	11.4	15.8	12.5
Multilateral to external debt stocks (%)	45.8	52.8	47.9	49.0	45.9	46.7	42.8	42.6
Reserves to external debt stocks (%)	14.5	27.7	44.6	37.8	44.8	49.1	41.5	49.4
Reserves to imports (months)	2.7	3.1	3.9	2.7	4.0	3.8	3.1	3.8

Notes:

Short-term debt is based on data from the BIS.

KOSOVO

(US$ million, unless otherwise indicated)

	2000	2005	2007	2008	2009	2010	2011	2012
Summary external debt data								
External debt stocks	..	..	..	**710**	**1,726**	**1,456**	**1,700**	**2,002**
Long-term external debt	..	..	..	430	818	886	1,130	1,116
Short-term external debt	..	..	..	194	821	455	456	652
interest arrears on long-term	..	..	..	0	0	0	0	0
Use of IMF credit	..	..	..	85	87	114	114	234
Long-term external debt								
Debt outstanding and disbursed	..	..	..	**430**	**818**	**886**	**1,130**	**1,116**
Public and publicly guaranteed	..	..	..	0	359	319	299	295
Official creditors	..	..	..	0	359	319	299	295
Private creditors	..	..	..	0	0	0	0	0
Private nonguaranteed	..	..	..	430	459	567	830	822
Disbursements	..	..	..	**161**	**90**	**169**	**158**	**93**
Public and publicly guaranteed	..	..	..	0	0	0	7	5
Official creditors	..	..	..	0	0	0	7	5
Private creditors	..	..	..	0	0	0	0	0
Private nonguaranteed	..	..	..	161	90	169	152	89
Principal repayments	..	..	..	**37**	**269**	**76**	**85**	**96**
Public and publicly guaranteed	..	..	..	0	208	14	17	15
Official creditors	..	..	..	0	208	14	17	15
Private creditors	..	..	..	0	0	0	0	0
Private nonguaranteed	..	..	..	37	61	61	68	82
Interest payments	..	..	..	**15**	**44**	**34**	**38**	**33**
Public and publicly guaranteed	..	..	..	0	23	11	12	11
Official creditors	..	..	..	0	23	11	12	11
Private creditors	..	..	..	0	0	0	0	0
Private nonguaranteed	..	..	..	15	22	23	26	22
Debt resource inflows								
Net debt inflows	..	..	..	177	448	-244	75	312
Official creditors (incl. IMF)	..	..	..	0	-208	14	-10	109
Private creditors	..	..	..	177	656	-258	85	203
Long-term	..	..	..	124	29	108	84	7
Public and publicly guaranteed	..	..	..	0	0	0	0	0
Private nonguaranteed	..	..	..	124	29	108	84	7
Short-term	..	..	..	54	627	-366	1	196
	..	..	..					
Non-debt resource inflows	..	..	..					
Foreign direct investment	..	..	..	537	408	487	546	293
Portfolio equity	..	..	..	..	..	..	..	1
Currency composition (%)								
Euro	..	..	..	..	..	..	..	1.6
U.S.dollars	..	..	..	..	100.0	100.0	100.0	98.4
Major economic aggregates								
Gross national income (GNI)	..	..	4,961	5,873	5,565	5,712	6,620	6,392
Exports of goods, services & prim. income	..	625	991	1,138	1,170	1,333	1,670	1,477
Personal transfers & comp. of employees	..	701	919	1,042	1,055	997	1,122	1,059
Imports of goods, services & prim. income	..	1,803	2,528	3,222	3,101	3,377	4,018	3,495
Primary income on FDI	..	28	59	88	102	130	148	64
Current account balance	..	-308	-485	-921	-547	-768	-1,028	-484
International reserves	..	..	952	892	830	846	742	1,108
Ratios								
External debt stocks to exports (%)	..	12.7	54.0	62.4	147.5	109.2	101.8	135.6
External debt stocks to GNI (%)	..	..	10.8	12.1	31.0	25.5	25.7	31.3
Debt service to exports (%)	..	0.4	0.3	4.6	26.8	8.3	7.4	8.8
Short-term to external debt stocks (%)	..	..	26.3	27.4	47.6	31.3	26.8	32.6
Multilateral to external debt stocks (%)	..	..	..	..	20.8	21.9	17.6	14.7
Reserves to external debt stocks (%)	..	..	178.0	125.7	48.1	58.2	43.6	55.3
Reserves to imports (months)	..	..	4.5	3.3	3.2	3.0	2.2	3.8

Notes:

Kosovo became independent in 2008.

KYRGYZ REPUBLIC

(US$ million, unless otherwise indicated)

	2000	2005	2007	2008	2009	2010	2011	2012
Summary external debt data								
External debt stocks	**1,938**	**2,257**	**2,881**	**3,628**	**4,119**	**4,114**	**5,486**	**6,026**
Long-term external debt	1,510	1,825	2,278	2,942	3,395	3,612	4,986	5,492
Short-term external debt	129	132	319	391	424	195	188	214
interest arrears on long-term	10	3	7	6	2	12	3	4
Use of IMF credit	298	299	284	295	300	307	312	321
Long-term external debt								
Debt outstanding and disbursed	**1,510**	**1,825**	**2,278**	**2,942**	**3,395**	**3,612**	**4,986**	**5,492**
Public and publicly guaranteed	1,220	1,665	1,898	1,963	2,320	2,442	2,618	2,840
Official creditors	1,184	1,665	1,898	1,963	2,320	2,442	2,618	2,840
Private creditors	37	0	0	0	0	0	0	0
Private nonguaranteed	290	161	380	980	1,076	1,171	2,368	2,652
Disbursements	**161**	**132**	**278**	**878**	**635**	**668**	**746**	**853**
Public and publicly guaranteed	153	76	66	51	378	147	211	344
Official creditors	149	76	66	51	378	147	211	344
Private creditors	4	0	0	0	0	0	0	0
Private nonguaranteed	8	56	212	827	257	521	535	510
Principal repayments	**86**	**73**	**127**	**261**	**200**	**462**	**314**	**266**
Public and publicly guaranteed	17	16	25	35	38	38	44	41
Official creditors	13	16	25	35	38	38	44	41
Private creditors	4	0	0	0	0	0	0	0
Private nonguaranteed	69	57	102	225	162	424	270	226
Interest payments	**69**	**21**	**23**	**42**	**37**	**69**	**70**	**58**
Public and publicly guaranteed	23	12	16	17	19	23	40	32
Official creditors	20	12	16	17	19	23	40	32
Private creditors	2	0	0	0	0	0	0	0
Private nonguaranteed	47	9	7	24	18	46	29	25
Debt resource inflows								
Net debt inflows	152	-150	241	709	472	-20	439	620
Official creditors (incl. IMF)	143	47	20	35	339	121	173	311
Private creditors	9	-196	221	674	132	-141	266	309
Long-term	-60	-1	110	601	96	97	265	284
Public and publicly guaranteed	0	..	..	..	..	..	..	..
Private nonguaranteed	-60	-1	110	601	96	97	265	284
Short-term	69	-195	111	73	37	-238	1	25
Non-debt resource inflows								
Foreign direct investment	-2	43	208	377	189	438	694	372
Portfolio equity	..	0	1	6	1	-18	5	0
Currency composition (%)								
Euro	..	2.8	4.3	4.0	3.5	3.1	2.8	2.8
U.S.dollars	67.9	69.5	68.0	65.3	69.2	68.9	68.9	71.5
Major economic aggregates								
Gross national income (GNI)	1,288	2,372	3,751	4,959	4,500	4,450	5,668	6,083
Exports of goods, services & prim. income	590	963	2,065	2,812	2,578	2,536	3,442	3,180
Personal transfers & comp. of employees	9	313	704	1,223	982	1,266	1,709	2,031
Imports of goods, services & prim. income	753	1,501	3,311	4,996	3,879	4,240	5,765	6,672
Primary income on FDI	37	36	39	178	118	248	611	86
Current account balance	-76	-37	-228	-708	-94	-312	-484	-1,431
International reserves	239	570	1,107	1,153	1,494	1,604	1,703	1,903
Ratios								
External debt stocks to exports (%)	328.5	234.4	139.5	129.0	159.8	162.2	159.4	189.5
External debt stocks to GNI (%)	150.5	95.1	76.8	73.2	91.5	92.5	96.8	99.1
Debt service to exports (%)	30.2	14.8	9.4	11.9	10.4	22.0	11.9	10.9
Short-term to external debt stocks (%)	6.7	5.9	11.1	10.8	10.3	4.7	3.4	3.5
Multilateral to external debt stocks (%)	37.3	48.7	44.4	35.6	31.8	31.5	24.5	23.0
Reserves to external debt stocks (%)	12.3	25.2	38.4	31.8	36.3	39.0	31.0	31.6
Reserves to imports (months)	3.8	4.6	4.0	2.8	4.6	4.5	3.5	3.4

Notes:

Long-term private nonguaranteed debt data are World Bank staff estimates based on reports provided by the country. Short-term debt is based on data from the National Statistical Committee of Kyrgyz Republic.

LAO PEOPLE'S DEMOCRATIC REPUBLIC

(US$ million, unless otherwise indicated)

	2000	2005	2007	2008	2009	2010	2011	2012
Summary external debt data								
External debt stocks	**2,520**	**2,912**	**4,606**	**5,189**	**5,737**	**5,655**	**6,158**	**6,372**
Long-term external debt	2,459	2,815	4,362	4,987	5,442	5,549	6,014	6,245
Short-term external debt	6	55	203	166	199	18	62	47
interest arrears on long-term	0	0	0	0	0	0	0	0
Use of IMF credit	55	43	41	35	95	88	83	79
Long-term external debt								
Debt outstanding and disbursed	**2,459**	**2,815**	**4,362**	**4,987**	**5,442**	**5,549**	**6,014**	**6,245**
Public and publicly guaranteed	2,459	1,989	2,515	2,720	2,818	2,939	2,889	2,745
Official creditors	2,459	1,989	2,515	2,720	2,818	2,939	2,889	2,745
Private creditors	0	0	0	0	0	0	0	0
Private nonguaranteed	..	825	1,847	2,267	2,625	2,610	3,125	3,500
Disbursements	**77**	**472**	**1,058**	**756**	**599**	**233**	**638**	**462**
Public and publicly guaranteed	77	150	201	174	152	89	23	12
Official creditors	77	150	201	174	152	89	23	12
Private creditors	0	0	0	0	0	0	0	0
Private nonguaranteed	..	321	857	581	447	144	615	450
Principal repayments	**23**	**79**	**132**	**143**	**146**	**221**	**199**	**179**
Public and publicly guaranteed	23	39	33	43	57	62	99	104
Official creditors	23	39	33	43	57	62	99	104
Private creditors	0	0	0	0	0	0	0	0
Private nonguaranteed	..	40	100	100	89	159	100	75
Interest payments	**9**	**47**	**54**	**60**	**69**	**79**	**77**	**56**
Public and publicly guaranteed	9	14	18	23	25	29	27	26
Official creditors	9	14	18	23	25	29	27	26
Private creditors	0	0	0	0	0	0	0	0
Private nonguaranteed	..	32	37	37	43	50	50	30
Debt resource inflows								
Net debt inflows	53	441	1,023	571	480	-175	477	265
Official creditors (incl. IMF)	47	105	166	127	90	21	-81	-95
Private creditors	6	336	857	445	391	-195	559	360
Long-term	0	281	757	482	358	-14	515	375
Public and publicly guaranteed	0	0	0	0	0	0	0	0
Private nonguaranteed	..	281	757	482	358	-14	515	375
Short-term	6	55	100	-37	33	-181	44	-15
Non-debt resource inflows								
Foreign direct investment	34	28	324	228	319	279	301	294
Portfolio equity	..	..	..	..	..	54	11	6
Currency composition (%)								
Euro	..	..	..	..	..	..	..	..
U.S.dollars	18.4	66.0	69.9	70.5	71.5	71.8	71.2	71.7
Major economic aggregates								
Gross national income (GNI)	1,660	2,670	4,075	5,188	5,668	6,713	7,741	8,676
Exports of goods, services & prim. income	513	762	1,244	1,526	1,492	2,308	2,452	2,917
Personal transfers & comp. of employees	1	1	6	18	38	42	110	59
Imports of goods, services & prim. income	638	1,003	1,202	1,589	1,685	2,457	2,881	3,584
Primary income on FDI	..	25	48	26	43	44	16	52
Current account balance	-8	-174	139	78	-61	29	-206	-415
International reserves	139	234	533	629	609	703	741	..
Ratios								
External debt stocks to exports (%)	490.9	382.0	370.1	340.1	384.6	245.0	251.2	218.4
External debt stocks to GNI (%)	151.7	109.1	113.0	100.0	101.2	84.2	79.6	73.4
Debt service to exports (%)	8.0	17.4	15.3	13.6	14.8	13.2	11.5	8.2
Short-term to external debt stocks (%)	0.3	1.9	4.4	3.2	3.5	0.3	1.0	0.7
Multilateral to external debt stocks (%)	41.3	52.4	40.1	37.9	34.4	35.1	31.8	29.0
Reserves to external debt stocks (%)	5.5	8.0	11.6	12.1	10.6	12.4	12.0	..
Reserves to imports (months)	2.6	2.8	5.3	4.7	4.3	3.4	3.1	..

Notes:

Long-term public and publicly guaranteed debt data are World Bank staff estimates based on reports provided by the country. Long-term private nonguaranteed debt data are World Bank staff estimates. Short-term debt is based on data from the BIS.

LEBANON

(US$ million, unless otherwise indicated)

	2000	2005	2007	2008	2009	2010	2011	2012
Summary external debt data								
External debt stocks	**10,250**	**23,334**	**25,642**	**24,328**	**24,803**	**24,591**	**24,767**	**28,950**
Long-term external debt	7,704	19,877	21,437	21,066	21,285	20,713	21,101	24,690
Short-term external debt	2,541	3,450	4,118	3,138	3,096	3,482	3,311	3,943
interest arrears on long-term	0	0	0	0	0	0	0	0
Use of IMF credit	6	6	87	124	422	395	355	317
Long-term external debt								
Debt outstanding and disbursed	**7,704**	**19,877**	**21,437**	**21,066**	**21,285**	**20,713**	**21,101**	**24,690**
Public and publicly guaranteed	6,968	18,866	20,907	20,596	20,615	20,213	20,601	23,990
Official creditors	1,290	2,172	2,437	2,432	2,356	2,226	2,088	1,999
Private creditors	5,677	16,694	18,470	18,165	18,259	17,987	18,513	21,991
Private nonguaranteed	736	1,011	530	470	670	500	500	700
Disbursements	**2,445**	**3,179**	**3,374**	**2,709**	**3,332**	**2,143**	**4,174**	**6,220**
Public and publicly guaranteed	2,330	2,649	3,374	2,709	3,132	2,143	4,174	5,720
Official creditors	238	106	287	421	223	199	206	229
Private creditors	2,092	2,543	3,087	2,288	2,909	1,943	3,968	5,491
Private nonguaranteed	115	530	0	0	200	0	0	500
Principal repayments	**884**	**2,172**	**3,078**	**2,905**	**3,096**	**2,632**	**3,743**	**2,642**
Public and publicly guaranteed	834	1,907	2,803	2,845	3,096	2,462	3,743	2,342
Official creditors	74	143	362	375	334	298	328	318
Private creditors	760	1,764	2,441	2,470	2,762	2,164	3,415	2,024
Private nonguaranteed	50	265	275	60	0	170	0	300
Interest payments	**475**	**1,287**	**1,430**	**1,442**	**1,475**	**1,454**	**1,491**	**1,484**
Public and publicly guaranteed	418	1,197	1,373	1,402	1,431	1,403	1,453	1,446
Official creditors	57	92	101	105	88	100	82	75
Private creditors	361	1,106	1,271	1,297	1,344	1,303	1,372	1,371
Private nonguaranteed	57	90	57	40	43	51	38	38
Debt resource inflows								
Net debt inflows	1,900	486	291	-1,136	195	-122	220	4,172
Official creditors (incl. IMF)	164	-37	3	87	-111	-117	-161	-128
Private creditors	1,735	524	288	-1,222	305	-5	382	4,300
Long-term	1,397	1,045	370	-242	347	-391	553	3,668
Public and publicly guaranteed	1,332	780	645	-182	147	-221	553	3,468
Private nonguaranteed	65	265	-275	-60	200	-170	0	200
Short-term	339	-521	-82	-980	-42	386	-171	632
Non-debt resource inflows								
Foreign direct investment	..	2,624	3,376	4,333	4,804	4,280	3,490	3,678
Portfolio equity	..	1,436	791	466	929	154	-145	-239
Currency composition (%)								
Euro	..	9.0	9.8	9.7	9.1	8.3	7.6	5.7
U.S.dollars	67.9	85.7	85.8	86.3	86.9	87.9	88.7	91.2
Major economic aggregates								
Gross national income (GNI)	17,581	21,674	25,797	30,517	34,423	36,615	39,916	42,322
Exports of goods, services & prim. income	..	14,958	19,445	24,813	23,137	22,177	26,687	29,639
Personal transfers & comp. of employees	..	4,924	5,769	7,181	7,558	6,914	6,913	6,918
Imports of goods, services & prim. income	..	18,768	23,819	31,276	31,705	32,179	34,071	33,969
Primary income on FDI	..	95	64	121	95	209	184	213
Current account balance	..	-2,748	-1,605	-4,103	-6,741	-7,552	-4,859	-1,663
International reserves	5,944	11,887	12,910	20,244	29,103	31,514	33,741	37,186
Ratios								
External debt stocks to exports (%)	..	156.0	131.9	98.0	107.2	110.9	92.8	97.7
External debt stocks to GNI (%)	58.3	107.7	99.4	79.7	72.1	67.2	62.0	68.4
Debt service to exports (%)	..	24.3	24.4	17.8	19.9	18.7	20.0	14.2
Short-term to external debt stocks (%)	24.8	14.8	16.1	12.9	12.5	14.2	13.4	13.6
Multilateral to external debt stocks (%)	8.7	5.1	5.6	5.5	5.4	5.4	5.0	3.9
Reserves to external debt stocks (%)	58.0	50.9	50.3	83.2	117.3	128.2	136.2	128.4
Reserves to imports (months)	..	7.6	6.5	7.8	11.0	11.8	11.9	13.1

Notes:

Long-term private nonguaranteed debt only cover Bonds. Short-term debt is based on data from the BIS.

LESOTHO

(US$ million, unless otherwise indicated)

	2000	2005	2007	2008	2009	2010	2011	2012
Summary external debt data								
External debt stocks	**676.7**	**667.3**	**683.5**	**694.6**	**756.3**	**776.7**	**794.8**	**860.2**
Long-term external debt	656.7	618.9	642.2	659.2	680.6	697.9	714.5	745.0
Short-term external debt	4.0	8.0	0.0	0.0	0.0	0.0	0.0	0.0
interest arrears on long-term	0.0	0.0	0.0	0.0	0.0	0.0	0.0	0.0
Use of IMF credit	16.0	40.4	41.3	35.4	75.7	78.8	80.3	115.2
Long-term external debt								
Debt outstanding and disbursed	**656.7**	**618.9**	**642.2**	**659.2**	**680.6**	**697.9**	**714.5**	**745.0**
Public and publicly guaranteed	656.7	618.9	642.2	659.2	680.6	697.9	714.5	745.0
Official creditors	580.9	590.6	624.6	646.6	667.1	684.3	702.8	733.8
Private creditors	75.8	28.4	17.5	12.5	13.6	13.6	11.7	11.2
Private nonguaranteed	..	..	..	..	..	..	..	..
Disbursements	**69.4**	**21.1**	**38.3**	**45.8**	**37.4**	**40.8**	**42.7**	**57.6**
Public and publicly guaranteed	69.4	21.1	38.3	45.8	37.4	40.8	42.7	57.6
Official creditors	67.4	21.1	38.3	45.8	37.4	40.8	42.7	57.6
Private creditors	2.0	0.0	0.0	0.0	0.0	0.0	0.0	0.0
Private nonguaranteed	..	..	..	..	..	..	..	..
Principal repayments	**33.2**	**65.3**	**31.1**	**24.5**	**24.6**	**19.4**	**23.3**	**24.3**
Public and publicly guaranteed	33.2	65.3	31.1	24.5	24.6	19.4	23.3	24.3
Official creditors	26.4	32.0	25.8	21.3	23.9	19.1	23.0	24.0
Private creditors	6.8	33.3	5.3	3.2	0.7	0.3	0.3	0.3
Private nonguaranteed	..	..	..	..	..	..	..	..
Interest payments	**22.9**	**13.7**	**64.3**	**7.8**	**7.4**	**7.5**	**8.8**	**9.2**
Public and publicly guaranteed	22.9	13.7	64.3	7.8	7.4	7.5	8.8	9.2
Official creditors	16.0	7.7	63.3	6.7	6.9	6.4	7.8	8.3
Private creditors	7.0	6.0	1.1	1.1	0.5	1.0	1.0	0.9
Private nonguaranteed	..	..	..	..	..	..	..	..
Debt resource inflows								
Net debt inflows	31.0	-43.2	4.5	16.3	6.8	25.8	21.1	67.8
Official creditors (incl. IMF)	35.9	-10.9	9.8	19.5	7.5	26.1	21.4	68.1
Private creditors	-4.9	-32.3	-5.3	-3.2	-0.7	-0.3	-0.3	-0.3
Long-term	-4.9	-33.3	-5.3	-3.2	-0.7	-0.3	-0.3	-0.3
Public and publicly guaranteed	-4.9	-33.3	-5.3	-3.2	-0.7	-0.3	-0.3	-0.3
Private nonguaranteed	..	..	..	..	..	..	..	..
Short-term	..	1.0	..	..	..	..	..	..
Non-debt resource inflows								
Foreign direct investment	32.4	70.3	104.3	194.0	177.5	177.7	200.3	197.8
Portfolio equity	..	0.0	..	..	..	..	..	..
Currency composition (%)								
Euro	..	9.8	9.2	7.5	6.8	5.5	7.3	9.2
U.S.dollars	26.9	39.3	43.2	43.8	43.6	45.3	43.7	41.8
Major economic aggregates								
Gross national income (GNI)	1,014.4	1,869.6	2,020.5	2,030.2	2,116.2	2,622.2	2,856.6	2,751.7
Exports of goods, services & prim. income	824.4	1,391.2	1,667.8	1,680.9	1,473.7	1,669.3	1,952.7	1,658.4
Personal transfers & comp. of employees	478.1	599.4	638.2	575.9	547.9	610.1	649.3	554.0
Imports of goods, services & prim. income	1,132.8	1,891.8	2,251.7	2,034.9	2,138.5	2,740.8	3,027.8	3,111.0
Primary income on FDI	68.3	196.2	305.6	91.4	116.6	317.8	386.4	406.8
Current account balance	-71.5	-26.6	111.5	338.9	59.7	-404.8	-460.5	-587.4
International reserves	417.9	519.1	1,002.8	971.5	1,179.8	1,071.0	919.1	1,027.9
Ratios								
External debt stocks to exports (%)	82.1	48.0	41.0	41.3	51.3	46.5	40.7	51.9
External debt stocks to GNI (%)	66.7	35.7	33.8	34.2	35.7	29.6	27.8	31.3
Debt service to exports (%)	7.5	5.7	5.9	2.2	2.6	2.1	2.0	2.3
Short-term to external debt stocks (%)	0.6	1.2	..	..	0.0	..	..	..
Multilateral to external debt stocks (%)	70.3	77.7	86.0	86.4	80.2	80.2	80.3	75.8
Reserves to external debt stocks (%)	61.8	77.8	146.7	139.9	156.0	137.9	115.6	119.5
Reserves to imports (months)	4.4	3.3	5.3	5.7	6.6	4.7	3.6	4.0

Notes:

Large interest payment was made during 2007 to a creditor country to settle a long standing claim. Short-term debt is based on data from the BIS.

LIBERIA

(US$ million, unless otherwise indicated)

	2000	2005	2007	2008	2009	2010	2011	2012
Summary external debt data								
External debt stocks	**2,836.3**	**3,950.6**	**3,778.0**	**3,160.8**	**1,850.3**	**418.9**	**448.4**	**487.0**
Long-term external debt	1,104.0	1,179.1	1,033.5	865.0	673.1	183.1	188.0	208.3
Short-term external debt	1,412.6	2,421.8	2,359.4	1,405.5	91.6	0.4	12.2	12.0
interest arrears on long-term	1,412.6	2,421.8	2,359.4	1,405.5	91.6	0.4	12.2	12.0
Use of IMF credit	319.7	349.7	385.1	890.3	1,085.5	235.3	248.2	266.7
Long-term external debt								
Debt outstanding and disbursed	**1,104.0**	**1,179.1**	**1,033.5**	**865.0**	**673.1**	**183.1**	**188.0**	**208.3**
Public and publicly guaranteed	1,104.0	1,179.1	1,033.5	865.0	673.1	183.1	188.0	208.3
Official creditors	907.3	981.3	831.0	669.8	652.6	183.1	188.0	208.3
Private creditors	196.8	197.7	202.5	195.2	20.5	0.0	0.0	0.0
Private nonguaranteed	0.0	0.0	0.0	0.0	0.0	0.0	0.0	0.0
Disbursements	**0.0**	**0.0**	**0.0**	**0.0**	**0.0**	**0.0**	**20.3**	**23.1**
Public and publicly guaranteed	0.0	0.0	0.0	0.0	0.0	0.0	20.3	23.1
Official creditors	0.0	0.0	0.0	0.0	0.0	0.0	20.3	23.1
Private creditors	0.0	0.0	0.0	0.0	0.0	0.0	0.0	0.0
Private nonguaranteed	0.0	0.0	0.0	0.0	0.0	0.0	0.0	0.0
Principal repayments	**0.0**	**0.0**	**260.7**	**37.5**	**36.3**	**3.7**	**2.6**	**3.7**
Public and publicly guaranteed	0.0	0.0	260.7	37.5	36.3	3.7	2.6	3.7
Official creditors	0.0	0.0	260.7	37.5	4.3	3.7	2.6	3.7
Private creditors	0.0	0.0	0.0	0.0	32.0	0.0	0.0	0.0
Private nonguaranteed	0.0	0.0	0.0	0.0	0.0	0.0	0.0	0.0
Interest payments	**0.0**	**0.0**	**380.5**	**69.0**	**16.8**	**0.6**	**0.4**	**1.1**
Public and publicly guaranteed	0.0	0.0	380.5	69.0	16.8	0.6	0.4	1.1
Official creditors	0.0	0.0	380.5	69.0	11.8	0.6	0.4	1.1
Private creditors	0.0	0.0	0.0	0.0	5.0	0.0	0.0	0.0
Private nonguaranteed	0.0	0.0	0.0	0.0	0.0	0.0	0.0	0.0
Debt resource inflows								
Net debt inflows	-0.6	-0.1	-261.4	491.1	-18.6	9.8	31.8	37.5
Official creditors (incl. IMF)	-0.6	-0.1	-261.4	491.1	13.3	9.8	31.8	37.5
Private creditors	0.0	0.0	0.0	0.0	-32.0	0.0	0.0	0.0
Long-term	0.0	0.0	0.0	0.0	-32.0	0.0	0.0	0.0
Public and publicly guaranteed	0.0	0.0	0.0	0.0	-32.0	0.0	0.0	0.0
Private nonguaranteed	..	..	..	..	..	..	..	..
Short-term	..	..	..	..	..	..	..	..
Non-debt resource inflows								
Foreign direct investment	20.8	82.8	131.6	283.5	127.8	452.3	1,312.7	1,354.1
Portfolio equity	..	..	..	..	..	..	..	..
Currency composition (%)								
Euro	..	11.6	16.5	2.4	2.6	..	..	..
U.S.dollars	56.8	53.7	64.8	82.7	88.9	95.2	96.1	96.5
Major economic aggregates								
Gross national income (GNI)	514.1	394.4	584.8	690.4	1,010.5	1,113.3	1,428.2	1,614.9
Exports of goods, services & prim. income	..	354.7	562.2	781.0	472.2	430.4	1,351.8	..
Personal transfers & comp. of employees	..	31.9	62.0	58.1	25.1	31.4	360.0	..
Imports of goods, services & prim. income	..	1,317.7	1,924.2	2,310.7	1,850.0	1,804.7	3,325.3	..
Primary income on FDI	..	7.1	14.7	22.5	5.8	0.1	11.7	..
Current account balance	..	-183.5	-223.2	-354.3	-277.2	-415.2	-755.7	-1,765.8
International reserves	0.3	25.4	119.4	160.9	372.5	465.9	512.8	497.2
Ratios								
External debt stocks to exports (%)	..	1113.7	672.0	404.7	391.9	97.3	33.2	..
External debt stocks to GNI (%)	551.7	1001.7	646.0	457.8	183.1	37.6	31.4	30.2
Debt service to exports (%)	..	0.5	114.4	119.7	13.6	1.4	0.2	..
Short-term to external debt stocks (%)	49.8	61.3	62.5	44.5	5.0	0.1	2.7	2.5
Multilateral to external debt stocks (%)	13.9	11.1	5.1	5.0	8.4	15.1	13.3	16.6
Reserves to external debt stocks (%)	0.0	0.6	3.2	5.1	20.1	111.2	114.4	102.1
Reserves to imports (months)	..	0.2	0.7	0.8	2.4	3.1	1.9	..

Notes:

Historical long-term public and publicly guaranteed debt data before 2011 are revised based on reports provided by the country. Data include the effects of Paris Club rescheduling agreement signed in 2008 and 2010, and HIPC and MDRI debt relief.

MACEDONIA, FYR

(US$ million, unless otherwise indicated)

	2000	2005	2007	2008	2009	2010	2011	2012
Summary external debt data								
External debt stocks	**1,480**	**2,981**	**4,174**	**4,457**	**5,247**	**5,344**	**6,304**	**6,678**
Long-term external debt	1,333	2,108	2,564	3,013	3,731	3,840	4,132	4,391
Short-term external debt	55	800	1,597	1,432	1,413	1,403	1,769	1,884
interest arrears on long-term	4	9	28	29	30	64	80	109
Use of IMF credit	92	74	13	13	103	101	403	404
Long-term external debt								
Debt outstanding and disbursed	**1,333**	**2,108**	**2,564**	**3,013**	**3,731**	**3,840**	**4,132**	**4,391**
Public and publicly guaranteed	1,206	1,637	1,520	1,574	1,874	1,880	2,110	2,270
Official creditors	921	1,202	1,239	1,277	1,321	1,369	1,392	1,453
Private creditors	284	435	281	297	552	512	717	817
Private nonguaranteed	127	471	1,044	1,438	1,858	1,959	2,022	2,121
Disbursements	**151**	**318**	**538**	**789**	**1,012**	**596**	**968**	**637**
Public and publicly guaranteed	98	293	142	174	347	197	414	303
Official creditors	96	104	138	137	103	190	155	176
Private creditors	1	189	3	37	244	7	259	127
Private nonguaranteed	54	25	396	615	665	399	555	334
Principal repayments	**74**	**171**	**485**	**293**	**375**	**443**	**739**	**479**
Public and publicly guaranteed	25	81	294	78	88	98	126	168
Official creditors	23	67	286	74	81	90	103	124
Private creditors	2	14	8	5	7	9	23	44
Private nonguaranteed	49	90	191	215	287	344	614	310
Interest payments	**37**	**54**	**88**	**104**	**93**	**128**	**129**	**125**
Public and publicly guaranteed	30	41	51	54	47	56	60	64
Official creditors	20	32	38	41	33	22	24	23
Private creditors	10	9	12	14	15	35	36	41
Private nonguaranteed	7	13	38	50	46	71	70	60
Debt resource inflows								
Net debt inflows	59	117	713	329	617	109	890	244
Official creditors (incl. IMF)	58	42	-204	64	22	101	362	51
Private creditors	2	75	917	265	595	9	528	193
Long-term	5	109	200	432	615	53	177	108
Public and publicly guaranteed	0	174	-5	32	237	-2	236	83
Private nonguaranteed	5	-65	205	400	378	55	-59	24
Short-term	-3	-34	717	-167	-20	-44	350	85
Non-debt resource inflows								
Foreign direct investment	215	145	733	612	260	301	495	283
Portfolio equity	..	54	170	-49	-14	-4	-8	-6
Currency composition (%)								
Euro	..	40.8	63.0	64.0	69.6	69.8	73.9	77.3
U.S.dollars	71.8	56.6	34.3	31.8	25.8	23.9	20.3	17.9
Major economic aggregates								
Gross national income (GNI)	3,517	5,877	7,770	9,714	9,231	9,215	10,266	9,545
Exports of goods, services & prim. income	1,679	2,196	3,831	4,540	3,186	3,825	5,031	4,544
Personal transfers & comp. of employees	81	227	345	407	381	388	434	394
Imports of goods, services & prim. income	2,391	3,408	5,820	7,234	5,397	5,828	7,367	6,939
Primary income on FDI	31	142	470	253	138	232	276	268
Current account balance	-103	-159	-606	-1,236	-610	-198	-261	-300
International reserves	429	1,229	2,082	1,920	2,051	1,970	2,331	2,528
Ratios								
External debt stocks to exports (%)	88.1	135.8	108.9	98.2	164.7	139.7	125.3	147.0
External debt stocks to GNI (%)	42.1	50.7	53.7	45.9	56.8	58.0	61.4	70.0
Debt service to exports (%)	8.3	12.5	18.4	10.2	16.7	16.5	18.9	15.1
Short-term to external debt stocks (%)	3.7	26.8	38.3	32.1	26.9	26.3	28.1	28.2
Multilateral to external debt stocks (%)	38.5	30.7	24.9	23.5	20.6	21.1	18.4	18.3
Reserves to external debt stocks (%)	29.0	41.2	49.9	43.1	39.1	36.9	37.0	37.9
Reserves to imports (months)	2.2	4.3	4.3	3.2	4.6	4.1	3.8	4.4

MADAGASCAR

(US$ million, unless otherwise indicated)

	2000	2005	2007	2008	2009	2010	2011	2012
Summary external debt data								
External debt stocks	**4,716**	**3,521**	**2,283**	**2,480**	**2,788**	**2,699**	**2,769**	**2,896**
Long-term external debt	4,286	3,182	1,411	1,738	1,855	1,997	2,066	2,166
Short-term external debt	301	99	799	613	649	425	430	463
interest arrears on long-term	203	72	189	188	189	188	188	192
Use of IMF credit	129	240	73	129	284	278	273	267
Long-term external debt								
Debt outstanding and disbursed	**4,286**	**3,182**	**1,411**	**1,738**	**1,855**	**1,997**	**2,066**	**2,166**
Public and publicly guaranteed	4,286	3,182	1,411	1,717	1,836	1,982	2,053	2,157
Official creditors	4,247	3,173	1,404	1,710	1,829	1,975	2,046	2,146
Private creditors	39	9	6	7	7	7	7	10
Private nonguaranteed	..	..	..	21	19	15	12	10
Disbursements	**150**	**249**	**261**	**345**	**126**	**198**	**90**	**138**
Public and publicly guaranteed	150	249	261	342	124	198	90	138
Official creditors	150	249	261	342	124	197	90	135
Private creditors	0	0	0	0	0	0	0	3
Private nonguaranteed	..	..	..	3	2	0	0	0
Principal repayments	**74**	**38**	**9**	**20**	**34**	**37**	**18**	**37**
Public and publicly guaranteed	74	38	9	20	32	36	18	35
Official creditors	73	37	8	20	32	36	18	35
Private creditors	0	1	1	0	0	0	0	0
Private nonguaranteed	..	..	..	1	1	1	1	2
Interest payments	**28**	**28**	**10**	**11**	**15**	**16**	**16**	**17**
Public and publicly guaranteed	28	28	10	11	15	16	16	17
Official creditors	28	28	10	11	15	16	16	17
Private creditors	0	0	0	0	0	0	0	0
Private nonguaranteed	..	..	..	0	0	0	0	0
Debt resource inflows								
Net debt inflows	45	244	839	198	127	-65	74	123
Official creditors (incl. IMF)	122	218	264	381	92	160	69	94
Private creditors	-77	26	575	-183	35	-225	5	29
Long-term	0	-1	-1	3	0	-1	-1	1
Public and publicly guaranteed	0	-1	-1	0	0	..	0	3
Private nonguaranteed	..	..	..	3	0	-1	-1	-2
Short-term	-76	27	575	-186	35	-224	6	29
Non-debt resource inflows								
Foreign direct investment	83	85	773	1,169	1,066	808	810	895
Portfolio equity	..	..	..	..	..	..	..	..
Currency composition (%)								
Euro	..	2.3	3.0	2.3	2.4	2.5	2.1	1.2
U.S.dollars	56.8	71.9	57.2	53.8	52.5	53.1	53.1	54.8
Major economic aggregates								
Gross national income (GNI)	3,807	4,960	7,287	9,344	8,498	8,750	9,724	9,686
Exports of goods, services & prim. income	1,210	954	2,342	2,614	1,982	1,653	1,965	..
Personal transfers & comp. of employees	11	11	..	..	..	..	..	..
Imports of goods, services & prim. income	1,584	1,743	3,606	4,805	4,134	2,744	3,003	..
Primary income on FDI	4	38	..	..	..	..	..	..
Current account balance	-260	-554	-898	-1,726	-1,840	-1,210	-979	..
International reserves	285	481	847	982	1,135	1,172	1,279	1,191
Ratios								
External debt stocks to exports (%)	389.7	369.2	97.5	94.9	140.7	163.3	140.9	..
External debt stocks to GNI (%)	123.9	71.0	31.3	26.5	32.8	30.8	28.5	29.9
Debt service to exports (%)	9.7	8.3	1.5	1.7	2.8	3.7	2.1	..
Short-term to external debt stocks (%)	6.4	2.8	35.0	24.7	23.3	15.7	15.5	16.0
Multilateral to external debt stocks (%)	38.7	80.6	47.9	55.6	51.9	57.0	58.0	58.1
Reserves to external debt stocks (%)	6.0	13.7	37.1	39.6	40.7	43.4	46.2	41.1
Reserves to imports (months)	2.2	3.3	2.8	2.5	3.3	5.1	5.1	..

Notes:

Data include the effects of HIPC and MDRI debt relief.

MALAWI

(US$ million, unless otherwise indicated)

	2000	2005	2007	2008	2009	2010	2011	2012
Summary external debt data								
External debt stocks	**2,719**	**3,196**	**869**	**996**	**1,144**	**1,039**	**1,203**	**1,314**
Long-term external debt	2,544	3,062	759	769	846	729	927	1,023
Short-term external debt	78	43	61	85	67	61	30	8
interest arrears on long-term	37	34	0	0	0	0	0	0
Use of IMF credit	97	91	48	142	231	248	247	283
Long-term external debt								
Debt outstanding and disbursed	**2,544**	**3,062**	**759**	**769**	**846**	**729**	**927**	**1,023**
Public and publicly guaranteed	2,544	3,062	759	769	846	729	927	1,023
Official creditors	2,526	3,043	752	763	841	724	921	1,017
Private creditors	18	18	7	6	6	5	5	5
Private nonguaranteed	..	..	..	..	..	..	..	..
Disbursements	**119**	**89**	**69**	**66**	**107**	**81**	**208**	**109**
Public and publicly guaranteed	119	89	69	66	107	81	208	109
Official creditors	119	89	69	66	107	81	208	109
Private creditors	0	0	0	0	0	0	0	0
Private nonguaranteed	..	..	..	..	..	..	..	..
Principal repayments	**33**	**38**	**20**	**17**	**22**	**13**	**14**	**15**
Public and publicly guaranteed	33	38	20	17	22	13	14	15
Official creditors	33	35	19	17	22	13	14	15
Private creditors	0	3	1	0	0	0	0	0
Private nonguaranteed	..	..	..	..	..	..	..	..
Interest payments	**18**	**22**	**11**	**15**	**15**	**7**	**7**	**9**
Public and publicly guaranteed	18	22	11	15	15	7	7	9
Official creditors	18	22	11	15	15	7	7	9
Private creditors	0	0	0	0	0	0	0	0
Private nonguaranteed	..	..	..	..	..	..	..	..
Debt resource inflows								
Net debt inflows	83	42	51	170	67	83	162	108
Official creditors (incl. IMF)	85	47	60	146	85	89	193	130
Private creditors	-2	-5	-9	24	-18	-6	-31	-22
Long-term	0	-3	-1	0	0	0	0	0
Public and publicly guaranteed	0	-3	-1	0	0	0	0	0
Private nonguaranteed	..	..	..	..	..	..	..	..
Short-term	-2	-2	-8	24	-18	-6	-31	-22
Non-debt resource inflows								
Foreign direct investment	26	140	124	195	49	97	129	129
Portfolio equity	..	-4	-2	-1	0	1	1	1
Currency composition (%)								
Euro	..	3.3	5.0	3.5	3.1	3.6	3.8	4.0
U.S.dollars	65.9	65.8	57.1	54.2	53.1	41.8	40.7	40.3
Major economic aggregates								
Gross national income (GNI)	1,707	2,713	3,626	4,254	4,959	5,272	5,493	4,139
Exports of goods, services & prim. income	471	609	879	1,026	1,348	1,224	1,632	1,397
Personal transfers & comp. of employees	1	23	21	17	17	22	25	28
Imports of goods, services & prim. income	680	1,390	1,619	2,127	2,298	2,650	2,917	2,646
Primary income on FDI	15	52	67	139	103	173	92	93
Current account balance	-73	-507	-418	-664	-482	-786	-766	-800
International reserves	243	159	217	243	149	307	197	223
Ratios								
External debt stocks to exports (%)	577.7	524.5	98.9	97.0	84.9	84.9	73.7	94.0
External debt stocks to GNI (%)	159.3	117.8	24.0	23.4	23.1	19.7	21.9	31.7
Debt service to exports (%)	13.5	12.5	3.8	3.1	2.9	1.7	1.4	2.0
Short-term to external debt stocks (%)	2.9	1.4	7.0	8.5	5.9	5.9	2.5	0.6
Multilateral to external debt stocks (%)	75.2	80.1	50.3	48.8	47.8	56.4	52.6	53.7
Reserves to external debt stocks (%)	8.9	5.0	24.9	24.4	13.1	29.6	16.4	17.0
Reserves to imports (months)	4.3	1.4	1.6	1.4	0.8	1.4	0.8	1.0

Notes:

Short-term debt is based on data from the BIS. Data include the effects of Paris Club rescheduling agreement signed in 2006 and HIPC and MDRI debt relief.

MALAYSIA

(US$ million, unless otherwise indicated)

	2000	2005	2007	2008	2009	2010	2011	2012
Summary external debt data								
External debt stocks	**41,946**	**52,054**	**63,091**	**67,674**	**69,784**	**85,126**	**94,468**	**103,950**
Long-term external debt	37,192	38,679	39,771	44,660	43,979	47,977	48,697	54,894
Short-term external debt	4,573	13,176	23,100	22,800	23,695	35,076	43,704	46,987
interest arrears on long-term	0	0	0	0	0	0	0	0
Use of IMF credit	181	199	220	214	2,110	2,073	2,067	2,069
Long-term external debt								
Debt outstanding and disbursed	**37,192**	**38,679**	**39,771**	**44,660**	**43,979**	**47,977**	**48,697**	**54,894**
Public and publicly guaranteed	19,125	22,324	19,745	22,742	22,647	27,351	27,156	27,119
Official creditors	4,950	6,542	4,374	5,164	4,092	3,750	3,263	2,468
Private creditors	14,175	15,782	15,372	17,578	18,555	23,601	23,893	24,651
Private nonguaranteed	18,067	16,356	20,026	21,918	21,332	20,626	21,541	27,775
Disbursements	**5,921**	**6,050**	**5,852**	**5,180**	**8,339**	**14,720**	**12,856**	**14,814**
Public and publicly guaranteed	3,460	2,182	1,373	1,942	5,319	6,014	3,311	3,439
Official creditors	1,446	981	206	98	47	18	10	2
Private creditors	2,015	1,201	1,166	1,844	5,271	5,996	3,301	3,436
Private nonguaranteed	2,461	3,868	4,479	3,238	3,020	8,706	9,545	11,375
Principal repayments	**4,146**	**7,192**	**7,819**	**6,258**	**9,793**	**11,349**	**8,981**	**7,357**
Public and publicly guaranteed	2,017	4,752	3,646	1,503	5,351	1,863	3,608	3,304
Official creditors	840	1,218	1,691	820	1,053	688	625	604
Private creditors	1,176	3,534	1,956	683	4,298	1,176	2,983	2,701
Private nonguaranteed	2,129	2,440	4,172	4,755	4,442	9,486	5,373	4,053
Interest payments	**2,021**	**1,858**	**2,035**	**2,112**	**1,746**	**1,708**	**1,563**	**1,967**
Public and publicly guaranteed	1,159	1,208	1,192	1,058	876	1,024	1,017	1,293
Official creditors	259	314	202	129	124	97	86	79
Private creditors	900	894	990	929	752	927	931	1,214
Private nonguaranteed	862	650	843	1,053	870	684	545	674
Debt resource inflows								
Net debt inflows	337	601	9,331	-1,378	-560	14,753	12,503	10,740
Official creditors (incl. IMF)	606	-238	-1,484	-722	-1,006	-669	-614	-602
Private creditors	-269	839	10,815	-656	446	15,423	13,117	11,341
Long-term	1,170	-904	-482	-356	-448	4,041	4,489	8,058
Public and publicly guaranteed	838	-2,333	-789	1,161	974	4,821	317	736
Private nonguaranteed	331	1,428	307	-1,517	-1,422	-780	4,172	7,323
Short-term	-1,439	1,744	11,297	-300	895	11,381	8,628	3,283
Non-debt resource inflows								
Foreign direct investment	3,788	3,925	9,071	7,573	115	10,886	15,119	9,734
Portfolio equity	..	-1,200	-669	-10,716	-449	..	..	..
Currency composition (%)								
Euro	..	4.2	5.8	4.7	0.1	0.1	0.0	0.0
U.S.dollars	63.1	71.2	65.9	68.7	78.2	82.3	83.0	85.9
Major economic aggregates								
Gross national income (GNI)	86,182	137,211	189,484	224,078	198,218	238,591	280,754	292,622
Exports of goods, services & prim. income	114,356	166,725	217,001	242,055	197,562	243,301	281,911	279,255
Personal transfers & comp. of employees	342	1,117	1,556	1,329	1,131	1,103	1,211	1,320
Imports of goods, services & prim. income	103,944	142,268	182,563	197,879	160,181	209,534	241,520	254,714
Primary income on FDI	7,173	8,330	9,932	13,838	11,119	15,298	18,105	18,385
Current account balance	8,488	19,980	29,770	38,914	31,801	26,998	33,508	18,638
International reserves	28,330	69,858	101,019	91,149	95,432	104,884	131,780	137,784
Ratios								
External debt stocks to exports (%)	36.7	31.2	29.1	28.0	35.3	35.0	33.5	37.2
External debt stocks to GNI (%)	48.7	37.9	33.3	30.2	35.2	35.7	33.6	35.5
Debt service to exports (%)	5.6	5.6	4.8	3.7	6.1	5.5	3.9	3.5
Short-term to external debt stocks (%)	10.9	25.3	36.6	33.7	34.0	41.2	46.3	45.2
Multilateral to external debt stocks (%)	3.1	1.8	0.7	0.6	0.4	0.3	0.2	0.2
Reserves to external debt stocks (%)	67.5	134.2	160.1	134.7	136.8	123.2	139.5	132.5
Reserves to imports (months)	3.3	5.9	6.6	5.5	7.1	6.0	6.5	6.5

Notes:

Long-term public and publicly guaranteed, long-term private nonguaranteed, and short-term debt data are World Bank staff estimates based on reports provided by the country.

MALDIVES

(US$ million, unless otherwise indicated)

	2000	2005	2007	2008	2009	2010	2011	2012
Summary external debt data								
External debt stocks	**206**	**389**	**853**	**922**	**985**	**1,011**	**988**	**1,027**
Long-term external debt	185	327	656	701	779	760	731	732
Short-term external debt	21	56	190	216	186	224	229	267
interest arrears on long-term	0	0	0	2	1	3	1	3
Use of IMF credit	0	6	7	4	21	28	28	28
Long-term external debt								
Debt outstanding and disbursed	**185**	**327**	**656**	**701**	**779**	**760**	**731**	**732**
Public and publicly guaranteed	185	327	438	493	563	645	689	732
Official creditors	155	277	354	379	465	539	579	644
Private creditors	30	50	84	114	97	105	110	87
Private nonguaranteed	0	0	218	209	216	115	42	0
Disbursements	**14**	**50**	**105**	**150**	**157**	**168**	**124**	**113**
Public and publicly guaranteed	14	50	71	105	112	142	116	113
Official creditors	6	33	43	58	107	108	83	112
Private creditors	7	16	29	47	5	34	33	2
Private nonguaranteed	0	0	34	45	45	26	9	0
Principal repayments	**14**	**25**	**52**	**65**	**68**	**63**	**73**	**69**
Public and publicly guaranteed	14	25	31	41	47	54	69	69
Official creditors	7	16	21	26	24	30	44	44
Private creditors	7	9	11	15	23	24	25	25
Private nonguaranteed	0	0	20	24	20	9	4	0
Interest payments	**5**	**9**	**18**	**20**	**17**	**11**	**11**	**10**
Public and publicly guaranteed	5	9	12	14	13	10	11	10
Official creditors	3	7	9	9	8	6	7	7
Private creditors	2	2	4	5	5	4	4	3
Private nonguaranteed	0	0	5	7	4	1	1	0
Debt resource inflows								
Net debt inflows	-4	55	143	107	64	149	58	80
Official creditors (incl. IMF)	0	23	22	29	88	85	39	68
Private creditors	-3	31	121	77	-23	63	19	12
Long-term	0	7	32	53	6	27	12	-24
Public and publicly guaranteed	0	7	18	32	-18	10	8	-24
Private nonguaranteed	..	..	14	21	24	17	5	..
Short-term	-3	24	89	24	-30	36	7	36
Non-debt resource inflows								
Foreign direct investment	22	53	132	181	158	216	256	284
Portfolio equity	..	..	0	14	-14	-10	0	0
Currency composition (%)								
Euro	..	8.6	20.8	22.5	18.9	18.5	18.9	16.0
U.S.dollars	53.3	55.3	47.8	46.6	53.3	46.9	43.6	40.5
Major economic aggregates								
Gross national income (GNI)	594	945	1,303	1,602	1,712	1,823	1,833	1,883
Exports of goods, services & prim. income	468	495	1,831	1,984	1,718	2,011	2,358	2,351
Personal transfers & comp. of employees	2	2	8	6	5	3	3	3
Imports of goods, services & prim. income	492	910	1,943	2,381	1,758	2,008	2,595	2,709
Primary income on FDI	34	31	242	249	236	272	280	281
Current account balance	-51	-273	-269	-612	-221	-196	-437	-600
International reserves	123	189	311	244	276	364	349	318
Ratios								
External debt stocks to exports (%)	44.1	78.5	46.6	46.5	57.3	50.3	41.9	43.7
External debt stocks to GNI (%)	34.7	41.2	65.5	57.5	57.5	55.5	53.9	54.5
Debt service to exports (%)	4.2	7.3	4.4	4.9	5.4	4.2	4.0	3.8
Short-term to external debt stocks (%)	10.3	14.5	22.2	23.4	18.8	22.1	23.2	26.0
Multilateral to external debt stocks (%)	57.5	44.7	30.5	30.3	29.1	30.3	30.9	31.4
Reserves to external debt stocks (%)	59.5	48.6	36.5	26.4	28.0	36.0	35.3	31.0
Reserves to imports (months)	3.0	2.5	1.9	1.2	1.9	2.2	1.6	1.4

Notes:

Long-term private nonguaranteed and short-term debt data from 2006 are World Bank staff estimates based on reports provided by the country.

MALI

(US$ million, unless otherwise indicated)

	2000	2005	2007	2008	2009	2010	2011	2012
Summary external debt data								
External debt stocks	**2,981**	**3,224**	**1,851**	**2,056**	**2,211**	**2,464**	**2,931**	**3,073**
Long-term external debt	2,671	3,036	1,807	1,985	2,002	2,271	2,508	2,797
Short-term external debt	114	55	6	7	25	6	193	39
interest arrears on long-term	42	6	6	7	1	0	18	26
Use of IMF credit	196	132	38	65	184	187	230	237
Long-term external debt								
Debt outstanding and disbursed	**2,671**	**3,036**	**1,807**	**1,985**	**2,002**	**2,271**	**2,508**	**2,797**
Public and publicly guaranteed	2,671	3,036	1,807	1,985	2,002	2,271	2,508	2,797
Official creditors	2,671	3,032	1,800	1,979	1,995	2,266	2,504	2,793
Private creditors	0	5	7	5	7	5	4	3
Private nonguaranteed	..	..	..	..	..	..	..	..
Disbursements	**100**	**280**	**257**	**234**	**494**	**312**	**293**	**275**
Public and publicly guaranteed	100	280	257	234	494	312	293	275
Official creditors	100	277	257	234	491	312	293	275
Private creditors	0	3	0	0	3	0	0	0
Private nonguaranteed	..	..	..	..	..	..	..	..
Principal repayments	**50**	**52**	**43**	**44**	**46**	**39**	**40**	**28**
Public and publicly guaranteed	50	52	43	44	46	39	40	28
Official creditors	50	52	42	43	45	38	39	27
Private creditors	0	0	1	1	1	1	1	0
Private nonguaranteed	..	..	..	..	..	..	..	..
Interest payments	**18**	**27**	**19**	**24**	**22**	**21**	**26**	**24**
Public and publicly guaranteed	18	27	19	24	22	21	26	24
Official creditors	18	27	19	24	21	21	25	24
Private creditors	0	0	0	0	0	0	0	0
Private nonguaranteed	..	..	..	..	..	..	..	..
Debt resource inflows								
Net debt inflows	-31	219	194	218	475	261	466	93
Official creditors (incl. IMF)	42	210	219	219	449	280	299	255
Private creditors	-73	8	-25	-1	25	-19	168	-162
Long-term	..	3	-1	-1	1	-1	-1	0
Public and publicly guaranteed	..	3	-1	-1	1	-1	-1	0
Private nonguaranteed	..	..	..	..	..	..	..	..
Short-term	-73	5	-24	..	24	-18	169	-162
Non-debt resource inflows								
Foreign direct investment	82	175	-50	100	103	27	556	310
Portfolio equity	0	9	-6	-3	-3	1	..	..
Currency composition (%)								
Euro	..	14.4	18.1	15.4	3.1	3.5	3.2	5.0
U.S.dollars	33.9	45.2	32.0	31.6	34.1	36.7	37.8	35.1
Major economic aggregates								
Gross national income (GNI)	2,392	5,099	6,847	8,425	8,508	9,003	10,195	9,808
Exports of goods, services & prim. income	665	1,443	2,004	2,653	2,210	2,508	2,838	..
Personal transfers & comp. of employees	73	177	344	431	454	473	..	..
Imports of goods, services & prim. income	1,046	2,108	2,985	4,171	3,351	4,236	4,338	..
Primary income on FDI	76	190	262	326	459	402	..	..
Current account balance	-255	-438	-581	-1,063	-655	-1,190	-652	..
International reserves	382	854	1,087	1,072	1,604	1,344	1,379	1,341
Ratios								
External debt stocks to exports (%)	448.5	223.4	92.3	77.5	100.1	98.3	103.3	..
External debt stocks to GNI (%)	124.6	63.2	27.0	24.4	26.0	27.4	28.7	31.3
Debt service to exports (%)	14.1	6.9	3.2	2.6	3.1	2.5	2.4	..
Short-term to external debt stocks (%)	3.8	1.7	0.3	0.3	1.1	0.2	6.6	1.3
Multilateral to external debt stocks (%)	50.8	69.5	52.1	55.8	70.8	72.6	68.3	70.0
Reserves to external debt stocks (%)	12.8	26.5	58.7	52.1	72.6	54.6	47.0	43.7
Reserves to imports (months)	4.4	4.9	4.4	3.1	5.7	3.8	3.8	..

Notes:

Short-term debt is based on data from the BIS. The data for Principal Arrears on long-term are revised from 2001. Data include the effects of HIPC and MDRI debt relief.

MAURITANIA

(US$ million, unless otherwise indicated)

	2000	2005	2007	2008	2009	2010	2011	2012
Summary external debt data								
External debt stocks	**2,390**	**2,322**	**1,719**	**2,001**	**2,289**	**2,705**	**2,867**	**3,348**
Long-term external debt	2,029	2,072	1,437	1,669	1,984	2,323	2,538	2,940
Short-term external debt	251	167	254	301	192	237	151	196
interest arrears on long-term	112	109	128	135	134	76	77	76
Use of IMF credit	111	83	29	31	113	145	178	211
Long-term external debt								
Debt outstanding and disbursed	**2,029**	**2,072**	**1,437**	**1,669**	**1,984**	**2,323**	**2,538**	**2,940**
Public and publicly guaranteed	2,029	2,072	1,437	1,669	1,984	2,323	2,538	2,940
Official creditors	2,009	2,048	1,417	1,655	1,972	2,322	2,538	2,940
Private creditors	19	23	20	14	12	1	0	0
Private nonguaranteed	..	..	..	..	..	..	..	..
Disbursements	**115**	**143**	**185**	**294**	**407**	**412**	**287**	**440**
Public and publicly guaranteed	115	143	185	294	407	412	287	440
Official creditors	115	128	185	294	407	412	287	440
Private creditors	0	15	0	0	0	0	0	0
Private nonguaranteed	..	..	..	..	..	..	..	..
Principal repayments	**46**	**33**	**93**	**38**	**53**	**76**	**79**	**85**
Public and publicly guaranteed	46	33	93	38	53	76	79	85
Official creditors	43	31	92	31	52	65	78	85
Private creditors	2	1	1	6	1	11	1	0
Private nonguaranteed	..	..	..	..	..	..	..	..
Interest payments	**20**	**20**	**23**	**21**	**23**	**35**	**41**	**55**
Public and publicly guaranteed	20	20	23	21	23	35	41	55
Official creditors	18	19	22	21	23	34	41	55
Private creditors	2	1	1	0	0	1	0	0
Private nonguaranteed	..	..	..	..	..	..	..	..
Debt resource inflows								
Net debt inflows	62	92	131	300	246	473	156	433
Official creditors (incl. IMF)	74	87	106	266	355	381	244	387
Private creditors	-11	5	26	34	-109	92	-88	46
Long-term	-2	14	-1	-6	-1	-11	-1	..
Public and publicly guaranteed	-2	14	-1	-6	-1	-11	-1	..
Private nonguaranteed	..	..	..	..	..	..	..	..
Short-term	-9	-9	27	40	-108	103	-87	46
Non-debt resource inflows								
Foreign direct investment	40	814	139	343	-3	131	589	1,204
Portfolio equity	..	..	..	..	..	..	..	..
Currency composition (%)								
Euro	..	2.2	8.3	9.4	7.6	6.3	6.3	7.7
U.S.dollars	40.9	49.3	35.9	37.7	36.1	41.5	43.2	49.1
Major economic aggregates								
Gross national income (GNI)	1,304	2,249	3,348	3,821	3,079	3,603	4,090	4,066
Exports of goods, services & prim. income	..	..	1,627	2,056	1,641	2,306	3,124	2,914
Personal transfers & comp. of employees	..	..	..	..	..	..	..	..
Imports of goods, services & prim. income	..	..	2,286	2,776	2,176	2,787	3,522	4,497
Primary income on FDI	..	..	..	..	..	..	..	..
Current account balance	..	..	144	-523	-405	-319	-248	-1,263
International reserves	46	64	198	189	225	272	485	949
Ratios								
External debt stocks to exports (%)	..	..	105.7	97.3	139.5	117.3	91.8	114.9
External debt stocks to GNI (%)	183.3	103.2	51.4	52.4	74.3	75.1	70.1	82.3
Debt service to exports (%)	..	..	7.5	3.1	4.7	4.9	3.9	4.9
Short-term to external debt stocks (%)	10.5	7.2	14.8	15.0	8.4	8.8	5.3	5.9
Multilateral to external debt stocks (%)	41.6	60.9	46.5	46.1	48.2	49.9	51.2	48.0
Reserves to external debt stocks (%)	1.9	2.8	11.5	9.4	9.8	10.0	16.9	28.4
Reserves to imports (months)	..	..	1.0	0.8	1.2	1.2	1.7	2.5

Notes:

Short-term debt is based on data from the BIS. Data include the effects of MDRI debt relief.

MAURITIUS

(US$ million, unless otherwise indicated)

	2000	2005	2007	2008	2009	2010	2011	2012
Summary external debt data								
External debt stocks	**967**	**805**	**714**	**669**	**978**	**1,225**	**3,133**	**4,459**
Long-term external debt	946	782	689	645	818	1,072	1,277	1,454
Short-term external debt	..	..	..	..	8	3	1,708	2,856
interest arrears on long-term	..	..	..	..	..	..	..	15
Use of IMF credit	21	23	25	24	152	149	149	149
Long-term external debt								
Debt outstanding and disbursed	**946**	**782**	**689**	**645**	**818**	**1,072**	**1,277**	**1,454**
Public and publicly guaranteed	828	716	627	596	737	972	1,166	1,343
Official creditors	494	504	497	500	652	884	1,100	1,290
Private creditors	334	213	130	96	85	88	66	53
Private nonguaranteed	118	66	62	49	81	100	111	111
Disbursements	**128**	**138**	**118**	**114**	**285**	**388**	**333**	**187**
Public and publicly guaranteed	119	126	89	86	217	319	283	136
Official creditors	43	62	89	86	197	292	281	136
Private creditors	76	64	0	0	19	27	1	0
Private nonguaranteed	9	11	29	28	69	69	51	51
Principal repayments	**401**	**197**	**126**	**145**	**121**	**113**	**139**	**120**
Public and publicly guaranteed	385	176	105	110	84	64	78	58
Official creditors	55	87	61	83	51	44	56	45
Private creditors	330	89	44	27	33	20	21	14
Private nonguaranteed	16	21	21	35	37	49	61	61
Interest payments	**52**	**30**	**28**	**26**	**21**	**17**	**23**	**26**
Public and publicly guaranteed	51	30	28	25	20	16	22	26
Official creditors	23	19	18	18	16	15	20	24
Private creditors	29	10	10	7	4	2	2	2
Private nonguaranteed	1	0	1	0	1	1	1	1
Debt resource inflows								
Net debt inflows	-273	-59	-8	-31	164	270	1,898	1,201
Official creditors (incl. IMF)	-12	-24	28	3	146	247	225	92
Private creditors	-261	-35	-36	-34	18	23	1,673	1,109
Long-term	-261	-35	-36	-34	18	27	-31	-24
Public and publicly guaranteed	-254	-25	-44	-27	-14	8	-20	-14
Private nonguaranteed	-6	-10	8	-7	32	20	-11	-11
Short-term	..	..	..	..	..	-4	1,704	1,134
Non-debt resource inflows								
Foreign direct investment	266	42	341	378	257	430	273	361
Portfolio equity	-4	36	50	34	..	..	..	..
Currency composition (%)								
Euro	..	49.1	50.1	45.4	40.8	32.0	29.7	28.7
U.S.dollars	47.1	25.8	21.8	24.9	32.6	31.4	35.0	40.7
Major economic aggregates								
Gross national income (GNI)	4,553	6,276	8,016	9,714	8,793	9,835	11,325	10,604
Exports of goods, services & prim. income	2,671	3,899	5,259	5,748	4,635	10,189	7,005	7,622
Personal transfers & comp. of employees	177	1	1	1	1	1	1	1
Imports of goods, services & prim. income	2,772	4,284	5,818	6,948	5,514	11,378	8,632	8,939
Primary income on FDI	8	34	90	163	195	4,639	547	569
Current account balance	-37	-324	-434	-976	-655	-1,006	-1,506	-1,175
International reserves	897	1,340	1,780	1,743	2,179	2,442	2,583	2,837
Ratios								
External debt stocks to exports (%)	36.2	20.6	13.6	11.6	21.1	12.0	44.7	58.5
External debt stocks to GNI (%)	21.2	12.8	8.9	6.9	11.1	12.5	27.7	42.0
Debt service to exports (%)	17.0	5.8	2.9	3.0	3.1	1.3	2.7	2.4
Short-term to external debt stocks (%)	..	..	..	..	0.8	0.3	54.5	64.1
Multilateral to external debt stocks (%)	22.3	31.1	35.5	40.3	38.5	40.9	18.7	14.1
Reserves to external debt stocks (%)	92.8	166.4	249.4	260.4	222.9	199.4	82.4	63.6
Reserves to imports (months)	3.9	3.8	3.7	3.0	4.7	2.6	3.6	3.8

Notes:

Long-term private nonguaranteed from 2009 are based on reports provided by the country and do not include offshore liabilities. Private nonguaranteed debt data for 2012 are World Bank staff estimates. Short-term debt data are based on reports provided by the country and data for 2009 and 2010 are public sector short-term debt only.

MEXICO

(US$ million, unless otherwise indicated)

	2000	2005	2007	2008	2009	2010	2011	2012
Summary external debt data								
External debt stocks	**152,260**	**175,918**	**199,218**	**206,736**	**199,807**	**243,635**	**286,382**	**354,897**
Long-term external debt	132,951	153,302	171,398	177,884	167,747	200,231	231,088	278,204
Short-term external debt	18,932	22,201	27,362	28,405	27,590	39,013	50,917	72,311
interest arrears on long-term	0	0	0	0	0	0	0	0
Use of IMF credit	378	415	458	447	4,470	4,391	4,377	4,382
Long-term external debt								
Debt outstanding and disbursed	**132,951**	**153,302**	**171,398**	**177,884**	**167,747**	**200,231**	**231,088**	**278,204**
Public and publicly guaranteed	82,470	118,145	125,525	133,102	123,226	150,603	171,586	208,649
Official creditors	20,892	18,789	11,019	12,424	21,082	25,973	28,161	29,848
Private creditors	61,577	99,356	114,506	120,679	102,144	124,630	143,426	178,801
Private nonguaranteed	50,481	35,158	45,872	44,782	44,521	49,628	59,502	69,555
Disbursements	**32,830**	**28,801**	**41,661**	**33,704**	**36,695**	**54,986**	**59,712**	**98,408**
Public and publicly guaranteed	11,483	17,995	23,952	24,746	26,616	42,142	34,063	47,826
Official creditors	2,855	2,309	2,165	2,761	8,572	6,166	4,518	3,099
Private creditors	8,628	15,686	21,786	21,985	18,044	35,976	29,546	44,727
Private nonguaranteed	21,346	10,806	17,710	8,958	10,079	12,844	25,649	50,582
Principal repayments	**38,967**	**25,101**	**24,288**	**24,565**	**22,318**	**21,683**	**28,708**	**35,413**
Public and publicly guaranteed	16,337	15,686	13,544	14,831	11,872	13,941	12,383	8,501
Official creditors	3,386	2,530	1,543	1,463	1,795	1,679	1,947	1,490
Private creditors	12,950	13,155	12,001	13,368	10,077	12,263	10,436	7,011
Private nonguaranteed	22,630	9,416	10,744	9,735	10,446	7,742	16,325	26,912
Interest payments	**12,174**	**9,398**	**11,717**	**9,975**	**8,792**	**8,345**	**10,887**	**32,204**
Public and publicly guaranteed	7,923	7,532	7,934	7,176	6,019	5,859	7,318	28,709
Official creditors	1,554	848	514	458	551	627	730	756
Private creditors	6,368	6,685	7,420	6,718	5,468	5,232	6,587	27,954
Private nonguaranteed	4,251	1,866	3,783	2,799	2,773	2,486	3,570	3,495
Debt resource inflows								
Net debt inflows	-15,566	5,588	18,477	10,181	13,562	44,726	42,907	84,390
Official creditors (incl. IMF)	-4,830	-221	623	1,298	6,777	4,487	2,570	1,609
Private creditors	-10,736	5,809	17,855	8,883	6,785	40,239	40,337	82,781
Long-term	-5,606	3,920	16,751	7,840	7,600	28,816	28,433	61,387
Public and publicly guaranteed	-4,322	2,530	9,785	8,617	7,966	23,713	19,110	37,717
Private nonguaranteed	-1,284	1,390	6,966	-777	-367	5,103	9,324	23,670
Short-term	-5,130	1,889	1,104	1,043	-815	11,423	11,904	21,395
Non-debt resource inflows								
Foreign direct investment	18,110	24,451	31,552	27,853	16,605	22,563	23,553	15,453
Portfolio equity	447	3,353	-482	-3,503	4,155	373	-6,566	10,038
Currency composition (%)								
Euro	..	1.0	1.0	0.8	6.0	4.8	4.2	3.5
U.S.dollars	84.0	87.9	81.8	83.7	69.4	63.3	59.0	52.3
Major economic aggregates								
Gross national income (GNI)	566,409	833,255	1,014,791	1,074,109	869,375	1,023,942	1,139,952	1,157,782
Exports of goods, services & prim. income	185,853	235,187	297,201	318,089	251,597	324,906	376,096	398,728
Personal transfers & comp. of employees	7,525	22,742	26,880	26,041	22,076	22,080	23,588	23,366
Imports of goods, services & prim. income	211,589	265,939	337,874	363,114	280,913	349,673	410,906	435,471
Primary income on FDI	6,076	8,145	13,443	11,201	8,084	7,918	11,633	13,402
Current account balance	-18,742	-8,614	-14,268	-19,557	-7,724	-3,230	-11,836	-14,184
International reserves	35,509	74,054	87,109	95,126	99,589	120,265	143,991	160,413
Ratios								
External debt stocks to exports (%)	81.9	74.8	67.0	65.0	79.4	75.0	76.1	89.0
External debt stocks to GNI (%)	26.9	21.1	19.6	19.2	23.0	23.8	25.1	30.7
Debt service to exports (%)	31.6	15.5	12.8	11.1	12.7	10.0	11.2	17.7
Short-term to external debt stocks (%)	12.4	12.6	13.7	13.7	13.8	16.0	17.8	20.4
Multilateral to external debt stocks (%)	11.3	9.4	4.6	5.2	8.6	8.8	8.1	7.1
Reserves to external debt stocks (%)	23.3	42.1	43.7	46.0	49.8	49.4	50.3	45.2
Reserves to imports (months)	2.0	3.3	3.1	3.1	4.3	4.1	4.2	4.4

MOLDOVA

(US$ million, unless otherwise indicated)

	2000	2005	2007	2008	2009	2010	2011	2012
Summary external debt data								
External debt stocks	**1,843**	**2,219**	**3,365**	**3,655**	**3,753**	**4,837**	**5,459**	**6,135**
Long-term external debt	1,047	1,238	1,941	2,019	2,011	2,745	2,899	3,205
Short-term external debt	489	718	1,079	1,289	1,403	1,583	1,906	2,137
interest arrears on long-term	22	56	21	22	38	37	42	52
Use of IMF credit	308	264	346	347	338	509	655	793
Long-term external debt								
Debt outstanding and disbursed	**1,047**	**1,238**	**1,941**	**2,019**	**2,011**	**2,745**	**2,899**	**3,205**
Public and publicly guaranteed	850	698	783	805	809	839	857	942
Official creditors	743	664	759	790	790	823	836	913
Private creditors	107	34	24	15	19	16	21	29
Private nonguaranteed	197	540	1,158	1,214	1,203	1,906	2,042	2,263
Disbursements	**164**	**237**	**588**	**484**	**284**	**464**	**530**	**648**
Public and publicly guaranteed	54	26	47	53	54	94	94	142
Official creditors	52	26	47	53	41	89	80	121
Private creditors	2	0	0	0	13	5	14	21
Private nonguaranteed	110	211	541	432	230	370	436	505
Principal repayments	**57**	**163**	**219**	**391**	**303**	**306**	**368**	**467**
Public and publicly guaranteed	30	42	43	44	55	55	71	65
Official creditors	27	35	34	35	46	47	63	51
Private creditors	3	7	9	8	9	8	8	14
Private nonguaranteed	28	120	176	347	248	251	297	402
Interest payments	**46**	**42**	**50**	**56**	**54**	**49**	**58**	**54**
Public and publicly guaranteed	39	22	18	17	22	16	16	16
Official creditors	28	20	16	15	21	16	16	15
Private creditors	11	2	2	1	1	1	0	1
Private nonguaranteed	7	20	33	39	32	33	42	38
Debt resource inflows								
Net debt inflows	560	157	611	313	65	514	632	539
Official creditors (incl. IMF)	13	-31	24	28	-21	217	169	207
Private creditors	547	188	587	285	86	297	463	332
Long-term	82	84	356	76	-13	117	145	111
Public and publicly guaranteed	0	-7	-9	-8	4	-3	6	7
Private nonguaranteed	82	91	365	85	-18	119	140	104
Short-term	465	104	231	208	99	180	318	221
Non-debt resource inflows								
Foreign direct investment	128	191	536	727	135	202	276	185
Portfolio equity	3	1	2	11	2	6	5	14
Currency composition (%)								
Euro	..	7.6	8.7	9.9	11.4	10.3	11.7	15.1
U.S.dollars	67.1	68.9	69.3	67.2	66.5	69.1	68.6	64.2
Major economic aggregates								
Gross national income (GNI)	1,310	3,347	4,819	6,653	5,742	6,297	7,580	7,820
Exports of goods, services & prim. income	780	1,871	2,456	3,056	2,308	2,745	3,656	3,818
Personal transfers & comp. of employees	179	915	1,491	1,888	1,199	1,351	1,600	1,786
Imports of goods, services & prim. income	1,089	2,673	4,359	5,670	3,975	4,523	5,957	5,923
Primary income on FDI	3	45	182	151	141	152	257	118
Current account balance	-98	-226	-671	-976	-447	-451	-784	-495
International reserves	222	597	1,334	1,672	1,480	1,718	1,965	2,511
Ratios								
External debt stocks to exports (%)	236.2	118.6	137.0	119.6	162.6	176.2	149.3	160.7
External debt stocks to GNI (%)	140.7	66.3	69.8	54.9	65.4	76.8	72.0	78.5
Debt service to exports (%)	20.0	13.6	14.1	16.5	16.9	14.5	12.8	15.1
Short-term to external debt stocks (%)	26.5	32.3	32.1	35.3	37.4	32.7	34.9	34.8
Multilateral to external debt stocks (%)	21.9	18.4	14.1	13.8	14.0	11.7	11.3	11.7
Reserves to external debt stocks (%)	12.1	26.9	39.6	45.8	39.4	35.5	36.0	40.9
Reserves to imports (months)	2.5	2.7	3.7	3.5	4.5	4.6	4.0	5.1

MONGOLIA

(US$ million, unless otherwise indicated)

	2000	2005	2007	2008	2009	2010	2011	2012
Summary external debt data								
External debt stocks	**960**	**1,396**	**1,759**	**1,908**	**2,215**	**2,506**	**2,564**	**5,080**
Long-term external debt	833	1,267	1,581	1,705	1,885	2,003	2,057	4,550
Short-term external debt	13	25	75	108	72	230	239	297
interest arrears on long-term	2	0	0	0	0	0	0	0
Use of IMF credit	114	105	103	95	258	273	268	234
Long-term external debt								
Debt outstanding and disbursed	**833**	**1,267**	**1,581**	**1,705**	**1,885**	**2,003**	**2,057**	**4,550**
Public and publicly guaranteed	833	1,267	1,576	1,657	1,817	1,782	1,826	3,242
Official creditors	831	1,266	1,487	1,571	1,733	1,775	1,814	1,736
Private creditors	3	0	89	86	84	7	12	1,506
Private nonguaranteed	..	..	5	48	68	221	231	1,307
Disbursements	**75**	**91**	**167**	**122**	**239**	**236**	**122**	**2,680**
Public and publicly guaranteed	75	91	165	75	212	66	87	1,562
Official creditors	75	91	87	75	212	66	83	62
Private creditors	0	0	79	0	0	0	5	1,500
Private nonguaranteed	..	..	2	47	27	170	35	1,118
Principal repayments	**22**	**17**	**30**	**41**	**70**	**139**	**78**	**138**
Public and publicly guaranteed	22	17	30	40	62	122	54	90
Official creditors	19	17	28	37	59	44	54	84
Private creditors	3	0	3	3	2	77	0	6
Private nonguaranteed	..	..	0	1	8	18	24	48
Interest payments	**9**	**15**	**15**	**30**	**29**	**24**	**20**	**63**
Public and publicly guaranteed	9	15	15	24	26	20	20	21
Official creditors	9	15	15	18	19	19	20	21
Private creditors	0	0	0	7	7	1	0	0
Private nonguaranteed	..	..	0	6	4	4	0	42
Debt resource inflows								
Net debt inflows	45	-73	160	109	292	274	49	2,566
Official creditors (incl. IMF)	58	69	52	33	312	40	24	-56
Private creditors	-12	-142	107	76	-20	234	25	2,622
Long-term	-3	0	78	43	16	76	16	2,564
Public and publicly guaranteed	-3	0	76	-3	-2	-77	5	1,494
Private nonguaranteed	..	..	2	46	18	153	11	1,070
Short-term	-9	-142	29	33	-36	158	9	58
Non-debt resource inflows								
Foreign direct investment	54	185	373	845	624	1,691	4,715	4,452
Portfolio equity	..	..	1	13	4	680	9	15
Currency composition (%)								
Euro	..	7.6	9.1	8.5	8.1	7.4	7.4	4.0
U.S.dollars	35.8	44.5	46.7	43.8	43.8	40.2	40.5	68.4
Major economic aggregates								
Gross national income (GNI)	1,132	2,472	4,137	5,450	4,388	5,640	7,918	9,592
Exports of goods, services & prim. income	627	1,494	2,586	3,045	2,322	3,423	5,481	5,402
Personal transfers & comp. of employees	12	180	178	225	200	266	279	320
Imports of goods, services & prim. income	791	1,635	2,627	3,956	2,850	4,496	8,480	9,004
Primary income on FDI	9	41	126	109	121	464	632	594
Current account balance	-70	84	172	-690	-342	-886	-2,760	-3,362
International reserves	179	333	802	561	1,294	2,197	2,275	3,930
Ratios								
External debt stocks to exports (%)	153.2	93.5	68.0	62.7	95.4	73.2	46.8	94.0
External debt stocks to GNI (%)	84.8	56.5	42.5	35.0	50.5	44.4	32.4	53.0
Debt service to exports (%)	6.6	3.0	2.2	2.7	4.6	5.0	2.0	4.5
Short-term to external debt stocks (%)	1.3	1.8	4.3	5.7	3.3	9.2	9.3	5.8
Multilateral to external debt stocks (%)	48.1	56.4	53.7	50.5	48.3	42.8	43.4	22.3
Reserves to external debt stocks (%)	18.6	23.9	45.6	29.4	58.4	87.7	88.7	77.4
Reserves to imports (months)	2.7	2.4	3.7	1.7	5.5	5.9	3.2	5.2

Notes:

Long-term private nonguaranteed debt data only cover European Bank for Reconstruction and Development lending and bonds.

MONTENEGRO

(US$ million, unless otherwise indicated)

	2000	2005	2007	2008	2009	2010	2011	2012
Summary external debt data								
External debt stocks	..	..	**1,299**	**1,502**	**2,357**	**1,603**	**2,354**	**2,833**
Long-term external debt	..	..	854	860	1,109	1,378	1,859	2,255
Short-term external debt	..	..	405	602	1,207	186	455	538
interest arrears on long-term	..	..	0	0	0	0	0	0
Use of IMF credit	..	..	41	40	40	40	40	40
Long-term external debt								
Debt outstanding and disbursed	..	..	**854**	**860**	**1,109**	**1,378**	**1,859**	**2,255**
Public and publicly guaranteed	..	..	844	851	1,094	1,359	1,805	2,161
Official creditors	..	..	827	836	894	846	1,012	1,145
Private creditors	..	..	17	15	201	512	792	1,016
Private nonguaranteed	..	..	10	9	15	19	54	94
Disbursements	..	..	**74**	**64**	**248**	**395**	**659**	**528**
Public and publicly guaranteed	..	..	73	60	242	383	619	482
Official creditors	..	..	73	60	61	35	258	164
Private creditors	..	..	0	0	181	348	361	319
Private nonguaranteed	..	..	1	4	7	12	40	46
Principal repayments	..	..	**109**	**28**	**25**	**61**	**127**	**174**
Public and publicly guaranteed	..	..	105	25	23	60	124	166
Official creditors	..	..	105	24	22	33	43	48
Private creditors	..	..	1	1	1	27	81	118
Private nonguaranteed	..	..	4	3	2	2	2	8
Interest payments	..	..	**35**	**28**	**28**	**34**	**79**	**87**
Public and publicly guaranteed	..	..	34	27	28	33	78	86
Official creditors	..	..	34	27	26	20	24	24
Private creditors	..	..	1	0	2	13	55	63
Private nonguaranteed	..	..	1	0	0	1	1	1
Debt resource inflows								
Net debt inflows	..	..	-36	233	829	-687	802	437
Official creditors (incl. IMF)	..	..	-32	36	38	2	214	116
Private creditors	..	..	-4	197	790	-689	587	322
Long-term	..	..	-4	0	185	332	318	239
Public and publicly guaranteed	..	..	-1	-1	180	322	280	201
Private nonguaranteed	..	..	-3	1	5	11	38	38
Short-term	..	..	..	197	605	-1,021	269	83
Non-debt resource inflows								
Foreign direct investment	..	..	938	975	1,549	758	556	618
Portfolio equity	..	..	3	-6	-5	-8	-15	0
Currency composition (%)								
Euro	..	..	50.7	51.1	62.5	71.4	77.6	80.7
U.S.dollars	..	..	41.6	39.5	29.7	21.7	17.1	14.7
Major economic aggregates								
Gross national income (GNI)	..	..	2,991	3,972	4,368	3,959	4,290	4,150
Exports of goods, services & prim. income	..	..	1,727	2,064	1,663	1,722	2,198	1,975
Personal transfers & comp. of employees	..	..	196	298	303	301	343	333
Imports of goods, services & prim. income	..	..	3,273	4,428	2,933	2,826	3,152	2,918
Primary income on FDI	..	..	16	43	91	99	45	33
Current account balance	..	..	-1,464	-2,258	-1,150	-952	-791	-769
International reserves	..	..	689	436	573	556	393	459
Ratios								
External debt stocks to exports (%)	..	..	75.3	72.8	141.7	93.1	107.1	143.5
External debt stocks to GNI (%)	..	..	43.4	37.8	54.0	40.5	54.9	68.3
Debt service to exports (%)	..	..	9.8	3.4	4.1	5.7	9.7	13.6
Short-term to external debt stocks (%)	..	..	31.2	40.1	51.2	11.6	19.3	19.0
Multilateral to external debt stocks (%)	..	..	42.0	37.0	25.1	34.7	28.6	27.8
Reserves to external debt stocks (%)	..	..	53.0	29.0	24.3	34.7	16.7	16.2
Reserves to imports (months)	..	..	2.5	1.2	2.3	2.4	1.5	1.9

Notes:

Long-term private nonguaranteed debt data (excluding bonds) only cover European Bank for Reconstruction and Development lending. Short-term debt is based on data from the BIS. Montenegro became independent in 2006 and started to report data in 2007.

MOROCCO

(US$ million, unless otherwise indicated)

	2000	2005	2007	2008	2009	2010	2011	2012
Summary external debt data								
External debt stocks	**20,790**	**16,297**	**20,679**	**20,957**	**24,631**	**26,303**	**29,096**	**33,816**
Long-term external debt	19,106	15,493	18,625	19,194	21,572	23,638	25,204	28,786
Short-term external debt	1,573	682	1,919	1,631	2,179	1,800	3,030	4,167
interest arrears on long-term	122	0	0	0	0	0	0	0
Use of IMF credit	112	122	135	132	880	865	862	863
Long-term external debt								
Debt outstanding and disbursed	**19,106**	**15,493**	**18,625**	**19,194**	**21,572**	**23,638**	**25,204**	**28,786**
Public and publicly guaranteed	17,244	12,442	15,650	16,538	19,218	21,049	22,371	25,087
Official creditors	12,759	10,119	13,084	14,543	16,713	17,269	18,628	19,839
Private creditors	4,485	2,323	2,566	1,994	2,504	3,780	3,743	5,248
Private nonguaranteed	1,862	3,051	2,975	2,656	2,354	2,589	2,833	3,699
Disbursements	**1,638**	**2,456**	**3,976**	**4,554**	**4,551**	**4,999**	**4,506**	**6,199**
Public and publicly guaranteed	980	1,658	2,714	3,093	3,468	3,882	3,285	4,191
Official creditors	631	1,562	1,810	2,800	2,868	2,258	2,995	2,539
Private creditors	349	97	904	292	600	1,625	290	1,652
Private nonguaranteed	658	798	1,262	1,461	1,083	1,116	1,222	2,008
Principal repayments	**1,632**	**2,139**	**3,325**	**3,452**	**2,709**	**2,428**	**2,436**	**2,845**
Public and publicly guaranteed	1,593	1,881	1,861	1,795	1,138	1,274	1,481	1,648
Official creditors	928	1,303	990	1,043	966	1,090	1,277	1,430
Private creditors	666	578	872	753	172	184	205	217
Private nonguaranteed	39	258	1,464	1,656	1,572	1,154	955	1,198
Interest payments	**949**	**569**	**590**	**709**	**678**	**850**	**757**	**783**
Public and publicly guaranteed	877	501	555	655	612	819	722	748
Official creditors	548	388	443	536	523	731	571	584
Private creditors	329	113	112	120	89	88	152	164
Private nonguaranteed	71	68	34	54	66	31	35	35
Debt resource inflows								
Net debt inflows	-449	831	838	814	2,390	2,192	3,300	4,491
Official creditors (incl. IMF)	-296	259	820	1,758	1,902	1,168	1,718	1,109
Private creditors	-153	573	17	-944	487	1,024	1,582	3,382
Long-term	302	59	-170	-656	-61	1,403	352	2,245
Public and publicly guaranteed	-317	-481	32	-460	428	1,441	85	1,435
Private nonguaranteed	619	540	-202	-195	-489	-37	267	810
Short-term	-455	514	187	-288	548	-379	1,230	1,137
Non-debt resource inflows								
Foreign direct investment	221	1,671	2,826	2,466	1,970	1,241	2,521	2,842
Portfolio equity	18	64	-64	148	-4	132	166	-108
Currency composition (%)								
Euro	..	43.4	54.6	53.0	54.5	55.6	56.4	55.2
U.S.dollars	37.6	23.8	12.6	11.9	10.4	10.3	9.2	13.7
Major economic aggregates								
Gross national income (GNI)	36,053	58,760	74,246	87,411	88,520	88,305	96,120	93,832
Exports of goods, services & prim. income	10,729	17,281	24,910	31,613	24,924	27,913	32,649	32,954
Personal transfers & comp. of employees	2,161	4,589	6,730	6,894	6,269	6,423	7,256	6,508
Imports of goods, services & prim. income	13,686	21,616	32,736	44,910	37,346	39,109	48,764	49,913
Primary income on FDI	268	594	730	835	1,753	1,445	2,086	2,092
Current account balance	-475	1,041	-122	-4,528	-4,971	-3,925	-8,000	-9,571
International reserves	4,823	16,187	24,123	22,104	22,797	22,613	19,526	16,356
Ratios								
External debt stocks to exports (%)	193.8	94.3	83.0	66.3	98.8	94.2	89.1	102.6
External debt stocks to GNI (%)	57.7	27.7	27.9	24.0	27.8	29.8	30.3	36.0
Debt service to exports (%)	25.3	15.8	16.2	13.3	13.7	11.8	9.9	11.2
Short-term to external debt stocks (%)	7.6	4.2	9.3	7.8	8.8	6.8	10.4	12.3
Multilateral to external debt stocks (%)	29.3	36.0	38.2	40.9	40.7	38.6	38.8	35.6
Reserves to external debt stocks (%)	23.2	99.3	116.7	105.5	92.6	86.0	67.1	48.4
Reserves to imports (months)	4.2	9.0	8.8	5.9	7.3	6.9	4.8	3.9

Notes:

Short-term debt is based on data from the BIS.

MOZAMBIQUE

(US$ million, unless otherwise indicated)

	2000	2005	2007	2008	2009	2010	2011	2012
Summary external debt data								
External debt stocks	**7,338**	**4,393**	**3,048**	**3,489**	**4,138**	**3,736**	**4,106**	**4,788**
Long-term external debt	6,410	3,367	2,344	2,726	3,165	2,898	3,617	4,245
Short-term external debt	567	714	516	580	632	480	134	190
interest arrears on long-term	411	525	387	449	465	381	5	20
Use of IMF credit	361	312	187	183	342	357	355	353
Long-term external debt								
Debt outstanding and disbursed	**6,410**	**3,367**	**2,344**	**2,726**	**3,165**	**2,898**	**3,617**	**4,245**
Public and publicly guaranteed	4,693	3,367	2,344	2,726	3,165	2,898	3,617	4,245
Official creditors	4,682	3,365	2,336	2,719	3,136	2,800	3,387	3,983
Private creditors	11	2	9	7	28	98	230	262
Private nonguaranteed	..	..	..	..	..	..	..	..
Disbursements	**131**	**326**	**329**	**399**	**446**	**368**	**524**	**648**
Public and publicly guaranteed	131	326	329	399	446	368	524	648
Official creditors	131	326	322	397	422	289	373	617
Private creditors	0	0	6	2	23	79	151	31
Private nonguaranteed	..	..	..	..	..	..	..	..
Principal repayments	**64**	**39**	**10**	**14**	**15**	**38**	**28**	**39**
Public and publicly guaranteed	34	18	10	14	15	38	28	39
Official creditors	33	18	10	11	12	30	21	36
Private creditors	1	0	0	3	3	8	6	4
Private nonguaranteed	..	..	..	..	..	..	..	..
Interest payments	**20**	**22**	**14**	**19**	**23**	**47**	**26**	**39**
Public and publicly guaranteed	20	22	14	19	23	47	26	39
Official creditors	20	22	14	19	23	46	26	39
Private creditors	0	0	0	0	0	0	0	0
Private nonguaranteed	..	..	..	..	..	..	..	..
Debt resource inflows								
Net debt inflows	53	104	371	387	620	284	525	648
Official creditors (incl. IMF)	157	297	318	386	564	281	350	579
Private creditors	-104	-193	53	1	56	3	174	68
Long-term	-31	-21	6	-1	20	71	144	27
Public and publicly guaranteed	-1	0	6	-1	20	71	144	27
Private nonguaranteed	..	..	..	..	..	..	..	..
Short-term	-73	-172	47	2	36	-68	30	41
Non-debt resource inflows								
Foreign direct investment	139	122	417	559	899	1,258	2,846	5,238
Portfolio equity	..	0	0	0	0	0	0	..
Currency composition (%)								
Euro	..	3.0	5.8	6.2	6.4	9.6	14.9	14.2
U.S.dollars	68.7	69.0	58.6	57.9	55.1	43.9	48.9	49.6
Major economic aggregates								
Gross national income (GNI)	4,075	6,219	7,450	9,263	9,430	9,192	12,379	14,540
Exports of goods, services & prim. income	769	2,186	3,064	3,270	2,909	3,102	4,002	5,127
Personal transfers & comp. of employees	37	59	99	116	111	139	157	220
Imports of goods, services & prim. income	1,763	3,350	4,453	5,325	4,893	5,245	7,891	12,253
Primary income on FDI	0	284	554	544	240	214	234	50
Current account balance	-764	-761	-786	-1,193	-1,221	-1,450	-2,997	-6,297
International reserves	723	1,054	1,445	1,578	2,099	2,159	2,469	2,770
Ratios								
External debt stocks to exports (%)	954.6	201.0	99.5	106.7	142.3	120.4	102.6	93.4
External debt stocks to GNI (%)	180.1	70.6	40.9	37.7	43.9	40.6	33.2	32.9
Debt service to exports (%)	13.4	4.2	1.2	1.1	1.4	2.8	1.4	1.6
Short-term to external debt stocks (%)	7.7	16.3	16.9	16.6	15.3	12.9	3.3	4.0
Multilateral to external debt stocks (%)	15.1	52.9	43.2	47.2	46.9	58.0	56.2	54.4
Reserves to external debt stocks (%)	9.9	24.0	47.4	45.2	50.7	57.8	60.1	57.9
Reserves to imports (months)	4.9	3.8	3.9	3.6	5.1	4.9	3.8	2.7

Notes:

Short-term debt is based on data from the BIS. Data include HIPC and MDRI debt relief.

MYANMAR

(US$ million, unless otherwise indicated)

	2000	2005	2007	2008	2009	2010	2011	2012
Summary external debt data								
External debt stocks	**5,832**	**6,337**	**7,250**	**7,136**	**7,702**	**7,789**	**7,770**	**2,563**
Long-term external debt	5,287	5,515	6,221	6,121	6,320	6,274	6,253	1,858
Short-term external debt	490	759	958	950	1,009	1,125	1,136	336
interest arrears on long-term	490	759	958	950	1,009	1,125	1,136	336
Use of IMF credit	55	63	71	65	373	390	381	368
Long-term external debt								
Debt outstanding and disbursed	**5,287**	**5,515**	**6,221**	**6,121**	**6,320**	**6,274**	**6,253**	**1,858**
Public and publicly guaranteed	5,287	5,515	6,221	6,121	6,320	6,274	6,253	1,858
Official creditors	4,262	4,568	5,218	5,155	5,345	5,823	5,809	1,528
Private creditors	1,026	947	1,002	966	976	451	443	331
Private nonguaranteed	..	..	..	..	..	..	..	..
Disbursements	**14**	**1**	**1**	**1**	**0**	**0**	**0**	**0**
Public and publicly guaranteed	14	1	1	1	0	0	0	0
Official creditors	12	1	1	1	0	0	0	0
Private creditors	3	0	0	0	0	0	0	0
Private nonguaranteed	..	..	..	..	..	..	..	..
Principal repayments	**22**	**25**	**11**	**10**	**9**	**553**	**6**	**736**
Public and publicly guaranteed	22	25	11	10	9	553	6	736
Official creditors	2	8	11	10	9	7	6	736
Private creditors	20	17	1	0	0	546	0	0
Private nonguaranteed	..	..	..	..	..	..	..	..
Interest payments	**2**	**1**	**2**	**2**	**2**	**11**	**1**	**180**
Public and publicly guaranteed	2	1	2	2	2	11	1	180
Official creditors	0	1	2	2	2	2	1	180
Private creditors	2	0	0	0	0	10	0	0
Private nonguaranteed	..	..	..	..	..	..	..	..
Debt resource inflows								
Net debt inflows	-7	-24	-10	-10	-9	-553	-6	-736
Official creditors (incl. IMF)	10	-7	-10	-10	-9	-7	-6	-736
Private creditors	-17	-17	-1	0	0	-546	0	0
Long-term	-17	-17	-1	0	0	-546	0	0
Public and publicly guaranteed	-17	-17	-1	0	0	-546	0	0
Private nonguaranteed	..	..	..	..	..	..	..	..
Short-term	..	..	..	..	..	..	..	..
Non-debt resource inflows								
Foreign direct investment	258	235	710	864	1,079	901	1,001	2,243
Portfolio equity	..	..	..	..	..	..	..	..
Currency composition (%)								
Euro	..	11.0	12.6	10.6	10.3	10.9	10.2	32.7
U.S.dollars	35.4	33.5	30.3	30.6	29.9	22.0	21.8	48.2
Major economic aggregates								
Gross national income (GNI)	..	..	..	..	..	..	..	..
Exports of goods, services & prim. income	2,145	3,838	5,911	6,439	6,347	7,851	8,566	..
Personal transfers & comp. of employees	104	129	81	55	54	115	127	..
Imports of goods, services & prim. income	2,627	3,429	4,735	5,500	5,794	6,516	10,379	..
Primary income on FDI	135	1,388	1,387	1,884	1,811	1,816	1,721	..
Current account balance	-210	582	1,381	1,247	986	1,574	-1,424	..
International reserves	223	771	3,089	3,717	5,252	5,717	7,004	6,964
Ratios								
External debt stocks to exports (%)	271.9	165.1	122.6	110.8	121.3	99.2	90.7	..
External debt stocks to GNI (%)	..	..	..	..	..	..	..	..
Debt service to exports (%)	1.2	0.7	0.3	0.2	0.2	7.2	0.1	..
Short-term to external debt stocks (%)	8.4	12.0	13.2	13.3	13.1	14.4	14.6	13.1
Multilateral to external debt stocks (%)	19.7	19.4	17.8	18.4	17.4	18.2	18.0	24.0
Reserves to external debt stocks (%)	3.8	12.2	42.6	52.1	68.2	73.4	90.1	271.7
Reserves to imports (months)	1.0	2.7	7.8	8.1	10.9	10.5	8.1	..

Notes:

Fiscal year-end for external debt data is March. Long-term public and publicly guaranteed and short-term debt data are World Bank staff estimates based on the original terms of the loans.

NEPAL

(US$ million, unless otherwise indicated)

	2000	2005	2007	2008	2009	2010	2011	2012
Summary external debt data								
External debt stocks	**2,878**	**3,191**	**3,615**	**3,698**	**3,778**	**3,789**	**3,828**	**3,818**
Long-term external debt	2,826	3,112	3,468	3,551	3,552	3,509	3,530	3,501
Short-term external debt	29	47	55	57	44	61	84	113
interest arrears on long-term	0	0	0	0	0	0	0	0
Use of IMF credit	23	32	92	89	183	219	214	204
Long-term external debt								
Debt outstanding and disbursed	**2,826**	**3,112**	**3,468**	**3,551**	**3,552**	**3,509**	**3,530**	**3,501**
Public and publicly guaranteed	2,826	3,112	3,468	3,551	3,552	3,509	3,530	3,501
Official creditors	2,821	3,108	3,463	3,547	3,548	3,506	3,528	3,499
Private creditors	5	5	5	4	4	3	2	2
Private nonguaranteed	..	..	..	..	..	..	..	..
Disbursements	**154**	**192**	**141**	**103**	**116**	**126**	**174**	**160**
Public and publicly guaranteed	154	192	141	103	116	126	174	160
Official creditors	154	192	141	103	116	126	174	160
Private creditors	0	0	0	0	0	0	0	0
Private nonguaranteed	..	..	..	..	..	..	..	..
Principal repayments	**67**	**85**	**113**	**127**	**140**	**149**	**154**	**175**
Public and publicly guaranteed	67	85	113	127	140	149	154	175
Official creditors	59	85	112	126	140	149	153	175
Private creditors	7	1	1	1	1	0	1	0
Private nonguaranteed	..	..	..	..	..	..	..	..
Interest payments	**28**	**30**	**30**	**34**	**32**	**33**	**35**	**33**
Public and publicly guaranteed	28	30	30	34	32	33	35	33
Official creditors	27	30	30	34	32	32	35	33
Private creditors	1	0	0	0	0	0	0	0
Private nonguaranteed	..	..	..	..	..	..	..	..
Debt resource inflows								
Net debt inflows	69	118	36	-21	-40	33	39	3
Official creditors (incl. IMF)	90	108	62	-23	-27	16	16	-25
Private creditors	-21	10	-26	1	-14	17	22	29
Long-term	-7	-1	0	-1	-1	0	-1	0
Public and publicly guaranteed	-7	-1	0	-1	-1	0	-1	0
Private nonguaranteed	..	..	..	..	..	..	..	..
Short-term	-14	11	-26	2	-13	17	23	29
Non-debt resource inflows								
Foreign direct investment	0	2	6	1	38	88	94	92
Portfolio equity	..	..	..	..	..	..	..	..
Currency composition (%)								
Euro	..	2.1	2.1	1.7	1.6	1.4	1.2	1.1
U.S.dollars	38.6	43.6	43.5	42.5	42.4	41.9	41.8	43.1
Major economic aggregates								
Gross national income (GNI)	5,514	8,153	10,440	12,661	13,007	16,078	19,083	19,561
Exports of goods, services & prim. income	1,354	1,423	1,661	1,946	1,753	1,783	2,150	2,177
Personal transfers & comp. of employees	111	1,212	1,734	2,727	2,985	3,469	4,217	4,793
Imports of goods, services & prim. income	1,825	2,803	3,743	4,456	5,160	6,004	6,588	6,969
Primary income on FDI	..	57	54	44	9	50	59	34
Current account balance	-131	153	6	733	18	-128	289	577
International reserves	945	1,499	2,014	2,458	2,769	2,937	3,631	4,307
Ratios								
External debt stocks to exports (%)	212.5	224.2	217.7	190.0	215.6	212.5	178.1	175.4
External debt stocks to GNI (%)	52.2	39.1	34.6	29.2	29.0	23.6	20.1	19.5
Debt service to exports (%)	7.5	8.4	8.9	8.5	10.1	10.6	9.2	10.3
Short-term to external debt stocks (%)	1.0	1.5	1.5	1.5	1.2	1.6	2.2	3.0
Multilateral to external debt stocks (%)	85.4	85.8	86.5	86.2	84.7	82.7	82.2	82.4
Reserves to external debt stocks (%)	32.9	47.0	55.7	66.5	73.3	77.5	94.8	112.8
Reserves to imports (months)	6.2	6.4	6.5	6.6	6.4	5.9	6.6	7.4

Notes:

Short-term debt is based on data from the BIS.

NICARAGUA

(US$ million, unless otherwise indicated)

	2000	2005	2007	2008	2009	2010	2011	2012
Summary external debt data								
External debt stocks	**6,823**	**5,000**	**4,105**	**4,715**	**5,842**	**6,961**	**7,881**	**8,858**
Long-term external debt	5,717	4,231	2,833	3,421	4,504	5,209	6,065	6,873
Short-term external debt	912	540	1,157	1,153	993	1,392	1,443	1,625
interest arrears on long-term	791	364	467	472	484	495	506	518
Use of IMF credit	194	229	116	141	346	359	373	361
Long-term external debt								
Debt outstanding and disbursed	**5,717**	**4,231**	**2,833**	**3,421**	**4,504**	**5,209**	**6,065**	**6,873**
Public and publicly guaranteed	5,435	3,939	2,171	2,253	2,505	2,683	2,846	3,055
Official creditors	5,220	3,867	2,165	2,249	2,502	2,680	2,843	3,051
Private creditors	216	72	5	4	4	3	3	3
Private nonguaranteed	281	292	662	1,168	1,999	2,526	3,219	3,818
Disbursements	**511**	**287**	**922**	**946**	**827**	**1,185**	**1,396**	**1,194**
Public and publicly guaranteed	226	226	368	183	291	267	239	258
Official creditors	220	226	368	183	291	267	239	258
Private creditors	6	0	0	0	0	0	0	0
Private nonguaranteed	285	61	554	763	536	918	1,157	936
Principal repayments	**184**	**110**	**313**	**309**	**365**	**456**	**539**	**431**
Public and publicly guaranteed	71	64	198	52	62	56	63	53
Official creditors	62	64	198	52	62	56	63	53
Private creditors	8	0	0	0	0	0	0	0
Private nonguaranteed	114	47	115	257	302	400	475	377
Interest payments	**91**	**46**	**64**	**98**	**121**	**104**	**121**	**140**
Public and publicly guaranteed	79	44	46	39	37	33	39	39
Official creditors	76	44	46	39	37	33	39	39
Private creditors	3	0	0	0	0	0	0	0
Private nonguaranteed	12	2	19	59	84	70	82	101
Debt resource inflows								
Net debt inflows	350	210	1,138	657	326	1,137	913	920
Official creditors (incl. IMF)	179	153	188	160	265	230	191	192
Private creditors	172	57	949	497	61	907	721	729
Long-term	169	14	439	506	234	518	682	559
Public and publicly guaranteed	-2	0	0	0	0	0	0	0
Private nonguaranteed	171	14	439	506	234	518	682	559
Short-term	3	43	511	-8	-173	389	40	170
Non-debt resource inflows								
Foreign direct investment	267	241	382	626	434	508	968	805
Portfolio equity	..	..	..	..	..	..	..	0
Currency composition (%)								
Euro	..	0.5	3.7	4.1	4.6	5.1	4.6	4.4
U.S.dollars	70.4	80.3	83.9	83.9	83.8	84.1	85.2	86.2
Major economic aggregates								
Gross national income (GNI)	4,906	6,173	7,223	8,031	7,901	8,344	9,381	10,216
Exports of goods, services & prim. income	1,133	1,434	2,303	2,835	2,765	3,455	4,460	5,018
Personal transfers & comp. of employees	320	616	740	820	770	825	914	1,016
Imports of goods, services & prim. income	2,479	3,075	4,621	5,491	4,675	5,490	6,973	7,708
Primary income on FDI	69	82	93	113	121	135	146	157
Current account balance	-936	-784	-1,243	-1,521	-791	-875	-1,284	-1,381
International reserves	488	728	1,103	1,141	1,573	1,799	1,892	1,887
Ratios								
External debt stocks to exports (%)	602.4	348.7	178.2	166.3	211.3	201.4	176.7	176.5
External debt stocks to GNI (%)	139.1	81.0	56.8	58.7	73.9	83.4	84.0	86.7
Debt service to exports (%)	25.6	12.1	17.4	15.2	18.3	16.9	15.7	12.3
Short-term to external debt stocks (%)	13.4	10.8	28.2	24.5	17.0	20.0	18.3	18.3
Multilateral to external debt stocks (%)	32.0	56.8	27.5	26.0	24.9	23.8	23.5	23.4
Reserves to external debt stocks (%)	7.2	14.6	26.9	24.2	26.9	25.8	24.0	21.3
Reserves to imports (months)	2.4	2.8	2.9	2.5	4.0	3.9	3.3	2.9

Notes:

Historical short-term debt until 2006 is based on data from the BIS. Data include the effects of HIPC and MDRI debt relief.

NIGER

(US$ million, unless otherwise indicated)

	2000	2005	2007	2008	2009	2010	2011	2012
Summary external debt data								
External debt stocks	**1,721**	**1,994**	**1,121**	**974**	**1,271**	**1,561**	**2,256**	**2,340**
Long-term external debt	1,563	1,812	805	816	985	1,231	1,948	2,079
Short-term external debt	72	41	261	93	131	172	156	98
interest arrears on long-term	60	38	38	19	17	23	21	23
Use of IMF credit	86	141	55	65	155	158	153	164
Long-term external debt								
Debt outstanding and disbursed	**1,563**	**1,812**	**805**	**816**	**985**	**1,231**	**1,948**	**2,079**
Public and publicly guaranteed	1,495	1,780	785	803	978	1,231	1,948	2,079
Official creditors	1,495	1,780	785	803	978	1,231	1,948	2,079
Private creditors	0	0	0	0	0	0	0	0
Private nonguaranteed	68	33	20	13	7	0	0	0
Disbursements	**76**	**122**	**80**	**96**	**214**	**283**	**754**	**146**
Public and publicly guaranteed	76	122	80	96	214	283	754	146
Official creditors	76	122	80	96	214	283	754	146
Private creditors	0	0	0	0	0	0	0	0
Private nonguaranteed	0	0	0	0	0	0	0	0
Principal repayments	**14**	**22**	**17**	**18**	**35**	**17**	**17**	**18**
Public and publicly guaranteed	12	15	10	11	28	10	17	18
Official creditors	12	15	10	11	28	10	17	18
Private creditors	0	0	0	0	0	0	0	0
Private nonguaranteed	2	7	7	7	7	7	0	0
Interest payments	**8**	**13**	**9**	**7**	**8**	**8**	**10**	**10**
Public and publicly guaranteed	8	11	7	6	8	8	10	10
Official creditors	8	11	7	6	8	8	10	10
Private creditors	0	0	0	0	0	0	0	0
Private nonguaranteed	0	2	2	1	0	0	0	0
Debt resource inflows								
Net debt inflows	52	109	289	-58	225	307	718	78
Official creditors (incl. IMF)	73	119	82	97	191	278	732	138
Private creditors	-22	-10	207	-156	33	28	-14	-60
Long-term	-2	-7	-7	-7	-7	-7	..	..
Public and publicly guaranteed	..	..	..	..	..	..	..	..
Private nonguaranteed	-2	-7	-7	-7	-7	-7	..	..
Short-term	-20	-3	214	-149	40	35	-14	-60
Non-debt resource inflows								
Foreign direct investment	8	50	99	282	631	796	1,066	793
Portfolio equity	0	1	0	1	9	6	..	..
Currency composition (%)								
Euro	..	11.3	0.2	0.2	0.4	0.6	4.2	5.5
U.S.dollars	46.7	58.7	49.4	48.4	53.4	61.3	67.7	63.7
Major economic aggregates								
Gross national income (GNI)	1,782	3,397	4,290	5,351	5,220	5,379	5,955	6,450
Exports of goods, services & prim. income	334	602	806	1,124	1,186	1,332	..	..
Personal transfers & comp. of employees	14	66	79	94	102	134	..	..
Imports of goods, services & prim. income	485	1,095	1,343	2,006	2,657	2,916	..	..
Primary income on FDI	2	21	28	23	84	17	..	..
Current account balance	-104	-312	-351	-651	-1,320	-1,136	..	..
International reserves	81	251	593	705	656	760	673	1,015
Ratios								
External debt stocks to exports (%)	515.7	331.1	139.1	86.6	107.2	117.2	..	..
External debt stocks to GNI (%)	96.6	58.7	26.1	18.2	24.3	29.0	37.9	36.3
Debt service to exports (%)	8.0	6.8	4.0	2.6	3.8	2.0	..	..
Short-term to external debt stocks (%)	4.2	2.0	23.3	9.5	10.3	11.0	6.9	4.2
Multilateral to external debt stocks (%)	59.8	79.2	53.2	61.9	49.7	43.3	37.4	41.1
Reserves to external debt stocks (%)	4.7	12.6	52.9	72.4	51.6	48.7	29.8	43.4
Reserves to imports (months)	2.0	2.7	5.3	4.2	3.0	3.1	..	..

Notes:

Short-term debt is based on data from the BIS. Data include the effects of HIPC and MDRI debt relief.

NIGERIA

(US$ million, unless otherwise indicated)

	2000	2005	2007	2008	2009	2010	2011	2012
Summary external debt data								
External debt stocks	**31,582**	**20,476**	**3,863**	**4,144**	**6,848**	**7,271**	**9,009**	**10,077**
Long-term external debt	30,257	20,248	3,614	3,902	4,221	4,691	6,437	7,502
Short-term external debt	1,120	3	0	0	0	0	0	0
interest arrears on long-term	43	3	0	0	0	0	0	0
Use of IMF credit	205	225	248	242	2,626	2,580	2,572	2,575
Long-term external debt								
Debt outstanding and disbursed	**30,257**	**20,248**	**3,614**	**3,902**	**4,221**	**4,691**	**6,437**	**7,502**
Public and publicly guaranteed	30,042	20,248	3,614	3,902	4,221	4,691	5,937	6,652
Official creditors	26,596	18,039	3,518	3,789	4,135	4,691	5,437	6,152
Private creditors	3,446	2,209	96	112	87	0	500	500
Private nonguaranteed	215	..	..	..	..	..	500	850
Disbursements	**153**	**379**	**532**	**409**	**519**	**1,057**	**2,087**	**1,155**
Public and publicly guaranteed	153	379	532	409	519	1,057	1,587	805
Official creditors	153	345	514	385	519	1,057	1,087	805
Private creditors	0	34	18	24	0	0	500	0
Private nonguaranteed	0	..	..	..	..	..	500	350
Principal repayments	**1,092**	**3,863**	**916**	**340**	**342**	**248**	**274**	**158**
Public and publicly guaranteed	1,057	3,863	916	340	342	248	274	158
Official creditors	915	3,685	320	333	316	244	274	158
Private creditors	142	179	596	8	26	4	0	0
Private nonguaranteed	35	..	..	..	..	..	0	0
Interest payments	**690**	**4,937**	**86**	**87**	**85**	**59**	**96**	**144**
Public and publicly guaranteed	673	4,937	86	87	85	59	77	94
Official creditors	516	4,717	80	86	78	59	61	60
Private creditors	157	220	6	1	6	0	17	34
Private nonguaranteed	18	..	..	..	..	..	19	50
Debt resource inflows								
Net debt inflows	-697	-3,484	-383	69	178	809	1,813	997
Official creditors (incl. IMF)	-762	-3,340	194	53	204	813	813	647
Private creditors	64	-145	-577	16	-26	-4	1,000	350
Long-term	-177	-145	-577	16	-26	-4	1,000	350
Public and publicly guaranteed	-142	-145	-577	16	-26	-4	500	0
Private nonguaranteed	-35	..	..	..	..	..	500	350
Short-term	241	..	..	..	..	..	..	0
Non-debt resource inflows								
Foreign direct investment	1,140	4,983	6,035	8,197	8,555	6,049	8,842	7,101
Portfolio equity	..	751	1,447	-954	487	2,161	2,571	10,003
Currency composition (%)								
Euro	..	36.3	3.9	3.5	5.3	3.9	2.6	2.0
U.S.dollars	85.0	27.3	58.6	61.5	58.8	61.6	68.9	69.5
Major economic aggregates								
Gross national income (GNI)	40,256	98,881	154,067	191,961	154,024	208,963	221,013	239,106
Exports of goods, services & prim. income	21,183	57,149	70,046	90,388	59,321	81,976	100,653	99,048
Personal transfers & comp. of employees	1,392	14,640	18,011	19,206	18,368	19,818	20,619	20,633
Imports of goods, services & prim. income	15,383	35,773	60,948	81,632	64,815	88,299	109,908	100,602
Primary income on FDI	2,279	2,603	13,056	17,000	15,042	20,032	23,072	22,430
Current account balance	7,427	36,529	27,643	29,154	13,868	14,459	12,554	20,353
International reserves	9,911	28,280	51,334	53,002	44,763	34,919	35,212	46,405
Ratios								
External debt stocks to exports (%)	149.1	35.8	5.5	4.6	11.5	8.9	9.0	10.2
External debt stocks to GNI (%)	78.5	20.7	2.5	2.2	4.4	3.5	4.1	4.2
Debt service to exports (%)	8.8	15.4	1.4	0.5	0.7	0.4	0.4	0.3
Short-term to external debt stocks (%)	3.5	0.0	0.0	0.0	0.0	0.0	0.0	..
Multilateral to external debt stocks (%)	10.5	12.5	75.9	73.0	51.4	59.3	53.3	53.1
Reserves to external debt stocks (%)	31.4	138.1	1,328.9	1,279.0	653.7	480.2	390.9	460.5
Reserves to imports (months)	7.7	9.5	10.1	7.8	8.3	4.7	3.8	5.5

Notes:

Long-term private nonguaranteed debt only cover Bonds. Short-term debt is revised from 2001 based on reports provided by the country.

PAKISTAN

(US$ million, unless otherwise indicated)

	2000	2005	2007	2008	2009	2010	2011	2012
Summary external debt data								
External debt stocks	**32,954**	**34,018**	**42,006**	**49,524**	**56,340**	**63,152**	**65,125**	**61,867**
Long-term external debt	29,684	31,053	38,128	43,540	45,829	50,603	52,628	51,585
Short-term external debt	1,519	1,230	2,228	1,370	1,466	2,291	2,535	2,598
interest arrears on long-term	0	0	0	0	0	0	0	0
Use of IMF credit	1,751	1,735	1,650	4,614	9,045	10,258	9,962	7,684
Long-term external debt								
Debt outstanding and disbursed	**29,684**	**31,053**	**38,128**	**43,540**	**45,829**	**50,603**	**52,628**	**51,585**
Public and publicly guaranteed	27,124	30,089	36,935	40,356	42,564	43,402	45,127	44,736
Official creditors	25,074	28,907	33,941	37,270	40,059	41,603	43,360	43,007
Private creditors	2,051	1,182	2,994	3,086	2,505	1,799	1,768	1,729
Private nonguaranteed	2,560	964	1,193	3,184	3,265	7,201	7,501	6,849
Disbursements	**1,644**	**2,831**	**3,725**	**3,596**	**4,414**	**6,669**	**3,154**	**2,312**
Public and publicly guaranteed	1,527	2,231	3,195	2,684	3,732	1,857	2,572	2,312
Official creditors	1,522	1,619	2,436	2,557	3,731	1,856	2,572	2,312
Private creditors	4	612	760	127	1	1	0	0
Private nonguaranteed	117	600	530	912	681	4,812	582	0
Principal repayments	**1,587**	**1,463**	**1,381**	**1,764**	**2,243**	**3,010**	**1,665**	**1,527**
Public and publicly guaranteed	1,143	1,136	1,110	1,307	1,637	2,134	1,383	1,395
Official creditors	1,105	993	1,103	1,272	1,055	1,427	1,351	1,356
Private creditors	37	143	7	35	582	707	32	39
Private nonguaranteed	445	327	272	456	606	876	282	132
Interest payments	**857**	**674**	**999**	**1,028**	**917**	**876**	**806**	**773**
Public and publicly guaranteed	641	598	868	880	812	786	711	686
Official creditors	527	548	694	683	643	654	594	583
Private creditors	114	50	174	197	169	131	117	103
Private nonguaranteed	217	76	132	147	105	90	95	87
Debt resource inflows								
Net debt inflows	-343	1,116	3,098	3,995	5,350	5,853	1,462	-1,427
Official creditors (incl. IMF)	330	389	1,181	4,306	5,760	1,798	950	-1,319
Private creditors	-672	727	1,917	-311	-410	4,055	512	-108
Long-term	-361	742	1,011	547	-506	3,230	268	-171
Public and publicly guaranteed	-33	469	753	92	-581	-706	-32	-39
Private nonguaranteed	-328	273	258	455	75	3,936	300	-132
Short-term	-311	-15	906	-858	96	825	244	63
Non-debt resource inflows								
Foreign direct investment	308	2,201	5,590	5,438	2,338	2,018	1,309	854
Portfolio equity	35	451	1,276	-270	-37	524	-37	178
Currency composition (%)								
Euro	..	12.0	11.6	10.0	9.8	8.8	8.2	8.4
U.S.dollars	41.6	42.2	44.6	44.3	46.5	44.8	45.7	48.0
Major economic aggregates								
Gross national income (GNI)	73,025	111,867	145,773	167,234	166,223	183,228	220,327	242,656
Exports of goods, services & prim. income	10,237	19,760	23,302	26,756	22,921	28,738	32,173	31,837
Personal transfers & comp. of employees	1,075	4,280	5,998	7,039	8,717	9,690	12,263	14,007
Imports of goods, services & prim. income	14,484	32,445	42,687	53,546	39,373	43,885	50,838	52,308
Primary income on FDI	429	1,871	2,974	3,203	2,548	2,140	2,102	2,375
Current account balance	-85	-3,606	-8,301	-15,655	-3,993	-1,354	-2,234	-2,025
International reserves	1,513	10,033	14,044	7,194	11,318	14,346	14,528	10,242
Ratios								
External debt stocks to exports (%)	321.9	172.2	180.3	185.1	245.8	219.8	202.4	194.3
External debt stocks to GNI (%)	45.1	30.4	28.8	29.6	33.9	34.5	29.6	25.5
Debt service to exports (%)	28.0	12.4	11.5	11.3	15.2	15.0	9.2	14.9
Short-term to external debt stocks (%)	4.6	3.6	5.3	2.8	2.6	3.6	3.9	4.2
Multilateral to external debt stocks (%)	40.9	46.9	47.6	44.6	42.0	39.0	39.0	40.6
Reserves to external debt stocks (%)	4.6	29.5	33.4	14.5	20.1	22.7	22.3	16.6
Reserves to imports (months)	1.3	3.7	3.9	1.6	3.4	3.9	3.4	2.3

Notes:

Long-term private nonguaranteed debt data from 2006 are World Bank staff estimates based on the reports provided by the country. Short-term debt is based on data from the BIS.

PANAMA

(US$ million, unless otherwise indicated)

	2000	2005	2007	2008	2009	2010	2011	2012
Summary external debt data								
External debt stocks	**6,606**	**8,108**	**8,785**	**9,280**	**11,243**	**11,382**	**12,583**	**12,294**
Long-term external debt	6,481	8,047	8,738	9,240	10,934	11,078	12,281	11,991
Short-term external debt	1	0	0	0	0	0	0	0
interest arrears on long-term	1	0	0	0	0	0	0	0
Use of IMF credit	124	61	47	41	309	303	302	303
Long-term external debt								
Debt outstanding and disbursed	**6,481**	**8,047**	**8,738**	**9,240**	**10,934**	**11,078**	**12,281**	**11,991**
Public and publicly guaranteed	5,700	6,305	7,677	8,129	9,798	10,087	10,890	9,723
Official creditors	1,289	1,306	1,407	1,529	1,833	2,126	2,399	2,732
Private creditors	4,411	4,999	6,270	6,600	7,965	7,961	8,491	6,992
Private nonguaranteed	780	1,742	1,061	1,111	1,136	991	1,391	2,268
Disbursements	**724**	**1,595**	**679**	**704**	**1,890**	**445**	**1,377**	**1,453**
Public and publicly guaranteed	486	1,325	199	654	1,865	440	973	537
Official creditors	97	94	199	254	461	440	438	537
Private creditors	388	1,231	0	400	1,404	0	535	0
Private nonguaranteed	238	270	480	50	25	5	404	915
Principal repayments	**411**	**1,207**	**171**	**659**	**190**	**320**	**185**	**1,908**
Public and publicly guaranteed	386	955	171	659	190	170	178	1,869
Official creditors	109	139	154	160	154	165	175	176
Private creditors	277	817	17	499	36	5	3	1,694
Private nonguaranteed	25	251	0	0	0	150	7	38
Interest payments	**418**	**541**	**607**	**641**	**684**	**726**	**745**	**691**
Public and publicly guaranteed	365	454	544	578	596	638	668	645
Official creditors	79	59	70	71	72	75	76	77
Private creditors	286	394	474	506	524	563	592	567
Private nonguaranteed	53	87	63	64	88	87	77	47
Debt resource inflows								
Net debt inflows	261	378	498	41	1,700	125	1,192	-455
Official creditors (incl. IMF)	-63	-55	35	89	307	275	263	362
Private creditors	324	433	463	-48	1,393	-150	929	-816
Long-term	324	433	463	-48	1,393	-150	929	-816
Public and publicly guaranteed	112	414	-17	-98	1,368	-5	531	-1,694
Private nonguaranteed	213	19	480	50	25	-145	397	877
Short-term	..	..	..	..	..	..	..	..
Non-debt resource inflows								
Foreign direct investment	624	1,104	2,023	2,534	1,086	2,195	3,223	3,383
Portfolio equity	..	..	..	..	..	..	..	..
Currency composition (%)								
Euro	..	0.0	0.0	0.0	0.0	0.0	0.0	0.0
U.S.dollars	91.8	95.9	97.4	97.8	98.2	97.4	92.2	92.2
Major economic aggregates								
Gross national income (GNI)	11,007	14,340	21,100	24,575	25,612	28,902	33,170	38,908
Exports of goods, services & prim. income	9,408	11,619	16,124	17,991	19,006	20,416	26,104	29,754
Personal transfers & comp. of employees	16	130	180	196	336	410	384	402
Imports of goods, services & prim. income	10,258	12,882	17,784	20,951	19,311	23,319	30,096	33,102
Primary income on FDI	562	1,048	1,521	1,748	1,310	1,829	2,096	2,873
Current account balance	-673	-1,022	-1,407	-2,722	-178	-2,765	-3,826	-3,267
International reserves	723	1,211	1,935	2,424	3,028	2,714	2,304	2,466
Ratios								
External debt stocks to exports (%)	70.2	69.8	54.5	51.6	59.2	55.7	48.2	41.3
External debt stocks to GNI (%)	60.0	56.5	41.6	37.8	43.9	39.4	37.9	31.6
Debt service to exports (%)	9.4	15.1	4.9	7.3	4.6	5.1	3.6	8.7
Short-term to external debt stocks (%)	0.0	..	..	..	..	..	..	..
Multilateral to external debt stocks (%)	15.5	13.7	13.9	14.4	14.5	15.9	16.1	19.4
Reserves to external debt stocks (%)	10.9	14.9	22.0	26.1	26.9	23.8	18.3	20.1
Reserves to imports (months)	0.8	1.1	1.3	1.4	1.9	1.4	0.9	0.9

Notes:

Long-term private nonguaranteed debt data only cover Bonds.

PAPUA NEW GUINEA

(US$ million, unless otherwise indicated)

	2000	2005	2007	2008	2009	2010	2011	2012
Summary external debt data								
External debt stocks	**2,305**	**1,896**	**1,448**	**1,435**	**1,787**	**5,965**	**12,584**	**23,128**
Long-term external debt	2,204	1,651	1,342	1,412	1,460	5,380	12,268	22,651
Short-term external debt	49	232	91	9	130	392	123	284
interest arrears on long-term	0	0	0	0	0	0	0	0
Use of IMF credit	51	13	15	14	197	193	193	193
Long-term external debt								
Debt outstanding and disbursed	**2,204**	**1,651**	**1,342**	**1,412**	**1,460**	**5,380**	**12,268**	**22,651**
Public and publicly guaranteed	1,454	1,264	1,129	1,067	1,045	1,042	1,069	1,130
Official creditors	1,394	1,213	1,087	1,023	1,008	1,009	1,043	1,114
Private creditors	60	51	42	44	36	33	26	16
Private nonguaranteed	750	387	213	345	415	4,337	11,199	21,521
Disbursements	**254**	**335**	**615**	**951**	**516**	**3,153**	**8,158**	**10,896**
Public and publicly guaranteed	219	45	40	26	33	37	94	161
Official creditors	206	44	39	26	33	37	94	161
Private creditors	13	1	0	0	0	0	0	0
Private nonguaranteed	35	290	575	925	483	3,116	8,064	10,735
Principal repayments	**196**	**183**	**947**	**932**	**513**	**758**	**1,076**	**349**
Public and publicly guaranteed	115	114	172	163	62	67	79	78
Official creditors	96	93	166	157	55	60	71	70
Private creditors	19	21	6	6	7	7	8	8
Private nonguaranteed	80	69	775	769	451	691	997	271
Interest payments	**85**	**54**	**55**	**40**	**28**	**50**	**104**	**131**
Public and publicly guaranteed	54	38	39	32	21	16	19	18
Official creditors	50	36	38	31	20	16	19	18
Private creditors	5	2	1	1	1	1	1	0
Private nonguaranteed	31	16	16	8	7	33	85	113
Debt resource inflows								
Net debt inflows	30	214	-408	-63	124	2,657	6,812	10,708
Official creditors (incl. IMF)	128	-110	-127	-131	-22	-23	23	91
Private creditors	-99	323	-281	67	146	2,680	6,790	10,617
Long-term	-51	200	-205	149	25	2,418	7,059	10,456
Public and publicly guaranteed	-5	-20	-5	-6	-7	-7	-8	-8
Private nonguaranteed	-45	221	-200	156	32	2,426	7,067	10,464
Short-term	-48	123	-76	-82	121	262	-269	161
Non-debt resource inflows								
Foreign direct investment	96	32	95	-31	419	29	-309	29
Portfolio equity	..	..	..	..	..	..	..	..
Currency composition (%)								
Euro	..	3.8	4.6	4.3	4.3	3.8	3.3	3.0
U.S.dollars	21.3	33.7	36.2	38.5	39.1	38.9	37.2	37.6
Major economic aggregates								
Gross national income (GNI)	3,303	4,531	6,261	7,931	7,855	9,262	12,003	15,024
Exports of goods, services & prim. income	2,369	3,649	5,205	6,259	4,624	6,097	..	..
Personal transfers & comp. of employees	7	7	8	7	5	3	..	..
Imports of goods, services & prim. income	2,013	3,368	5,399	5,713	5,382	6,920	..	..
Primary income on FDI	198	511	674	611	537	466	..	..
Current account balance	351	539	56	708	-585	-633	..	..
International reserves	287	718	2,054	1,953	2,561	3,033	4,256	3,930
Ratios								
External debt stocks to exports (%)	97.3	52.0	27.8	22.9	38.6	97.8	..	..
External debt stocks to GNI (%)	69.8	41.8	23.1	18.1	22.8	64.4	104.8	153.9
Debt service to exports (%)	12.9	8.4	19.4	15.6	11.7	13.3	..	..
Short-term to external debt stocks (%)	2.1	12.2	6.3	0.6	7.3	6.6	1.0	1.2
Multilateral to external debt stocks (%)	35.9	44.1	51.8	50.2	40.5	11.9	5.6	3.4
Reserves to external debt stocks (%)	12.4	37.9	141.8	136.1	143.3	50.8	33.8	17.0
Reserves to imports (months)	1.7	2.6	4.6	4.1	5.7	5.3	..	..

Notes:

Short-term debt is based on data from the BIS. Long-term private nonguaranteed debt data for 2011 include a huge outstanding loan about $18.5 billion.

PARAGUAY

(US$ million, unless otherwise indicated)

	2000	2005	2007	2008	2009	2010	2011	2012
Summary external debt data								
External debt stocks	**3,135**	**3,249**	**3,591**	**4,182**	**4,134**	**5,076**	**5,918**	**6,331**
Long-term external debt	2,537	2,716	2,767	3,015	3,233	3,782	3,869	4,668
Short-term external debt	580	513	803	1,146	752	1,147	1,903	1,517
interest arrears on long-term	11	0	0	0	0	0	0	0
Use of IMF credit	18	20	22	21	149	147	146	146
Long-term external debt								
Debt outstanding and disbursed	**2,537**	**2,716**	**2,767**	**3,015**	**3,233**	**3,782**	**3,869**	**4,668**
Public and publicly guaranteed	2,087	2,266	2,195	2,263	2,261	2,361	2,305	2,245
Official creditors	1,639	1,845	1,843	1,940	1,979	2,094	2,072	2,051
Private creditors	449	421	352	323	282	267	233	194
Private nonguaranteed	450	450	572	751	972	1,421	1,564	2,423
Disbursements	**192**	**210**	**206**	**376**	**489**	**826**	**512**	**1,118**
Public and publicly guaranteed	192	144	111	196	248	303	163	227
Official creditors	192	141	111	196	248	303	163	227
Private creditors	0	3	0	0	0	0	0	0
Private nonguaranteed	0	66	95	180	241	523	349	891
Principal repayments	**207**	**332**	**258**	**296**	**308**	**313**	**299**	**626**
Public and publicly guaranteed	114	205	206	237	262	239	244	240
Official creditors	107	176	177	208	221	224	211	201
Private creditors	7	29	29	29	41	15	34	39
Private nonguaranteed	93	126	52	59	46	75	55	386
Interest payments	**116**	**115**	**135**	**136**	**122**	**131**	**140**	**141**
Public and publicly guaranteed	100	94	104	96	97	65	66	59
Official creditors	70	77	80	78	83	63	61	55
Private creditors	30	17	24	18	14	2	4	4
Private nonguaranteed	16	21	31	40	25	66	75	82
Debt resource inflows								
Net debt inflows	-187	-275	39	423	-213	907	969	105
Official creditors (incl. IMF)	85	-35	-67	-11	27	79	-47	26
Private creditors	-272	-239	106	434	-241	828	1,016	80
Long-term	-100	-86	14	91	153	433	260	466
Public and publicly guaranteed	-7	-26	-29	-29	-41	-15	-34	-39
Private nonguaranteed	-93	-60	43	120	195	448	294	505
Short-term	-173	-153	92	343	-394	395	756	-386
Non-debt resource inflows								
Foreign direct investment	104	7	105	261	49	356	134	363
Portfolio equity	..	..	..	..	..	..	..	..
Currency composition (%)								
Euro	..	2.6	2.8	2.8	2.6	1.7	1.5	1.4
U.S.dollars	59.2	68.4	68.8	66.1	67.5	70.3	72.6	77.2
Major economic aggregates								
Gross national income (GNI)	7,085	7,360	12,840	17,379	14,774	18,617	24,841	23,324
Exports of goods, services & prim. income	3,185	5,182	7,970	10,278	8,386	11,135	13,371	12,725
Personal transfers & comp. of employees	278	161	341	363	377	410	541	634
Imports of goods, services & prim. income	3,524	5,473	7,564	10,503	8,421	11,758	13,796	13,368
Primary income on FDI	84	158	365	505	555	760	534	861
Current account balance	-163	-68	779	189	484	-66	289	116
International reserves	763	1,297	2,461	2,845	3,839	4,137	4,950	4,557
Ratios								
External debt stocks to exports (%)	98.4	62.7	45.1	40.7	49.3	45.6	44.3	49.8
External debt stocks to GNI (%)	44.2	44.1	28.0	24.1	28.0	27.3	23.8	27.1
Debt service to exports (%)	11.2	9.2	5.3	4.5	5.3	4.1	3.4	6.3
Short-term to external debt stocks (%)	18.5	15.8	22.4	27.4	18.2	22.6	32.2	24.0
Multilateral to external debt stocks (%)	37.3	38.9	36.1	31.0	32.7	29.5	25.6	25.2
Reserves to external debt stocks (%)	24.3	39.9	68.5	68.0	92.8	81.5	83.6	72.0
Reserves to imports (months)	2.6	2.8	3.9	3.3	5.5	4.2	4.3	4.1

Notes:

Short-term debt is based on data from the BIS.

PERU

(US$ million, unless otherwise indicated)

	2000	2005	2007	2008	2009	2010	2011	2012
Summary external debt data								
External debt stocks	**28,813**	**29,508**	**32,239**	**34,720**	**37,390**	**42,154**	**45,012**	**54,148**
Long-term external debt	24,208	26,109	26,761	29,159	31,649	34,822	37,751	44,679
Short-term external debt	3,928	3,212	5,334	5,420	4,784	6,393	6,325	8,532
interest arrears on long-term	14	4	17	22	1	1	0	0
Use of IMF credit	677	188	144	141	956	939	936	937
Long-term external debt								
Debt outstanding and disbursed	**24,208**	**26,109**	**26,761**	**29,159**	**31,649**	**34,822**	**37,751**	**44,679**
Public and publicly guaranteed	19,270	22,537	19,854	19,415	20,788	20,009	20,142	19,965
Official creditors	14,439	13,830	11,315	12,358	11,727	10,555	10,721	9,981
Private creditors	4,830	8,706	8,539	7,056	9,061	9,454	9,422	9,984
Private nonguaranteed	4,938	3,572	6,907	9,744	10,862	14,813	17,608	24,714
Disbursements	**2,066**	**3,721**	**7,149**	**4,630**	**4,772**	**8,296**	**3,386**	**6,866**
Public and publicly guaranteed	1,489	2,635	3,299	1,165	3,232	3,862	1,003	1,348
Official creditors	1,454	985	1,180	1,165	1,232	1,601	1,003	448
Private creditors	35	1,650	2,119	0	2,000	2,261	0	900
Private nonguaranteed	577	1,086	3,849	3,466	1,539	4,434	2,382	5,518
Principal repayments	**1,003**	**4,189**	**6,747**	**3,265**	**2,221**	**4,060**	**1,402**	**2,990**
Public and publicly guaranteed	986	3,033	5,865	2,618	1,833	3,490	892	1,350
Official creditors	840	2,918	3,498	1,255	1,808	2,971	867	1,015
Private creditors	146	114	2,366	1,363	25	518	25	335
Private nonguaranteed	17	1,156	882	647	389	570	509	1,640
Interest payments	**1,174**	**1,718**	**2,110**	**1,808**	**1,976**	**2,550**	**1,789**	**3,326**
Public and publicly guaranteed	1,105	1,403	1,512	1,185	1,084	1,096	1,001	969
Official creditors	917	807	818	572	452	346	288	275
Private creditors	188	596	694	613	632	750	712	694
Private nonguaranteed	69	314	598	623	892	1,454	788	2,357
Debt resource inflows								
Net debt inflows	283	-46	2,704	1,447	1,935	5,845	1,918	6,083
Official creditors (incl. IMF)	473	-1,972	-2,339	-91	-575	-1,370	136	-567
Private creditors	-190	1,927	5,042	1,538	2,511	7,215	1,781	6,650
Long-term	448	1,465	2,720	1,457	3,126	5,606	1,848	4,443
Public and publicly guaranteed	-111	1,536	-247	-1,363	1,975	1,742	-25	565
Private nonguaranteed	560	-70	2,967	2,819	1,151	3,864	1,873	3,878
Short-term	-638	461	2,322	81	-615	1,608	-67	2,207
Non-debt resource inflows								
Foreign direct investment	810	2,579	5,491	6,924	6,431	8,455	8,233	12,244
Portfolio equity	123	769	70	85	47	87	147	-32
Currency composition (%)								
Euro	..	7.0	8.2	11.1	7.2	4.4	4.7	4.6
U.S.dollars	73.5	80.4	78.7	72.6	77.9	83.6	84.0	85.7
Major economic aggregates								
Gross national income (GNI)	51,878	74,970	98,934	118,081	118,538	142,406	163,216	184,410
Exports of goods, services & prim. income	9,247	20,006	32,511	36,144	31,801	39,986	51,046	51,215
Personal transfers & comp. of employees	718	1,440	2,131	2,444	2,409	2,534	2,697	2,788
Imports of goods, services & prim. income	11,794	20,631	33,558	44,404	35,411	46,794	57,586	61,647
Primary income on FDI	344	4,030	7,788	8,346	8,172	10,714	12,866	11,748
Current account balance	-1,546	1,148	1,460	-5,318	-723	-3,782	-3,341	-7,136
International reserves	8,374	13,599	26,856	30,271	32,013	42,648	47,206	62,300
Ratios								
External debt stocks to exports (%)	311.6	147.5	99.2	96.1	117.6	105.4	88.2	105.7
External debt stocks to GNI (%)	55.5	39.4	32.6	29.4	31.5	29.6	27.6	29.4
Debt service to exports (%)	27.9	30.3	27.9	14.6	13.4	16.7	6.4	12.5
Short-term to external debt stocks (%)	13.6	10.9	16.5	15.6	12.8	15.2	14.1	15.8
Multilateral to external debt stocks (%)	19.3	26.8	24.6	23.1	22.5	18.7	17.7	14.0
Reserves to external debt stocks (%)	29.1	46.1	83.3	87.2	85.6	101.2	104.9	115.1
Reserves to imports (months)	8.5	7.9	9.6	8.2	10.8	10.9	9.8	12.1

Notes:

Long-term private nonguaranteed debt data for 2012 are World Bank staff estimates based on market data. Short-term debt is based on data from the BIS.

PHILIPPINES

(US$ million, unless otherwise indicated)

	2000	2005	2007	2008	2009	2010	2011	2012
Summary external debt data								
External debt stocks	**58,456**	**58,693**	**59,115**	**58,206**	**55,711**	**60,775**	**61,023**	**61,390**
Long-term external debt	50,777	51,742	51,847	51,026	50,395	53,189	52,723	51,619
Short-term external debt	5,495	6,395	7,084	7,001	4,002	6,295	7,013	8,483
interest arrears on long-term	0	0	0	0	0	0	0	0
Use of IMF credit	2,183	555	184	180	1,314	1,290	1,287	1,288
Long-term external debt								
Debt outstanding and disbursed	**50,777**	**51,742**	**51,847**	**51,026**	**50,395**	**53,189**	**52,723**	**51,619**
Public and publicly guaranteed	33,744	35,364	38,077	39,195	41,923	44,727	44,579	43,037
Official creditors	19,890	18,580	19,574	21,599	22,054	23,210	23,587	21,934
Private creditors	13,855	16,784	18,503	17,596	19,870	21,517	20,992	21,103
Private nonguaranteed	17,033	16,378	13,770	11,831	8,472	8,462	8,144	8,582
Disbursements	**5,747**	**5,544**	**3,802**	**4,293**	**8,767**	**10,928**	**7,954**	**5,761**
Public and publicly guaranteed	5,228	3,874	2,767	2,130	8,124	8,251	4,999	3,828
Official creditors	1,528	1,144	1,655	1,454	2,349	1,370	1,709	1,436
Private creditors	3,701	2,730	1,112	677	5,776	6,881	3,290	2,392
Private nonguaranteed	519	1,670	1,034	2,163	642	2,677	2,954	1,933
Principal repayments	**4,047**	**5,748**	**4,739**	**6,995**	**5,675**	**8,341**	**6,311**	**2,725**
Public and publicly guaranteed	2,515	3,353	2,549	3,592	3,841	6,813	4,887	2,629
Official creditors	1,572	1,788	1,668	2,322	1,722	1,818	2,007	1,756
Private creditors	943	1,566	881	1,270	2,120	4,996	2,880	873
Private nonguaranteed	1,533	2,395	2,190	3,402	1,833	1,527	1,424	96
Interest payments	**2,469**	**3,152**	**3,206**	**3,376**	**3,266**	**3,112**	**3,195**	**2,973**
Public and publicly guaranteed	1,882	2,409	2,527	2,865	2,841	2,977	2,850	2,844
Official creditors	841	584	614	612	542	498	489	431
Private creditors	1,041	1,825	1,913	2,253	2,299	2,479	2,361	2,414
Private nonguaranteed	586	743	679	511	425	135	345	129
Debt resource inflows								
Net debt inflows	2,551	828	1,138	-2,785	93	4,880	2,360	4,505
Official creditors (incl. IMF)	261	-961	-13	-868	627	-447	-298	-320
Private creditors	2,290	1,788	1,151	-1,917	-534	5,328	2,658	4,826
Long-term	1,744	439	-924	-1,834	2,465	3,035	1,941	3,356
Public and publicly guaranteed	2,758	1,164	231	-594	3,656	1,885	410	1,520
Private nonguaranteed	-1,014	-725	-1,155	-1,240	-1,191	1,149	1,530	1,836
Short-term	546	1,349	2,075	-83	-2,998	2,293	718	1,470
Non-debt resource inflows								
Foreign direct investment	2,240	1,664	3,245	1,436	2,712	1,635	1,816	2,797
Portfolio equity	-202	1,465	3,178	-1,289	-1,096	503	1,046	1,728
Currency composition (%)								
Euro	..	5.5	5.9	5.1	5.1	3.7	3.3	2.9
U.S.dollars	42.2	49.5	52.9	49.8	55.8	56.1	58.4	63.1
Major economic aggregates								
Gross national income (GNI)	80,996	102,768	148,461	173,708	168,141	200,094	225,008	249,394
Exports of goods, services & prim. income	44,060	37,031	51,227	52,392	47,317	59,105	63,337	72,658
Personal transfers & comp. of employees	6,961	13,561	16,285	18,628	19,726	21,369	23,058	24,641
Imports of goods, services & prim. income	51,931	46,442	58,268	64,012	54,238	66,831	74,747	84,704
Primary income on FDI	230	1,391	2,133	1,675	2,150	2,125	2,925	4,237
Current account balance	-2,228	1,980	7,112	3,627	9,358	8,922	6,970	7,126
International reserves	13,090	15,926	30,211	33,193	38,783	55,363	67,290	73,478
Ratios								
External debt stocks to exports (%)	132.7	158.5	115.4	111.1	117.7	102.8	96.3	84.5
External debt stocks to GNI (%)	72.2	57.1	39.8	33.5	33.1	30.4	27.1	24.6
Debt service to exports (%)	16.0	25.7	16.2	20.6	19.2	19.4	15.3	8.0
Short-term to external debt stocks (%)	9.4	10.9	12.0	12.0	7.2	10.4	11.5	13.8
Multilateral to external debt stocks (%)	12.3	11.3	12.2	12.7	15.2	13.8	14.8	15.3
Reserves to external debt stocks (%)	22.4	27.1	51.1	57.0	69.6	91.1	110.3	119.7
Reserves to imports (months)	3.0	4.1	6.2	6.2	8.6	9.9	10.8	10.4

Notes:

Long-term private nonguaranteed debt data no longer include unregistered debt and are revised from 2005 based on the reports provided by the country.

ROMANIA

(US$ million, unless otherwise indicated)

	2000	2005	2007	2008	2009	2010	2011	2012
Summary external debt data								
External debt stocks	**11,259**	**38,884**	**84,381**	**102,539**	**120,092**	**124,358**	**129,822**	**131,889**
Long-term external debt	9,945	31,102	54,935	73,761	86,545	81,627	82,331	89,135
Short-term external debt	763	7,413	29,326	28,660	22,459	26,122	29,752	27,006
interest arrears on long-term	12	13	6	2	1	1	1	1
Use of IMF credit	552	369	120	117	11,088	16,609	17,738	15,748
Long-term external debt								
Debt outstanding and disbursed	**9,945**	**31,102**	**54,935**	**73,761**	**86,545**	**81,627**	**82,331**	**89,135**
Public and publicly guaranteed	6,583	13,330	15,299	15,256	18,248	20,801	24,870	29,695
Official creditors	4,149	6,152	7,315	8,042	11,321	14,280	16,888	17,600
Private creditors	2,434	7,177	7,984	7,214	6,927	6,520	7,982	12,095
Private nonguaranteed	3,362	17,773	39,636	58,505	68,297	60,826	57,462	59,440
Disbursements	**3,144**	**12,909**	**21,016**	**32,747**	**23,271**	**17,435**	**17,847**	**20,896**
Public and publicly guaranteed	1,937	2,637	1,371	3,059	3,938	5,623	6,177	6,483
Official creditors	1,083	1,016	731	1,543	3,735	4,128	3,900	1,242
Private creditors	854	1,621	640	1,516	204	1,495	2,277	5,241
Private nonguaranteed	1,207	10,272	19,645	29,688	19,332	11,812	11,670	14,413
Principal repayments	**1,706**	**5,170**	**8,239**	**14,475**	**13,169**	**15,784**	**15,729**	**15,887**
Public and publicly guaranteed	984	1,697	1,469	2,543	1,423	2,150	1,274	2,083
Official creditors	493	590	585	685	671	668	767	744
Private creditors	491	1,107	884	1,858	752	1,482	507	1,338
Private nonguaranteed	721	3,473	6,770	11,932	11,746	13,633	14,454	13,804
Interest payments	**632**	**1,247**	**1,961**	**2,926**	**2,775**	**2,180**	**2,454**	**2,314**
Public and publicly guaranteed	439	672	805	901	741	617	751	972
Official creditors	269	229	316	347	328	297	421	472
Private creditors	171	443	489	553	413	320	330	500
Private nonguaranteed	193	575	1,156	2,025	2,034	1,563	1,703	1,342
Debt resource inflows								
Net debt inflows	1,843	10,619	25,431	17,611	13,292	10,979	6,961	264
Official creditors (incl. IMF)	608	275	40	857	12,454	9,124	4,346	-1,500
Private creditors	1,235	10,344	25,391	16,753	838	1,855	2,616	1,764
Long-term	849	7,312	12,631	17,415	7,038	-1,808	-1,015	4,511
Public and publicly guaranteed	363	513	-244	-342	-548	13	1,770	3,903
Private nonguaranteed	486	6,799	12,874	17,757	7,586	-1,821	-2,784	609
Short-term	386	3,032	12,760	-662	-6,200	3,663	3,630	-2,747
Non-debt resource inflows								
Foreign direct investment	1,037	6,866	10,290	13,849	4,926	3,204	2,557	2,024
Portfolio equity	58	229	746	23	7	4	-37	403
Currency composition (%)								
Euro	..	58.9	68.8	70.7	77.6	81.5	86.1	82.2
U.S.dollars	42.5	26.9	18.8	17.0	13.1	10.4	7.6	13.1
Major economic aggregates								
Gross national income (GNI)	36,768	98,008	169,088	198,413	162,112	162,477	187,306	167,254
Exports of goods, services & prim. income	12,438	25,693	46,509	59,740	47,150	54,951	69,663	64,738
Personal transfers & comp. of employees	96	4,708	8,461	9,285	4,881	3,879	3,889	3,541
Imports of goods, services & prim. income	14,653	38,645	76,207	92,343	59,813	66,966	82,653	75,400
Primary income on FDI	72	2,926	5,988	4,362	1,212	717	674	-378
Current account balance	-1,355	-8,504	-23,080	-23,719	-6,955	-7,258	-8,344	-6,346
International reserves	2,470	19,872	37,194	36,868	40,757	43,361	42,939	41,162
Ratios								
External debt stocks to exports (%)	90.5	151.3	181.4	171.6	254.7	226.3	186.4	203.7
External debt stocks to GNI (%)	30.6	39.7	49.9	51.7	74.1	76.5	69.3	78.9
Debt service to exports (%)	20.1	26.9	24.9	30.3	34.7	33.8	27.4	34.2
Short-term to external debt stocks (%)	6.8	19.1	34.8	28.0	18.7	21.0	22.9	20.5
Multilateral to external debt stocks (%)	29.9	14.4	8.0	7.1	8.9	10.8	12.3	12.7
Reserves to external debt stocks (%)	21.9	51.1	44.1	36.0	33.9	34.9	33.1	31.2
Reserves to imports (months)	2.0	6.2	5.9	4.8	8.2	7.8	6.2	6.6

RWANDA

(US$ million, unless otherwise indicated)

	2000	2005	2007	2008	2009	2010	2011	2012
Summary external debt data								
External debt stocks	**1,289**	**1,528**	**606**	**684**	**869**	**913**	**1,103**	**1,269**
Long-term external debt	1,148	1,415	566	646	724	765	971	1,048
Short-term external debt	38	17	11	6	10	14	0	89
interest arrears on long-term	16	13	11	1	0	0	0	0
Use of IMF credit	104	97	30	33	136	133	132	131
Long-term external debt								
Debt outstanding and disbursed	**1,148**	**1,415**	**566**	**646**	**724**	**765**	**971**	**1,048**
Public and publicly guaranteed	1,148	1,415	566	646	724	765	971	1,048
Official creditors	1,147	1,415	566	646	724	765	971	1,048
Private creditors	1	0	0	0	0	0	0	0
Private nonguaranteed	..	..	..	..	..	..	..	..
Disbursements	**40**	**85**	**82**	**111**	**85**	**61**	**223**	**97**
Public and publicly guaranteed	40	85	82	111	85	61	223	97
Official creditors	40	85	82	111	85	61	223	97
Private creditors	0	0	0	0	0	0	0	0
Private nonguaranteed	..	..	..	..	..	..	..	..
Principal repayments	**13**	**13**	**16**	**9**	**5**	**8**	**12**	**13**
Public and publicly guaranteed	13	13	16	9	5	8	12	13
Official creditors	13	13	16	9	5	8	12	13
Private creditors	0	0	0	0	0	0	0	0
Private nonguaranteed	..	..	..	..	..	..	..	..
Interest payments	**8**	**10**	**6**	**6**	**6**	**6**	**7**	**8**
Public and publicly guaranteed	8	10	6	6	6	6	7	8
Official creditors	8	10	6	6	6	6	7	8
Private creditors	0	0	0	0	0	0	0	0
Private nonguaranteed	..	..	..	..	..	..	..	..
Debt resource inflows								
Net debt inflows	24	67	63	111	88	57	197	172
Official creditors (incl. IMF)	41	70	70	106	83	53	211	83
Private creditors	-16	-3	-7	5	5	4	-14	89
Long-term	0	0	0	0	0	0	0	0
Public and publicly guaranteed	0	0	0	0	0	0	0	0
Private nonguaranteed	..	..	..	..	..	..	..	..
Short-term	-16	-3	-7	5	5	4	-14	89
Non-debt resource inflows								
Foreign direct investment	8	8	82	103	119	42	106	160
Portfolio equity	..	..	..	..	..	21	31	7
Currency composition (%)								
Euro	..	4.2	5.1	6.8	6.7	5.5	3.8	3.3
U.S.dollars	58.5	63.8	44.4	41.9	41.2	40.1	46.8	47.7
Major economic aggregates								
Gross national income (GNI)	1,719	2,554	3,721	4,676	5,216	5,582	6,302	..
Exports of goods, services & prim. income	142	260	487	726	611	639	933	1,027
Personal transfers & comp. of employees	7	9	121	68	93	106	174	182
Imports of goods, services & prim. income	452	693	1,033	1,487	1,594	1,710	2,291	2,570
Primary income on FDI	3	5	12	16	5	4	12	1
Current account balance	-94	-65	-85	-242	-379	-414	-477	-821
International reserves	191	406	553	596	743	813	1,050	848
Ratios								
External debt stocks to exports (%)	911.2	587.3	124.6	94.2	142.2	142.9	118.3	123.5
External debt stocks to GNI (%)	75.0	59.8	16.3	14.6	16.7	16.4	17.5	..
Debt service to exports (%)	25.7	10.8	4.8	2.0	1.9	2.3	2.1	2.2
Short-term to external debt stocks (%)	2.9	1.1	1.7	0.8	1.2	1.5	0.0	7.0
Multilateral to external debt stocks (%)	77.3	88.8	77.1	82.2	70.8	70.0	74.3	69.1
Reserves to external debt stocks (%)	14.8	26.5	91.2	87.2	85.4	89.0	95.2	66.8
Reserves to imports (months)	5.1	7.0	6.4	4.8	5.6	5.7	5.5	4.0

Notes:

Data include the effects of HIPC and MDRI debt relief.

SAMOA

(US$ million, unless otherwise indicated)

	2000	2005	2007	2008	2009	2010	2011	2012
Summary external debt data								
External debt stocks	**139.2**	**169.1**	**187.7**	**207.4**	**252.9**	**325.1**	**368.3**	**422.9**
Long-term external debt	137.7	167.5	185.9	205.6	226.4	299.1	342.4	396.9
Short-term external debt	0.0	0.0	0.0	0.0	0.0	0.0	0.0	0.0
interest arrears on long-term	0.0	0.0	0.0	0.0	0.0	0.0	0.0	0.0
Use of IMF credit	1.5	1.6	1.8	1.8	26.5	26.0	25.9	26.0
Long-term external debt								
Debt outstanding and disbursed	**137.7**	**167.5**	**185.9**	**205.6**	**226.4**	**299.1**	**342.4**	**396.9**
Public and publicly guaranteed	137.7	167.5	185.9	205.6	226.4	299.1	342.4	396.9
Official creditors	137.7	167.5	185.9	205.6	226.4	299.1	342.4	396.9
Private creditors	0.0	0.0	0.0	0.0	0.0	0.0	0.0	0.0
Private nonguaranteed	..	..	..	..	..	..	..	..
Disbursements	**6.7**	**10.4**	**17.8**	**25.5**	**25.2**	**78.9**	**47.6**	**64.3**
Public and publicly guaranteed	6.7	10.4	17.8	25.5	25.2	78.9	47.6	64.3
Official creditors	6.7	10.4	17.8	25.5	25.2	78.9	47.6	64.3
Private creditors	0.0	0.0	0.0	0.0	0.0	0.0	0.0	0.0
Private nonguaranteed	..	..	..	..	..	..	..	..
Principal repayments	**4.2**	**4.3**	**5.3**	**6.0**	**6.0**	**7.2**	**7.7**	**8.6**
Public and publicly guaranteed	4.2	4.3	5.3	6.0	6.0	7.2	7.7	8.6
Official creditors	4.2	4.3	5.3	6.0	6.0	7.2	7.7	8.6
Private creditors	0.0	0.0	0.0	0.0	0.0	0.0	0.0	0.0
Private nonguaranteed	..	..	..	..	..	..	..	..
Interest payments	**1.3**	**1.5**	**1.6**	**2.1**	**2.5**	**3.3**	**4.1**	**4.7**
Public and publicly guaranteed	1.3	1.5	1.6	2.1	2.5	3.3	4.1	4.7
Official creditors	1.3	1.5	1.6	2.1	2.5	3.3	4.1	4.7
Private creditors	0.0	0.0	0.0	0.0	0.0	0.0	0.0	0.0
Private nonguaranteed	..	..	..	..	..	..	..	..
Debt resource inflows								
Net debt inflows	2.5	6.1	12.6	19.6	28.1	71.6	39.8	55.7
Official creditors (incl. IMF)	2.5	6.1	12.6	19.6	28.1	71.6	39.8	55.7
Private creditors	0.0	0.0	0.0	0.0	0.0	0.0	0.0	0.0
Long-term	0.0	0.0	0.0	0.0	0.0	0.0	0.0	0.0
Public and publicly guaranteed	0.0	0.0	0.0	0.0	0.0	0.0	0.0	0.0
Private nonguaranteed	..	..	..	..	..	..	..	..
Short-term	..	..	..	..	..	..	..	..
Non-debt resource inflows								
Foreign direct investment	-1.5	3.8	6.8	45.9	9.9	1.0	15.2	23.5
Portfolio equity	..	..	..	..	..	..	..	..
Currency composition (%)								
Euro	..	1.7	1.4	0.9	0.8	0.4	0.3	0.2
U.S.dollars	41.0	43.7	45.7	41.1	36.8	33.7	29.0	25.1
Major economic aggregates								
Gross national income (GNI)	239.7	388.2	452.9	545.5	473.6	554.0	607.7	640.5
Exports of goods, services & prim. income	..	147.3	188.5	193.5	181.4	210.4	217.6	250.8
Personal transfers & comp. of employees	45.0	81.6	96.6	109.0	119.5	122.1	139.1	158.8
Imports of goods, services & prim. income	..	300.2	344.3	376.8	319.8	386.4	434.2	459.6
Primary income on FDI	..	30.0	37.9	50.5	27.4	17.8	29.2	36.0
Current account balance	..	-47.3	-45.7	-57.7	-12.7	-43.4	-65.9	-35.4
International reserves	63.7	81.8	95.4	87.1	165.8	209.4	166.8	168.7
Ratios								
External debt stocks to exports (%)	..	114.8	99.6	107.2	139.4	154.5	169.3	168.6
External debt stocks to GNI (%)	58.1	43.6	41.4	38.0	53.4	58.7	60.6	66.0
Debt service to exports (%)	..	3.9	3.7	4.2	4.7	5.0	5.5	5.3
Short-term to external debt stocks (%)	..	..	..	..	0.0	..	..	..
Multilateral to external debt stocks (%)	92.9	91.7	94.2	84.9	71.2	67.4	60.8	56.7
Reserves to external debt stocks (%)	45.7	48.4	50.8	42.0	65.6	64.4	45.3	39.9
Reserves to imports (months)	..	3.3	3.3	2.8	6.2	6.5	4.6	4.4

Notes:

Short-term debt data are excluded since BIS data include debt liabilities of offshore centers located in the country. BIS short-term debt data for 2010, 2011, and 2012 are $2.1 billion, $2.5 billion, and $3.0 billion respectively.

SAO TOME AND PRINCIPE

(US$ million, unless otherwise indicated)

	2000	2005	2007	2008	2009	2010	2011	2012
Summary external debt data								
External debt stocks	**303.8**	**335.0**	**165.8**	**131.4**	**159.6**	**180.9**	**230.8**	**201.6**
Long-term external debt	277.3	316.5	143.0	108.4	124.7	145.1	189.1	169.3
Short-term external debt	23.3	14.4	19.2	18.2	19.4	19.9	25.9	15.9
interest arrears on long-term	11.3	14.4	8.2	8.2	8.4	5.9	5.9	7.9
Use of IMF credit	3.3	4.1	3.5	4.8	15.6	15.9	15.8	16.4
Long-term external debt								
Debt outstanding and disbursed	**277.3**	**316.5**	**143.0**	**108.4**	**124.7**	**145.1**	**189.1**	**169.3**
Public and publicly guaranteed	277.3	316.5	143.0	108.4	124.7	145.1	189.1	169.3
Official creditors	277.3	316.5	143.0	108.4	124.7	145.1	189.1	169.3
Private creditors	0.0	0.0	0.0	0.0	0.0	0.0	0.0	0.0
Private nonguaranteed	..	..	..	..	..	..	..	..
Disbursements	**9.4**	**5.4**	**4.2**	**5.2**	**18.8**	**19.8**	**47.6**	**14.9**
Public and publicly guaranteed	9.4	5.4	4.2	5.2	18.8	19.8	47.6	14.9
Official creditors	9.4	5.4	4.2	5.2	18.8	19.8	47.6	14.9
Private creditors	0.0	0.0	0.0	0.0	0.0	0.0	0.0	0.0
Private nonguaranteed	..	..	..	..	..	..	..	..
Principal repayments	**2.2**	**4.3**	**4.2**	**1.6**	**1.7**	**1.1**	**1.0**	**1.5**
Public and publicly guaranteed	2.2	4.3	4.2	1.6	1.7	1.1	1.0	1.5
Official creditors	2.2	4.3	4.2	1.6	1.7	1.1	1.0	1.5
Private creditors	0.0	0.0	0.0	0.0	0.0	0.0	0.0	0.0
Private nonguaranteed	..	..	..	..	..	..	..	..
Interest payments	**1.2**	**2.0**	**1.1**	**0.3**	**0.3**	**0.3**	**0.3**	**0.5**
Public and publicly guaranteed	1.2	2.0	1.1	0.3	0.3	0.3	0.3	0.5
Official creditors	1.2	2.0	1.1	0.3	0.3	0.3	0.3	0.5
Private creditors	0.0	0.0	0.0	0.0	0.0	0.0	0.0	0.0
Private nonguaranteed	..	..	..	..	..	..	..	..
Debt resource inflows								
Net debt inflows	9.7	1.6	10.6	3.9	18.7	22.2	52.6	2.0
Official creditors (incl. IMF)	9.7	1.6	0.6	4.9	17.7	19.2	46.6	14.0
Private creditors	0.0	0.0	10.0	-1.0	1.0	3.0	6.0	-12.0
Long-term	0.0	0.0	0.0	0.0	0.0	0.0	0.0	0.0
Public and publicly guaranteed	0.0	0.0	0.0	0.0	0.0	0.0	0.0	0.0
Private nonguaranteed	..	..	..	..	..	..	..	..
Short-term	..	..	10.0	-1.0	1.0	3.0	6.0	-12.0
Non-debt resource inflows								
Foreign direct investment	3.8	15.7	36.0	79.1	15.5	50.6	32.2	22.5
Portfolio equity	..	..	..	..	..	..	..	..
Currency composition (%)								
Euro	..	6.2	3.8	4.5	3.8	14.9	26.5	23.6
U.S.dollars	43.5	44.9	64.6	53.5	58.7	50.8	45.3	40.9
Major economic aggregates								
Gross national income (GNI)	73.7	111.8	149.4	183.4	196.2	200.7	247.9	263.8
Exports of goods, services & prim. income	17.1	18.1	20.3	19.4	21.3	26.2	31.2	30.8
Personal transfers & comp. of employees	0.5	1.5	2.0	3.0	2.0	6.4	6.9	6.4
Imports of goods, services & prim. income	42.0	57.8	85.8	115.6	104.7	122.8	149.4	144.4
Primary income on FDI	..	..	..	..	..	..	..	..
Current account balance	-20.5	-36.3	-64.3	-93.5	-78.8	-87.6	-105.8	-99.5
International reserves	11.6	26.7	39.3	61.3	66.7	48.2	52.3	51.6
Ratios								
External debt stocks to exports (%)	1772.0	1853.8	817.6	675.6	751.0	690.1	739.7	654.8
External debt stocks to GNI (%)	412.2	299.6	110.9	71.6	81.4	90.1	93.1	76.4
Debt service to exports (%)	25.4	36.3	31.5	11.5	9.4	6.0	5.0	6.9
Short-term to external debt stocks (%)	7.7	4.3	11.6	13.9	12.1	11.0	11.2	7.9
Multilateral to external debt stocks (%)	55.4	58.8	22.5	27.0	22.8	20.5	18.0	18.7
Reserves to external debt stocks (%)	3.8	8.0	23.7	46.6	41.8	26.6	22.7	25.6
Reserves to imports (months)	3.3	5.5	5.5	6.4	7.6	4.7	4.2	4.3

Notes:

Short-term debt is based on data from the BIS. Data include HIPC and MDRI debt relief.

SENEGAL

(US$ million, unless otherwise indicated)

	2000	2005	2007	2008	2009	2010	2011	2012
Summary external debt data								
External debt stocks	**3,653**	**3,862**	**2,586**	**2,851**	**3,739**	**3,908**	**4,324**	**4,900**
Long-term external debt	3,221	3,643	2,188	2,552	3,312	3,457	3,877	4,317
Short-term external debt	146	36	332	197	18	0	0	141
interest arrears on long-term	1	0	0	0	0	0	0	0
Use of IMF credit	286	183	66	102	409	451	447	442
Long-term external debt								
Debt outstanding and disbursed	**3,221**	**3,643**	**2,188**	**2,552**	**3,312**	**3,457**	**3,877**	**4,317**
Public and publicly guaranteed	3,208	3,501	1,988	2,372	2,954	3,149	3,612	4,051
Official creditors	3,203	3,492	1,981	2,367	2,752	2,949	3,112	3,695
Private creditors	5	9	7	4	202	200	500	357
Private nonguaranteed	13	141	200	180	357	308	265	266
Disbursements	**137**	**382**	**497**	**522**	**837**	**434**	**1,009**	**746**
Public and publicly guaranteed	136	333	472	518	628	352	928	672
Official creditors	131	333	472	518	428	352	428	670
Private creditors	5	0	0	0	200	0	500	2
Private nonguaranteed	1	49	24	4	208	83	81	74
Principal repayments	**127**	**112**	**126**	**126**	**146**	**229**	**236**	**211**
Public and publicly guaranteed	125	83	72	87	97	84	140	138
Official creditors	124	81	68	85	94	83	140	138
Private creditors	0	2	4	3	3	2	0	0
Private nonguaranteed	3	29	54	39	49	144	96	73
Interest payments	**58**	**55**	**50**	**49**	**50**	**75**	**122**	**102**
Public and publicly guaranteed	58	45	34	36	41	64	108	85
Official creditors	58	44	33	36	41	46	57	48
Private creditors	0	1	1	0	0	18	51	37
Private nonguaranteed	0	10	16	13	9	11	15	17
Debt resource inflows								
Net debt inflows	-153	242	618	299	612	236	770	671
Official creditors (incl. IMF)	5	224	405	471	434	318	285	527
Private creditors	-158	18	214	-172	178	-81	485	144
Long-term	3	18	-34	-37	357	-63	485	3
Public and publicly guaranteed	5	-2	-4	-3	197	-2	500	2
Private nonguaranteed	-1	20	-30	-34	159	-62	-15	2
Short-term	-161	..	248	-135	-179	-18	..	141
Non-debt resource inflows								
Foreign direct investment	63	168	351	454	330	275	338	338
Portfolio equity	-2	-6	8	-93	-2	23	..	..
Currency composition (%)								
Euro	..	10.9	9.9	15.9	17.8	18.9	17.3	20.8
U.S.dollars	45.0	59.5	41.0	37.0	39.5	38.4	43.8	35.9
Major economic aggregates								
Gross national income (GNI)	4,589	8,544	11,224	13,339	12,591	12,722	14,282	13,969
Exports of goods, services & prim. income	1,383	2,562	3,075	3,785	3,286	3,407	4,025	..
Personal transfers & comp. of employees	233	789	1,192	1,476	1,350	1,478	..	..
Imports of goods, services & prim. income	1,929	3,991	5,676	7,353	5,613	5,557	6,917	..
Primary income on FDI	75	173	141	178	147	135	..	..
Current account balance	-332	-676	-1,311	-1,884	-854	-600	-1	..
International reserves	388	1,186	1,660	1,602	2,123	2,047	1,946	2,082
Ratios								
External debt stocks to exports (%)	264.2	150.8	84.1	75.3	113.8	114.7	107.4	..
External debt stocks to GNI (%)	79.6	45.2	23.0	21.4	29.7	30.7	30.3	35.1
Debt service to exports (%)	16.3	7.9	6.2	4.8	6.0	8.9	9.0	..
Short-term to external debt stocks (%)	4.0	0.9	12.8	6.9	0.5	..	..	2.9
Multilateral to external debt stocks (%)	52.4	72.9	53.4	54.4	48.3	50.5	51.8	51.6
Reserves to external debt stocks (%)	10.6	30.7	64.2	56.2	56.8	52.4	45.0	42.5
Reserves to imports (months)	2.4	3.6	3.5	2.6	4.5	4.4	3.4	..

Notes:

Short-term debt is based on data from the BIS. Data include the effects of Paris Club debt restructuring agreement and HIPC and MDRI debt relief.

SERBIA

(US$ million, unless otherwise indicated)

	2000	2005	2007	2008	2009	2010	2011	2012
Summary external debt data								
External debt stocks	**11,573**	**16,159**	**26,212**	**30,493**	**33,814**	**32,935**	**31,724**	**34,438**
Long-term external debt	6,789	12,970	23,873	26,719	27,915	27,417	27,779	30,904
Short-term external debt	4,558	2,242	2,249	3,687	3,600	2,798	1,162	1,018
interest arrears on long-term	3,668	728	703	704	712	352	324	367
Use of IMF credit	226	947	90	87	2,299	2,720	2,783	2,517
Long-term external debt								
Debt outstanding and disbursed	**6,789**	**12,970**	**23,873**	**26,719**	**27,915**	**27,417**	**27,779**	**30,904**
Public and publicly guaranteed	6,178	7,756	8,469	8,399	8,839	9,504	11,339	13,695
Official creditors	4,243	6,679	7,289	7,223	7,664	8,172	8,738	9,318
Private creditors	1,935	1,077	1,180	1,175	1,175	1,332	2,601	4,378
Private nonguaranteed	611	5,214	15,404	18,320	19,076	17,912	16,440	17,208
Disbursements	**222**	**2,904**	**6,661**	**6,996**	**4,533**	**4,617**	**6,280**	**6,371**
Public and publicly guaranteed	222	311	316	294	971	1,388	2,541	2,843
Official creditors	187	311	275	291	971	1,149	1,137	954
Private creditors	35	0	41	3	0	239	1,404	1,889
Private nonguaranteed	0	2,593	6,345	6,703	3,562	3,230	3,739	3,528
Principal repayments	**0**	**570**	**2,334**	**3,486**	**3,613**	**3,431**	**4,257**	**4,585**
Public and publicly guaranteed	0	48	184	181	158	351	451	617
Official creditors	0	48	184	180	154	275	350	488
Private creditors	0	0	0	1	4	76	101	129
Private nonguaranteed	0	522	2,149	3,305	3,454	3,081	3,806	3,968
Interest payments	**0**	**367**	**840**	**1,136**	**916**	**759**	**905**	**983**
Public and publicly guaranteed	0	237	415	354	348	321	348	430
Official creditors	0	194	369	328	303	241	257	268
Private creditors	0	44	46	26	45	80	91	162
Private nonguaranteed	0	129	425	782	568	438	557	552
Debt resource inflows								
Net debt inflows	51	2,827	4,216	4,948	2,401	1,201	489	1,330
Official creditors (incl. IMF)	268	241	91	111	2,392	1,332	861	198
Private creditors	-217	2,586	4,126	4,837	9	-130	-372	1,133
Long-term	35	2,071	4,237	3,400	104	312	1,235	1,320
Public and publicly guaranteed	35	0	41	1	-4	163	1,303	1,760
Private nonguaranteed	..	2,071	4,196	3,398	108	149	-68	-440
Short-term	-252	515	-112	1,437	-95	-442	-1,607	-188
Non-debt resource inflows								
Foreign direct investment	52	2,051	3,432	2,996	1,936	1,340	2,700	355
Portfolio equity	..	..	772	-57	22	84	69	-24
Currency composition (%)								
Euro	..	32.3	37.8	37.6	42.4	46.7	47.5	44.3
U.S.dollars	24.6	62.5	55.3	55.0	50.6	46.2	46.5	50.6
Major economic aggregates								
Gross national income (GNI)	6,082	24,910	38,137	46,395	39,560	36,099	42,238	36,318
Exports of goods, services & prim. income	..	..	12,579	15,792	12,544	13,916	16,561	16,012
Personal transfers & comp. of employees	..	..	3,062	2,708	3,933	3,349	3,271	2,763
Imports of goods, services & prim. income	..	..	23,401	29,927	20,348	20,884	24,773	23,788
Primary income on FDI	..	..	596	890	451	552	531	602
Current account balance	..	..	-6,890	-10,395	-2,867	-2,550	-3,834	-4,002
International reserves	392	5,628	13,893	11,123	14,769	12,715	14,877	13,585
Ratios								
External debt stocks to exports (%)	..	..	208.4	193.1	269.6	236.7	191.6	215.1
External debt stocks to GNI (%)	190.3	64.9	68.7	65.7	85.5	91.2	75.1	94.8
Debt service to exports (%)	..	..	25.7	30.0	37.0	30.9	31.5	36.7
Short-term to external debt stocks (%)	39.4	13.9	8.6	12.1	10.6	8.5	3.7	3.0
Multilateral to external debt stocks (%)	12.4	22.0	17.2	14.9	13.0	14.8	17.1	17.6
Reserves to external debt stocks (%)	3.4	34.8	53.0	36.5	43.7	38.6	46.9	39.4
Reserves to imports (months)	..	..	7.1	4.5	8.7	7.3	7.2	6.9

Notes:

Beginning 2006, the data for Serbia exclude Montenegro.

SEYCHELLES

(US$ million, unless otherwise indicated)

	2000	2005	2007	2008	2009	2010	2011	2012
Summary external debt data								
External debt stocks	**304**	**672**	**1,410**	**1,502**	**1,707**	**1,487**	**1,778**	**2,024**
Long-term external debt	220	398	626	650	708	463	457	475
Short-term external debt	84	273	784	842	968	980	1,272	1,494
interest arrears on long-term	5	57	60	78	110	24	16	13
Use of IMF credit	1	1	1	10	32	44	49	54
Long-term external debt								
Debt outstanding and disbursed	**220**	**398**	**626**	**650**	**708**	**463**	**457**	**475**
Public and publicly guaranteed	220	398	626	650	708	463	457	475
Official creditors	159	224	210	196	271	213	209	228
Private creditors	61	175	416	453	436	250	249	247
Private nonguaranteed	..	..	..	..	..	..	..	..
Disbursements	**38**	**59**	**151**	**84**	**34**	**49**	**7**	**23**
Public and publicly guaranteed	38	59	151	84	34	49	7	23
Official creditors	19	8	11	4	25	33	6	20
Private creditors	19	51	140	80	9	16	1	3
Private nonguaranteed	..	..	..	..	..	..	..	..
Principal repayments	**10**	**41**	**46**	**53**	**43**	**9**	**8**	**9**
Public and publicly guaranteed	10	41	46	53	43	9	8	9
Official creditors	5	11	20	15	18	6	7	5
Private creditors	5	30	26	38	25	3	1	5
Private nonguaranteed	..	..	..	..	..	..	..	..
Interest payments	**7**	**11**	**28**	**21**	**8**	**28**	**9**	**12**
Public and publicly guaranteed	7	11	28	21	8	28	9	12
Official creditors	2	3	3	4	4	2	3	4
Private creditors	5	8	25	18	4	26	6	8
Private nonguaranteed	..	..	..	..	..	..	..	..
Debt resource inflows								
Net debt inflows	71	180	284	81	93	151	305	244
Official creditors (incl. IMF)	14	-3	-9	-1	15	40	4	20
Private creditors	57	183	292	82	78	111	300	224
Long-term	15	21	113	42	-16	13	0	-1
Public and publicly guaranteed	15	21	113	42	-16	13	0	-1
Private nonguaranteed	..	..	..	..	..	..	..	..
Short-term	42	162	179	40	94	98	300	225
Non-debt resource inflows								
Foreign direct investment	24	86	26	21	13	13	139	12
Portfolio equity	..	..	..	..	..	..	..	..
Currency composition (%)								
Euro	..	13.7	23.1	20.0	26.1	17.5	17.0	18.6
U.S.dollars	35.6	55.3	61.5	65.8	57.6	62.9	63.9	63.4
Major economic aggregates								
Gross national income (GNI)	582	879	970	899	801	926	1,009	985
Exports of goods, services & prim. income	492	729	129	102	65	71	77	69
Personal transfers & comp. of employees	3	12	1	0	1	1	2	1
Imports of goods, services & prim. income	545	935	152	133	80	89	101	92
Primary income on FDI	8	20	2	2	1	-1	4	3
Current account balance	-43	-174	-28	-32	-15	-18	-23	-20
International reserves	44	56	41	64	191	236	290	319
Ratios								
External debt stocks to exports (%)	61.9	92.1	1,096.9	1,466.4	2,624.8	2,108.9	2,296.8	2,912.4
External debt stocks to GNI (%)	52.3	76.4	145.5	167.0	213.1	160.5	176.3	205.6
Debt service to exports (%)	4.2	8.1	85.6	90.2	94.5	68.7	44.7	64.3
Short-term to external debt stocks (%)	27.6	40.6	55.6	56.1	56.7	65.9	71.5	73.8
Multilateral to external debt stocks (%)	18.9	10.7	3.6	2.9	2.6	5.0	4.1	4.4
Reserves to external debt stocks (%)	14.4	8.4	2.9	4.2	11.2	15.8	16.3	15.7
Reserves to imports (months)	1.0	0.7	3.2	5.7	28.5	31.9	34.6	41.7

Notes:

Short-term debt is based on data from the BIS.

SIERRA LEONE

(US$ million, unless otherwise indicated)

	2000	2005	2007	2008	2009	2010	2011	2012
Summary external debt data								
External debt stocks	**1,213**	**1,776**	**551**	**634**	**857**	**931**	**1,051**	**1,121**
Long-term external debt	973	1,538	482	545	605	661	742	833
Short-term external debt	44	21	5	9	23	4	35	14
interest arrears on long-term	36	11	0	0	0	0	0	0
Use of IMF credit	196	217	64	80	229	266	274	274
Long-term external debt								
Debt outstanding and disbursed	**973**	**1,538**	**482**	**545**	**605**	**661**	**742**	**833**
Public and publicly guaranteed	973	1,538	482	545	605	661	742	833
Official creditors	967	1,325	271	334	394	450	534	624
Private creditors	5	213	211	211	211	211	208	210
Private nonguaranteed	..	..	..	..	..	..	..	..
Disbursements	**77**	**51**	**31**	**69**	**62**	**66**	**95**	**107**
Public and publicly guaranteed	77	51	31	69	62	66	95	107
Official creditors	77	51	31	69	62	66	95	107
Private creditors	0	0	0	0	0	0	0	0
Private nonguaranteed	..	..	..	..	..	..	..	..
Principal repayments	**10**	**5**	**5**	**2**	**3**	**5**	**7**	**8**
Public and publicly guaranteed	10	5	5	2	3	5	7	8
Official creditors	10	5	5	2	3	5	7	8
Private creditors	0	0	0	0	0	0	0	0
Private nonguaranteed	..	..	..	..	..	..	..	..
Interest payments	**9**	**9**	**4**	**3**	**4**	**4**	**6**	**6**
Public and publicly guaranteed	9	9	4	3	4	4	6	6
Official creditors	9	9	4	3	4	4	6	6
Private creditors	0	0	0	0	0	0	0	0
Private nonguaranteed	..	..	..	..	..	..	..	..
Debt resource inflows								
Net debt inflows	57	54	31	89	92	83	128	78
Official creditors (incl. IMF)	55	64	26	85	78	102	97	99
Private creditors	1	-10	5	4	14	-19	31	-21
Long-term	0	0	0	0	0	0	0	0
Public and publicly guaranteed	0	0	0	0	0	0	0	0
Private nonguaranteed	..	..	..	..	..	..	..	..
Short-term	1	-10	5	4	14	-19	31	-21
Non-debt resource inflows								
Foreign direct investment	39	91	95	53	110	238	715	548
Portfolio equity	..	..	..	..	6	0	0	7
Currency composition (%)								
Euro	..	10.4	5.1	3.9	3.2	2.4	1.7	1.9
U.S.dollars	44.9	55.0	68.4	64.5	64.0	64.4	64.8	62.7
Major economic aggregates								
Gross national income (GNI)	616	1,590	2,054	2,430	2,419	2,526	2,903	3,796
Exports of goods, services & prim. income	62	267	374	348	380	427	548	1,350
Personal transfers & comp. of employees	7	2	42	23	36	44	59	61
Imports of goods, services & prim. income	262	509	637	685	797	1,191	2,711	2,689
Primary income on FDI	2	41	122	76	39	46	219	130
Current account balance	-112	-105	-160	-225	-327	-585	-1,914	-1,102
International reserves	49	171	217	220	405	409	439	478
Ratios								
External debt stocks to exports (%)	1,941.0	664.7	147.4	182.1	225.7	218.3	191.8	83.1
External debt stocks to GNI (%)	196.8	111.7	26.8	26.1	35.4	36.9	36.2	29.5
Debt service to exports (%)	76.4	6.9	2.9	1.7	2.1	2.7	3.4	1.5
Short-term to external debt stocks (%)	3.6	1.2	0.9	1.4	2.7	0.4	3.3	1.2
Multilateral to external debt stocks (%)	47.5	48.6	40.4	43.1	37.6	39.9	39.6	42.9
Reserves to external debt stocks (%)	4.1	9.6	39.3	34.7	47.3	43.9	41.8	42.6
Reserves to imports (months)	2.3	4.0	4.1	3.9	6.1	4.1	1.9	2.1

Notes:

Short-term debt is based on data from the BIS. Data include the effects of Paris Club debt restructuring agreement and HIPC and MDRI debt relief.

SOLOMON ISLANDS

(US$ million, unless otherwise indicated)

	2000	2005	2007	2008	2009	2010	2011	2012
Summary external debt data								
External debt stocks	**156.2**	**167.4**	**178.3**	**166.9**	**172.4**	**230.8**	**257.5**	**228.1**
Long-term external debt	152.1	151.2	173.9	162.8	154.4	201.9	210.3	191.5
Short-term external debt	3.2	15.3	3.4	3.1	2.5	4.0	12.9	2.0
interest arrears on long-term	1.8	12.3	3.4	3.1	1.5	4.0	8.9	0.0
Use of IMF credit	0.9	0.9	1.0	1.0	15.5	24.9	34.4	34.6
Long-term external debt								
Debt outstanding and disbursed	**152.1**	**151.2**	**173.9**	**162.8**	**154.4**	**201.9**	**210.3**	**191.5**
Public and publicly guaranteed	120.7	144.2	148.1	137.1	132.9	125.3	117.8	110.2
Official creditors	117.3	143.8	147.5	136.6	132.7	125.2	117.8	110.2
Private creditors	3.4	0.4	0.6	0.4	0.2	0.1	0.0	0.0
Private nonguaranteed	31.5	7.0	25.9	25.8	21.5	76.6	92.4	81.3
Disbursements	**3.4**	**5.7**	**24.5**	**1.1**	**13.7**	**36.8**	**27.3**	**2.2**
Public and publicly guaranteed	3.4	5.7	4.5	0.1	0.0	0.0	0.0	0.0
Official creditors	3.4	5.3	4.5	0.1	0.0	0.0	0.0	0.0
Private creditors	0.0	0.4	0.0	0.0	0.0	0.0	0.0	0.0
Private nonguaranteed	0.0	0.0	20.0	1.0	13.7	36.8	27.3	2.2
Principal repayments	**6.2**	**10.0**	**10.7**	**10.8**	**7.6**	**17.5**	**12.6**	**21.8**
Public and publicly guaranteed	2.7	5.8	8.3	10.8	6.5	8.6	6.6	6.5
Official creditors	2.7	3.2	7.9	10.7	6.3	8.4	6.5	6.5
Private creditors	0.0	2.6	0.4	0.1	0.2	0.2	0.1	0.0
Private nonguaranteed	3.5	4.2	2.4	0.0	1.1	8.9	6.0	15.3
Interest payments	**2.7**	**3.9**	**3.2**	**4.3**	**2.4**	**3.2**	**2.6**	**8.1**
Public and publicly guaranteed	0.8	1.7	3.2	4.3	1.8	1.7	1.7	1.5
Official creditors	0.8	1.7	3.2	4.3	1.8	1.7	1.7	1.5
Private creditors	0.0	0.0	0.0	0.0	0.0	0.0	0.0	0.0
Private nonguaranteed	1.9	2.3	0.0	0.0	0.5	1.5	0.9	6.5
Debt resource inflows								
Net debt inflows	-4.4	-2.3	11.8	-9.7	7.1	27.9	28.5	-21.3
Official creditors (incl. IMF)	0.6	2.1	-3.4	-10.6	-6.3	1.1	3.3	-6.3
Private creditors	-5.0	-4.4	15.2	0.9	13.4	26.8	25.2	-15.1
Long-term	-3.5	-6.4	17.2	0.9	12.4	27.8	21.2	-13.1
Public and publicly guaranteed	..	-2.1	-0.4	-0.1	-0.2	-0.2	-0.1	0.0
Private nonguaranteed	-3.5	-4.2	17.6	1.0	12.6	28.0	21.3	-13.1
Short-term	-1.5	2.0	-2.0	..	1.0	-1.0	4.0	-2.0
Non-debt resource inflows								
Foreign direct investment	13.0	0.5	42.8	90.6	115.4	121.6	105.4	68.3
Portfolio equity	..	..	..	..	..	..	..	..
Currency composition (%)								
Euro	..	7.1	9.2	7.2	7.3	5.1	3.7	3.7
U.S.dollars	67.1	73.7	75.4	78.0	77.7	79.2	80.6	81.4
Major economic aggregates								
Gross national income (GNI)	435.5	415.5	549.7	551.5	473.1	554.7	673.3	699.5
Exports of goods, services & prim. income	128.8	154.9	237.7	289.7	247.5	347.8	582.9	665.1
Personal transfers & comp. of employees	4.3	7.2	2.1	1.7	2.5	1.7	1.9	17.2
Imports of goods, services & prim. income	176.4	250.1	411.4	524.0	492.5	690.3	771.9	761.3
Primary income on FDI	8.3	5.3	41.0	103.5	135.5	127.0	133.5	84.2
Current account balance	-41.0	-90.2	-80.9	-124.4	-128.7	-210.1	-60.3	2.2
International reserves	32.0	94.8	120.5	88.8	146.0	265.8	412.3	469.5
Ratios								
External debt stocks to exports (%)	121.3	108.1	75.0	57.6	69.7	66.4	44.2	34.3
External debt stocks to GNI (%)	35.9	40.3	32.4	30.3	36.5	41.6	38.2	32.6
Debt service to exports (%)	7.1	9.1	5.9	5.2	4.0	6.0	2.6	4.5
Short-term to external debt stocks (%)	2.1	9.1	1.9	1.8	1.5	1.7	5.0	0.9
Multilateral to external debt stocks (%)	64.3	63.9	68.2	68.1	64.6	45.8	38.8	41.2
Reserves to external debt stocks (%)	20.5	56.7	67.6	53.2	84.7	115.2	160.1	205.8
Reserves to imports (months)	2.2	4.5	3.5	2.0	3.6	4.6	6.4	7.4

Notes:

Short-term debt is based on data from the BIS.

SOMALIA

(US$ million, unless otherwise indicated)

	2000	2005	2007	2008	2009	2010	2011	2012
Summary external debt data								
External debt stocks	**2,579**	**2,770**	**2,965**	**2,970**	**3,046**	**3,045**	**3,053**	**3,055**
Long-term external debt	1,825	1,882	1,979	1,983	1,987	1,990	1,992	1,985
Short-term external debt	591	709	788	793	810	811	818	827
interest arrears on long-term	569	709	788	793	810	811	818	827
Use of IMF credit	164	180	199	194	248	244	243	243
Long-term external debt								
Debt outstanding and disbursed	**1,825**	**1,882**	**1,979**	**1,983**	**1,987**	**1,990**	**1,992**	**1,985**
Public and publicly guaranteed	1,825	1,882	1,979	1,983	1,987	1,990	1,992	1,985
Official creditors	1,792	1,846	1,940	1,946	1,950	1,954	1,955	1,948
Private creditors	33	35	38	37	38	37	36	36
Private nonguaranteed	..	..	..	..	..	..	..	..
Disbursements	**0**	**0**	**0**	**0**	**0**	**0**	**0**	**0**
Public and publicly guaranteed	0	0	0	0	0	0	0	0
Official creditors	0	0	0	0	0	0	0	0
Private creditors	0	0	0	0	0	0	0	0
Private nonguaranteed	..	..	..	..	..	..	..	..
Principal repayments	**0**	**0**	**0**	**0**	**0**	**0**	**0**	**0**
Public and publicly guaranteed	0	0	0	0	0	0	0	0
Official creditors	0	0	0	0	0	0	0	0
Private creditors	0	0	0	0	0	0	0	0
Private nonguaranteed	..	..	..	..	..	..	..	..
Interest payments	**0**	**0**	**0**	**0**	**0**	**0**	**0**	**0**
Public and publicly guaranteed	0	0	0	0	0	0	0	0
Official creditors	0	0	0	0	0	0	0	0
Private creditors	0	0	0	0	0	0	0	0
Private nonguaranteed	..	..	..	..	..	..	..	..
Debt resource inflows								
Net debt inflows	-7	0	0	0	0	0	0	0
Official creditors (incl. IMF)	0	0	0	0	0	0	0	0
Private creditors	-7	0	0	0	0	0	0	0
Long-term	0	0	0	0	0	0	0	0
Public and publicly guaranteed	0	0	0	0	0	0	0	0
Private nonguaranteed	..	..	..	..	..	..	..	..
Short-term	-7	..	..	..	..	..	..	..
Non-debt resource inflows								
Foreign direct investment	0	24	141	87	108	112	102	107
Portfolio equity	..	..	..	..	..	..	..	..
Currency composition (%)								
Euro	..	5.6	6.6	6.3	6.5	6.0	5.8	5.9
U.S.dollars	52.0	51.8	50.6	50.4	50.4	50.0	49.9	50.1
Major economic aggregates								
Gross national income (GNI)	..	..	..	..	..	..	..	..
Exports of goods, services & prim. income	..	..	..	..	..	..	..	..
Personal transfers & comp. of employees	..	..	..	..	..	..	..	..
Imports of goods, services & prim. income	..	..	..	..	..	..	..	..
Primary income on FDI	..	..	..	..	..	..	..	..
Current account balance	..	..	..	..	..	..	..	..
International reserves	..	..	..	..	..	..	..	..
Ratios								
External debt stocks to exports (%)	..	..	..	..	..	..	..	..
External debt stocks to GNI (%)	..	..	..	..	..	..	..	..
Debt service to exports (%)	..	..	..	..	..	..	..	..
Short-term to external debt stocks (%)	22.9	25.6	26.6	26.7	26.6	26.6	26.8	27.1
Multilateral to external debt stocks (%)	27.5	27.3	27.3	27.0	26.4	26.3	26.2	26.1
Reserves to external debt stocks (%)	..	..	..	..	..	..	..	..
Reserves to imports (months)	..	..	..	..	..	..	..	..

Notes:

Long-term public and publicly guaranteed debt data are World Bank staff estimates based on the original terms of the loans.

SOUTH AFRICA

(US$ million, unless otherwise indicated)

	2000	2005	2007	2008	2009	2010	2011	2012
Summary external debt data								
External debt stocks	**25,148**	**48,044**	**69,364**	**68,052**	**77,275**	**102,348**	**115,184**	**137,501**
Long-term external debt	15,308	33,453	44,972	42,251	53,190	77,869	91,909	106,889
Short-term external debt	9,553	14,276	24,044	25,462	21,286	21,730	20,534	27,868
interest arrears on long-term	..	..	..	..	..	..	..	..
Use of IMF credit	287	315	348	339	2,799	2,750	2,741	2,744
Long-term external debt								
Debt outstanding and disbursed	**15,308**	**33,453**	**44,972**	**42,251**	**53,190**	**77,869**	**91,909**	**106,889**
Public and publicly guaranteed	9,088	21,834	19,707	20,016	24,658	39,017	46,669	57,351
Official creditors	145	286	291	259	227	1,139	1,449	2,782
Private creditors	8,943	21,547	19,416	19,757	24,430	37,878	45,220	54,568
Private nonguaranteed	6,220	11,619	25,265	22,235	28,532	38,852	45,240	49,538
Disbursements	**3,611**	**5,641**	**8,727**	**1,871**	**4,339**	**5,698**	**8,036**	**9,312**
Public and publicly guaranteed	1,597	2,678	1,870	1,219	2,332	3,777	5,050	3,915
Official creditors	91	58	0	3	32	913	490	1,415
Private creditors	1,506	2,620	1,870	1,216	2,300	2,864	4,560	2,500
Private nonguaranteed	2,014	2,963	6,857	652	2,007	1,921	2,986	5,397
Principal repayments	**2,631**	**3,124**	**2,306**	**3,677**	**2,127**	**2,608**	**2,482**	**4,937**
Public and publicly guaranteed	1,649	2,870	808	2,353	1,419	1,278	1,165	2,514
Official creditors	0	27	26	26	38	40	42	37
Private creditors	1,649	2,844	782	2,327	1,381	1,238	1,123	2,477
Private nonguaranteed	982	254	1,498	1,324	708	1,330	1,317	2,423
Interest payments	**746**	**1,321**	**1,694**	**1,623**	**1,557**	**2,949**	**3,419**	**3,197**
Public and publicly guaranteed	549	1,109	1,281	1,192	1,097	1,573	2,061	2,567
Official creditors	1	12	18	16	10	20	40	62
Private creditors	548	1,098	1,264	1,176	1,087	1,553	2,021	2,505
Private nonguaranteed	196	212	413	431	460	1,377	1,358	631
Debt resource inflows								
Net debt inflows	-282	5,597	9,899	-388	-1,964	3,534	4,358	11,709
Official creditors (incl. IMF)	91	31	-26	-23	-6	873	448	1,378
Private creditors	-373	5,566	9,925	-365	-1,958	2,661	3,910	10,331
Long-term	889	2,485	6,447	-1,783	2,218	2,217	5,106	2,997
Public and publicly guaranteed	-143	-224	1,088	-1,111	919	1,626	3,437	23
Private nonguaranteed	1,032	2,709	5,359	-672	1,299	591	1,669	2,974
Short-term	-1,262	3,081	3,478	1,418	-4,176	444	-1,196	7,334
Non-debt resource inflows								
Foreign direct investment	969	6,522	6,587	9,885	7,624	3,693	5,889	4,644
Portfolio equity	4,169	7,230	8,670	-4,707	9,364	5,826	-3,769	-679
Currency composition (%)								
Euro	..	9.6	19.1	14.2	11.9	7.0	5.7	4.7
U.S.dollars	92.0	55.9	51.1	53.5	49.8	36.6	40.9	26.5
Major economic aggregates								
Gross national income (GNI)	129,704	242,110	276,404	264,199	277,670	356,012	392,634	375,786
Exports of goods, services & prim. income	39,507	72,202	97,135	104,867	82,551	104,355	122,985	114,567
Personal transfers & comp. of employees	344	614	792	783	862	1,070	1,158	1,085
Imports of goods, services & prim. income	38,771	78,267	114,803	122,644	91,219	112,194	134,696	134,834
Primary income on FDI	2,329	4,320	8,666	8,031	5,279	6,165	8,375	8,144
Current account balance	-191	-8,518	-20,018	-20,110	-11,353	-10,117	-13,683	-24,069
International reserves	6,083	18,579	29,589	30,584	35,237	38,175	42,595	43,995
Ratios								
External debt stocks to exports (%)	63.7	66.5	71.4	64.9	93.6	98.1	93.7	120.0
External debt stocks to GNI (%)	19.4	19.8	25.1	25.8	27.8	28.7	29.3	36.6
Debt service to exports (%)	9.9	6.9	5.0	5.8	5.4	6.0	5.3	7.9
Short-term to external debt stocks (%)	38.0	29.7	34.7	37.4	27.5	21.2	17.8	20.3
Multilateral to external debt stocks (%)	0.6	0.6	0.4	0.4	0.3	1.1	1.3	2.0
Reserves to external debt stocks (%)	24.2	38.7	42.7	44.9	45.6	37.3	37.0	32.0
Reserves to imports (months)	1.9	2.8	3.1	3.0	4.6	4.1	3.8	3.9

Notes:

Long-term public and publicly guaranteed and long-term private nonguaranteed debt data are World Bank staff estimates based on reports provided by the country.

SRI LANKA

(US$ million, unless otherwise indicated)

	2000	2005	2007	2008	2009	2010	2011	2012
Summary external debt data								
External debt stocks	**9,173**	**11,472**	**14,468**	**15,710**	**17,833**	**21,125**	**24,003**	**25,382**
Long-term external debt	8,236	9,997	12,473	13,345	14,642	17,392	19,747	20,377
Short-term external debt	685	992	1,632	2,087	1,849	1,813	1,931	1,887
interest arrears on long-term	112	0	0	0	0	0	0	0
Use of IMF credit	253	483	363	278	1,341	1,920	2,325	3,118
Long-term external debt								
Debt outstanding and disbursed	**8,236**	**9,997**	**12,473**	**13,345**	**14,642**	**17,392**	**19,747**	**20,377**
Public and publicly guaranteed	7,868	9,609	11,834	12,611	13,676	16,473	18,734	20,374
Official creditors	6,928	8,982	10,372	11,285	11,933	13,603	14,793	15,878
Private creditors	940	627	1,462	1,327	1,743	2,870	3,941	4,497
Private nonguaranteed	368	388	639	734	967	919	1,013	3
Disbursements	**732**	**929**	**1,698**	**1,238**	**2,209**	**3,086**	**2,990**	**3,312**
Public and publicly guaranteed	563	818	1,524	1,083	1,822	2,989	2,746	3,312
Official creditors	348	670	754	789	1,160	1,805	1,607	2,143
Private creditors	215	149	769	293	662	1,183	1,138	1,169
Private nonguaranteed	169	111	174	156	387	97	244	0
Principal repayments	**453**	**228**	**534**	**804**	**967**	**715**	**805**	**1,200**
Public and publicly guaranteed	439	209	506	743	812	570	651	1,199
Official creditors	216	123	449	518	555	507	587	604
Private creditors	223	86	57	224	257	64	64	595
Private nonguaranteed	14	19	28	61	154	145	154	0
Interest payments	**213**	**106**	**218**	**286**	**325**	**616**	**448**	**515**
Public and publicly guaranteed	178	84	191	251	285	596	405	515
Official creditors	125	65	164	178	227	308	268	292
Private creditors	54	19	27	73	58	288	137	223
Private nonguaranteed	35	22	26	35	40	20	43	0
Debt resource inflows								
Net debt inflows	-25	1,160	1,935	811	1,545	2,931	2,725	2,854
Official creditors (incl. IMF)	45	661	300	193	1,145	1,895	1,443	2,325
Private creditors	-70	499	1,636	619	399	1,036	1,283	529
Long-term	148	155	859	164	637	1,072	1,165	574
Public and publicly guaranteed	-7	63	713	69	405	1,120	1,075	574
Private nonguaranteed	155	92	146	95	233	-48	90	0
Short-term	-218	344	777	455	-238	-36	118	-44
Non-debt resource inflows								
Foreign direct investment	173	272	603	752	404	478	956	898
Portfolio equity	..	-216	-322	-488	-382	-1,049	-171	305
Currency composition (%)								
Euro	..	7.8	9.5	9.2	9.5	8.0	6.9	6.9
U.S.dollars	38.4	40.8	44.3	40.4	42.7	47.7	51.7	56.8
Major economic aggregates								
Gross national income (GNI)	16,016	24,107	31,997	39,744	41,581	48,948	58,535	58,258
Exports of goods, services & prim. income	6,527	7,963	9,864	10,338	9,099	11,423	14,109	13,802
Personal transfers & comp. of employees	1,166	1,976	2,507	2,925	3,337	4,123	5,153	6,000
Imports of goods, services & prim. income	8,554	10,441	13,575	16,889	12,318	16,159	23,368	23,198
Primary income on FDI	109	115	349	470	230	303	385	445
Current account balance	-1,044	-650	-1,401	-3,885	-215	-1,075	-4,615	-4,003
International reserves	1,039	2,650	3,380	2,469	4,616	6,710	6,248	6,378
Ratios								
External debt stocks to exports (%)	140.5	144.1	146.7	152.0	196.0	184.9	170.1	183.9
External debt stocks to GNI (%)	57.3	47.6	45.2	39.5	42.9	43.2	41.0	43.6
Debt service to exports (%)	12.1	5.3	8.5	11.9	15.6	12.3	9.4	13.3
Short-term to external debt stocks (%)	7.5	8.6	11.3	13.3	10.4	8.6	8.0	7.4
Multilateral to external debt stocks (%)	37.2	39.7	37.1	35.4	32.9	28.8	26.4	26.1
Reserves to external debt stocks (%)	11.3	23.1	23.4	15.7	25.9	31.8	26.0	25.1
Reserves to imports (months)	1.5	3.0	3.0	1.8	4.5	5.0	3.2	3.3

ST. LUCIA

(US$ million, unless otherwise indicated)

	2000	2005	2007	2008	2009	2010	2011	2012
Summary external debt data								
External debt stocks	**222.2**	**415.7**	**474.9**	**832.4**	**433.1**	**579.6**	**451.0**	**472.8**
Long-term external debt	153.5	238.6	300.4	316.3	314.9	321.3	309.9	289.0
Short-term external debt	67.8	176.0	173.3	514.9	84.6	225.3	99.9	142.6
interest arrears on long-term	0.0	0.0	0.3	0.9	2.6	5.3	3.9	1.6
Use of IMF credit	1.0	1.1	1.2	1.1	33.6	33.0	41.2	41.2
Long-term external debt								
Debt outstanding and disbursed	**153.5**	**238.6**	**300.4**	**316.3**	**314.9**	**321.3**	**309.9**	**289.0**
Public and publicly guaranteed	153.5	238.6	300.4	316.3	314.9	321.3	309.9	289.0
Official creditors	120.7	164.6	201.8	232.7	239.8	258.0	258.6	249.6
Private creditors	32.8	74.0	98.6	83.6	75.1	63.3	51.4	39.5
Private nonguaranteed	..	..	..	..	..	..	..	..
Disbursements	**48.7**	**12.6**	**24.4**	**13.0**	**25.8**	**36.4**	**20.0**	**7.0**
Public and publicly guaranteed	48.7	12.6	24.4	13.0	25.8	36.4	20.0	7.0
Official creditors	16.8	12.6	24.4	13.0	22.4	36.4	20.0	7.0
Private creditors	31.9	0.0	0.0	0.0	3.4	0.0	0.0	0.0
Private nonguaranteed	..	..	..	..	..	..	..	..
Principal repayments	**20.9**	**14.2**	**26.4**	**32.4**	**27.8**	**29.9**	**31.4**	**28.0**
Public and publicly guaranteed	20.9	14.2	26.4	32.4	27.8	29.9	31.4	28.0
Official creditors	11.7	9.5	14.5	17.5	16.0	18.0	19.6	16.1
Private creditors	9.2	4.7	11.9	15.0	11.9	11.9	11.9	11.9
Private nonguaranteed	..	..	..	..	..	..	..	..
Interest payments	**6.4**	**12.8**	**14.9**	**15.1**	**13.4**	**10.6**	**11.3**	**10.5**
Public and publicly guaranteed	6.4	12.8	14.9	15.1	13.4	10.6	11.3	10.5
Official creditors	5.2	6.3	6.2	8.3	7.4	7.4	6.7	6.4
Private creditors	1.2	6.5	8.7	6.9	6.1	3.2	4.6	4.1
Private nonguaranteed	..	..	..	..	..	..	..	..
Debt resource inflows								
Net debt inflows	40.3	65.4	54.1	321.6	-423.4	144.5	-127.0	23.9
Official creditors (incl. IMF)	5.1	3.1	10.0	-4.5	17.1	18.4	8.9	-9.2
Private creditors	35.2	62.3	44.1	326.0	-440.5	126.1	-135.9	33.1
Long-term	22.7	-4.7	-11.9	-15.0	-8.5	-11.9	-11.9	-11.9
Public and publicly guaranteed	22.7	-4.7	-11.9	-15.0	-8.5	-11.9	-11.9	-11.9
Private nonguaranteed	..	..	..	..	..	..	..	..
Short-term	12.5	67.0	56.0	341.0	-432.0	138.0	-124.0	45.0
Non-debt resource inflows								
Foreign direct investment	53.7	78.2	271.9	161.2	146.4	121.3	112.4	109.4
Portfolio equity	..	..	..	..	..	..	..	..
Currency composition (%)								
Euro	..	6.6	8.1	6.0	5.6	4.3	3.8	3.6
U.S.dollars	55.0	69.0	67.5	71.1	71.4	73.4	72.8	70.6
Major economic aggregates								
Gross national income (GNI)	719.9	836.0	1,057.2	1,093.2	1,121.7	1,160.0	1,195.4	1,172.4
Exports of goods, services & prim. income	380.6	533.0	469.5	544.3	560.5	626.6	588.4	605.7
Personal transfers & comp. of employees	26.4	27.1	28.6	28.9	28.0	29.0	29.4	29.8
Imports of goods, services & prim. income	494.2	675.5	827.8	900.4	709.6	844.7	852.0	807.7
Primary income on FDI	33.4	51.1	45.1	52.5	35.3	31.7	12.0	12.2
Current account balance	-94.8	-129.5	-344.7	-339.9	-136.7	-202.8	-243.7	-184.4
International reserves	78.8	116.4	153.7	142.8	174.8	206.3	213.4	232.0
Ratios								
External debt stocks to exports (%)	58.4	78.0	101.1	152.9	77.3	92.5	76.7	78.1
External debt stocks to GNI (%)	30.9	49.7	44.9	76.1	38.6	50.0	37.7	40.3
Debt service to exports (%)	7.9	6.0	10.0	10.6	7.7	7.4	7.7	6.9
Short-term to external debt stocks (%)	30.5	42.3	36.5	61.9	19.5	38.9	22.2	30.2
Multilateral to external debt stocks (%)	44.8	34.7	35.8	24.7	49.8	40.9	52.7	47.9
Reserves to external debt stocks (%)	35.5	28.0	32.4	17.2	40.4	35.6	47.3	49.1
Reserves to imports (months)	1.9	2.1	2.2	1.9	3.0	2.9	3.0	3.4

Notes:

Short-term debt is based on data from the BIS.

ST. VINCENT AND THE GRENADINES

(US$ million, unless otherwise indicated)

	2000	2005	2007	2008	2009	2010	2011	2012
Summary external debt data								
External debt stocks	**195.1**	**252.6**	**201.9**	**204.6**	**222.0**	**273.4**	**282.8**	**266.9**
Long-term external debt	163.3	247.8	199.8	203.9	203.2	255.5	259.8	243.9
Short-term external debt	31.4	4.3	1.6	0.2	0.5	0.0	0.0	0.0
interest arrears on long-term	0.4	4.3	1.6	0.2	0.5	0.0	0.0	0.0
Use of IMF credit	0.5	0.5	0.6	0.5	18.3	17.9	23.0	23.0
Long-term external debt								
Debt outstanding and disbursed	**163.3**	**247.8**	**199.8**	**203.9**	**203.2**	**255.5**	**259.8**	**243.9**
Public and publicly guaranteed	163.3	247.8	199.8	203.9	203.2	255.5	259.8	243.9
Official creditors	104.8	114.8	135.1	133.3	143.3	206.7	222.0	218.5
Private creditors	58.5	133.0	64.7	70.6	59.8	48.7	37.8	25.4
Private nonguaranteed	0.0	0.0	0.0	0.0	0.0	0.0	0.0	0.0
Disbursements	**8.5**	**42.4**	**15.4**	**23.4**	**20.2**	**76.2**	**25.9**	**10.3**
Public and publicly guaranteed	8.5	42.4	15.4	23.4	20.2	76.2	25.9	10.3
Official creditors	8.5	12.4	15.4	7.4	20.2	76.2	25.9	10.3
Private creditors	0.0	30.0	0.0	16.0	0.0	0.0	0.0	0.0
Private nonguaranteed	0.0	0.0	0.0	0.0	0.0	0.0	0.0	0.0
Principal repayments	**6.1**	**15.5**	**18.3**	**18.7**	**21.4**	**22.7**	**21.4**	**26.3**
Public and publicly guaranteed	6.1	15.5	18.3	18.7	21.4	22.7	21.4	26.3
Official creditors	5.7	7.7	7.1	8.6	10.6	11.6	10.5	13.9
Private creditors	0.4	7.7	11.3	10.1	10.7	11.1	10.9	12.4
Private nonguaranteed	0.0	0.0	0.0	0.0	0.0	0.0	0.0	0.0
Interest payments	**5.1**	**8.2**	**9.5**	**10.7**	**9.7**	**8.7**	**8.9**	**7.2**
Public and publicly guaranteed	5.1	8.2	9.5	10.7	9.7	8.7	8.9	7.2
Official creditors	3.3	3.5	3.6	5.6	4.4	4.4	5.4	4.4
Private creditors	1.8	4.7	5.9	5.1	5.4	4.3	3.4	2.8
Private nonguaranteed	0.0	0.0	0.0	0.0	0.0	0.0	0.0	0.0
Debt resource inflows								
Net debt inflows	1.6	26.9	-2.9	4.7	4.6	53.5	9.8	-16.0
Official creditors (incl. IMF)	2.8	4.6	8.3	-1.2	15.4	64.6	20.7	-3.6
Private creditors	-1.2	22.3	-11.3	5.9	-10.7	-11.1	-10.9	-12.4
Long-term	-0.4	22.3	-11.3	5.9	-10.7	-11.1	-10.9	-12.4
Public and publicly guaranteed	-0.4	22.3	-11.3	5.9	-10.7	-11.1	-10.9	-12.4
Private nonguaranteed	..	..	..	..	..	..	..	..
Short-term	-0.8	..	..	..	..	..	..	..
Non-debt resource inflows								
Foreign direct investment	37.7	40.1	119.4	159.2	110.2	97.2	85.6	125.3
Portfolio equity	..	..	..	..	..	..	..	..
Currency composition (%)								
Euro	..	5.4	7.5	6.3	5.6	3.2	2.4	2.1
U.S.dollars	82.2	73.8	71.2	75.0	77.7	85.3	88.4	90.4
Major economic aggregates								
Gross national income (GNI)	378.3	521.8	662.0	672.6	661.2	668.7	678.2	700.9
Exports of goods, services & prim. income	182.6	208.9	225.6	220.3	206.0	195.9	192.3	201.7
Personal transfers & comp. of employees	22.5	22.4	28.9	26.8	29.1	29.1	29.2	29.7
Imports of goods, services & prim. income	222.8	329.2	437.5	463.8	414.7	414.1	399.1	424.9
Primary income on FDI	12.7	22.1	19.6	18.1	12.4	11.0	7.4	7.7
Current account balance	-23.9	-102.2	-191.7	-230.3	-197.3	-208.3	-198.9	-215.9
International reserves	55.2	69.5	87.0	83.7	87.8	112.7	89.6	111.0
Ratios								
External debt stocks to exports (%)	106.9	120.9	89.5	92.9	107.7	139.6	147.0	132.3
External debt stocks to GNI (%)	51.6	48.4	30.5	30.4	33.6	40.9	41.7	38.1
Debt service to exports (%)	7.2	11.3	12.3	13.4	15.1	16.1	15.8	16.6
Short-term to external debt stocks (%)	16.1	1.7	0.8	0.1	0.2	0.0	0.0	0.0
Multilateral to external debt stocks (%)	33.9	32.8	52.4	52.7	54.5	69.0	73.1	75.5
Reserves to external debt stocks (%)	28.3	27.5	43.1	40.9	39.6	41.2	31.7	41.6
Reserves to imports (months)	3.0	2.5	2.4	2.2	2.5	3.3	2.7	3.1

Notes:

Short-term debt data are excluded since BIS data include debt liabilities of offshore centers located in the country. BIS short-term debt data for 2010, 2011, and 2012 are $482 million, $393 million, and $361 million respectively.

SUDAN

(US$ million, unless otherwise indicated)

	2000	2005	2007	2008	2009	2010	2011	2012
Summary external debt data								
External debt stocks	**16,085**	**17,613**	**19,633**	**20,280**	**21,128**	**22,233**	**21,146**	**21,840**
Long-term external debt	10,647	11,232	12,738	13,120	13,707	14,444	15,093	15,744
Short-term external debt	4,745	5,788	6,331	6,673	6,740	7,126	5,402	5,452
interest arrears on long-term	4,474	5,377	6,057	6,197	6,523	6,772	4,891	5,090
Use of IMF credit	693	593	565	486	682	664	651	645
Long-term external debt								
Debt outstanding and disbursed	**10,647**	**11,232**	**12,738**	**13,120**	**13,707**	**14,444**	**15,093**	**15,744**
Public and publicly guaranteed	10,151	11,232	12,738	13,120	13,707	14,444	15,093	15,744
Official creditors	8,393	9,145	10,405	10,730	11,258	11,815	11,350	11,413
Private creditors	1,758	2,087	2,333	2,390	2,449	2,629	3,743	4,331
Private nonguaranteed	496	0	0	0	0	0	0	0
Disbursements	**861**	**387**	**717**	**673**	**971**	**935**	**793**	**405**
Public and publicly guaranteed	861	387	717	673	971	935	793	405
Official creditors	318	387	717	673	971	935	793	405
Private creditors	543	0	0	0	0	0	0	0
Private nonguaranteed	..	..	..	..	..	..	..	..
Principal repayments	**143**	**291**	**216**	**219**	**362**	**397**	**416**	**313**
Public and publicly guaranteed	143	291	216	219	362	397	416	313
Official creditors	143	291	216	219	362	397	416	313
Private creditors	0	0	0	0	0	0	0	0
Private nonguaranteed	..	..	..	..	..	..	..	..
Interest payments	**42**	**67**	**87**	**68**	**111**	**83**	**100**	**77**
Public and publicly guaranteed	42	67	87	68	111	83	100	77
Official creditors	42	67	87	68	111	83	100	77
Private creditors	0	0	0	0	0	0	0	0
Private nonguaranteed	..	..	..	..	..	..	..	..
Debt resource inflows								
Net debt inflows	625	76	379	591	339	669	524	-64
Official creditors (incl. IMF)	121	67	441	389	598	532	367	85
Private creditors	504	9	-62	202	-259	137	157	-149
Long-term	543	0	0	0	0	0	0	0
Public and publicly guaranteed	543	0	0	0	0	0	0	0
Private nonguaranteed	..	..	..	..	..	..	..	..
Short-term	-39	9	-62	202	-259	137	157	-149
Non-debt resource inflows								
Foreign direct investment	392	3,312	4,240	6,705	5,566	6,114	2,616	2,488
Portfolio equity	..	78	1	72	0	7	13	2
Currency composition (%)								
Euro	..	8.5	9.7	9.6	9.6	9.3	8.5	8.2
U.S.dollars	60.3	53.6	50.3	49.1	50.5	50.8	51.9	53.4
Major economic aggregates								
Gross national income (GNI)	11,535	25,190	41,554	48,722	48,443	59,579	58,475	54,227
Exports of goods, services & prim. income	1,839	5,051	9,432	12,167	8,685	11,790	10,505	4,539
Personal transfers & comp. of employees	641	704	1,000	1,591	2,135	1,100	442	401
Imports of goods, services & prim. income	2,594	8,904	12,634	14,809	13,543	14,601	10,850	10,684
Primary income on FDI	..	1,099	2,252	4,312	2,911	3,224	384	5
Current account balance	-518	-2,555	-2,622	-2,256	-3,846	-680	768	-5,282
International reserves	138	1,869	1,378	1,399	1,094	1,036	193	193
Ratios								
External debt stocks to exports (%)	874.8	348.7	208.1	166.7	243.3	188.6	201.3	481.2
External debt stocks to GNI (%)	139.4	69.9	47.2	41.6	43.6	37.3	36.2	40.3
Debt service to exports (%)	13.5	7.9	4.0	3.0	5.6	4.2	5.1	8.9
Short-term to external debt stocks (%)	29.5	32.9	32.2	32.9	31.9	32.0	25.5	25.0
Multilateral to external debt stocks (%)	12.2	14.6	15.9	16.2	15.7	15.0	16.5	15.9
Reserves to external debt stocks (%)	0.9	10.6	7.0	6.9	5.2	4.7	0.9	0.9
Reserves to imports (months)	0.6	2.5	1.3	1.1	1.0	0.9	0.2	0.2

Notes:

Data include South Sudan. Long-term public and publicly guaranteed debt data exclude penalty interest. Short-term debt is based on data from the BIS.

SWAZILAND

(US$ million, unless otherwise indicated)

	2000	2005	2007	2008	2009	2010	2011	2012
Summary external debt data								
External debt stocks	**273.2**	**451.6**	**414.4**	**436.7**	**493.3**	**689.6**	**634.7**	**460.3**
Long-term external debt	262.9	362.3	368.8	354.8	390.6	384.6	359.6	320.1
Short-term external debt	1.8	80.1	35.5	72.0	27.0	230.7	201.0	66.0
interest arrears on long-term	0.0	15.1	5.5	15.0	25.0	35.7	48.0	41.0
Use of IMF credit	8.4	9.2	10.2	9.9	75.7	74.4	74.1	74.2
Long-term external debt								
Debt outstanding and disbursed	**262.9**	**362.3**	**368.8**	**354.8**	**390.6**	**384.6**	**359.6**	**320.1**
Public and publicly guaranteed	262.9	362.3	368.8	354.8	390.6	384.6	359.6	320.1
Official creditors	243.1	338.6	346.7	338.7	370.3	362.0	341.2	302.5
Private creditors	19.8	23.7	22.0	16.1	20.3	22.6	18.4	17.6
Private nonguaranteed	..	..	..	..	..	..	..	..
Disbursements	**15.8**	**51.1**	**12.4**	**56.3**	**33.2**	**8.0**	**28.6**	**3.1**
Public and publicly guaranteed	15.8	51.1	12.4	56.3	33.2	8.0	28.6	3.1
Official creditors	15.8	51.1	12.4	56.3	33.2	8.0	28.6	3.1
Private creditors	0.0	0.0	0.0	0.0	0.0	0.0	0.0	0.0
Private nonguaranteed	..	..	..	..	..	..	..	..
Principal repayments	**12.4**	**18.1**	**22.4**	**33.6**	**28.4**	**27.3**	**25.6**	**34.4**
Public and publicly guaranteed	12.4	18.1	22.4	33.6	28.4	27.3	25.6	34.4
Official creditors	12.4	18.1	22.4	33.6	28.4	27.3	25.6	34.4
Private creditors	0.0	0.0	0.0	0.0	0.0	0.0	0.0	0.0
Private nonguaranteed	..	..	..	..	..	..	..	..
Interest payments	**16.1**	**13.6**	**23.4**	**18.8**	**15.8**	**13.0**	**13.8**	**15.1**
Public and publicly guaranteed	16.1	13.6	23.4	18.8	15.8	13.0	13.8	15.1
Official creditors	10.2	10.5	20.5	16.3	14.6	13.0	13.8	12.7
Private creditors	5.9	3.2	2.9	2.5	1.2	0.0	0.0	2.4
Private nonguaranteed	..	..	..	..	..	..	..	..
Debt resource inflows								
Net debt inflows	-47.5	54.1	-11.0	49.7	-50.2	173.8	-39.0	-159.3
Official creditors (incl. IMF)	3.4	33.1	-10.0	22.7	4.8	-19.2	3.0	-31.3
Private creditors	-50.9	21.0	-1.0	27.0	-55.0	193.0	-42.0	-128.0
Long-term	0.0	0.0	0.0	0.0	0.0	0.0	0.0	0.0
Public and publicly guaranteed	0.0	0.0	0.0	0.0	0.0	0.0	0.0	0.0
Private nonguaranteed	..	..	..	..	..	..	..	..
Short-term	-50.9	21.0	-1.0	27.0	-55.0	193.0	-42.0	-128.0
Non-debt resource inflows								
Foreign direct investment	90.7	-45.9	37.5	105.7	65.7	135.7	93.2	89.6
Portfolio equity	1.4	0.8	1.0	43.9	-6.6	4.7	..	..
Currency composition (%)								
Euro	..	11.6	12.2	18.2	17.5	15.5	15.0	15.2
U.S.dollars	10.4	16.5	14.5	14.1	15.6	14.9	16.9	18.5
Major economic aggregates								
Gross national income (GNI)	1,558.7	2,762.4	3,094.9	3,014.6	3,085.4	3,465.0	3,718.3	3,456.2
Exports of goods, services & prim. income	1,376.4	2,075.9	2,399.7	2,042.3	2,066.2	2,275.3	2,267.9	2,268.6
Personal transfers & comp. of employees	56.9	95.4	95.1	89.6	93.5	54.7	..	..
Imports of goods, services & prim. income	1,522.9	2,276.0	2,659.2	2,483.4	2,672.4	3,063.4	3,127.8	3,085.6
Primary income on FDI	65.9	44.0	160.0	252.7	352.5	401.6	..	..
Current account balance	-45.9	-102.6	-65.5	-231.2	-414.3	-388.3	-352.8	128.0
International reserves	351.8	243.9	774.2	751.9	958.9	756.3	600.5	741.0
Ratios								
External debt stocks to exports (%)	19.8	21.8	17.3	21.4	23.9	30.3	28.0	20.3
External debt stocks to GNI (%)	17.5	16.3	13.4	14.5	16.0	19.9	17.1	13.3
Debt service to exports (%)	2.2	1.7	2.0	2.7	2.2	1.9	1.9	2.2
Short-term to external debt stocks (%)	0.7	17.7	8.6	16.5	5.5	33.4	31.7	14.3
Multilateral to external debt stocks (%)	54.9	53.0	60.8	55.2	51.6	34.7	36.2	46.4
Reserves to external debt stocks (%)	128.8	54.0	186.8	172.2	194.4	109.7	94.6	161.0
Reserves to imports (months)	2.8	1.3	3.5	3.6	4.3	3.0	2.3	2.9

Notes:

Short-term debt is based on data from the BIS.

SYRIAN ARAB REPUBLIC

(US$ million, unless otherwise indicated)

	2000	2005	2007	2008	2009	2010	2011	2012
Summary external debt data								
External debt stocks	**22,203**	**5,583**	**5,683**	**5,374**	**5,674**	**5,263**	**4,968**	**4,736**
Long-term external debt	16,464	5,025	4,976	4,737	4,480	4,276	3,998	3,948
Short-term external debt	5,692	506	649	581	756	558	542	359
interest arrears on long-term	2,372	193	142	145	206	217	218	316
Use of IMF credit	48	52	58	56	438	430	429	429
Long-term external debt								
Debt outstanding and disbursed	**16,464**	**5,025**	**4,976**	**4,737**	**4,480**	**4,276**	**3,998**	**3,948**
Public and publicly guaranteed	16,464	5,025	4,976	4,737	4,480	4,276	3,998	3,948
Official creditors	15,502	5,025	4,976	4,737	4,480	4,276	3,998	3,948
Private creditors	962	0	0	0	0	0	0	0
Private nonguaranteed	..	..	..	..	..	..	..	..
Disbursements	**18**	**189**	**425**	**282**	**281**	**286**	**222**	**0**
Public and publicly guaranteed	18	189	425	282	281	286	222	0
Official creditors	18	189	425	282	281	286	222	0
Private creditors	0	0	0	0	0	0	0	0
Private nonguaranteed	..	..	..	..	..	..	..	..
Principal repayments	**239**	**439**	**546**	**560**	**499**	**508**	**509**	**0**
Public and publicly guaranteed	239	439	546	560	499	508	509	0
Official creditors	224	428	546	560	499	508	509	0
Private creditors	16	11	0	0	0	0	0	0
Private nonguaranteed	..	..	..	..	..	..	..	..
Interest payments	**127**	**110**	**114**	**125**	**119**	**111**	**109**	**0**
Public and publicly guaranteed	127	110	114	125	119	111	109	0
Official creditors	126	110	114	125	119	111	109	0
Private creditors	1	0	0	0	0	0	0	0
Private nonguaranteed	..	..	..	..	..	..	..	..
Debt resource inflows								
Net debt inflows	-826	-357	-8	-350	-104	-430	-304	-281
Official creditors (incl. IMF)	-205	-239	-121	-279	-218	-221	-287	..
Private creditors	-621	-118	113	-71	114	-209	-17	-281
Long-term	-16	-11	0	0	0	0	0	0
Public and publicly guaranteed	-16	-11	0	0	0	0	0	0
Private nonguaranteed	..	..	..	..	..	..	..	..
Short-term	-605	-107	113	-71	114	-209	-17	-281
Non-debt resource inflows								
Foreign direct investment	270	500	1,242	1,466	2,570	1,469	..	..
Portfolio equity	..	..	..	..	..	..	..	..
Currency composition (%)								
Euro	..	12.4	21.6	22.4	26.1	27.3	27.0	27.9
U.S.dollars	84.1	49.1	36.6	33.3	31.0	28.6	26.7	27.0
Major economic aggregates								
Gross national income (GNI)	18,446	27,980	39,716	51,433	52,828	57,266	..	70,501
Exports of goods, services & prim. income	7,190	11,907	16,211	20,289	16,026	19,919	..	..
Personal transfers & comp. of employees	180	823	1,030	1,325	1,350	1,623	..	..
Imports of goods, services & prim. income	6,614	12,359	16,572	20,967	18,118	21,235	..	..
Primary income on FDI	..	1,220	1,085	1,527	1,301	1,684	..	..
Current account balance	1,061	299	460	472	-1,030	-367	..	..
International reserves	126	17,347	17,013	17,062	17,398	19,465	..	..
Ratios								
External debt stocks to exports (%)	308.8	46.9	35.1	26.5	35.4	26.4	..	..
External debt stocks to GNI (%)	120.4	20.0	14.3	10.4	10.7	9.2	..	6.7
Debt service to exports (%)	6.8	4.8	4.2	3.4	3.9	3.1	..	..
Short-term to external debt stocks (%)	25.6	9.1	11.4	10.8	13.3	10.6	10.9	7.6
Multilateral to external debt stocks (%)	2.6	18.2	26.6	28.7	29.2	32.2	32.8	34.7
Reserves to external debt stocks (%)	0.6	310.7	299.4	317.5	306.6	369.8	..	..
Reserves to imports (months)	0.2	16.8	12.3	9.8	11.5	11.0	..	..

Notes:

Long-term public and publicly guaranteed debt data are World Bank staff estimates. Short-term debt is based on data from the BIS.

TAJIKISTAN

(US$ million, unless otherwise indicated)

	2000	2005	2007	2008	2009	2010	2011	2012
Summary external debt data								
External debt stocks	**1,141**	**1,121**	**1,344**	**2,493**	**2,666**	**3,082**	**3,323**	**3,648**
Long-term external debt	846	850	1,096	2,261	2,423	2,734	2,948	3,346
Short-term external debt	77	27	72	90	74	122	129	16
interest arrears on long-term	45	2	0	0	0	0	0	16
Use of IMF credit	218	244	176	142	170	227	246	287
Long-term external debt								
Debt outstanding and disbursed	**846**	**850**	**1,096**	**2,261**	**2,423**	**2,734**	**2,948**	**3,346**
Public and publicly guaranteed	755	826	1,063	1,374	1,606	1,806	1,969	2,007
Official creditors	704	817	1,063	1,374	1,606	1,806	1,969	2,007
Private creditors	51	8	0	0	0	0	0	0
Private nonguaranteed	91	24	33	887	816	927	979	1,339
Disbursements	**37**	**108**	**264**	**379**	**518**	**924**	**725**	**560**
Public and publicly guaranteed	36	105	250	356	211	251	202	109
Official creditors	36	105	250	356	211	251	202	109
Private creditors	0	0	0	0	0	0	0	0
Private nonguaranteed	1	2	14	24	307	673	523	451
Principal repayments	**28**	**42**	**39**	**64**	**409**	**630**	**513**	**334**
Public and publicly guaranteed	15	37	29	52	35	37	34	74
Official creditors	15	37	29	52	35	37	34	74
Private creditors	0	0	0	0	0	0	0	0
Private nonguaranteed	12	5	11	12	374	593	479	261
Interest payments	**21**	**10**	**20**	**28**	**41**	**54**	**64**	**94**
Public and publicly guaranteed	7	9	18	26	24	23	28	30
Official creditors	4	9	18	26	24	23	28	30
Private creditors	4	0	0	0	0	0	0	0
Private nonguaranteed	14	1	2	2	17	31	36	63
Debt resource inflows								
Net debt inflows	-4	23	267	302	119	401	240	137
Official creditors (incl. IMF)	36	84	221	273	202	274	188	76
Private creditors	-40	-61	46	29	-83	127	52	61
Long-term	-11	-3	3	12	-67	80	44	190
Public and publicly guaranteed	0	0	0	0	0	0	0	0
Private nonguaranteed	-11	-3	3	12	-67	80	44	190
Short-term	-29	-58	43	18	-16	47	7	-129
Non-debt resource inflows								
Foreign direct investment	24	54	360	376	16	-16	67	198
Portfolio equity	..	..	..	..	..	..	..	..
Currency composition (%)								
Euro	..	6.1	3.9	2.8	2.8	2.6	2.7	2.8
U.S.dollars	97.9	86.3	86.2	86.3	82.9	81.4	81.0	79.2
Major economic aggregates								
Gross national income (GNI)	824	2,234	3,634	5,108	4,907	5,571	6,441	6,919
Exports of goods, services & prim. income	..	1,264	1,728	1,776	1,225	899	1,198	1,684
Personal transfers & comp. of employees	..	467	1,691	2,544	1,748	2,306	3,060	3,626
Imports of goods, services & prim. income	..	1,733	3,780	4,227	3,141	3,458	4,319	5,383
Primary income on FDI	..	2	26	4	5	9	7	33
Current account balance	..	-19	-495	48	-180	-370	-171	-248
International reserves	93	168	40	104	175	324	289	298
Ratios								
External debt stocks to exports (%)	..	88.7	77.8	140.3	217.6	342.8	277.4	216.6
External debt stocks to GNI (%)	138.4	50.2	37.0	48.8	54.3	55.3	51.6	52.7
Debt service to exports (%)	..	5.8	3.7	7.1	38.0	76.3	48.3	25.5
Short-term to external debt stocks (%)	6.8	2.4	5.4	3.6	2.8	3.9	3.9	0.4
Multilateral to external debt stocks (%)	16.3	46.3	49.6	29.4	31.1	30.7	29.3	26.9
Reserves to external debt stocks (%)	8.1	15.0	3.0	4.2	6.5	10.5	8.7	8.2
Reserves to imports (months)	..	1.2	0.1	0.3	0.7	1.1	0.8	0.7

Notes:

Short-term debt is based on data from the BIS. Data include MDRI debt relief.

TANZANIA

(US$ million, unless otherwise indicated)

	2000	2005	2007	2008	2009	2010	2011	2012
Summary external debt data								
External debt stocks	**7,183**	**8,400**	**5,057**	**6,012**	**7,624**	**8,987**	**9,940**	**11,581**
Long-term external debt	5,969	7,006	3,925	4,600	5,656	6,824	7,686	8,830
Short-term external debt	849	1,006	1,065	1,346	1,341	1,515	1,611	2,110
interest arrears on long-term	647	615	628	763	836	908	989	1,054
Use of IMF credit	364	387	67	66	628	647	643	641
Long-term external debt								
Debt outstanding and disbursed	**5,969**	**7,006**	**3,925**	**4,600**	**5,656**	**6,824**	**7,686**	**8,830**
Public and publicly guaranteed	5,969	6,446	3,181	3,711	4,640	5,601	6,438	7,366
Official creditors	5,776	6,341	3,079	3,613	4,522	5,488	6,030	6,761
Private creditors	194	105	102	98	118	113	408	604
Private nonguaranteed	..	560	744	889	1,016	1,224	1,248	1,465
Disbursements	**211**	**466**	**649**	**523**	**1,065**	**1,254**	**1,179**	**978**
Public and publicly guaranteed	211	466	649	523	919	1,038	872	794
Official creditors	206	447	646	523	889	1,021	568	791
Private creditors	5	19	3	0	30	17	304	2
Private nonguaranteed	..	0	0	0	146	216	307	184
Principal repayments	**94**	**31**	**20**	**22**	**105**	**131**	**76**	**78**
Public and publicly guaranteed	94	31	20	13	26	52	33	35
Official creditors	77	31	19	13	13	35	26	27
Private creditors	17	0	1	0	13	17	7	7
Private nonguaranteed	..	0	0	9	79	79	44	43
Interest payments	**51**	**44**	**26**	**27**	**45**	**50**	**53**	**60**
Public and publicly guaranteed	51	42	23	21	27	32	39	43
Official creditors	49	42	22	21	24	31	36	39
Private creditors	2	0	1	0	3	2	3	4
Private nonguaranteed	..	2	2	6	18	17	14	17
Debt resource inflows								
Net debt inflows	205	459	665	647	1,188	1,255	1,116	1,331
Official creditors (incl. IMF)	172	378	632	510	1,182	1,016	540	761
Private creditors	33	81	33	137	6	239	576	569
Long-term	-12	19	2	-9	84	137	561	135
Public and publicly guaranteed	-12	19	2	0	17	0	297	-5
Private nonguaranteed	..	0	0	-9	67	137	264	140
Short-term	44	62	31	146	-78	102	15	434
Non-debt resource inflows								
Foreign direct investment	463	936	582	1,383	953	1,840	1,229	1,707
Portfolio equity	..	3	3	3	3	3	3	4
Currency composition (%)								
Euro	..	2.9	6.6	5.6	4.6	3.5	2.9	2.5
U.S.dollars	51.9	54.1	40.1	41.2	44.5	48.1	50.3	51.6
Major economic aggregates								
Gross national income (GNI)	10,114	13,836	16,666	20,425	21,093	22,607	23,609	27,989
Exports of goods, services & prim. income	1,411	3,053	4,210	5,700	5,314	6,530	7,582	8,675
Personal transfers & comp. of employees	8	19	25	37	40	55	78	67
Imports of goods, services & prim. income	2,230	4,641	6,664	9,111	8,015	9,541	12,477	13,106
Primary income on FDI	13	319	309	318	342	365	309	268
Current account balance	-428	-1,093	-1,715	-2,577	-1,810	-1,960	-3,992	-3,640
International reserves	974	2,049	2,886	2,863	3,470	3,905	3,726	4,052
Ratios								
External debt stocks to exports (%)	509.0	275.2	120.1	105.5	143.5	137.6	131.1	133.5
External debt stocks to GNI (%)	71.0	60.7	30.3	29.4	36.1	39.8	42.1	41.4
Debt service to exports (%)	11.9	4.4	1.6	1.1	3.1	3.0	1.9	1.9
Short-term to external debt stocks (%)	11.8	12.0	21.1	22.4	17.6	16.9	16.2	18.2
Multilateral to external debt stocks (%)	45.5	58.0	43.1	44.5	46.9	48.7	47.9	47.0
Reserves to external debt stocks (%)	13.6	24.4	57.1	47.6	45.5	43.4	37.5	35.0
Reserves to imports (months)	5.2	5.3	5.2	3.8	5.2	4.9	3.6	3.7

Notes:

Long-term public and publicly guaranteed debt data include debt liabilities of Zanzibar. Long-term private nonguaranteed debt data from 2004 to 2007 are World Bank staff estimates and from 2008 are reported by Central Bank. Short-term debt is based on data from the BIS. Data include the effects of HIPC and MDRI debt relief.

THAILAND

(US$ million, unless otherwise indicated)

	2000	2005	2007	2008	2009	2010	2011	2012
Summary external debt data								
External debt stocks	**79,830**	**58,600**	**62,741**	**66,583**	**77,187**	**102,552**	**107,609**	**134,223**
Long-term external debt	61,778	42,465	44,312	45,997	45,981	54,172	61,132	75,764
Short-term external debt	14,880	16,014	18,295	20,455	29,685	46,886	44,988	56,968
interest arrears on long-term	0	0	0	4	8	2	5	2
Use of IMF credit	3,172	121	134	130	1,521	1,494	1,490	1,491
Long-term external debt								
Debt outstanding and disbursed	**61,778**	**42,465**	**44,312**	**45,997**	**45,981**	**54,172**	**61,132**	**75,764**
Public and publicly guaranteed	29,463	17,585	14,812	14,659	14,707	21,172	26,445	34,731
Official creditors	20,820	7,862	6,297	6,947	6,468	6,843	6,865	6,327
Private creditors	8,643	9,723	8,515	7,711	8,239	14,329	19,580	28,403
Private nonguaranteed	32,316	24,880	29,500	31,338	31,274	33,000	34,687	41,033
Disbursements	**4,031**	**17,083**	**18,630**	**13,526**	**12,989**	**16,838**	**17,452**	**29,509**
Public and publicly guaranteed	3,031	2,521	274	1,638	1,716	6,442	6,128	9,735
Official creditors	2,156	434	274	74	76	160	493	735
Private creditors	876	2,086	0	1,564	1,640	6,282	5,635	9,000
Private nonguaranteed	1,000	14,562	18,356	11,888	11,273	10,396	11,324	19,775
Principal repayments	**8,945**	**16,464**	**20,333**	**15,417**	**11,313**	**9,386**	**8,815**	**9,516**
Public and publicly guaranteed	3,010	2,709	1,845	2,721	1,590	803	1,197	757
Official creditors	1,666	2,321	1,178	819	468	534	779	619
Private creditors	1,344	388	667	1,902	1,122	269	418	137
Private nonguaranteed	5,935	13,755	18,488	12,696	9,723	8,582	7,618	8,760
Interest payments	**3,776**	**1,074**	**882**	**1,091**	**1,085**	**1,075**	**1,176**	**1,354**
Public and publicly guaranteed	1,577	437	320	255	231	230	263	409
Official creditors	1,008	234	150	121	112	113	114	111
Private creditors	569	202	170	134	119	118	149	298
Private nonguaranteed	2,199	637	562	836	855	845	913	944
Debt resource inflows								
Net debt inflows	-13,649	5,145	-1,219	265	10,902	24,659	6,736	31,976
Official creditors (incl. IMF)	292	-1,886	-904	-744	-392	-374	-285	115
Private creditors	-13,942	7,031	-316	1,009	11,294	25,033	7,022	31,861
Long-term	-5,404	2,505	-799	-1,147	2,068	7,826	8,923	19,878
Public and publicly guaranteed	-469	1,698	-667	-339	518	6,012	5,217	8,863
Private nonguaranteed	-4,935	807	-131	-808	1,550	1,813	3,706	11,015
Short-term	-8,538	4,526	483	2,156	9,226	17,207	-1,901	11,983
Non-debt resource inflows								
Foreign direct investment	3,366	8,055	11,327	8,538	4,854	9,104	9,005	10,689
Portfolio equity	900	5,121	4,268	-3,802	1,695	3,215	-406	2,663
Currency composition (%)								
Euro	..	1.6	1.9	1.6	1.5	0.8	0.5	0.3
U.S.dollars	46.3	52.3	54.5	53.4	52.9	65.2	73.2	82.2
Major economic aggregates								
Gross national income (GNI)	120,809	167,799	237,961	262,864	253,430	305,181	333,324	351,347
Exports of goods, services & prim. income	85,997	131,744	187,047	214,536	186,028	231,029	267,630	283,282
Personal transfers & comp. of employees	1,697	1,187	1,635	1,898	2,776	3,580	4,554	4,713
Imports of goods, services & prim. income	77,269	143,591	176,962	218,993	169,485	227,130	274,331	296,929
Primary income on FDI	..	10,812	14,286	15,171	13,283	18,845	18,658	22,596
Current account balance	9,313	-7,647	15,678	2,211	21,891	9,946	4,134	-1,431
International reserves	32,016	50,691	85,221	108,661	135,483	167,530	167,389	173,328
Ratios								
External debt stocks to exports (%)	92.8	44.5	33.5	31.0	41.5	44.4	40.2	47.4
External debt stocks to GNI (%)	66.1	34.9	26.4	25.3	30.5	33.6	32.3	38.2
Debt service to exports (%)	16.3	13.7	11.8	7.9	6.8	4.7	3.9	4.1
Short-term to external debt stocks (%)	18.6	27.3	29.2	30.7	38.5	45.7	41.8	42.4
Multilateral to external debt stocks (%)	6.7	1.4	0.5	0.4	0.3	0.2	0.2	0.4
Reserves to external debt stocks (%)	40.1	86.5	135.8	163.2	175.5	163.4	155.6	129.1
Reserves to imports (months)	5.0	4.2	5.8	6.0	9.6	8.9	7.3	7.0

Notes:

Long-term private nonguaranteed debt data for 2012 are World Bank staff estimates based on creditors and market data.

TOGO

(US$ million, unless otherwise indicated)

	2000	2005	2007	2008	2009	2010	2011	2012
Summary external debt data								
External debt stocks	**1,446.0**	**1,686.9**	**1,969.9**	**1,641.7**	**1,730.1**	**1,284.6**	**629.4**	**754.1**
Long-term external debt	1,229.6	1,439.5	1,640.6	1,468.8	1,481.9	1,004.2	369.4	450.0
Short-term external debt	132.5	217.7	310.3	107.8	47.0	38.9	5.8	49.6
interest arrears on long-term	62.6	166.7	234.3	23.8	30.0	9.9	2.8	3.6
Use of IMF credit	83.8	29.7	19.1	65.0	201.2	241.5	254.2	254.5
Long-term external debt								
Debt outstanding and disbursed	**1,229.6**	**1,439.5**	**1,640.6**	**1,468.8**	**1,481.9**	**1,004.2**	**369.4**	**450.0**
Public and publicly guaranteed	1,229.6	1,439.5	1,640.6	1,468.8	1,481.9	1,004.2	369.4	450.0
Official creditors	1,229.6	1,439.5	1,640.6	1,468.8	1,481.9	1,004.2	369.4	450.0
Private creditors	0.0	0.0	0.0	0.0	0.0	0.0	0.0	0.0
Private nonguaranteed	..	..	..	..	..	..	..	..
Disbursements	**24.4**	**9.9**	**3.1**	**2.2**	**34.6**	**82.8**	**30.0**	**126.6**
Public and publicly guaranteed	24.4	9.9	3.1	2.2	34.6	82.8	30.0	126.6
Official creditors	24.4	9.9	3.1	2.2	34.6	82.8	30.0	126.6
Private creditors	0.0	0.0	0.0	0.0	0.0	0.0	0.0	0.0
Private nonguaranteed	..	..	..	..	..	..	..	..
Principal repayments	**9.9**	**7.9**	**3.8**	**140.1**	**39.5**	**28.3**	**10.0**	**13.0**
Public and publicly guaranteed	9.9	7.9	3.8	140.1	39.5	28.3	10.0	13.0
Official creditors	9.9	7.9	3.8	140.1	39.5	28.3	10.0	13.0
Private creditors	0.0	0.0	0.0	0.0	0.0	0.0	0.0	0.0
Private nonguaranteed	..	..	..	..	..	..	..	..
Interest payments	**4.6**	**0.3**	**1.5**	**51.3**	**13.1**	**8.0**	**4.6**	**9.3**
Public and publicly guaranteed	4.6	0.3	1.5	51.3	13.1	8.0	4.6	9.3
Official creditors	4.6	0.3	1.5	51.3	13.1	8.0	4.6	9.3
Private creditors	0.0	0.0	0.0	0.0	0.0	0.0	0.0	0.0
Private nonguaranteed	..	..	..	..	..	..	..	..
Debt resource inflows								
Net debt inflows	-44.3	15.8	43.7	-82.2	-30.6	110.2	7.9	156.7
Official creditors (incl. IMF)	5.1	-9.2	-7.3	-90.2	36.4	98.2	33.9	113.7
Private creditors	-49.4	25.0	51.0	8.0	-67.0	12.0	-26.0	43.0
Long-term	0.0	0.0	0.0	0.0	0.0	0.0	0.0	0.0
Public and publicly guaranteed	0.0	0.0	0.0	0.0	0.0	0.0	0.0	0.0
Private nonguaranteed	..	..	..	..	..	..	..	..
Short-term	-49.4	25.0	51.0	8.0	-67.0	12.0	-26.0	43.0
Non-debt resource inflows								
Foreign direct investment	41.9	96.0	62.3	50.7	46.1	124.9	171.0	166.3
Portfolio equity	6.1	16.0	6.3	1.4	2.1	4.5	..	..
Currency composition (%)								
Euro	..	18.7	20.4	15.1	15.3	7.0	11.7	8.2
U.S.dollars	52.5	49.7	46.9	58.6	58.5	62.9	39.5	47.3
Major economic aggregates								
Gross national income (GNI)	1,265.3	2,079.9	2,493.2	2,794.2	2,803.4	2,761.6	3,197.5	3,331.3
Exports of goods, services & prim. income	456.5	857.3	974.2	1,216.8	1,265.0	1,395.8	..	..
Personal transfers & comp. of employees	34.2	192.5	284.4	337.1	334.5	336.6	..	..
Imports of goods, services & prim. income	664.1	1,249.0	1,468.9	1,762.6	1,777.3	1,951.3	..	..
Primary income on FDI	17.2	47.2	44.0	51.5	41.5	67.0	..	..
Current account balance	-139.6	-203.9	-215.8	-222.0	-176.7	-199.7	..	..
International reserves	140.9	191.5	438.1	581.8	703.2	714.9	774.3	441.6
Ratios								
External debt stocks to exports (%)	316.7	196.8	202.2	134.9	136.8	92.0	..	..
External debt stocks to GNI (%)	114.3	81.1	79.0	58.8	61.7	46.5	19.7	22.6
Debt service to exports (%)	6.6	2.5	1.6	16.0	4.3	2.6	..	..
Short-term to external debt stocks (%)	9.2	12.9	15.8	6.6	2.7	3.0	0.9	6.6
Multilateral to external debt stocks (%)	53.0	52.1	50.5	51.6	47.9	66.2	33.5	27.2
Reserves to external debt stocks (%)	9.7	11.4	22.2	35.4	40.6	55.7	123.0	58.6
Reserves to imports (months)	2.5	1.8	3.6	4.0	4.7	4.4	..	..

Notes:

Short-term debt is based on data from the BIS. Data include the effects of Paris Club debt restructuring agreement and HIPC and MDRI debt relief.

TONGA

(US$ million, unless otherwise indicated)

	2000	2005	2007	2008	2009	2010	2011	2012
Summary external debt data								
External debt stocks	**73.8**	**89.0**	**96.9**	**99.0**	**114.9**	**153.7**	**190.6**	**197.4**
Long-term external debt	65.0	79.5	86.5	88.8	104.6	143.5	180.5	187.2
Short-term external debt	0.2	0.1	0.0	0.0	0.0	0.0	0.0	0.0
interest arrears on long-term	0.2	0.1	0.0	0.0	0.0	0.0	0.0	0.0
Use of IMF credit	8.6	9.4	10.4	10.1	10.3	10.1	10.1	10.1
Long-term external debt								
Debt outstanding and disbursed	**65.0**	**79.5**	**86.5**	**88.8**	**104.6**	**143.5**	**180.5**	**187.2**
Public and publicly guaranteed	65.0	79.5	86.5	88.8	104.6	143.5	180.5	187.2
Official creditors	65.0	79.5	86.5	88.8	103.7	142.4	180.0	186.9
Private creditors	0.0	0.0	0.0	0.0	0.9	1.1	0.4	0.3
Private nonguaranteed	..	..	..	..	..	..	..	..
Disbursements	**5.4**	**4.5**	**4.5**	**8.5**	**17.4**	**40.9**	**36.9**	**9.9**
Public and publicly guaranteed	5.4	4.5	4.5	8.5	17.4	40.9	36.9	9.9
Official creditors	5.4	4.5	4.5	8.5	16.5	40.7	36.9	9.9
Private creditors	0.0	0.0	0.0	0.0	0.8	0.2	0.0	0.0
Private nonguaranteed	..	..	..	..	..	..	..	..
Principal repayments	**3.7**	**3.7**	**3.6**	**3.7**	**2.4**	**2.7**	**3.3**	**3.4**
Public and publicly guaranteed	3.7	3.7	3.6	3.7	2.4	2.7	3.3	3.4
Official creditors	2.4	3.7	3.6	3.7	2.4	2.6	3.3	3.3
Private creditors	1.3	0.0	0.0	0.0	0.0	0.1	0.0	0.2
Private nonguaranteed	..	..	..	..	..	..	..	..
Interest payments	**0.9**	**1.2**	**1.1**	**1.7**	**1.4**	**2.4**	**2.6**	**2.9**
Public and publicly guaranteed	0.9	1.2	1.1	1.7	1.4	2.4	2.6	2.9
Official creditors	0.8	1.2	1.1	1.7	1.4	2.3	2.6	2.9
Private creditors	0.1	0.0	0.0	0.0	0.0	0.1	0.0	0.0
Private nonguaranteed	..	..	..	..	..	..	..	..
Debt resource inflows								
Net debt inflows	1.8	0.9	0.9	4.8	14.9	38.2	33.6	6.5
Official creditors (incl. IMF)	3.0	0.9	0.9	4.8	14.2	38.1	33.7	6.6
Private creditors	-1.3	0.0	0.0	0.0	0.8	0.1	0.0	-0.2
Long-term	-1.3	0.0	0.0	0.0	0.8	0.1	0.0	-0.2
Public and publicly guaranteed	-1.3	0.0	0.0	0.0	0.8	0.1	0.0	-0.2
Private nonguaranteed	..	..	..	..	..	..	..	..
Short-term	..	..	..	..	..	..	..	..
Non-debt resource inflows								
Foreign direct investment	4.8	7.2	27.7	4.2	0.0	7.3	19.2	6.6
Portfolio equity	..	..	..	..	..	..	..	..
Currency composition (%)								
Euro	..	7.3	3.6	0.1	0.1	0.0	0.0	..
U.S.dollars	4.8	28.0	35.1	33.8	30.3	21.4	16.6	15.5
Major economic aggregates								
Gross national income (GNI)	191.0	264.7	308.2	354.4	324.9	372.7	438.8	482.5
Exports of goods, services & prim. income	..	59.0	51.0	59.8	51.9	55.0	65.0	80.9
Personal transfers & comp. of employees	..	68.6	101.0	93.7	71.4	..	..	..
Imports of goods, services & prim. income	..	156.8	181.3	222.2	192.7	160.5	193.1	177.3
Primary income on FDI	..	..	..	0.0	0.0	..	..	..
Current account balance	..	-21.3	-19.4	-66.0	-54.2	-26.9	-38.0	-31.6
International reserves	24.6	46.9	65.2	69.8	95.7	104.5	143.3	152.4
Ratios								
External debt stocks to exports (%)	..	151.0	189.8	165.5	221.4	279.5	293.0	243.9
External debt stocks to GNI (%)	38.6	33.6	31.4	27.9	35.4	41.2	43.4	40.9
Debt service to exports (%)	..	8.8	9.8	9.3	7.4	9.2	9.1	7.8
Short-term to external debt stocks (%)	0.3	0.1	..	..	..	0.0	0.0	0.0
Multilateral to external debt stocks (%)	72.4	75.4	77.7	72.9	63.5	46.0	35.7	33.1
Reserves to external debt stocks (%)	33.4	52.6	67.3	70.5	83.3	68.0	75.2	77.2
Reserves to imports (months)	..	3.6	4.3	3.8	6.0	7.8	8.9	10.3

TUNISIA

(US$ million, unless otherwise indicated)

	2000	2005	2007	2008	2009	2010	2011	2012
Summary external debt data								
External debt stocks	**11,355**	**17,926**	**20,504**	**21,378**	**22,688**	**22,472**	**22,849**	**25,475**
Long-term external debt	9,688	14,742	16,466	16,998	17,459	17,073	17,481	18,826
Short-term external debt	1,590	3,135	3,984	4,327	4,801	4,979	4,949	6,230
interest arrears on long-term	0	0	0	0	0	0	0	0
Use of IMF credit	77	49	54	53	428	420	419	419
Long-term external debt								
Debt outstanding and disbursed	**9,688**	**14,742**	**16,466**	**16,998**	**17,459**	**17,073**	**17,481**	**18,826**
Public and publicly guaranteed	8,888	13,001	14,517	14,451	14,852	14,671	15,138	16,782
Official creditors	6,093	8,421	9,566	9,286	9,979	10,220	11,502	12,714
Private creditors	2,795	4,580	4,950	5,165	4,873	4,451	3,636	4,068
Private nonguaranteed	800	1,741	1,949	2,547	2,607	2,402	2,343	2,044
Disbursements	**1,542**	**1,256**	**1,625**	**1,225**	**1,548**	**1,642**	**2,466**	**3,417**
Public and publicly guaranteed	1,242	1,126	1,436	915	1,371	1,545	2,379	3,361
Official creditors	709	843	1,103	831	1,315	1,507	2,352	2,047
Private creditors	533	283	333	84	56	39	26	1,314
Private nonguaranteed	300	130	189	310	177	97	87	56
Principal repayments	**1,296**	**1,187**	**1,588**	**1,170**	**1,350**	**1,617**	**1,905**	**1,897**
Public and publicly guaranteed	1,264	1,129	1,493	1,057	1,233	1,397	1,759	1,607
Official creditors	662	873	1,099	958	837	887	860	878
Private creditors	602	255	393	99	396	510	899	729
Private nonguaranteed	32	58	95	112	117	220	146	290
Interest payments	**489**	**686**	**743**	**745**	**700**	**670**	**678**	**610**
Public and publicly guaranteed	479	584	619	630	598	546	559	500
Official creditors	297	334	356	366	335	309	330	342
Private creditors	182	249	264	264	263	237	230	158
Private nonguaranteed	10	102	123	115	102	124	119	110
Debt resource inflows								
Net debt inflows	258	-141	664	399	673	203	531	2,800
Official creditors (incl. IMF)	7	-31	3	-126	478	619	1,492	1,169
Private creditors	251	-111	661	525	195	-417	-961	1,631
Long-term	199	99	34	182	-280	-594	-931	351
Public and publicly guaranteed	-69	27	-60	-16	-340	-471	-872	585
Private nonguaranteed	268	72	94	198	60	-123	-59	-234
Short-term	52	-210	627	343	474	177	-29	1,280
Non-debt resource inflows								
Foreign direct investment	752	713	1,515	2,601	1,525	1,334	433	1,554
Portfolio equity	-18	12	30	-39	-89	-26	-44	-15
Currency composition (%)								
Euro	..	40.1	50.1	48.4	49.0	49.0	45.1	45.3
U.S.dollars	30.0	20.3	14.3	12.9	12.6	12.4	15.2	16.3
Major economic aggregates								
Gross national income (GNI)	20,525	30,645	36,825	42,244	41,370	42,121	44,116	43,638
Exports of goods, services & prim. income	8,701	14,884	20,527	25,602	20,133	22,556	22,950	22,600
Personal transfers & comp. of employees	796	1,393	1,716	1,977	1,964	2,063	2,004	2,266
Imports of goods, services & prim. income	10,347	16,495	23,063	29,235	23,318	26,595	28,235	28,523
Primary income on FDI	468	962	1,523	1,958	1,588	1,658	1,716	1,533
Current account balance	-821	-299	-917	-1,711	-1,234	-2,104	-3,386	-3,773
International reserves	1,811	4,437	7,851	8,849	11,057	9,459	7,454	8,357
Ratios								
External debt stocks to exports (%)	130.5	120.4	99.9	83.5	112.7	99.6	99.6	112.7
External debt stocks to GNI (%)	55.3	58.5	55.7	50.6	54.8	53.4	51.8	58.4
Debt service to exports (%)	21.9	13.7	12.3	7.9	10.5	10.4	11.5	11.5
Short-term to external debt stocks (%)	14.0	17.5	19.4	20.2	21.2	22.2	21.7	24.5
Multilateral to external debt stocks (%)	30.6	30.9	30.7	28.0	29.0	30.2	33.5	34.4
Reserves to external debt stocks (%)	15.9	24.8	38.3	41.4	48.7	42.1	32.6	32.8
Reserves to imports (months)	2.1	3.2	4.1	3.6	5.7	4.3	3.2	3.5

Notes:

Long-term private nonguaranteed debt data from 2008 to 2012 are World Bank staff estimates based on reports provided by the country.

TURKEY

(US$ million, unless otherwise indicated)

	2000	2005	2007	2008	2009	2010	2011	2012
Summary external debt data								
External debt stocks	**116,787**	**172,131**	**258,443**	**288,978**	**277,270**	**299,183**	**305,481**	**337,492**
Long-term external debt	83,552	118,408	207,959	227,759	218,639	214,580	219,026	234,150
Short-term external debt	28,912	38,916	43,148	52,522	48,993	77,326	81,934	100,832
interest arrears on long-term	0	0	0	0	0	0	0	0
Use of IMF credit	4,323	14,807	7,336	8,697	9,638	7,277	4,521	2,510
Long-term external debt								
Debt outstanding and disbursed	**83,552**	**118,408**	**207,959**	**227,759**	**218,639**	**214,580**	**219,026**	**234,150**
Public and publicly guaranteed	55,724	62,965	81,096	82,313	85,609	91,501	94,759	98,922
Official creditors	12,537	12,435	17,083	19,719	23,109	26,427	28,221	29,416
Private creditors	43,187	50,530	64,013	62,595	62,500	65,074	66,538	69,506
Private nonguaranteed	27,828	55,443	126,863	145,446	133,030	123,080	124,267	135,228
Disbursements	**22,949**	**41,260**	**72,632**	**65,149**	**39,688**	**48,617**	**54,358**	**64,378**
Public and publicly guaranteed	14,069	7,756	13,300	10,679	9,842	14,578	11,049	12,268
Official creditors	2,393	1,001	3,119	3,850	4,749	5,561	4,008	2,940
Private creditors	11,676	6,754	10,181	6,829	5,093	9,017	7,042	9,328
Private nonguaranteed	8,881	33,504	59,332	54,470	29,846	34,039	43,308	52,110
Principal repayments	**13,744**	**24,649**	**31,717**	**40,169**	**49,657**	**45,489**	**38,665**	**41,206**
Public and publicly guaranteed	6,268	7,957	6,491	7,736	6,469	6,013	5,010	5,571
Official creditors	1,745	1,653	1,674	1,570	1,650	1,788	1,714	1,739
Private creditors	4,523	6,303	4,816	6,166	4,819	4,225	3,296	3,832
Private nonguaranteed	7,476	16,693	25,226	32,433	43,188	39,476	33,654	35,635
Interest payments	**5,000**	**6,396**	**10,300**	**11,396**	**10,421**	**8,703**	**12,006**	**8,541**
Public and publicly guaranteed	3,467	4,471	5,288	5,169	4,785	4,526	4,594	4,752
Official creditors	659	596	661	703	650	488	580	611
Private creditors	2,807	3,875	4,626	4,466	4,135	4,038	4,014	4,141
Private nonguaranteed	1,533	1,925	5,013	6,227	5,635	4,177	7,412	3,789
Debt resource inflows								
Net debt inflows	18,017	19,346	37,191	35,941	-14,203	29,290	17,494	40,067
Official creditors (incl. IMF)	4,020	-5,972	-2,572	3,868	2,392	1,602	-513	-803
Private creditors	13,997	25,317	39,763	32,073	-16,596	27,688	18,007	40,870
Long-term	8,557	17,262	39,470	22,700	-13,067	-645	13,399	21,972
Public and publicly guaranteed	7,152	451	5,365	663	274	4,792	3,745	5,497
Private nonguaranteed	1,405	16,811	34,106	22,037	-13,342	-5,437	9,654	16,475
Short-term	5,440	8,055	293	9,374	-3,529	28,333	4,608	18,898
Non-debt resource inflows								
Foreign direct investment	982	10,031	22,047	19,760	8,663	9,036	16,047	12,519
Portfolio equity	489	5,669	5,138	716	2,827	3,468	-986	6,274
Currency composition (%)								
Euro	..	24.0	27.2	27.8	30.0	31.6	31.8	31.4
U.S.dollars	58.0	71.3	69.0	67.5	65.5	63.2	60.6	60.7
Major economic aggregates								
Gross national income (GNI)	262,566	477,141	640,031	721,974	606,354	724,027	766,862	782,277
Exports of goods, services & prim. income	53,189	109,975	151,809	184,839	150,653	161,919	188,423	212,052
Personal transfers & comp. of employees	4,560	887	1,248	1,476	1,050	993	1,087	1,015
Imports of goods, services & prim. income	67,873	132,878	191,815	227,409	165,230	208,889	265,273	261,185
Primary income on FDI	279	1,051	2,213	2,953	2,929	2,867	2,924	2,193
Current account balance	-9,920	-21,449	-37,781	-40,438	-12,168	-45,447	-75,092	-47,750
International reserves	22,488	50,579	73,384	70,428	70,874	80,713	78,322	99,943
Ratios								
External debt stocks to exports (%)	219.6	156.5	170.2	156.3	184.0	184.8	162.1	159.2
External debt stocks to GNI (%)	44.5	36.1	40.4	40.0	45.7	41.3	39.8	43.1
Debt service to exports (%)	38.9	37.4	32.4	30.2	41.6	36.6	29.9	26.1
Short-term to external debt stocks (%)	24.8	22.6	16.7	18.2	17.7	25.8	26.8	29.9
Multilateral to external debt stocks (%)	4.9	4.4	4.7	4.8	6.1	6.6	7.0	6.9
Reserves to external debt stocks (%)	19.3	29.4	28.4	24.4	25.6	27.0	25.6	29.6
Reserves to imports (months)	4.0	4.6	4.6	3.7	5.1	4.6	3.5	4.6

Notes:

Long-term public and publicly guaranteed debt data include nonresident deposits made under the Dresdner Bank scheme, amounting to $6.1 billion at end-2012.

TURKMENISTAN

(US$ million, unless otherwise indicated)

	2000	2005	2007	2008	2009	2010	2011	2012
Summary external debt data								
External debt stocks	**2,609.3**	**1,157.8**	**853.7**	**745.7**	**661.5**	**529.1**	**454.3**	**492.4**
Long-term external debt	2,288.1	911.0	649.9	587.4	477.2	366.8	299.3	293.3
Short-term external debt	230.3	147.0	93.5	50.8	74.8	54.8	47.8	91.8
interest arrears on long-term	5.0	5.0	3.5	0.8	0.8	0.8	0.8	0.8
Use of IMF credit	91.0	99.8	110.3	107.5	109.5	107.5	107.2	107.3
Long-term external debt								
Debt outstanding and disbursed	**2,288.1**	**911.0**	**649.9**	**587.4**	**477.2**	**366.8**	**299.3**	**293.3**
Public and publicly guaranteed	2,271.3	877.8	648.2	586.8	463.3	359.5	265.5	270.6
Official creditors	838.6	685.9	523.4	500.2	409.5	341.6	265.5	270.6
Private creditors	1,432.7	192.0	124.8	86.5	53.9	17.8	0.0	0.0
Private nonguaranteed	16.7	33.1	1.8	0.6	13.9	7.4	33.8	22.7
Disbursements	**430.1**	**89.0**	**38.9**	**25.9**	**35.2**	**25.5**	**44.4**	**45.6**
Public and publicly guaranteed	420.9	24.9	38.9	25.6	22.4	17.9	13.6	45.6
Official creditors	292.6	24.9	38.9	25.6	22.4	17.9	13.6	45.6
Private creditors	128.3	0.0	0.0	0.0	0.0	0.0	0.0	0.0
Private nonguaranteed	9.2	64.1	0.0	0.3	12.8	7.5	30.9	0.0
Principal repayments	**353.0**	**261.4**	**166.3**	**140.8**	**146.4**	**142.8**	**120.9**	**48.4**
Public and publicly guaranteed	347.4	189.1	164.3	139.3	146.4	129.8	118.4	37.1
Official creditors	44.0	112.6	124.6	104.3	112.4	96.7	100.0	37.1
Private creditors	303.4	76.5	39.7	35.0	34.0	33.1	18.4	0.0
Private nonguaranteed	5.5	72.3	2.0	1.5	0.0	13.0	2.5	11.3
Interest payments	**101.9**	**39.1**	**29.8**	**26.7**	**17.6**	**10.8**	**9.6**	**7.2**
Public and publicly guaranteed	101.2	37.3	29.6	26.6	17.1	10.3	9.0	7.1
Official creditors	27.8	23.9	19.8	20.1	14.3	9.6	8.7	7.1
Private creditors	73.4	13.4	9.7	6.6	2.8	0.8	0.3	0.0
Private nonguaranteed	0.7	1.8	0.3	0.1	0.4	0.4	0.6	0.1
Debt resource inflows								
Net debt inflows	-1.6	-280.4	-185.4	-154.9	-87.2	-137.3	-83.5	41.1
Official creditors (incl. IMF)	248.6	-87.7	-85.7	-78.7	-90.0	-78.7	-86.4	8.5
Private creditors	-250.2	-192.7	-99.7	-76.2	2.8	-58.6	3.0	32.7
Long-term	-171.5	-84.7	-41.7	-36.2	-21.2	-38.6	10.0	-11.3
Public and publicly guaranteed	-175.2	-76.5	-39.7	-35.0	-34.0	-33.1	-18.4	..
Private nonguaranteed	3.7	-8.1	-2.0	-1.2	12.8	-5.5	28.4	-11.3
Short-term	-78.8	-108.0	-58.0	-40.0	24.0	-20.0	-7.0	44.0
Non-debt resource inflows								
Foreign direct investment	131.0	418.2	856.0	1,277.0	4,553.0	3,631.0	3,399.0	3,159.0
Portfolio equity	..	..	..	..	..	..	..	..
Currency composition (%)								
Euro	..	31.8	35.6	30.9	32.5	29.1	25.3	19.0
U.S.dollars	51.5	18.2	9.8	7.9	6.4	3.6	4.4	16.7
Major economic aggregates								
Gross national income (GNI)	2,727.4	7,541.4	12,299.8	18,235.7	18,957.5	20,689.3	26,362.8	30,678.9
Exports of goods, services & prim. income	..	..	..	..	..	..	..	..
Personal transfers & comp. of employees	..	..	..	..	..	..	..	..
Imports of goods, services & prim. income	..	..	..	..	..	..	..	..
Primary income on FDI	..	..	..	..	..	..	..	..
Current account balance	..	..	..	..	..	..	..	..
International reserves	..	..	..	..	..	..	..	..
Ratios								
External debt stocks to exports (%)	..	..	..	..	..	..	..	..
External debt stocks to GNI (%)	95.7	15.4	6.9	4.1	3.5	2.6	1.7	1.6
Debt service to exports (%)	..	..	..	..	..	..	..	..
Short-term to external debt stocks (%)	8.8	12.7	10.9	6.8	11.3	10.4	10.5	18.6
Multilateral to external debt stocks (%)	1.9	3.5	2.7	2.7	2.6	2.7	2.5	8.8
Reserves to external debt stocks (%)	..	..	..	..	..	..	..	..
Reserves to imports (months)	..	..	..	..	..	..	..	..

Notes:

Long-term public and publicly guaranteed debt from 2010 are World Bank staff estimates. Long-term private nonguaranteed debt data (excluding bonds) only cover European Bank for Reconstruction and Development lending.

UGANDA

(US$ million, unless otherwise indicated)

	2000	2005	2007	2008	2009	2010	2011	2012
Summary external debt data								
External debt stocks	**3,535**	**4,437**	**1,629**	**2,267**	**2,736**	**2,972**	**3,261**	**3,769**
Long-term external debt	3,051	4,184	1,546	1,754	2,221	2,671	2,961	3,471
Short-term external debt	129	79	26	458	235	26	26	26
interest arrears on long-term	58	29	26	26	26	26	26	26
Use of IMF credit	354	173	56	55	281	275	273	272
Long-term external debt								
Debt outstanding and disbursed	**3,051**	**4,184**	**1,546**	**1,754**	**2,221**	**2,671**	**2,961**	**3,471**
Public and publicly guaranteed	3,051	4,184	1,546	1,754	2,221	2,671	2,961	3,471
Official creditors	3,027	4,182	1,545	1,753	2,220	2,671	2,961	3,471
Private creditors	24	2	1	0	0	0	0	0
Private nonguaranteed	..	..	..	..	..	..	..	..
Disbursements	**219**	**224**	**473**	**275**	**493**	**486**	**334**	**554**
Public and publicly guaranteed	219	224	473	275	493	486	334	554
Official creditors	219	224	473	275	493	486	334	554
Private creditors	0	0	0	0	0	0	0	0
Private nonguaranteed	..	..	..	..	..	..	..	..
Principal repayments	**26**	**99**	**50**	**52**	**49**	**40**	**35**	**37**
Public and publicly guaranteed	26	99	50	52	49	40	35	37
Official creditors	25	98	49	52	49	39	35	37
Private creditors	1	1	1	1	0	0	0	0
Private nonguaranteed	..	..	..	..	..	..	..	..
Interest payments	**21**	**33**	**12**	**15**	**18**	**21**	**26**	**28**
Public and publicly guaranteed	21	33	12	15	18	21	26	28
Official creditors	20	32	12	15	18	21	26	28
Private creditors	0	0	0	0	0	0	0	0
Private nonguaranteed	..	..	..	..	..	..	..	..
Debt resource inflows								
Net debt inflows	177	85	303	655	221	237	298	514
Official creditors (incl. IMF)	184	95	424	224	445	447	298	514
Private creditors	-7	-10	-122	431	-223	-209	0	0
Long-term	-1	-1	-1	-1	0	0	0	0
Public and publicly guaranteed	-1	-1	-1	-1	0	0	0	0
Private nonguaranteed	..	..	..	..	..	..	..	..
Short-term	-6	-10	-121	432	-223	-209	..	..
Non-debt resource inflows								
Foreign direct investment	161	380	792	729	842	544	894	1,721
Portfolio equity	..	..	-23	13	131	-70	106	5
Currency composition (%)								
Euro	..	2.8	10.3	7.5	5.1	3.4	2.6	2.2
U.S.dollars	62.5	67.8	48.1	46.5	47.6	47.2	46.8	48.0
Major economic aggregates								
Gross national income (GNI)	6,086	8,749	10,579	12,919	13,366	15,813	15,671	16,760
Exports of goods, services & prim. income	716	1,591	2,466	3,137	3,361	3,430	4,271	4,760
Personal transfers & comp. of employees	238	322	452	724	781	771	816	733
Imports of goods, services & prim. income	1,574	2,653	4,275	5,691	5,647	6,495	7,856	8,243
Primary income on FDI	19	202	262	250	247	183	262	369
Current account balance	-359	-26	-701	-1,314	-1,139	-1,752	-2,160	-2,222
International reserves	808	1,344	2,560	2,301	2,994	2,706	2,617	3,167
Ratios								
External debt stocks to exports (%)	493.6	278.9	66.0	72.3	81.4	86.7	76.3	79.2
External debt stocks to GNI (%)	58.1	50.7	15.4	17.5	20.5	18.8	20.8	22.5
Debt service to exports (%)	10.6	10.8	2.7	2.4	2.1	1.8	1.5	1.4
Short-term to external debt stocks (%)	3.7	1.8	1.6	20.2	8.6	0.9	0.8	0.7
Multilateral to external debt stocks (%)	74.5	88.6	82.0	68.8	73.7	81.3	83.0	80.5
Reserves to external debt stocks (%)	22.9	30.3	157.2	101.5	109.4	91.0	80.3	84.0
Reserves to imports (months)	6.2	6.1	7.2	4.9	6.4	5.0	4.0	4.6

Notes:

Long-term private nonguaranteed debt data from 2010 are World Bank staff estimates based on reports provided by the country. Data include the effects of HIPC and MDRI debt relief.

UKRAINE

(US$ million, unless otherwise indicated)

	2000	2005	2007	2008	2009	2010	2011	2012
Summary external debt data								
External debt stocks	**13,890**	**33,721**	**78,975**	**98,328**	**104,347**	**124,968**	**135,296**	**135,067**
Long-term external debt	9,664	18,599	53,561	70,966	71,447	81,442	86,358	87,521
Short-term external debt	447	12,063	22,914	20,636	19,873	27,264	32,727	34,750
interest arrears on long-term	183	110	199	335	650	1,671	13	1,518
Use of IMF credit	3,779	3,059	2,501	6,726	13,027	16,262	16,212	12,795
Long-term external debt								
Debt outstanding and disbursed	**9,664**	**18,599**	**53,561**	**70,966**	**71,447**	**81,442**	**86,358**	**87,521**
Public and publicly guaranteed	8,123	9,069	14,171	14,708	18,107	24,967	25,473	31,481
Official creditors	5,000	5,021	5,369	5,859	11,093	14,731	12,528	14,436
Private creditors	3,123	4,048	8,802	8,848	7,014	10,236	12,945	17,045
Private nonguaranteed	1,541	9,530	39,390	56,258	53,340	56,476	60,885	56,040
Disbursements	**1,401**	**7,853**	**28,390**	**31,483**	**22,241**	**33,946**	**28,446**	**20,564**
Public and publicly guaranteed	173	1,411	4,318	990	5,581	7,944	3,352	7,961
Official creditors	141	563	807	985	5,581	4,259	600	3,109
Private creditors	32	847	3,511	4	0	3,685	2,753	4,853
Private nonguaranteed	1,228	6,442	24,072	30,493	16,661	26,002	25,094	12,602
Principal repayments	**2,114**	**4,018**	**8,097**	**13,595**	**17,855**	**23,458**	**24,054**	**21,178**
Public and publicly guaranteed	1,250	1,193	850	482	1,721	895	2,836	2,056
Official creditors	1,208	546	498	456	475	477	2,818	1,288
Private creditors	42	647	352	26	1,246	418	18	768
Private nonguaranteed	864	2,825	7,248	13,113	16,134	22,563	21,218	19,122
Interest payments	**447**	**894**	**2,307**	**3,200**	**4,171**	**3,494**	**4,302**	**4,472**
Public and publicly guaranteed	375	424	607	587	681	555	832	908
Official creditors	148	130	185	165	204	225	263	219
Private creditors	228	294	423	422	478	330	569	689
Private nonguaranteed	72	470	1,699	2,613	3,490	2,938	3,470	3,564
Debt resource inflows								
Net debt inflows	-1,285	5,234	27,370	19,875	9,390	20,291	11,513	-3,509
Official creditors (incl. IMF)	-1,666	-283	-118	4,930	11,187	7,215	-2,218	-1,593
Private creditors	380	5,516	27,488	14,945	-1,797	13,076	13,731	-1,917
Long-term	354	3,818	19,984	17,359	-719	6,706	6,610	-2,435
Public and publicly guaranteed	-10	201	3,160	-21	-1,246	3,267	2,735	4,085
Private nonguaranteed	364	3,617	16,825	17,380	527	3,439	3,876	-6,519
Short-term	26	1,698	7,504	-2,414	-1,078	6,370	7,121	518
Non-debt resource inflows								
Foreign direct investment	595	7,808	10,193	10,700	4,769	6,451	7,207	7,833
Portfolio equity	146	82	715	388	105	290	519	516
Currency composition (%)								
Euro	..	19.8	17.3	15.6	13.6	9.3	6.3	14.1
U.S.dollars	53.2	68.0	69.7	71.9	53.9	53.5	63.2	64.2
Major economic aggregates								
Gross national income (GNI)	30,320	85,157	140,602	178,452	114,788	134,410	161,449	173,344
Exports of goods, services & prim. income	19,665	43,384	65,068	87,899	56,704	70,341	89,137	93,326
Personal transfers & comp. of employees	33	2,408	5,290	6,782	5,941	6,535	7,822	8,449
Imports of goods, services & prim. income	19,032	43,695	73,858	103,807	61,101	76,332	103,078	111,079
Primary income on FDI	43	268	1,178	2,506	2,542	2,218	4,084	4,775
Current account balance	1,481	2,534	-5,251	-12,781	-1,736	-3,016	-10,233	-14,777
International reserves	1,353	18,988	31,786	30,801	25,557	33,327	30,409	22,656
Ratios								
External debt stocks to exports (%)	70.6	77.7	121.4	111.9	184.0	177.7	151.8	144.7
External debt stocks to GNI (%)	45.8	39.6	56.2	55.1	90.9	93.0	83.8	77.9
Debt service to exports (%)	18.4	13.2	17.8	20.0	39.7	39.2	32.7	31.5
Short-term to external debt stocks (%)	3.2	35.8	29.0	21.0	19.0	21.8	24.2	25.7
Multilateral to external debt stocks (%)	17.1	7.9	4.4	4.2	9.1	10.7	8.3	9.9
Reserves to external debt stocks (%)	9.7	56.3	40.2	31.3	24.5	26.7	22.5	16.8
Reserves to imports (months)	0.9	5.2	5.2	3.6	5.0	5.2	3.5	2.4

UZBEKISTAN

(US$ million, unless otherwise indicated)

	2000	2005	2007	2008	2009	2010	2011	2012
Summary external debt data								
External debt stocks	**4,980**	**4,656**	**4,642**	**5,100**	**6,950**	**7,782**	**8,417**	**8,853**
Long-term external debt	4,228	4,168	4,028	4,474	6,375	7,140	7,648	8,112
Short-term external debt	282	112	198	221	163	238	366	337
interest arrears on long-term	3	8	2	10	19	70	70	0
Use of IMF credit	469	376	415	405	412	405	403	404
Long-term external debt								
Debt outstanding and disbursed	**4,228**	**4,168**	**4,028**	**4,474**	**6,375**	**7,140**	**7,648**	**8,112**
Public and publicly guaranteed	3,762	3,626	3,166	3,168	3,257	3,410	3,738	3,987
Official creditors	2,117	2,451	2,489	2,686	2,923	3,184	3,511	3,824
Private creditors	1,645	1,175	677	482	335	226	227	163
Private nonguaranteed	467	542	863	1,306	3,117	3,730	3,910	4,125
Disbursements	**770**	**404**	**665**	**1,003**	**2,610**	**1,188**	**942**	**1,051**
Public and publicly guaranteed	713	262	237	309	472	452	598	610
Official creditors	409	200	217	272	464	437	523	600
Private creditors	304	62	21	37	8	15	75	10
Private nonguaranteed	57	142	428	694	2,138	736	344	441
Principal repayments	**584**	**620**	**646**	**710**	**713**	**493**	**461**	**517**
Public and publicly guaranteed	443	510	494	460	386	370	296	294
Official creditors	148	177	218	242	225	256	226	218
Private creditors	295	333	276	219	161	114	69	76
Private nonguaranteed	141	110	152	250	327	123	165	224
Interest payments	**206**	**140**	**167**	**141**	**120**	**118**	**158**	**172**
Public and publicly guaranteed	182	117	141	114	82	63	68	75
Official creditors	75	63	97	84	71	59	62	66
Private creditors	108	53	45	30	12	4	6	9
Private nonguaranteed	24	23	26	26	38	55	90	97
Debt resource inflows								
Net debt inflows	-223	-301	58	308	1,830	719	610	575
Official creditors (incl. IMF)	196	5	-1	31	238	181	297	382
Private creditors	-419	-305	59	278	1,591	538	313	193
Long-term	-75	-239	21	263	1,658	514	185	152
Public and publicly guaranteed	9	-271	-256	-181	-153	-99	6	-66
Private nonguaranteed	-84	32	276	444	1,811	613	179	218
Short-term	-344	-66	38	15	-67	24	128	41
Non-debt resource inflows								
Foreign direct investment	75	192	705	711	842	1,628	1,467	1,094
Portfolio equity	..	..	..	..	..	..	..	..
Currency composition (%)								
Euro	..	17.9	17.4	14.1	11.8	9.5	9.1	7.9
U.S.dollars	56.7	52.8	49.2	48.0	53.0	54.2	56.1	60.5
Major economic aggregates								
Gross national income (GNI)	13,541	14,283	23,242	29,656	33,714	40,492	47,104	53,362
Exports of goods, services & prim. income	..	..	..	..	..	..	..	..
Personal transfers & comp. of employees	..	..	..	..	..	..	..	..
Imports of goods, services & prim. income	..	..	..	..	..	..	..	..
Primary income on FDI	..	..	..	..	..	..	..	..
Current account balance	..	..	..	..	..	..	..	..
International reserves	..	..	..	..	..	..	..	..
Ratios								
External debt stocks to exports (%)	..	..	..	..	..	..	..	..
External debt stocks to GNI (%)	36.8	32.6	20.0	17.2	20.6	19.2	17.9	16.6
Debt service to exports (%)	..	..	..	..	..	..	..	..
Short-term to external debt stocks (%)	5.7	2.4	4.3	4.3	2.4	3.1	4.3	3.8
Multilateral to external debt stocks (%)	9.1	17.1	19.4	18.6	15.8	15.6	15.7	19.3
Reserves to external debt stocks (%)	..	..	..	..	..	..	..	..
Reserves to imports (months)	..	..	..	..	..	..	..	..

VANUATU

(US$ million, unless otherwise indicated)

	2000	2005	2007	2008	2009	2010	2011	2012
Summary external debt data								
External debt stocks	**95.7**	**105.3**	**123.9**	**150.9**	**155.3**	**173.3**	**201.8**	**369.2**
Long-term external debt	73.1	71.9	78.1	89.7	98.8	99.3	98.8	92.2
Short-term external debt	1.4	10.2	20.1	36.1	31.0	49.0	78.0	252.0
interest arrears on long-term	0.0	0.2	0.1	0.1	0.0	0.0	0.0	0.0
Use of IMF credit	21.2	23.3	25.7	25.1	25.5	25.1	25.0	25.0
Long-term external debt								
Debt outstanding and disbursed	**73.1**	**71.9**	**78.1**	**89.7**	**98.8**	**99.3**	**98.8**	**92.2**
Public and publicly guaranteed	73.1	71.9	78.1	89.7	98.8	99.3	98.8	92.2
Official creditors	73.1	71.9	78.1	89.7	98.8	99.3	98.8	92.2
Private creditors	0.0	0.0	0.0	0.0	0.0	0.0	0.0	0.0
Private nonguaranteed	..	..	..	..	..	..	..	..
Disbursements	**14.2**	**0.0**	**3.9**	**10.1**	**11.7**	**0.0**	**0.0**	**0.0**
Public and publicly guaranteed	14.2	0.0	3.9	10.1	11.7	0.0	0.0	0.0
Official creditors	14.2	0.0	3.9	10.1	11.7	0.0	0.0	0.0
Private creditors	0.0	0.0	0.0	0.0	0.0	0.0	0.0	0.0
Private nonguaranteed	..	..	..	..	..	..	..	..
Principal repayments	**0.9**	**1.1**	**2.1**	**2.5**	**3.5**	**3.6**	**3.4**	**3.8**
Public and publicly guaranteed	0.9	1.1	2.1	2.5	3.5	3.6	3.4	3.8
Official creditors	0.9	1.1	2.1	2.5	3.5	3.6	3.4	3.8
Private creditors	0.0	0.0	0.0	0.0	0.0	0.0	0.0	0.0
Private nonguaranteed	..	..	..	..	..	..	..	..
Interest payments	**0.6**	**0.7**	**0.9**	**1.1**	**1.4**	**1.4**	**1.3**	**1.2**
Public and publicly guaranteed	0.6	0.7	0.9	1.1	1.4	1.4	1.3	1.2
Official creditors	0.6	0.7	0.9	1.1	1.4	1.4	1.3	1.2
Private creditors	0.0	0.0	0.0	0.0	0.0	0.0	0.0	0.0
Private nonguaranteed	..	..	..	..	..	..	..	..
Debt resource inflows								
Net debt inflows	13.6	-28.1	10.8	23.6	3.1	14.4	25.6	170.2
Official creditors (incl. IMF)	13.4	-1.1	1.8	7.6	8.1	-3.6	-3.4	-3.8
Private creditors	0.3	-27.0	9.0	16.0	-5.0	18.0	29.0	174.0
Long-term	0.0	0.0	0.0	0.0	0.0	0.0	0.0	0.0
Public and publicly guaranteed	0.0	0.0	0.0	0.0	0.0	0.0	0.0	0.0
Private nonguaranteed	..	..	..	..	..	..	..	..
Short-term	0.3	-27.0	9.0	16.0	-5.0	18.0	29.0	174.0
Non-debt resource inflows								
Foreign direct investment	20.3	13.3	34.2	37.7	32.1	41.5	58.1	37.7
Portfolio equity	..	..	..	..	..	..	..	..
Currency composition (%)								
Euro	..	13.6	12.5	9.2	7.1	5.2	4.1	3.6
U.S.dollars	56.8	54.0	51.3	47.1	41.6	42.3	42.2	41.6
Major economic aggregates								
Gross national income (GNI)	259.0	369.0	498.8	603.2	586.8	679.1	766.2	766.7
Exports of goods, services & prim. income	175.7	204.6	255.7	313.7	330.9	365.5	396.1	413.9
Personal transfers & comp. of employees	34.7	5.1	5.5	8.9	11.5	11.8	21.8	22.0
Imports of goods, services & prim. income	178.8	258.6	313.2	492.8	345.5	419.6	465.7	480.8
Primary income on FDI	21.9	35.3	45.6	29.7	41.7	48.0	52.7	76.8
Current account balance	5.0	-34.0	-34.4	-141.6	10.3	-34.9	-57.6	-50.3
International reserves	38.9	67.2	119.6	115.2	148.6	161.4	173.8	..
Ratios								
External debt stocks to exports (%)	54.4	51.5	48.4	48.1	46.9	47.4	50.9	89.2
External debt stocks to GNI (%)	36.9	28.5	24.8	25.0	26.5	25.5	26.3	48.2
Debt service to exports (%)	1.6	1.6	1.8	1.5	1.7	1.6	1.6	2.1
Short-term to external debt stocks (%)	1.5	9.7	16.2	23.9	20.0	28.3	38.7	68.2
Multilateral to external debt stocks (%)	67.0	64.0	55.9	47.0	44.2	39.7	33.4	16.7
Reserves to external debt stocks (%)	40.7	63.8	96.5	76.4	95.7	93.1	86.1	..
Reserves to imports (months)	2.6	3.1	4.6	2.8	5.2	4.6	4.5	..

Notes:

Long-term public and publicly guaranteed debt data from 2010 are World Bank staff estimates. Short-term debt is based on data from the BIS.

VENEZUELA, REPUBLICA BOLIVARIANA de

(US$ million, unless otherwise indicated)

	2000	2005	2007	2008	2009	2010	2011	2012
Summary external debt data								
External debt stocks	**42,753**	**45,355**	**48,714**	**53,871**	**61,410**	**65,149**	**70,339**	**72,097**
Long-term external debt	33,952	34,794	30,512	33,199	38,508	40,572	47,324	48,796
Short-term external debt	8,186	10,108	17,701	20,184	18,915	20,660	19,110	19,393
interest arrears on long-term	59	5	0	0	7	7	7	1
Use of IMF credit	616	453	501	488	3,987	3,917	3,905	3,909
Long-term external debt								
Debt outstanding and disbursed	**33,952**	**34,794**	**30,512**	**33,199**	**38,508**	**40,572**	**47,324**	**48,796**
Public and publicly guaranteed	27,820	31,092	27,552	29,889	35,198	37,512	44,264	46,236
Official creditors	6,180	3,434	3,410	3,550	4,144	5,382	6,719	8,724
Private creditors	21,640	27,658	24,142	26,339	31,054	32,130	37,546	37,511
Private nonguaranteed	6,132	3,702	2,960	3,310	3,310	3,060	3,060	2,560
Disbursements	**2,343**	**7,250**	**2,053**	**5,490**	**6,068**	**4,729**	**9,266**	**2,661**
Public and publicly guaranteed	2,343	7,250	2,053	4,840	6,068	4,729	9,266	2,661
Official creditors	787	406	535	645	1,035	1,707	2,060	2,514
Private creditors	1,556	6,844	1,518	4,196	5,033	3,023	7,206	147
Private nonguaranteed	0	0	0	650	0	0	0	0
Principal repayments	**2,921**	**2,385**	**2,109**	**2,745**	**812**	**1,135**	**2,515**	**1,190**
Public and publicly guaranteed	2,265	1,698	1,835	2,445	812	885	2,515	690
Official creditors	613	739	992	527	450	479	726	504
Private creditors	1,652	959	843	1,918	362	406	1,790	186
Private nonguaranteed	655	687	274	300	0	250	0	500
Interest payments	**2,435**	**2,656**	**2,585**	**2,859**	**2,765**	**3,089**	**3,398**	**4,274**
Public and publicly guaranteed	1,867	2,308	2,314	2,525	2,441	2,789	3,119	4,002
Official creditors	343	204	243	235	186	177	205	207
Private creditors	1,524	2,103	2,070	2,290	2,255	2,612	2,914	3,795
Private nonguaranteed	568	349	271	334	324	301	278	272
Debt resource inflows								
Net debt inflows	-384	7,136	6,122	5,228	3,980	5,340	5,201	1,760
Official creditors (incl. IMF)	-333	-333	-457	118	585	1,228	1,334	2,010
Private creditors	-52	7,469	6,579	5,111	3,395	4,112	3,866	-250
Long-term	-752	5,198	401	2,628	4,671	2,367	5,416	-539
Public and publicly guaranteed	-96	5,885	675	2,278	4,671	2,617	5,416	-39
Private nonguaranteed	-655	-687	-274	350	0	-250	0	-500
Short-term	700	2,271	6,178	2,483	-1,276	1,745	-1,550	289
Non-debt resource inflows								
Foreign direct investment	4,701	2,706	2,517	1,258	-2,553	1,903	3,889	2,199
Portfolio equity	-574	28	50	1	118	10	..	-50
Currency composition (%)								
Euro	..	11.5	14.8	8.2	6.7	5.8	3.6	3.6
U.S.dollars	83.3	83.6	81.5	88.7	91.0	92.6	95.5	95.8
Major economic aggregates								
Gross national income (GNI)	115,760	143,314	233,063	316,093	325,894	387,524	309,380	372,396
Exports of goods, services & prim. income	37,760	61,208	81,937	106,204	62,445	69,584	97,042	101,543
Personal transfers & comp. of employees	17	148	151	137	131	143	138	118
Imports of goods, services & prim. income	25,737	36,093	65,201	73,145	59,517	59,879	71,865	89,549
Primary income on FDI	1,424	3,895	4,498	5,297	3,139	4,877	4,810	5,757
Current account balance	11,853	25,053	15,981	32,146	2,258	8,812	24,387	11,016
International reserves	13,088	23,919	24,196	33,098	21,703	13,137	9,930	9,900
Ratios								
External debt stocks to exports (%)	113.2	74.1	59.5	50.7	98.3	93.6	72.5	71.0
External debt stocks to GNI (%)	36.9	31.6	20.9	17.0	18.8	16.8	22.7	19.4
Debt service to exports (%)	16.9	8.7	7.0	5.7	6.1	6.5	6.4	5.6
Short-term to external debt stocks (%)	19.1	22.3	36.3	37.5	30.8	31.7	27.2	26.9
Multilateral to external debt stocks (%)	7.5	6.2	5.1	5.0	5.1	6.8	7.9	7.8
Reserves to external debt stocks (%)	30.6	52.7	49.7	61.4	35.3	20.2	14.1	13.7
Reserves to imports (months)	6.1	8.0	4.5	5.4	4.4	2.6	1.7	1.3

Notes:

Short-term debt from 1997 is based on Central Bank data.

VIETNAM

(US$ million, unless otherwise indicated)

	2000	2005	2007	2008	2009	2010	2011	2012
Summary external debt data								
External debt stocks	**12,859**	**19,039**	**23,285**	**26,488**	**33,084**	**44,923**	**53,080**	**59,133**
Long-term external debt	11,558	16,193	18,416	22,014	27,320	37,444	42,620	48,760
Short-term external debt	923	2,574	4,630	4,279	5,186	6,949	9,964	9,889
interest arrears on long-term	78	74	0	1	0	0	0	0
Use of IMF credit	378	272	239	195	578	529	496	484
Long-term external debt								
Debt outstanding and disbursed	**11,558**	**16,193**	**18,416**	**22,014**	**27,320**	**37,444**	**42,620**	**48,760**
Public and publicly guaranteed	11,558	16,193	18,416	22,014	27,320	32,764	36,758	39,954
Official creditors	8,680	14,259	16,261	19,370	23,938	27,435	31,085	33,480
Private creditors	2,878	1,934	2,155	2,644	3,382	5,329	5,673	6,475
Private nonguaranteed	..	..	..	..	..	4,680	5,862	8,806
Disbursements	**1,272**	**2,047**	**2,440**	**2,799**	**4,730**	**6,878**	**6,976**	**8,981**
Public and publicly guaranteed	1,272	2,047	2,440	2,799	4,730	5,593	4,759	5,955
Official creditors	1,176	1,261	2,006	2,202	4,104	3,675	4,009	4,708
Private creditors	96	786	433	597	627	1,918	750	1,247
Private nonguaranteed	..	..	..	..	..	1,285	2,217	3,026
Principal repayments	**937**	**480**	**617**	**770**	**915**	**1,048**	**3,082**	**4,055**
Public and publicly guaranteed	937	480	617	770	915	1,048	1,201	1,473
Official creditors	134	303	456	587	687	735	823	1,024
Private creditors	802	177	161	183	228	313	378	449
Private nonguaranteed	..	..	..	..	..	0	1,881	2,582
Interest payments	**296**	**317**	**418**	**464**	**476**	**707**	**902**	**1,217**
Public and publicly guaranteed	296	317	418	464	476	563	689	744
Official creditors	77	256	300	329	344	398	457	494
Private creditors	218	61	118	135	132	165	232	250
Private nonguaranteed	..	..	..	..	..	144	213	473
Debt resource inflows								
Net debt inflows	472	1,926	4,001	1,638	4,685	7,554	6,876	4,838
Official creditors (incl. IMF)	1,020	904	1,525	1,575	3,378	2,902	3,154	3,671
Private creditors	-548	1,022	2,475	62	1,307	4,652	3,722	1,167
Long-term	-706	609	272	414	399	2,889	707	1,242
Public and publicly guaranteed	-706	609	272	414	399	1,605	371	798
Private nonguaranteed	..	..	..	..	..	1,285	336	444
Short-term	158	413	2,203	-352	908	1,763	3,015	-75
Non-debt resource inflows								
Foreign direct investment	1,298	1,954	6,700	9,579	7,600	8,000	7,430	8,368
Portfolio equity	..	115	6,243	-578	128	2,383	1,064	1,887
Currency composition (%)								
Euro	..	5.7	7.3	6.7	8.2	9.1	8.2	7.6
U.S.dollars	43.2	44.7	41.8	39.5	43.3	48.1	47.9	49.2
Major economic aggregates								
Gross national income (GNI)	30,726	51,859	68,845	88,145	92,614	102,008	117,759	134,161
Exports of goods, services & prim. income	17,481	36,987	55,757	71,048	63,615	80,153	106,180	124,468
Personal transfers & comp. of employees	..	3,150	6,180	6,805	6,020	8,260	8,600	..
Imports of goods, services & prim. income	18,107	40,927	69,140	89,182	76,671	92,314	114,629	123,618
Primary income on FDI	..	..	..	..	..	..	..	..
Current account balance	1,106	-560	-6,953	-10,823	-6,608	-4,276	236	9,062
International reserves	3,417	9,051	23,479	23,890	16,447	12,467	13,539	25,573
Ratios								
External debt stocks to exports (%)	73.6	51.5	41.8	37.3	52.0	56.0	50.0	47.5
External debt stocks to GNI (%)	41.9	36.7	33.8	30.1	35.7	44.0	45.1	44.1
Debt service to exports (%)	7.5	2.6	2.3	2.0	2.3	2.3	3.9	4.4
Short-term to external debt stocks (%)	7.2	13.5	19.9	16.2	15.7	15.5	18.8	16.7
Multilateral to external debt stocks (%)	14.7	27.0	30.6	30.4	31.9	27.9	27.1	27.1
Reserves to external debt stocks (%)	26.6	47.5	100.8	90.2	49.7	27.8	25.5	43.2
Reserves to imports (months)	2.3	2.7	4.1	3.2	2.6	1.6	1.4	2.5

Notes:

Arrears were removed from 2006 based on reports provided by the country. Short-term debt is based on data from the BIS.

YEMEN, REPUBLIC OF

(US$ million, unless otherwise indicated)

	2000	2005	2007	2008	2009	2010	2011	2012
Summary external debt data								
External debt stocks	**5,162**	**5,501**	**6,152**	**6,319**	**6,734**	**6,682**	**6,418**	**7,555**
Long-term external debt	4,109	4,814	5,524	5,696	5,875	5,933	5,876	6,911
Short-term external debt	699	353	413	483	442	313	131	140
interest arrears on long-term	27	94	107	112	117	124	131	140
Use of IMF credit	355	333	215	140	417	436	410	504
Long-term external debt								
Debt outstanding and disbursed	**4,109**	**4,814**	**5,524**	**5,696**	**5,875**	**5,933**	**5,876**	**6,911**
Public and publicly guaranteed	4,109	4,814	5,524	5,696	5,875	5,933	5,876	6,911
Official creditors	4,046	4,807	5,517	5,690	5,871	5,930	5,874	6,909
Private creditors	63	7	7	6	5	3	2	1
Private nonguaranteed	..	..	..	..	..	..	..	..
Disbursements	**137**	**265**	**390**	**285**	**332**	**287**	**101**	**1,250**
Public and publicly guaranteed	137	265	390	285	332	287	101	1,250
Official creditors	137	265	390	285	332	287	101	1,250
Private creditors	0	0	0	0	0	0	0	0
Private nonguaranteed	..	..	..	..	..	..	..	..
Principal repayments	**81**	**94**	**113**	**134**	**140**	**155**	**175**	**181**
Public and publicly guaranteed	81	94	113	134	140	155	175	181
Official creditors	81	94	112	133	139	154	174	180
Private creditors	0	0	1	1	1	1	1	1
Private nonguaranteed	..	..	..	..	..	..	..	..
Interest payments	**45**	**55**	**65**	**70**	**72**	**74**	**75**	**73**
Public and publicly guaranteed	45	55	65	70	72	74	75	73
Official creditors	45	55	65	70	72	74	74	73
Private creditors	0	0	0	0	0	0	0	0
Private nonguaranteed	..	..	..	..	..	..	..	..
Debt resource inflows								
Net debt inflows	270	176	278	145	102	22	-288	1,162
Official creditors (incl. IMF)	-15	116	191	81	149	159	-98	1,163
Private creditors	285	61	87	64	-47	-137	-190	-1
Long-term	0	0	-1	-1	-1	-1	-1	-1
Public and publicly guaranteed	0	0	-1	-1	-1	-1	-1	-1
Private nonguaranteed	..	..	..	..	..	..	..	..
Short-term	285	61	88	65	-46	-136	-189	..
Non-debt resource inflows								
Foreign direct investment	6	-302	917	1,555	129	-93	-713	349
Portfolio equity	..	..	..	..	..	..	..	..
Currency composition (%)								
Euro	..	1.7	1.9	1.8	1.9	1.8	1.8	1.5
U.S.dollars	68.2	67.3	61.8	59.5	58.8	57.3	56.6	61.7
Major economic aggregates								
Gross national income (GNI)	8,863	15,139	20,249	24,957	23,436	29,922	29,442	33,649
Exports of goods, services & prim. income	4,158	6,963	8,158	10,504	7,207	9,316	9,963	..
Personal transfers & comp. of employees	1,288	1,283	1,322	1,411	1,160	1,526	1,404	..
Imports of goods, services & prim. income	4,221	7,745	11,092	13,918	11,287	12,821	13,126	..
Primary income on FDI	855	1,603	1,390	1,875	927	1,408	2,240	..
Current account balance	1,337	624	-1,508	-1,251	-2,565	-1,381	-1,029	..
International reserves	2,900	6,115	7,715	8,111	6,936	5,868	4,449	6,068
Ratios								
External debt stocks to exports (%)	124.2	79.0	75.4	60.2	93.4	71.7	64.4	..
External debt stocks to GNI (%)	58.2	36.3	30.4	25.3	28.7	22.3	21.8	22.5
Debt service to exports (%)	5.9	3.1	3.3	2.7	3.7	2.8	2.8	..
Short-term to external debt stocks (%)	13.5	6.4	6.7	7.7	6.6	4.7	2.0	1.9
Multilateral to external debt stocks (%)	32.5	40.3	47.2	48.1	46.9	49.1	50.6	44.3
Reserves to external debt stocks (%)	56.2	111.2	125.4	128.4	103.0	87.8	69.3	80.3
Reserves to imports (months)	8.2	9.5	8.3	7.0	7.4	5.5	4.1	..

Notes:

Short-term debt is based on data from the BIS.

ZAMBIA

(US$ million, unless otherwise indicated)

	2000	2005	2007	2008	2009	2010	2011	2012
Summary external debt data								
External debt stocks	**5,811**	**5,461**	**2,857**	**3,080**	**3,774**	**4,419**	**4,944**	**5,385**
Long-term external debt	4,508	4,538	2,087	2,205	2,220	2,111	3,482	3,929
Short-term external debt	76	234	575	674	474	1,191	326	330
interest arrears on long-term	33	90	149	152	154	167	167	171
Use of IMF credit	1,227	689	195	201	1,080	1,117	1,137	1,126
Long-term external debt								
Debt outstanding and disbursed	**4,508**	**4,538**	**2,087**	**2,205**	**2,220**	**2,111**	**3,482**	**3,929**
Public and publicly guaranteed	4,444	3,942	1,107	1,157	1,200	1,317	1,964	3,166
Official creditors	4,412	3,646	1,059	1,108	1,158	1,284	1,857	2,347
Private creditors	31	295	48	48	42	33	108	820
Private nonguaranteed	65	596	981	1,049	1,020	794	1,517	763
Disbursements	**261**	**218**	**315**	**239**	**126**	**203**	**789**	**1,333**
Public and publicly guaranteed	251	114	118	118	91	176	696	1,300
Official creditors	251	114	118	108	91	176	605	566
Private creditors	0	0	0	10	0	0	91	734
Private nonguaranteed	10	105	197	121	35	27	93	33
Principal repayments	**98**	**136**	**75**	**114**	**122**	**86**	**139**	**143**
Public and publicly guaranteed	79	71	32	61	59	47	56	101
Official creditors	79	59	32	52	52	38	40	78
Private creditors	1	12	0	8	7	8	16	23
Private nonguaranteed	18	66	43	53	63	40	82	42
Interest payments	**80**	**58**	**32**	**39**	**36**	**29**	**48**	**59**
Public and publicly guaranteed	76	29	9	14	13	11	13	41
Official creditors	76	29	9	14	13	11	13	41
Private creditors	0	0	0	0	0	0	0	0
Private nonguaranteed	4	28	23	24	24	18	35	18
Debt resource inflows								
Net debt inflows	159	88	405	232	45	876	-192	1,179
Official creditors (incl. IMF)	198	-8	127	67	283	193	589	476
Private creditors	-39	96	277	166	-238	683	-780	702
Long-term	-9	27	154	70	-36	-21	85	702
Public and publicly guaranteed	-1	-12	0	2	-7	-8	75	712
Private nonguaranteed	-8	39	154	68	-29	-13	10	-9
Short-term	-30	69	123	96	-202	704	-865	0
Non-debt resource inflows								
Foreign direct investment	122	357	1,324	939	695	1,729	1,108	1,066
Portfolio equity	6	5	4	-6	-13	101	25	26
Currency composition (%)								
Euro	..	5.9	18.2	14.8	13.3	10.5	6.0	3.7
U.S.dollars	61.7	72.9	41.3	39.3	37.4	33.8	49.1	64.6
Major economic aggregates								
Gross national income (GNI)	3,097	6,547	9,997	13,242	12,386	14,827	18,049	19,542
Exports of goods, services & prim. income	891	2,533	4,818	5,291	4,564	7,733	9,046	9,891
Personal transfers & comp. of employees	..	53	59	68	41	44	46	73
Imports of goods, services & prim. income	1,567	3,239	6,047	6,890	4,498	6,959	8,724	10,346
Primary income on FDI	71	461	1,474	1,346	265	1,303	1,093	1,033
Current account balance	-662	-600	-698	-1,039	582	1,206	700	-1
International reserves	245	560	1,090	1,096	1,892	2,094	2,324	3,042
Ratios								
External debt stocks to exports (%)	652.0	215.6	59.3	58.2	82.7	57.1	54.7	54.4
External debt stocks to GNI (%)	187.6	83.4	28.6	23.3	30.5	29.8	27.4	27.6
Debt service to exports (%)	21.2	11.2	2.6	3.2	3.7	1.9	2.2	2.2
Short-term to external debt stocks (%)	1.3	4.3	20.1	21.9	12.6	26.9	6.6	6.1
Multilateral to external debt stocks (%)	41.4	57.2	26.7	26.6	23.1	20.9	19.5	20.0
Reserves to external debt stocks (%)	4.2	10.3	38.1	35.6	50.1	47.4	47.0	56.5
Reserves to imports (months)	1.9	2.1	2.2	1.9	5.0	3.6	3.2	3.5

Notes:

Long-term private nonguaranteed before 2011 are World Bank staff estimates based on reports provided by the country. Short-term debt data before 2011 are from the BIS. Short-term debt from 2011 only include private nonguaranteed short-term debt. Data include the effects of HIPC and MDRI debt relief.

ZIMBABWE

(US$ million, unless otherwise indicated)

	2000	2005	2007	2008	2009	2010	2011	2012
Summary external debt data								
External debt stocks	**3,843**	**4,225**	**5,358**	**5,271**	**5,428**	**5,863**	**6,494**	**7,713**
Long-term external debt	2,981	3,209	3,768	3,743	3,824	4,259	4,724	5,715
Short-term external debt	568	891	1,456	1,398	1,062	1,075	1,243	1,477
interest arrears on long-term	55	534	753	807	915	938	1,052	1,141
Use of IMF credit	294	125	134	129	542	529	527	520
Long-term external debt								
Debt outstanding and disbursed	**2,981**	**3,209**	**3,768**	**3,743**	**3,824**	**4,259**	**4,724**	**5,715**
Public and publicly guaranteed	2,776	3,177	3,693	3,654	3,734	3,663	3,820	3,884
Official creditors	2,439	2,771	3,226	3,227	3,287	3,230	3,389	3,447
Private creditors	337	406	467	427	448	433	431	437
Private nonguaranteed	205	32	75	89	89	596	904	1,831
Disbursements	**185**	**25**	**227**	**105**	**79**	**847**	**1,584**	**1,433**
Public and publicly guaranteed	139	24	160	39	13	4	186	70
Official creditors	125	16	160	25	13	4	181	70
Private creditors	15	8	0	14	0	0	5	0
Private nonguaranteed	46	0	68	66	66	843	1,398	1,363
Principal repayments	**211**	**45**	**55**	**54**	**66**	**337**	**1,096**	**440**
Public and publicly guaranteed	146	31	36	2	0	1	6	5
Official creditors	113	21	36	2	0	1	6	5
Private creditors	33	10	0	0	0	0	0	0
Private nonguaranteed	65	14	19	52	66	336	1,091	435
Interest payments	**81**	**7**	**14**	**10**	**30**	**31**	**43**	**273**
Public and publicly guaranteed	64	3	13	5	14	13	14	14
Official creditors	50	2	13	5	14	13	14	14
Private creditors	13	1	0	0	0	0	0	0
Private nonguaranteed	17	4	1	5	16	18	29	259
Debt resource inflows								
Net debt inflows	-329	-225	386	-63	-431	496	542	1,130
Official creditors (incl. IMF)	-58	-169	124	21	13	-1	175	57
Private creditors	-271	-56	263	-84	-444	497	367	1,072
Long-term	-37	-16	49	28	0	507	313	927
Public and publicly guaranteed	-19	-2	0	14	0	0	5	0
Private nonguaranteed	-19	-14	49	14	0	507	308	927
Short-term	-233	-40	214	-112	-444	-10	54	145
Non-debt resource inflows								
Foreign direct investment	23	103	69	52	105	166	387	400
Portfolio equity	..	..	..	..	..	..	..	..
Currency composition (%)								
Euro	..	31.6	33.8	32.6	33.2	31.4	29.4	29.5
U.S.dollars	29.9	28.7	29.5	30.4	30.0	30.3	30.4	30.7
Major economic aggregates								
Gross national income (GNI)	6,329	5,479	5,198	4,181	5,714	7,012	9,137	10,210
Exports of goods, services & prim. income	..	..	..	..	..	..	..	..
Personal transfers & comp. of employees	..	..	..	..	..	..	..	..
Imports of goods, services & prim. income	..	..	..	..	..	..	..	..
Primary income on FDI	..	..	..	..	..	..	..	..
Current account balance	..	-532	-342	-762	..	..	..	..
International reserves	193	97	145	76	822	732	659	574
Ratios								
External debt stocks to exports (%)	..	..	..	..	..	..	..	..
External debt stocks to GNI (%)	60.7	77.1	103.1	126.1	95.0	83.6	71.1	75.5
Debt service to exports (%)	..	..	..	..	..	..	..	..
Short-term to external debt stocks (%)	14.8	21.1	27.2	26.5	19.6	18.3	19.1	19.2
Multilateral to external debt stocks (%)	35.2	35.1	30.1	30.5	29.9	27.2	24.6	21.1
Reserves to external debt stocks (%)	5.0	2.3	2.7	1.4	15.1	12.5	10.2	7.4
Reserves to imports (months)	..	..	..	..	..	..	..	..

Notes:

Short-term debt is based on data from the BIS.

About the Data

Data Sources and Methodology

Data Sources

The principal sources of information for the tables in *International Debt Statistics 2014* are reports to the World Bank through the World Bank's Debtor Reporting System (DRS) from member countries that have received either International Bank for Reconstruction and Development (IBRD) loans or International Development Association (IDA) credits. The DRS has its origin in the World Bank's need to monitor and assess the financial position of its borrowers. Since 1951, borrowers have been required to provide statistics on their public external debt and private sector debt that benefit from a public guarantee. In its design, consistency, and continuity of coverage, the DRS is a unique resource. Reporting countries submit detailed reports on the annual status, transactions, and terms of the long-term external debt of public agencies and that of private ones guaranteed by a public agency in the debtor country. The DRS maintains these records on a loan-by-loan basis. In 1973, coverage of the DRS was expanded to include private sector nonguaranteed borrowing, but for this category of debt, data are provided by borrowers in aggregate rather than loan by loan.

Data submitted to the DRS are processed in the World Bank External Debt (WBXD) system, along with additional information received from the files of the African Development Bank, the Asian Development Bank, the Inter-American Development Bank (IDB), the International Monetary Fund (IMF), institutions of the World Bank Group (IBRD and IDA), and the European Bank for Reconstruction and Development (EBRD). The WBXD is an internal system of the World Bank. Among its outputs is the International Debt Statistics (IDS) database, from which the tables in this publication and online database are produced.

Data on exports and imports (on a balance of payments basis), international reserves, current account balances, foreign direct investment (FDI), portfolio equity flows, and primary income of FDI are drawn mainly from the files of the IMF, supplemented by United Nations Conference on Trade and Development (UNCTAD) reports and country data. Balance of payments data are presented according to the sixth edition of the IMF's *Balance of Payments Manual* (BPM6). Official aid flows come from data collected and published by the Development Assistance Committee (DAC) of the Organisation for Economic Co-operation and Development (OECD). Short-term external debt data are as reported by debtor countries or are estimates based on the Bank for International Settlements (BIS) quarterly series of commercial banks' claims on developing countries. For some countries, estimates were prepared by pooling creditor and debtor information. Data on the gross national income of most developing countries are collected from national statistical organizations or central banks by visiting and resident World Bank missions.

Every effort has been made to ensure the accuracy and completeness of the external debt statistics. Coverage has been improved through the efforts of the reporting agencies and close collaboration between the Bank and our partners, Commonwealth Secretariat (COMSEC) and UNCTAD, which provide debt recording and reporting systems across the globe, as well as through the work of the World Bank missions, which visit member countries to gather data and to provide technical assistance on debt issues. Nevertheless, quality and coverage vary among debtors and may also vary for the same debtor from year to year. Data on long-term external debt reported by member countries are checked against, and supplemented by, data from several other sources. Among these sources are the statements and reports of several regional development banks, government lending agencies, and official government Web sites.

Methodology

Aggregations

Total debt stock and other aggregate measures are derived from the summation of loan-level data on stocks and flows after conversion to a common currency. Other tabulations are compiled using terms and conditions reported in the loan-level data, such as currency composition, cancellations, rescheduling of other liabilities into long-term public and publicly guaranteed external debt, and debt buybacks.

Aggregates for regional and income groups are based on the World Bank's operational classifications, which may differ from common geographic usage or income groups used by other organizations. Country classifications of DRS reporting countries in 2012 are shown in country groups in the back of the publication. The same classification is used for all historical data shown in *International Debt Statistics* and the online tables and online database.

Currency Conversion

Data on external obligations are normally reported to the World Bank in the currency of repayment and are converted into a common currency (U.S. dollars) using official exchange rates published by the IMF.

Commitments, disbursements, and debt service payments (flows) are converted to U.S. dollars at the annual average exchange rate for the year. Debt outstanding (disbursed and undisbursed) at the end of a given year (stock) is converted at the exchange rate in effect at the end of the relevant year. Consequently, year-to-year changes in debt outstanding and disbursed may not be equal to net flows (disbursements less principal repayments); similarly, changes in debt outstanding (including undisbursed debt) may not equal commitments less repayments. Discrepancies will be particularly significant when exchange rates have moved sharply during the year. Projected debt service is converted to U.S. dollars at rates in effect at the end of December 2012.

Beginning with 1991, all ruble debt owed to the former Soviet Union has been converted at a rate of US$1 = 0.6 ruble, except in cases where a bilateral agreement specifying a different conversion rate is in place. Adoption of this methodology does not constitute an endorsement by the World Bank staff of the appropriateness or validity of the exchange rate used. This matter must be resolved bilaterally between the Russian Federation and its debtor countries.

Starting with the 1988–89 edition of World Debt Tables (the predecessor of IDS), all data pertaining to IBRD loans from 1985 onward are recorded at their current market value. Starting with the 1991–92 edition, all data pertaining to Asian Development Bank loans from 1989 onward are recorded at their current market value. Starting with the 1998 edition, all data pertaining to African Development Bank and African Development Fund loans from 1997 onward are recorded at their current market value.

Debt Stock and Flow Reconciliation

Because of currency conversions and the timing of transactions, there may be differences between the change in aggregate stocks from one period to the next and flows during the relevant period; changes in debt outstanding, including undisbursed amounts, will therefore differ from commitments less repayments.

Changes in the stock of debt from one period to the next can be attributed to five factors: the net flow of debt, the net change in interest arrears, the capitalization of interest, a reduction in debt resulting from debt forgiveness or other debt reduction mechanisms, and cross-currency valuation effects. Any residual difference in the change in stock not explained by one of those five factors may indicate inconsistencies in the reported data or specific phenomena prevailing in an individual country (for example, an incomplete historical series for all categories of debt). Starting in 1989, the IDS includes the debt stock reconciliation, but not all components are shown in the IDS print edition and online tables.

External Debt Restructuring

Starting in 1985, the WBXD includes information on restructuring of debt by official creditors in the context of the Paris Club, restructuring by commercial creditors, debt swap operations, buybacks, and bond exchanges. It attempts to capture accurately the effect of debt restructuring on both external debt stocks and external debt flows, consistent with the terms on which the restructuring takes place. In the compilation and presentation of external debt data, a distinction is made between cash flows and imputed flows. According to this criterion, restructured service payments and the shift in liabilities from one financial instrument to another as a result of debt restructuring are considered to be imputed flows. Both cash flows and imputed flows are recorded separately in WBXD.

The imputed flows and stock changes associated with debt restructuring are included in the IDS tables and online database to complement the cash-basis transactions recorded in the main body of the data. Such data encompass information on the debt stock and debt flows restructured each year, the amount of principal forgiven (interest forgiven is shown as a memorandum item), and the amount of external debt stock reduced either by forgiveness or by a debt buyback operation. Changes in creditors and debtors that result from debt restructuring are also reflected. For example, when insured commercial credits are rescheduled, the creditor classification shifts from private to official (bilateral), reflecting the assumption of the assets by the official credit insurance agencies in the creditor country. The IDS data will show a reduction in the external debt owed to the original private creditors equal or similar to the amount of debt restructured and a corresponding increase in the debt owed to the new official creditor. Similarly on the debtor side, when a government accepts responsibility for the payment of restructured debt previously owed by a private enterprise, the relevant change in the debtor category will be reflected. Likewise, if short-term external debt is restructured into a long-term obligation, the stock of short-term external debt will decline and the stock of long-term external debt will rise by the amount of short-term debt restructured. In the event of a debt swap of long-term external debt (external debt to equity, external debt for nature, or external debt for development), the face value of the external debt swapped will be recorded as a decline in long-term external debt stock, but no flow transaction (principal repayment) will be recorded.

Projections of Future Disbursements and Debt Service Payments

The WBXD system projects future disbursements and future debt service payments on the assumption that every existing loan commitment will be fully used and repaid in full.

Future Disbursements

Disbursement projections are made using one of the following methods:

- *Specific schedules.* Debtor countries are requested to submit a schedule of future disbursements, if available, at the time each new loan is first reported.
- *Standard schedules.* In the absence of specific schedules, the WBXD system projects the future disbursement schedule according to the undisbursed balance of each loan at the end of the most recent reporting period.

These projected schedules are based on profiles derived from the disbursement pattern of comparable loans that fully disbursed. Thirty different profiles have been compiled corresponding to each category of creditor and, in the case of official creditors, for concessional and nonconcessional loans. Each profile is derived by applying regression analysis techniques to a body of data on actual disbursements for each fully disbursed loan in the WBXD database. The profiles are periodically updated to take into account the evolving pattern of disbursements observed for fully disbursed loans.

Future principal payments are generated by the WBXD system according to the repayment terms of each loan. Principal repayments (amortization) are based on the amount of the loan commitment. If the amortization schedule follows a set pattern (for example, equal semiannual payments), the WBXD system calculates repayments automatically using the loan commitment amount, the first and final payment dates, and the frequency of the payments. If future payments are irregular, the WBXD system requires a schedule.

Future interest payments are generated by the WBXD system according to the disbursed and outstanding balance of the loan at the beginning of the period. Using the interest rate specified in the loan contract, the first and final interest payment dates, and the frequency of payments, the WBXD system calculates the stream of future interest payments due. If interest payments are irregular, the WBXD system requires a schedule.

Future debt service payments are the sum of future principal and interest payments due on existing commitments, including the undisbursed portion. They do not include debt service payments that may become due as a result of new loans contracted in subsequent years, nor do they take into account the effect of any change to future debt service obligations resulting from actions such as prepayment or rescheduling or from cancellations that occurred after the most recent year-end data reported to the DRS.

Both projected disbursements and future debt service payments are converted into U.S. dollars using end-December 2012 exchange rates. Likewise, future interest payments on loans with a variable interest rate (for example, loans from commercial banks tied to the London Interbank Offered Rate [LIBOR]) are based on the interest rate prevailing at end-December 2012.

Treatment of Arrears

The DRS collects information on arrears of both principal and interest. Principal in arrears is included in the amount of long-term external debt outstanding and is shown separately. Interest in arrears on long-term external debt and interest in arrears on the use of IMF credit are included as part of short-term external debt outstanding and are shown separately. Clearance of interest in arrears by repayment will be recorded as an interest payment in the relevant creditor category of the loan (or loans) on which the arrears were incurred, as a corresponding reduction in the level of short-term debt outstanding, and as a net reduction in interest arrears. Clearance of interest arrears through debt restructuring or forgiveness will be recorded as a reduction in the level of short-term debt outstanding and a net reduction in interest arrears. When interests are rescheduled, they will be capitalized: This change will be recorded as an increase in long-term debt outstanding equal to the amount of interest capitalized and the reduction in short-term debt outstanding noted previously.

External Debt and Its Components

This section describes the compilation of the major components of external debt included in the IDS tables and database and the relationship between them, as shown in figure 1 on the next page. Information about general methods of compiling external debt data is discussed in the previuos section titled "Methodology." For concise definitions, see the Glossary.

Total External Debt

Total external debt shown in the IDS is the sum of long-term external debt, short-term debt, and IMF credit. It represents the total debt owed to nonresident creditors and is repayable in both foreign and domestic currency.

Short-Term Debt

Short-term debt is defined as external debt with an original maturity of one year or less. The DRS requires debtor countries to report only on their long-term external debt. However, to gain a comprehensive picture of total external obligations, the World Bank encourages debtor countries to voluntarily provide information on their short-term external obligations.

By its nature, short-term external debt is difficult to monitor: Loan-by-loan registration is normally impractical, and monitoring systems typically rely on information requested periodically by the central bank from the banking sector. The World Bank regards the debtor country as the authoritative source of information on its short-term debt. Unless otherwise specified in the country tables the data for short-term debt are derived from the data provided by quarterly external debt statistics (QEDS) database. QEDS was jointly developed by the World Bank and the IMF and provides detailed external debt data of countries that subscribe to the IMF's Special Data Dissemination Standard (SDDS) and a selected number of countries that participate in the IMF's General Data Dissemination System (GDDS). The data are compiled according to the External Debt Statistics, Guide for Compilers and Users., BIS data on international bank lending is the second source of the short-term debt. These data are reported on the basis of residual maturity, but an estimate of short-term external liabilities by original maturity can be derived by deducting from claims due in one year those that, 12 months

Figure 1. **External Debt and Its Components**

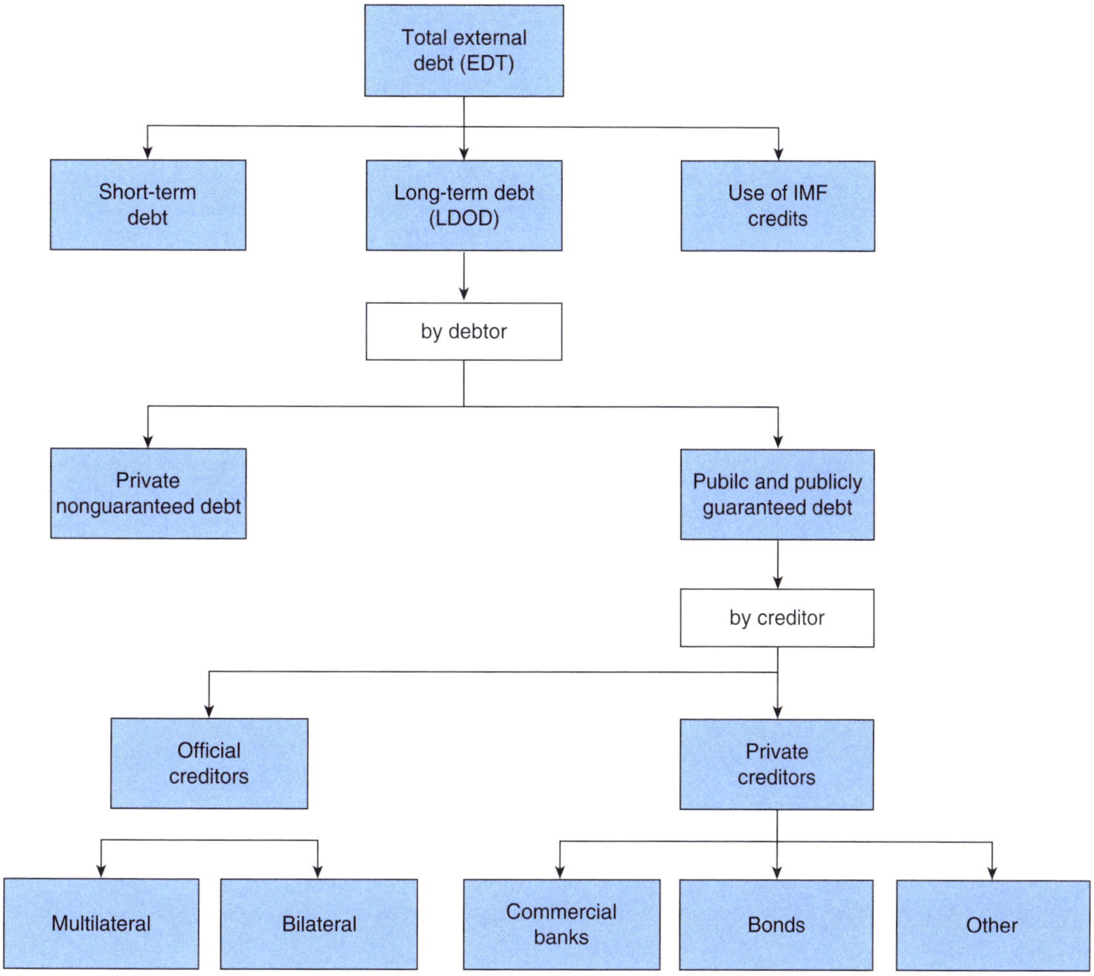

earlier, had a maturity of between one and two years. However, not all commercial banks report to the BIS in a way that allows the full maturity distribution to be determined, and the BIS data include liabilities only to banks within the BIS reporting area. Consequently, the results should be interpreted with caution.

The flow of short-term debt may be derived from the change in claims (stock) data in the BIS quarterly series over consecutive periods, but valuation adjustments resulting from exchange rate movements will affect the calculations, as will prepayment and refinancing of long-term maturities falling due. When short-term external debt has been rescheduled, lags in reporting and differences in the treatment of the rescheduled external debt by debtors and creditors may result in double counting.

Interest in arrears on long-term external debt and interest in arrears on the use of IMF credit are added to short-term debt and are separately identified.

Use of IMF Credit

Data related to the operations of the IMF are provided by the IMF Treasurer's Department. They are converted from special drawing rights (SDR) into dollars using end-of-period exchange rates for stocks and average-over-the-period exchange rates for flows. IMF trust fund operations under the Enhanced Structural Adjustment Facility, Extended Fund Facility, Poverty Reduction and Growth Facility, and Structural Adjustment Facility (Enhanced Structural Adjustment Facility in 1999) are presented together with all of the IMF's special facilities (buffer stock, supplemental reserve, compensatory and contingency facilities, oil facilities, and other facilities). SDR allocations are also included in this category. According to the BPM6, SDR allocations are recorded as the incurrence of a debt liability of the member receiving them (because of a requirement to repay the allocation in certain circumstances, and also because interest accrues). This debt item was introduced for the first time this year with historical data starting in 1999.

Long-Term Debt

Long-term debt has an original maturity of more than one year. It comprises the obligations of both public and private debtors. Private nonguaranteed debt comprises the external obligations of private debtors that are not guaranteed for repayment by a public entity in the debtor country.

Public and publicly guaranteed debt comprises the external obligations of public debtors and has two components: (a) public debt, which is borrowing by the national government or agency, by a political subdivision or agency, or by autonomous public bodies, and (b) publicly guaranteed debt, which is borrowing by a private agency that is guaranteed for repayment by a public entity.

Private Nonguaranteed Debt

The DRS reporting requirements were expanded in 1973 to include long-term private nonguaranteed debt. Data are reported annually on an aggregate basis and include, for the reporting year, the total amount of disbursed and outstanding debt; the amount of disbursements, principal repayments, and interest payments; the principal and interest rescheduled; and the projected principal and interest payments for future years. The aggregate data are usually reported in U.S. dollars, and no information on the underlying currency composition is given.

DRS reporting countries recognize the importance of monitoring borrowing by their private sector, particularly when it constitutes a significant portion of total external debt, but many countries acknowledge the difficulty of this process. Detailed data are available only when countries have registration requirements for private nonguaranteed debt in place, most commonly in connection with exchange controls. When formal registration of private nonguaranteed debt is not mandatory, compilers must rely on balance of payments data and financial surveys.

The data on private nonguaranteed debt in this publication is as reported or as estimated for countries where this type of external debt is known to be significant. The estimation of private nonguaranteed debt is based on the national data on quarterly external debt statistics (QEDS) or IMF data. Flows are derived from the change in stock over consecutive periods and are adjusted for the effects of exchange rate movements (assuming the currency composition mirrors that of public and publicly guaranteed debt) and for any known debt restructuring. Principal repayments are estimated on the basis of the average maturity observed for loans to private sector borrowers in countries reporting to the DRS and on the basis of the stock of debt outstanding. Interest payments are estimated on the basis of the stock of debt outstanding and interest rates prevailing in international capital markets.

Balance of payments data provide a useful guideline in the estimation process: private nonguaranteed external debt may be derived as a residual between net long-term external borrowing recorded in the balance of payments and net long-term public and publicly guaranteed external debt reported to the DRS.

Public and Publicly Guaranteed Debt

Data related to public and publicly guaranteed debt are reported to the DRS on a loan-by-loan basis. The data provide annual information on the disbursed and outstanding balance and the undisbursed balance of each loan, the cumulative disbursements, the principal and interest paid and principal and interest restructured in the reporting year, and the stock of any outstanding payment's arrears of principal and interest. Detailed information on the terms and conditions of each loan is also reported. Public debt and publicly guaranteed debt are shown as a single line in this publication and then further disaggregated by creditor type and, in the case of private creditors, by type of credit instrument.

Official Creditors

Official creditors include multilateral and bilateral lenders. In general, official creditors provide loans (and, in some cases, provide grants) to public bodies, although in some cases they may lend to other entities with a public guarantee.

Multilateral creditors are international financial institutions such as the World Bank, regional development banks, and other multilateral and intergovernmental agencies whose lending is administered on a multilateral basis. Funds administered by an international financial organization on behalf of a single donor government constitute bilateral loans (or grants). For lending by a number of multilateral creditors, the data presented in this publication are taken from the creditors' records. Such creditors include the African Development Bank, the Asian Development Bank, the IDB, the IBRD, and the IDA. (IBRD and IDA are institutions of the World Bank.)

Bilateral creditors are governments and their agencies, including central banks, aid agencies, official export credit agencies, and autonomous agencies such as the U.S. Department of Agriculture or the Federal Home Loan Bank. Member countries of the OECD DAC and some other countries also report information on loans extended bilaterally or officially guaranteed to the Creditor Reporting System of the OECD.

Private Creditors

Private creditors include commercial banks, bondholders, and other private creditors. This line includes only publicly guaranteed creditors. Nonguaranteed private creditors are shown separately.

Bonds include publicly issued or privately placed bonds.

Commercial bank loans are loans from private banks and other private financial institutions.

Credits of other private creditors include credits from manufacturers, exporters, and other suppliers of goods, plus bank credits covered by a guarantee of an export credit agency. This line is included in the online database but is not shown in the published tables. It can be obtained as the difference between (a) credits of total private creditors and (b) bonds and commercial bank loans.

Sources of the Macroeconomic Indicators

The macroeconomic data are prepared by The World Bank from a variety of sources. Data on Personal Transfers and Compensation of Employees are prepared by World Bank staff based on IMF balance of payments statistics. Data on foreign direct investments are prepared by World Bank staff based on IMF balance of payments statistics and UNCTAD publication. Other macroeconomic data are from IMF balance of payments statistics.

Data on Exports of Goods, Services, and Primary Income are gap-filled with countries' balance of payments statistics for the following countries:

Comoros (from 2005)
Madagascar (from 2006)
Mauritania (from 2006)
Mali (2011)
Senegal (2011)
Swaziland (from 2011)
Tonga (from 2010)

Data on Imports of Goods, Services, and Primary Income are gap-filled with countries' balance of payments statistics for the following countries:

Comoros (from 2005)
Madagascar (from 2006)
Mauritania (from 2006)
Mali (2011)
Senegal (2011)
Swaziland (from 2011)
Tonga (from 2010)

Data for Current Account Balance are based on countries' balance of payments statistics for the following countries:

Benin (2011)
Central African Republic (from 2005)
Chad (from 2005)
Comoros (from 2005)
Fiji (from 2011)
Gabon (from 2006)
Guinea-Bissau (2011)
Liberia (2012)
Madagascar (from 2006)
Mali (2011)
Mauritania (from 2007)
Senegal (2011)
Swaziland (from 2011)
Tonga (from 2010)
Tunisia
Zimbabwe (from 2005)

Country Groups

Regional Groups

East Asia and Pacific

Cambodia (A)
China (E)
Fiji (A)
Indonesia (A)
Lao PDR (P)
Malaysia (E)
Mongolia (P)
Myanmar (E)
Papua New Guinea (A)
Philippines (A)
Samoa (A)
Solomon Islands (A)
Thailand (A)
Tonga (A)
Vanuatu (E)
Vietnam (A)

Europe and Central Asia

Albania (A)
Armenia (A)
Azerbaijan (A)
Belarus (A)
Bosnia and Herzegovina[a] (A)
Bulgaria (A)
Georgia (A)
Hungary (A)
Kazakhstan (A)
Kosovo (A)
Kyrgyz Republic (A)
Macedonia, FYR (A)
Moldova (A)
Montenegro (A)
Romania (A)
Serbia[a, b] (A)
Tajikistan (A)
Turkey (A)
Turkmenistan (E)
Ukraine (A)
Uzbekistan (A)

Latin America and the Caribbean

Argentina (A)
Belize (A)
Bolivia (E)
Brazil (A)
Colombia (A)
Costa Rica (A)
Dominica (A)
Dominican Republic (A)
Ecuador (A)
El Salvador (A)
Grenada (A)
Guatemala (E)
Guyana (A)
Haiti (A)
Honduras (A)
Jamaica (A)
Mexico (A)
Nicaragua (A)
Panama (A)
Paraguay (A)
Peru (A)
St. Lucia (A)
St. Vincent and the Grenadines (A)
Venezuela, RB (A)

Middle East and North Africa

Algeria (A)
Djibouti (A)
Egypt, Arab Rep. (A)
Iran, Islamic Rep. (A)
Jordan (A)
Lebanon (A)
Morocco (A)
Syrian Arab Republic (E)
Tunisia (A)
Yemen, Rep. (A)

South Asia

Afghanistan (A)
Bangladesh (A)
Bhutan (A)
India (A)
Maldives (A)
Nepal (A)
Pakistan (A)
Sri Lanka(A)

Sub-Saharan Africa

Angola (A)
Benin (A)
Botswana (A)
Burkina Faso (A)
Burundi (A)
Cameroon (A)
Cape Verde (A)
Central African Republic (A)
Chad (E)
Comoros (A)
Congo, Dem. Rep. (P)
Congo, Rep. (P)
Côte d'Ivoire (E)
Eritrea (E)
Ethiopia (A)
Gabon (A)
Gambia, The (A)
Ghana (E)
Guinea (E)
Guinea-Bissau (E)
Kenya (A)
Lesotho (A)
Liberia (A)
Madagascar (A)
Malawi (A)
Mali (A)
Mauritania (A)
Mauritius (A)
Mozambique (A)
Niger (A)
Nigeria (A)
Rwanda (A)
São Tomé and Principe (A)
Senegal (A)
Seychelles (A)
Sierra Leone (A)
Somalia (E)
South Africa (E)
Sudan[c] (A)
Swaziland (A)
Tanzania (A)
Togo (A)
Uganda (A)
Zambia (A)
Zimbabwe (A)

Note: Letters in parenthesis indicate DRS reporters' status: (A) as reported, (P) preliminary, and (E) estimated. The status "as reported" indicates that the country was fully current in its reporting under the DRS and that World Bank staff are satisfied that the reported data give an adequate and fair representation of the country's total public debt. "Preliminary" data are based on reported or collected information, but because of incompleteness or other reasons, an element of staff estimation is included. "Estimated" data indicate that countries are not current in their reporting and that a significant element of staff estimation has been necessary in producing the data tables.
a. For Bosnia and Herzegovina, total debt before 1999, excluding IBRD and IMF obligations and short-term debt, is included under Serbia.
b. Data prior to 2006 include Montenegro.
c. Data include South Sudan.

Income Groups

Low-income economies

Afghanistan
Bangladesh
Benin
Burkina Faso
Burundi
Cambodia
Central African Republic
Chad
Comoros
Congo, Dem. Rep.
Eritrea
Ethiopia
Gambia, The
Guinea
Guinea-Bissau
Haiti
Kenya
Kyrgyz Republic
Liberia
Madagascar
Malawi
Mali
Mozambique
Myanmar
Nepal
Niger
Rwanda
Sierra Leone
Somalia
Tajikistan
Tanzania
Togo
Uganda
Zimbabwe

Middle-income economies

Albania
Algeria
Angola
Argentina
Armenia
Azerbaijan
Belarus
Belize
Bhutan
Bolivia
Bosnia and Herzegovina
Botswana
Brazil
Bulgaria
Cameroon
Cape Verde
China
Colombia
Congo, Rep.
Costa Rica
Côte d'Ivoire
Djibouti
Dominica
Dominican Republic
Ecuador
Egypt, Arab Rep.
El Salvador
Fiji
Gabon
Georgia
Ghana
Grenada
Guatemala
Guyana
Honduras
Hungary
India
Indonesia
Iran, Islamic Rep.
Jamaica
Jordan
Kazakhstan
Kosovo
Lao PDR
Lebanon
Lesotho
Macedonia, FYR
Malaysia
Maldives
Mauritania Mauritius
Mexico
Moldova
Mongolia
Montenegro
Morocco
Nicaragua
Nigeria
Pakistan
Panama
Papua New Guinea
Paraguay
Peru
Philippines
Romania
Samoa
São Tomé and Principe
Senegal
Serbia
Seychelles
Solomon Islands
South Africa
Sri Lanka
St. Lucia
St. Vincent and the Grenadines
Sudan
Swaziland
Syrian Arab Republic
Thailand
Tonga
Tunisia
Turkey
Turkmenistan
Ukraine
Uzbekistan
Vanuatu
Venezuela, RB
Vietnam
Yemen, Rep.
Zambia

Note: Low-income economies are those with a GNI per capita of $1,035 or less in 2012. Middle-income economies are those with a GNI per capita of more than $1,036 but less than $12,615.

Glossary

Debt Reporting System (DRS)

Average terms of new commitments provide information on the interest rate, maturity, and grace period of new commitments on public and publicly guaranteed external debt contracted with public and private creditors. Averages are weighted by the amounts of the loans.

Bilateral official creditors are official agencies that make loans on behalf of one government to another government or to public (and, in some cases, private) borrowers in another country.

Bonds are debt instruments issued by public and publicly guaranteed or private debtors with durations of one year or longer. Bonds usually give the holder the unconditional right to fixed money income or contractually determined, variable money income.

Commercial banks are private banks that provide loans and other financial services.

Commitments of public and publicly guaranteed debt constitute the total amount of new long-term loans to public sector borrowers or borrowers with a public sector guarantee extended by official and private lenders and for which contracts were signed in the year specified.

Concessional debt conveys information about the borrower's receipt of aid from official lenders at concessional terms as defined by the DAC, that is, loans with an original grant element of 25 percent or more. Loans from major regional development banks—African Development Bank, Asian Development Bank, and the Inter-American Development Bank—and from the World Bank are classified as concessional according to each institution's classification and not according to the DAC definition, as was the practice in earlier reports.

Contractual obligations on outstanding long-term external debt are the anticipated debt service payments on long-term external debt contracted up to December 31 of the reporting year.

Currency composition of public and publicly guaranteed debt provides information on the share of loans outstanding and disbursed by currency of repayment. For major multilateral creditors, the currency composition of the relevant unit of account is also taken into account. The principal currencies in which the external debt of low- and middle-income countries is contracted (the euro, Japanese yen, U.S. dollar, SDR, and all other currencies) are separately identified. Beginning in 2001, debt denominated in the currencies of the members in the Euro Area is included under the euro rather than the national currencies that previously prevailed.

Current account balance shows the difference between the sum of exports and income receivable and the sum of imports and income payable (exports and imports refer to both goods and services, while income refers to both primary and secondary income).

Debt buyback is the repurchase by a debtor of its own debt, either at a discount price or at par value. In the event of a buyback of long-term debt, the face value of the debt bought back will be recorded as a decline in stock outstanding of long-term debt, and the cash amount received by creditors will be recorded as a principal repayment. For example, if a country buys back long term external debt of face value B at a price P, then long-term external debt will decline by B, and principal repayment will increase by P. The difference between the price at which the debt was bought back and the face value is recorded as a debt stock write-off (the related transactions are not separately identified in the International Debt Statistics (IDS) publication but are available in the online database).

Debt forgiveness grants include both debts canceled by agreement between debtor and creditor and reductions in the net present value of official nonconcessional loans resulting from concessional rescheduling or refinancing. Data are recorded on a disbursement basis and include debt forgiveness from bilateral and multilateral creditors.

Debt outstanding and disbursed is the value at year's end of long-term external debt owed by public and publicly guaranteed debtors and private nonguaranteed debtors.

Debt restructurings are revisions to debt service obligations agreed on by creditors and debtors. Such agreements change the amount and timing of future principal and interest payments.

Debt service to exports is the ratio of the sum of principal repayments and interest paid on total long-term debt (public and publicly guaranteed debt and private nonguaranteed debt) to the value of exports of goods and services and receipts of primary income from abroad.

Debt stock-flow reconciliation shows the indicators that affect the change in debt stocks from one period to the next.

Disbursements are drawings during the year specified on loan commitments contracted by the borrower.

Exports of goods, services, and primary income constitute the total value of exports of goods and services, receipts of compensation of nonresident workers, and investment income from abroad.

External debt flows are debt-related transactions during the year specified. They include disbursements, principal repayments, and interest payments.

External debt stocks comprise public and publicly guaranteed long-term external debt, private nonguaranteed long-term external debt, use of IMF credit, and short-term external debt, including interest arrears on long-term debt. The relation between external debt stock and its components is illustrated on page 171 (figure 1).

External debt stocks to exports is the ratio of outstanding external debt to the value of exports of goods and services and receipts of primary income from abroad.

External debt stocks to GNI is the ratio of outstanding external debt to gross national income.

Foreign direct investment refers to direct investment flows in the reporting economy. It is the sum of equity capital, reinvestment earnings, and other capital. Direct investment is a category of cross-border investment associated with a resident in one economy having control or a significant degree of influence on the management of an enterprise that is resident in another economy. Ownership of 10 percent or more of the ordinary shares or voting stock is the criterion for determining the existence of a direct investment relationship.

Grace period is the time between the date on which a loan is committed and the date on which the first principal payment is due. The information presented in International Debt Statistics is the average grace period on all public and publicly guaranteed debt committed during the specified period.

Grants are legally binding commitments that obligate a specific value of funds available for disbursement for which there is no payment requirement. They include debt forgiveness grants and grants from bilateral and multilateral agencies (such as the International Development Association).

Gross national income (GNI) is the sum of value added by all resident producers, plus any product taxes (less subsidies) not included in the valuation of output, plus net receipts of primary income compensation of employees and property income from abroad. Yearly average exchange rates are used to convert GNI from local currency to U.S. dollars.

Heavily Indebted Poor Country (HIPC) Initiative is a program of the World Bank and the International Monetary Fund to provide debt relief to qualifying countries with unsustainable debt burdens.

Imports of goods, services, and primary income constitute the total value of goods and services imported and income payable to nonresidents. Interest arrears on long-term debt are interest payments due but not paid, shown on a cumulative basis.

Interest arrears are due and payable immediately and are therefore regarded as short-term obligations. Thus, an increase in interest arrears on long-term debt will be recorded as an increase in short-term debt. Interest in arrears on the use of IMF credit is also considered to be part of short-term external debt.

Interest payments are the amounts of interest paid in foreign currency, goods, or services in the year specified.

Interest rate is the interest rate applicable to a loan commitment as specified in the loan contract. The information presented in International Debt Statistics is the average interest on all public and publicly guaranteed debt committed during the specified period.

International Bank for Reconstruction and Development (IBRD) is a multilateral official creditor. It is the nonconcessional lending arm of the World Bank Group.

International Development Association (IDA) is a multilateral official creditor. It is the concessional financing arm of the World Bank Group. IDA also provides grant financing to qualified borrowers.

International Monetary Fund (IMF) charges are the amounts of interest paid in foreign currency in the year specified for transactions with the IMF.

International Monetary Fund (IMF) purchases are the total drawings on the general resources account of the IMF during the year specified, excluding drawings in the reserve tranche.

International Monetary Fund (IMF) repurchases are the amounts of principal (amortization) paid in foreign currency in the year specified for transactions with the IMF.

International reserves constitute the sum of a country's monetary authority's holdings of special drawing rights, its reserve position in the IMF, its holdings of foreign exchange, and its holdings of gold (valued at year-end London prices).

Long-term external debt is debt that has an original or extended maturity of more than one year and that is owed to nonresidents by residents of an economy and is repayable in foreign currency, goods, or services.

Long-term private sector debt is long-term debt owed by the private sector, whether publicly guaranteed or not.

Long-term public sector debt is long-term external debt owed by the public sector.

Maturity is the date on which the final principal repayment on a loan is due. It is the sum of the grace and repayment periods. The information presented in International Debt Statistics is the average maturity on all public and publicly guaranteed debt committed during the specified period.

Multilateral Debt Relief Initiative (MDRI) is a program of the World Bank, the IMF, the Inter-American Development Bank, and the African Development Bank that provides additional debt relief to countries that have completed the HIPC process.

Multilateral official creditors are official agencies owned or governed by more than one country that provide loan financing. They include international financial institutions such as the World Bank, regional development banks, and other intergovernmental agencies.

Multilateral to external debt stocks is the ratio of the stock of debt owed to multilateral creditors to total external debt.

Net flows on external debt are disbursements on long-term external debt and IMF purchases minus principal repayments on long-term external debt and IMF repurchases. Up to 1984, this calculation included only long-term external debt and IMF flows. Since 1985, the calculation includes the change in stock of short-term debt (excluding interest arrears on long-term external debt).

Official creditors are governments or other bilateral public entities, such as export-import agencies, development agencies, and multilateral financial institutions, such as the World Bank and regional development banks.

Personal transfers consist of all current transfers in cash or in kind made or received by resident households to or from nonresident households. Personal transfers thus include all current transfers between resident and nonresident individuals. Compensation of employees refers to the income of border, seasonal, and other short-term workers who are employed in an economy where they are not resident and of residents employed by nonresident entities.

Portfolio equity is the category of international investment that covers investment in equity securities. Equity securities include shares, stocks, participation, or similar documents (such as American Depositary Receipts) that usually denote ownership of equity.

Present value of debt outstanding is the nominal value of all future debt service obligations on existing debt discounted at prevailing market rates of interest. The interest rates used in this calculation are the Commercial Interest Reference Rates (CIRR) for each relevant currency compiled and published by the Organisation for Economic Cooperation and Development.

Primary income on FDI are payments of direct investment income (debit side), which consist of income on equity (dividends, branch profits, and reinvested earnings) and income on the intercompany debt (interest).

Principal arrears on long-term debt are principal repayments due but not paid on long-term external debt, shown on a cumulative basis.

Principal repayments are the amounts of principal (amortization) paid in foreign currency, goods, or services in the year specified with respect to long-term external debt.

Private creditors are bondholders, commercial banks, and other trade-related lenders.

Private nonguaranteed debt is debt owed by private sector borrowers to external creditors on loans that do not benefit from a public sector guarantee by the debtor country.

Public and publicly guaranteed debt outstanding and disbursed is the value of debt at year's end of public sector borrowers, or borrowers with a public sector guarantee, owed to official and private lenders.

Public and publicly guaranteed external debt comprises public debt (an external obligation of a public debtor, such as the national government or agency, a political subdivision or agency, or an autonomous public body) and publicly guaranteed external debt (an external obligation of a private debtor that is guaranteed for repayment by a public entity).

Public debt is an external obligation of public debtor, including the national government, a political subdivision (or an agency of either), and autonomous public bodies.

Publicly guaranteed debt is an external obligation of a private debtor that is guaranteed for repayment by a public entity.

Reserves to external debt stocks is the ratio of international reserves to outstanding external debt.

Reserves to imports (months) is the ratio of international reserves to the value of imports of goods, services, and primary income in the year shown and is expressed in months:

$$\frac{\text{Reserves}}{\text{Imports/12}}$$

Short-term external debt has an original maturity of one year or less. Available data permit no distinction among public, publicly guaranteed, and private nonguaranteed short-term external debt.

Short-term to external debt stock ratio is the ratio of short-term external debt to total outstanding external debt.

Special Drawing Rights (SDRs) refer to an international reserve asset that was created by the IMF in 1969 to supplement its member countries' official reserves. The value of SDRs is based on a basket of four key international currencies: the U.S. dollar, the pound sterling, the Japanese yen, and the euro. In addition to playing a role as a supplementary reserve asset, SDRs serve as the unit of account for the IMF and some other international organizations.

Technical cooperation grants include (a) free-standing technical cooperation grants, which are intended to finance the transfer of technical and managerial skills or of technology for the purpose of building up general national capacity without reference to any specific investment projects, and (b) investment-related technical cooperation grants, which are aimed at strengthening the capacity to execute specific investment projects.

Total amount forgiven is the total amount of principal and interest due, principal and interest in arrears, and debt stock forgiven in the year specified.

Total amount rescheduled is the total amount of external debt rescheduled, including principal and interest due, principal and interest in arrears, charges, penalties, and debt stock in the year specified.

Total change in external debt stocks is the difference in the external debt stock between two consecutive years.

Use of IMF credit denotes members' drawings on the IMF other than amounts drawn against the country's reserve tranche position. Use of IMF credit includes purchases and drawings under Stand-By, Extended, Structural Adjustment, Enhanced Structural Adjustment, and Systemic Transformation Facility Arrangements as well as trust fund loans. SDR allocations are also included in this category.

Quarterly Debt Statistics

Banking sector is identical with the "other (than the central bank) depository corporations" subsector of the financial corporate sector in the SNA. The banking sector includes commercial banks, institutions such as savings banks, savings and loan associations, credit unions or cooperatives, building societies, and post office savings banks, or other government-controlled savings banks (if such banks are institutional units separate from the government).

Central government subsector consists of the institutional unit(s) of the central government plus those nonmarket NPIs that are controlled by the central government. The political authority of the central government extends over the entire territory of the country.

Currency and deposits consist of notes and coins and deposits (both transferable and other). Notes and coins represent claims of a fixed nominal value usually on a central bank or government; commemorative coins are excluded. Deposits include all claims that are (a) on the central bank, deposit-taking corporations other than the central bank, and, in some cases, other institutional units; and (b) represented by evidence of deposit.

Debt liabilities owed by residents to residents of the same economy are classified as *domestic debt*, and debt liabilities owed by residents to nonresidents are classified as *external debt*. The definition of residence follows the current international standards (the System of National Accounts 2008 (2008 SNA) and the *Balance of Payments and International Investment Position Manual*, Sixth Edition (BPM6)).

Debt securities are negotiable financial instruments serving as evidence of a debt. The security normally specifies a schedule for interest payments and principal repayments. Examples of debt securities are bills, bonds, and debentures, including bonds that are convertible into shares, commercial paper, negotiable certificates of deposit, loans that have become negotiable from one holder to another, nonparticipating preferred stocks or shares, asset-backed securities and collateralized debt obligations, banker's acceptances, and similar instruments normally traded in the financial markets.

General government agencies that are residents of an economy include all departments, establishments, and bodies located in the economic territory of an economy's central, state, and local governments and all embassies, consulates, military establishments, and other entities, which are located elsewhere, of an economy's general government.

Insurance, pension, and standardized guarantee schemes comprise (a) nonlife insurance technical reserves, (b) life insurance and annuity entitlements, (c) pension entitlements, claims of pension funds on pension managers, and entitlements to nonpension funds, and (d) provisions for calls under standardized guarantees.

Loans include those financial assets created through the direct lending of funds by a creditor (lender) to a debtor (borrower) through an arrangement in which the lender either receives no security evidencing the transactions or receives a nonnegotiable document or instrument.

Monetary authorities sector includes the central bank (or currency board, monetary agency, etc.) and certain operations that are usually attributed to the central bank but are sometimes carried out by other government institutions or commercial banks.

Other accounts receivable/payable covers items other than equity; currency and deposits; loans; insurance, pension, and standardized guarantee schemes; trade credit and advances; and SDRs.

Other sectors category is comprised of nonfinancial corporations (private, public, and quasi-corporations), insurance companies, pension funds, other nondepository financial intermediaries, private nonprofit institutions, and households.

SDR allocations are recorded as the incurrence of a debt liability of the member receiving them (because of a requirement to repay the allocation in certain circumstances, and also because of interest accrues).

Trade credit and advances consist of liabilities arising from the direct extension of credit by suppliers for transactions in goods and services, and advance payments by buyers for goods and services and for work in progress (or to be undertaken).

ECO-AUDIT

Environmental Benefits Statement

The World Bank is committed to preserving endangered forests and natural resources. The Office of the Publisher has chosen to print ***International Debt Statistics 2014*** on recycled paper with 50 percent post-consumer waste, in accordance with the recommended standards for paper usage set by the Green Press Initiative, a non-profit program supporting publishers in using fiber that is not sourced from endangered forests. For more information, visit www.greenpressinitiative.org.

Saved:

- 13 trees
- 8 million BTUs of total energy
- 1,424 lbs. of net greenhouse gases
- 7,724 gallons of water
- 517 lbs. of solid waste

green press INITIATIVE